198

Islam and Capitalism

Israel and the Arabs
Mohammed

Maxime Rodinson

ISLAM AND CAPITALISM

Translated from the French by Brian Pearce

PANTHEON BOOKS

A Division of Random House, New York

FIRST AMERICAN EDITION

Translation Copyright © 1973 by Penguin Books Ltd.

All rights reserved under International and Pan-American Copyright Conventions. Published in the United States by Pantheon Books, a division of Random House, Inc., New York. Originally published in France as *Islam et le capitalisme* by Éditions du Seuil, Paris. Copyright © 1966 by Éditions du Seuil. This translation first published in Great Britain by Allen Lane, a division of Penguin Books Ltd., London.

Library of Congress Cataloging in Publication Data

Rodinson, Maxime.
Islam and Capitalism.

Includes bibliographical references.
1. Islam and economics.   I. Title.
BP173.75.R613   1974   297′.197′85   73-17297
ISBN 0-394-46719-1

Manufactured in the United States of America

Contents

Foreword

This book, by a sociologist specializing in Islamic studies, is written with the high ambition to be of service to intellectuals in the countries that belong to the Muslim faith and civilization, by helping them to understand their situation. It is not that I presume myself superior, by virtue of 'being European', to the best among them in learning or intelligence. I lay claim to no advantage of that sort. It is merely that circumstances have enabled me to escape sooner than them from certain social impediments that obstruct their understanding of their own problems. I have had the good fortune to be given free access to the acquisition of a knowledge of their past that is clear of myths, and I have sought to rid myself of the myths that are hindrances to understanding their present. It must be added that I am in a position to speak out and say what they are often obliged to keep to themselves. This is a freedom that has to be paid for, like all freedoms, but the price, in my case, is not excessive; whereas they, generally speaking, have to pay a great deal more for it.

My book is also intended to help European readers, similarly. I do not subscribe to the mystique of the Third World, now so widespread in Left circles, and do not beat my breast daily in despair at not having been born in the Congo or somewhere like that. Nevertheless, the problems of the Third World are indeed of major significance, and my studies and concerns during the last thirty years and more have given me special knowledge of an important region of the Third World which shares the problems common to the latter but also possesses problems peculiar to itself. I put before the reader the ideas that the study and reflection I have undertaken have left with me. It is for him to judge and dispose of them as he sees fit: no one has a key to fit all locks.

Of what use can a foreword be? It can endeavour to introduce a book as a whole, explaining how the author has approached his subject, in order, so far as is possible, to prevent misunderstandings. What authors, and even people in general, are most commonly blamed for is not having done something they never set out to do.

This book is neither a textbook of the economic history of the Muslim world nor a popular outline of what might have been such a textbook. Incidentally, I regret that no such textbook or outline is available.[1] On particular points which seem to me of fundamental importance, I have indeed summarized what historical studies have now established, to the best of my knowledge. But I have not sought to deal with the subject in general. In other words, what will be found here is not, in the main, a description, whether complete or incomplete, of the facts in all their many-sided diversity. The references I provide will enable, where the need arises, those who may wish to inform themselves on these details to look up the books and articles that deal with them.

My purpose has been to write a theoretical study; what does this mean? I start from the facts which have been established by scientific research and of which I have tried to keep myself informed, so far as possible, through making use of my knowledge of languages and the greater or lesser familiarity I have with the techniques of Oriental studies, history and sociology. Above all I have tried to draw conclusions on the plane of general problems, more precisely on the plane of certain general problems that have appeared to me as being especially important. Where does the Muslim world (in the different phases of its history) belong in the general typology of systems of production and distribution of goods? Do the answers that can be given to this question, the phenomena observed in this field, enable us to understand better the evolution that may take place within these systems, and from one of them to another? Or the factors in this development, or these developments? Or the relations between the economic facts and the other aspects of the total culture of a given society, in particular the ideological aspects, and most particularly, religion?

These large problems can be regarded as belonging to the domain of the philosophy of history or to that of sociology. This question of nomenclature seems to me of little interest. What is essential is that the problems exist.

It is clear, too, that these problems possess topical significance, just because they are general in character. *Pace* the specialists, they are significant politically. This does not mean that solving them necessarily depends on a certain political attitude or activity, nor that whoever deals with them has perforce to submit himself to taking a particular standpoint. It was a great misfortune for scientific activity (then called philosophy) that it was for so long the handmaid of theology. The misfortune would be no less if it were now to be turned into the handmaid of political ideology, which has taken the place of theology. Attempts to do this (in which I myself have participated) have turned out badly for scientific work and even for politics too. There is no need to dwell on it: the facts are plain enough.

An enlightened political outlook should merely take account of whatever conclusions research may lead to where these problems are concerned. It is even to its interest that this research should be as independent as possible. Furthermore, any socio-political ideology needs to be constructed exclusively from sound materials. Political leaders and activists, citizens who seek to find their way in the labyrinth of facts and ideas, often adopt – as the basis for their decisions – ideas, attitudes and conceptions that are lamentably inaccurate. This is to a large extent inevitable; in great part it is also due, however, to the failure of those who know and who could do more to communicate what they know. The specialists who smile or grimace at the myths that are widely accepted by the public (concerning matters in their special field, since they themselves belong to 'the public' in relation to everything else) ought to appreciate that they are not always free from responsibility for these infatuations.

I am well aware that often it is a matter of ideas whose strength lies in some emotional source and which cannot be shaken by any argument, experience, or information. But this is never more than partly true, and the introduction of a little lucid and well-informed consciousness into an ideological magma is still a task to which it is worth applying oneself, and not so utterly hopeless that one can feel exempt from undertaking it when one has the means to do so.

I know, too, that the educator himself greatly needs to be educated, that he is never so free as he supposes of preconceptions that determine the direction taken by his deductions. Here too, however, the power exercised by the adverse force is not so complete as ideologists imagine. It is possible to attain a certain degree of objectivity. It is inexcusable to use the pretext that complete objectivity is an unattainable ideal in order to submit willingly to an equally complete ideological control over one's thinking. This is like deliberately jumping into a river so as to avoid getting wet.

My book is, then, of a theoretical character. Consequently, it is polemical. The conclusions at which I have arrived do indeed conflict with views that are very widely held. I have done all I can to avoid letting strictness on the plane of concepts lead me into writing anything hurtful to individuals. Perhaps I have not always succeeded in this. War has its own laws, which apply even to the battle of ideas, and one is always led into going a little too far. It is hard to wage a polemic against someone without seeming to despise him. Nevertheless, I am too firmly convinced of the determinism that dominates men's thoughts and actions to be, at bottom, contemptuous of them. At all events, I give notice of this to my opponents and to my readers.

I have in particular attacked myths that are highly current among the Muslim public. Undoubtedly, many people in the Muslim world will on this account accuse me of spiteful hidden motives of a racialist or colonialist order. The political attitudes I have adopted provide, I think, an adequate reply to any such charges. It is behind complaisance towards accepted ideas that contempt and calculation hide themselves; besides, I have dealt no less roughly with some very European myths.

To attempt to unite, as I have, exact knowledge of the essential facts with a certain capacity for generalization presents a basic difficulty that the public does not always appreciate. I do not know whether or not I have coped more or less satisfactorily with this difficulty. Books of this kind struggle amid dilemmas that are hard to resolve and that specialists frequently decide cannot be overcome. The latter resign themselves, either in desperation or quite happily, to writing only for a narrow readership which is already well enough informed on the problems in their field. I have tried to avoid writing a book of the type that specialists rightly regret to see so widely read, consisting of rash theorizing on the basis of facts drawn from too small a part of the field that the theory seeks to cover, or of no less audacious deduction of particular judgements from general conceptions (whether the latter are valid or not) without regard to the actual facts – not to mention that irresponsible philosophico-literary chatter which these same specialists denounce with equal justification and which they see flourishing so frequently in the bastard *genre* of the essay. However, the wide prevalence of these types of general dissertation does not imply, as specialists often think (or appear to think), that attempts to generalize can be dispensed with, or that such attempts are always premature and constitute a mere waste of time in pursuit of ends that are intrinsically unattainable. The general public, specialists in other fields, and even practical workers in the sphere of social activity have need of syntheses, even if these are inevitably only provisional. If the experts do not provide such syntheses, these people will turn to less qualified authorities, and the results will be lamentable – indeed, they are already bad enough. Moreover, the advance of learning itself requires that attempts be made at well-thought-out surveys of work in progress.

On their part, those who like generalizations have their – often justified – complaints. They have the right to insist that whoever plunges into these dangerous attempts shall possess at least some notion of the development of general ideas, of the way of approaching problems that modern thought has worked out, and of the major problematics to which reference needs to be made. The great difficulty is, precisely, that of keeping up to date, broadly at any rate, without losing contact with specialized research. This is a practical difficulty and in trying to avoid succumbing to it I have sought to meet a challenge – presuming too much, perhaps, upon my talents and my capacity for work. All I can say is that I have made this attempt honestly and without trickery.

Finally, the public interested in these matters has a right not to find itself subjected to an unnecessary display of erudition. I have therefore used in the course of my argument only those facts that are strictly necessary for my purposes. The notes (to which the reader is free not to refer) are there simply to provide those who object to what I say with the possibility of checking and examining my statements on the basis of my sources, and to help those who may wish to obtain further information on some point that I have not been able to deal with fully. In some cases the notes also include brief discussions on matters of secondary interest that would have overloaded the main argument.

One question remains, on which I ought, it seems to me, to offer some explanation here. The present essay is intended and affirmed to be Marxist in orientation. This does not mean, as many will suppose, that I have subordinated my research to dogmas of doubtful validity and suspect origins, but only that I have tried to think out the problems arising from my study in the light of some very general socio-historical hypotheses that seem to me to give direction to a whole field of study where scientific exploration is only beginning, and which I consider have so far been confirmed by the concrete knowledge we have obtained. I do not bring forward in support of them any argument that is not drawn from facts or from reasoning of the kind that is normal in scientific research, and I am ready to abandon them if facts or scientific reasoning show me that they are futile. Furthermore, I deny that one can get very far along the path of generalization without broad hypotheses of this kind. Those who claim to be able to do without them end up with an unintelligible accumulation of facts; or, more frequently, employ, without being conscious of them, different hypotheses, which seem to me to be much less solidly based, in order to construct their own often highly subtle systems of categories.

A little more needs, nevertheless, to be said on this point. Anti-Marxists will be sure in advance that this book contains attitudes of a kind that they denounce (sometimes rightly) but which are in fact not to be found in it. The Marxists, *marxisants*, semi-Marxists and pseudo-Marxists, on the other hand, who are so plentiful in the Third World and in the European Left, will be disappointed at not finding in it attitudes that they are used to regarding as inseparable from the very concept of Marxism.

There are a score, a hundred, nay, a thousand varieties of Marxism. Marx said many things, and it is easy to find in his work, just as in the Bible, something to provide support for any idea whatever: 'The devil himself can cite Scripture for his purpose.' I make no claim to impose as the only correct one my own understanding of the Marxist orientation, as I have been accused of doing by a distinguished writer; and I hold no authority to excommunicate anybody, as another no less distinguished writer has blamed me for doing. I am myself the one excommunicated. I desire only to assert the right to define my own line of thought. I am even ready to proclaim that Marx would not completely agree with this line.

My Marxism is not institutionalized Marxism. The latter is certainly not *arrêté*, to employ Sartre's expression, except in a sense. Important work is being carried on in its light (or in its shadow) in the Communist countries and even elsewhere – in France, for example. It will be seen that I have made use of some of this work in my book. But a set of taboos stands in the way of a free approach to the great (and sometimes even small) problems on which the only answer permitted is that which is laid down in dogma. Or, at least, one has to observe so many precautions regarding both form and content that the flight of one's thought is heavily fettered thereby. Many powerful minds in the Communist countries inwardly escape from these fetters by means of the 'double-think' that is traditional in countries where a state ideology prevails. I have not seen the need, in France, to subject myself to this method, which is always equivocal and which brings with it, whatever anyone may say, more or less disastrous consequences for the free play of ideas. The advantage of seeing my book praised, or even merely quoted, in some journal or other has not seemed to me to be worth the price of this compromise.

I understand, often respect, and sometimes admire my former comrades who have considered that devotion to a cause, attachment to a group, or loyalty to an allegiance of their youth, must take precedence over the free expression of their thought, without their always seeing that the restrictions on expression that they accept often result in fettering the development of their thought. I have eventually decided that, as far as I personally am concerned, what is at stake does not justify the sacrifice.

This book does not belong, either, to the category I call pragmatic Marxism, which embraces institutionalized Marxism but is wider than that. In this category I include the many types of Marxist ideology which, concentrating on tasks of social action that, though various, are always of capital importance in the eyes of those who hold these views, subordinate to the tasks in question all theoretical and intellectual activity in general. This does not mean that I deny the usefulness of some of these tasks. While, however, the smallness of the groups that incarnate these ideologies (apart from the Communist organizations, which belong to the category previously discussed), often saves them from showing the disagreeable characteristics of institutionalized Marxism – in particular the massive weight of dogma, the 'official' mentality of the cadres that lay down the law on intellectual matters, the display of a policy of strength that is both repulsive to sincere minds and attractive to those who respect strength wherever it is to be found – they nevertheless contain within themselves an infantile, perhaps foetal, form of this same development. Inevitably they tend to reproduce its features. In some cases I value their activity, and I am not without hope of rendering service to it on some limited points, in endeavouring, for my own part, to engage in militancy, in radical activism. I do not, however, intend to adhere to the utopian aspirations to which this tendency almost inevitably gives rise, nor to subordinate my scientific work to the purposes of these groups.

The connection between truth and practice is a serious and complex question to which Marxists have hitherto replied a little too lightly in favour of political practice. I do not claim to be able to solve this problem in three sentences. I merely believe that I have noted that the search for truth has frequently been hindered through being tied up too directly with political action, and that this has occurred even in the best of cases. What can be said of the worst? Eventually, moreover, in the long run, it is to the advantage even of politicians if an activity carried on parallel to their own is exclusively concerned with discovering truth. A narrowly pragmatic and polemical conception of things usually gives rise to illusions, and illusions in the end prove fatal.

Finally, the Marxism that influences me is not the philosophical Marxism now in fashion, especially in France. Let there be no misunderstanding here. I am not a positivist as a matter of principle. I am convinced of the usefulness, the necessity, the fundamental and inescapable nature of philosophical reflection. Nor am I blind to the implicit philosophical presuppositions that are hidden in every piece of research, even if this be in intention objective in the highest degree. It is more than obvious, in particular, that Marx's scientific procedure was guided by the philosophical decisions from which he began. All the same, there remains a very large area of the field of learning that can and must be explored with these philosophical presuppositions provisionally suspended, and in accordance with methods that can be approved (in principle, at least) by all investigators, however different their philosophical viewpoints may be, within a given culture. This is the field of science in which so philosophical a thinker as Sartre acknowledges that the positivist procedure is the one to follow.

Now, whatever some Marxists may say, there is a problematic peculiar to the humane sciences, or to the social sciences, or to sociology in the broadest sense, whatever name one may give to this field. It is in this field that Marx established the presence of certain laws, made certain discoveries, put forward certain hypotheses which are, properly speaking, independent of his philosophical attitude and on which thinkers of very divergent philosophical schools can agree. This is the field in which I take my stand in the present work. It is harmful (and I think experience confirms my view here) to the philosopher, even the Marxist philosopher, to enter into this field of research, as he often does, without troubling to acquaint himself with the concepts, methods and problematic that are special to it.

To deduce directly from a general philosophical thesis, even if this be a correct one, consequences relating to the special problems of sociology or history, without going through the mediation of the laws or constants that are distinctively socio-historical, without taking account of the mass of empirical data or partial generalizations accumulated by researchers, and without using the special methods they have worked out, may occasionally enable someone to achieve brilliant and thought-provoking insights. Usually, however, it leads only to discoveries that are banal, insubstantial or even absurd. I recall an apocryphal story told me in Poland about a great Western philosopher arriving in Warsaw and questioning with curiosity a local intellectual: 'You are in a socialist country. Do you still feel alienated?'

Though there are many reasons for admiring Marx, I put this one first and foremost. Originally a philosopher, he realized that before he could put forward well-founded propositions on social evolution he must devote a lifetime of study to mastering political economy, social history and what today we call sociology, or the humane sciences. And this he did.

I do not believe in the unity of Marxism. Among Marxist ideas I distinguish *inter alia* between a philosophical approach, some sociological propositions, and an ideological inspiration. There is, of course, a certain connection between them in Marx's thought and even in the nature of things. But from the standpoint of methodology they can be dissociated. I will here put on one side the philosophical approach, while acknowledging the difficulties it contributes to my conception of a non-utopian radical activism. This means, indeed, tending, in contrast to Marx, to contemplate an ideal that is not necessarily something demanded by reality.

Here I base myself exclusively, or almost exclusively, on the great sociological or socio-historical theses worked out by Marx, which seem to me to be solidly established and acceptable to all thinkers on the scientific plane. This does not mean denying the ideological obstacles that have stood in the way of their general acceptance, and which still stand in their way. There were also ideological obstacles to acceptance of the law of how bodies fall. It is enough, however, to observe the extent to which these theses are nowadays currently accepted in circles most thoroughly opposed to Marxist ideology and philosophy in order to appreciate what a strong scientific foundation they possess. True, they are still contested (my book will show numerous examples of this), not only among ideologists but also among scholars. Nevertheless, the latter, at least (even those who are most hostile to these theses on the theoretical plane), have been compelled to swallow a big dose of Marxist theses, the origin of which they have sometimes forgotten. Ordinary scholars who take no interest in theory usually work on the basis of general ideas which were first put forward by Marxism and were then vigorously combated, but which have become the common property of science.

I apply the term 'Marxist ideology' to the ideological *ensemble* grouped around the values that were brought to the fore by Marx and by Marxist tradition, and which have been exalted even by those Marxists who most cynically trampled upon them in practice. Actually there is nothing specifically Marxist about them. They are the universalistic values that were already put forward by the liberal-humanitarian ideology (to employ Mannheim's terminology) of the eighteenth century. They are derived from a long moral tradition – philosophical and, in part, religious. I remain consciously faithful to them. Ought this to be taken into consideration in a book that is intended to be a scientific work? Yes, in so far as the book fights against conceptions that, in challenging scientific facts, are inspired by hostile ideologies, with the intention of attacking the values that Marxism exalts. This applies, for example, and above all, to the ideology that ascribes absolute supremacy to 'national' values, or 'communal' ones (when what is meant is religious communities).

This is why it is still meaningful to proclaim oneself a Marxist on the plane of socio-historical studies. This view is challenged by good historians and good sociologists who think that all the valid elements in the Marxist theses have been incorporated in science in general. That is true to a large extent, as has already been said. But also, in many sectors of the humane sciences, those most favourable to the development of irresponsible philosophico-literary chatter, in the sector of generalization (where poorly-equipped researchers easily tend to rely on bad philosophy; or else, as Engels well put it, while wishing not to concern themselves with philosophy at all, automatically secrete bad philosophy); and, finally, in the sectors that are directly linked with the preoccupations of the conflicting ideologies, an anti-scientific, and thereby anti-Marxist, tendency is continually reappearing. So long as this goes on making itself felt – and that, I fear, will be for a long time yet – there will be justification for proclaiming oneself a Marxist in this field.

I have been helped by many friends with whom I have discussed the problems brought up in this book. I can only thank them collectively. They are too numerous for me to list, and to make a selection among them would misrepresent the matter. They are well aware how grateful I am to them, as I am also to those who have helped me bring this book into existence – most particularly my wife, and also Jean Lacouture, who was the first to suggest that I expand a score of lines I had written on this subject as a contribution to a colloquium, to the dimensions of an article – which in turn grew into a book. I set forth the substance of it in a series of lectures at the Faculty of Arts in Algiers in March 1965, and the subsequent discussions also proved very helpful to me.

I, better than anyone else, realize the shortcomings of this work – so ambitious in its aim. I am too well aware of the gaps in my knowledge to enjoy that peace of mind that ignorance confers on so many authors of presumptuous essays. My excuse is that there were things that needed to be said and that I saw nobody saying them to the public interested in the matter, both in an accessible way and on the basis of an adequately sound and extensive documentation. Others, I hope, will do better than I. May I at least, in the words of a Finnish folk-song, have succeeded in blazing 'a fresh trail for more illustrious singers to follow, men richer in songs, from among the young people now growing up, in the rising generation'.

1 The Problem Stated

One thing is now clear to us all: the problem of the under-developed countries, of the growing contrast between the prosperous and sated world of the industrialized communities and the hungry universe in which the remainder of mankind struggles for life, is one of the two or three major problems of our time. In discussing it, a mass of other crucial questions arise in turn. The whole of this Third World, as it is called, is obsessed by the desire to draw level as soon as possible, in some respects at least, with the industrialized world in one or other of its two forms, or in a mixture of both. What does this really imply? How far is it necessary to go in the process of drawing level in order to achieve the enviable prosperity of the industrialized countries? Must one go so far as to sacrifice values that are specially cherished, those that constitute the particularity, the individuality, the identity of the peoples concerned? And what if these values (or some of them at least) are precisely the factor responsible for the backwardness that is now so obvious?

The problem has been widely argued about, with the heat and feeling that are aroused only by something that is of really vital importance to everyone. This is especially true of that very considerable section of the underdeveloped countries that make up the Muslim world – or to be precise, the world where for the last few centuries the Muslim religion has been predominant (for one cannot be too precise with regard to this matter: it is the unity of this world on every level that is just what is in question). Throughout these countries the discussion concentrates around certain key ideas: economic development, socialism, capitalism, the nation, Islam – how are these different concepts to be related together? Politics in the most immediate, practical and everyday meaning of the word demands that this question be clarified and answers found. Rulers act, ideologists and politicians put forward programmes in accordance with the answers (whether implicit or explicit, carefully thought out or inspired by violent feelings, theoretical or pragmatic) that they give to this question.

Moreover, in considering this matter one soon becomes involved in problems that transcend the present period and that draw one into discussions of a more theoretical and fundamental character. What are the connections, the exact relations, between economic activity; political activity; ideology (whether religious or otherwise); and cultural tradition? Here we find theories in conflict: philosophers, sociologists, scholars enter the game, advancing their views which are no doubt partly inspired by the facts that they study (or are supposed to study!) but which yet owe something to the passions, interests and aspirations of the circles in which they live, the ways of thinking handed down to them by their predecessors, and sometimes (more often than is thought) to sheer desire to shine in some salon, lecture-theatre or meeting-hall. Yet it is possible to discover here the same general tendencies that have always conflicted with each other in connection with our understanding of the phenomena of human society.

This book, which is intended to contribute to elucidating these problems, considers both the phenomena of the present time and the great fundamental issues. Although I have approached these from one particular angle only, I have realized in the course of writing that – all the same – everything was being called in question.

Capitalism and Islam: here was a problem that had been discussed by Muslims and by orientalists, by economists and by historians in Europe. The debate was far from lacking in a basis. The Muslims, moved either by piety or nationalism (or both), were concerned to show that nothing in their religious tradition was opposed to the adoption of modern and progressive economic methods,[1] or else to show that this tradition tended to favour economic and social justice.[2] Some European scholars who are sympathetic towards Islam also uphold one or other of these views.[3] Others who are, on the contrary, hostile to Islam (and who are backed by a horde of publicists who know nothing whatsoever about the subject), endeavour to show that this religion, by forbidding those who hold it to engage in any progressive economic initiative, dooms them to stagnation[4] – or else (a recent variant of the same theory) fatally predisposes them to a satanic alliance with Communism, itself intrinsically evil.[5] The conclusion to be drawn is that these (Muslim) peoples must be vigorously combated, in the interest of the progress of civilization in general. All these views, however they may contradict each other, are based, it should be observed, upon the same implicit presupposition. They assume that the men of a given epoch and a given region, that whole societies give strict obedience to a previously formed doctrine, which has taken shape independently of them; that they follow its precepts (and soak themselves in its spirit) without these undergoing any essential transformation, and without these men adapting them to their conditions of life and the attendant modes of thought. This presupposition, of which the supporters of these views are usually not even aware, seems to me to distort the whole problematic of this discussion. Nevertheless I shall examine their ideas without taking account of this basic objection, since not everyone will agree to it.

Only a few serious writers,[6] mostly inspired by Marxism, have looked at the problem in a manner that is both impartial and also in conformity with a sounder sociological idea of the relations between ideological doctrines and social realities.[7] Why, in fact, did capitalism triumph in modern times in Europe, and not in the Muslim countries (among others)? But also – why has European capitalism been able to penetrate the Muslim world so easily? In the past and in the present, has Islam, or at least, the cultural tradition of the Muslim countries, favoured (or does it favour?) capitalism, or socialism, or a backward economy of the 'feudal' type? Or does it urge those who are influenced by it in a quite different direction, a new economic system specific to Islam?

What is capitalism?

It may seem odd that most of those who have dealt with the
problem of capitalism (and they are legion) have omitted to
stop and define the concept they were employing. Actually,
this is odd only for those who have a naïve notion about scholar-
ship and scholars. One of the favourite procedures of present-
day obscurantism consists in playing upon the vagueness in
which the concepts employed have deliberately been allowed
to remain. Against this tendency we need to get back to the
eighteenth century's insistence – which is indeed a requirement
for any scientific work worthy of the name – upon always defining the words one uses and using them only in the meaning thus
defined.

It must be plainly understood that the term 'capitalism' has
been used in two different senses. More precisely, it has been
used in a wide variety of senses which can be grouped in two
different semantic fields; a great deal of the argument that has
gone on, for example, about whether or not classical antiquity
experienced capitalism, can be reduced to a confusion between
these two groups of meanings.

On the one hand, the term 'capitalism' has been used to
signify certain economic institutions taken in isolation, or a
combination of several of these; or else a state of mind that may
accompany and inspire operations carried on within the framework of these institutions. In all such cases the writers who
used the concept in this way did not consider that it necessarily
applied to a society as a whole. Capitalist institutions or a
capitalist mentality can coexist with institutions or a mentality
of a different type within one and the same society. They can
exist as 'minorities' in such a society. Among these institutions
and mental characteristics that are, at least partially, capitalist
in type have been mentioned: private ownership of the means of
production, free enterprise, striving-for-profit as the chief
motive force in economic activity, production for the market,
money economy, the mechanism of competition, rationality in
the conduct of an enterprise, and so on.

On the other hand, the description 'capitalist' has been given
to a society, taken as a whole, in which institutions or a mentality

defined as capitalist are predominant. Thus, in particular, this description has been applied to Western European society (with its American extensions) since a date which varies from writer to writer – the beginning of the nineteenth century, the sixteenth century, etc. – and sometimes to other societies as well, such as the Roman Empire at a certain period.[8]

It is obviously difficult to discuss a problem such as the one being considered here when the concept that is first and foremost in question is subject to so many divergent definitions – if one wants to take all these definitions into account. Contrariwise, it would be too easy to adopt one particular definition, as so many dogmatic Marxists have done, and settle the matter on the basis of this definition. One may prove, for instance, that a certain society is not capitalist *in this sense*. But that will not convince in the least those who hold to another definition of capitalism. Moreover, it must be appreciated (as the dogmatic Marxists in question do not appreciate) that no definition is *in itself* more 'scientific' than another. In any scientific discussion anyone is free to choose the definition he prefers, provided this is logically coherent and he sticks to it throughout the discussion. Choice between definitions is a matter chiefly important for teaching purposes, or in relation to the greater or lesser convenience of certain definitions in argument and research. It is therefore preferable to employ definitions that demarcate concepts that are useful in analysing phenomena in depth.

A choice has to be made. I have chosen definitions that belong to the framework of Marxist economic and sociological thought. A further distinction is called for, however. Marx and the Marxists have used the terms 'capitalism' and 'capitalist' more coherently than many non-Marxist writers. Nevertheless, it is also true that they have applied these terms both to particular economic institutions and to the society of modern Europe where these institutions have developed to an especially high degree. It is thus possible to distinguish between uses of these terms in different (although closely connected) senses in Marxist writings. The distinction was implicit between the concepts to which they were applied, but it is of some importance in a discussion of this sort to separate them quite sharply.[9] I have adopted, in order to distinguish between these concepts, the terminology of the Polish sociologist Julian Hochfeld, who has, I think, gone further than anyone else up to now towards achieving precision in these matters.[10] Here, then, are some of the notions between which I shall distinguish.

On the one hand, capitalism is a 'mode of production' in the strict sense of the word, that is, an economic model in accordance with which production can be carried on in an 'enterprise' (in the widest sense of this term). An owner of means of production pays a wage to free workers in order that the latter may, using the aforesaid means of production, produce commodities which the owner will sell for his own profit. He is an 'industrial capitalist'.[11]

In the second place, it is possible to talk of a capitalist 'sector' in the economic system of a given society, in order to indicate all the enterprises in which, in this society, the capitalist mode of production is operative; this was the usage in Soviet Russia in the period of the New Economic Policy.[12]

Finally, there is a capitalist 'socio-economic formation'. This is what one usually has in mind when speaking of capitalism; it is the formation in which we are living. It is marked by a particular 'economic system' in which the capitalist sector occupies a predominant place, and by an ideological and institutional superstructure corresponding to this.

However, these definitions leave open an important question in a field which, *inter alia*, we are going to study here. Marx explains, in Volume III of *Capital*, that 'not commerce alone, but also merchant's capital, is older than the capitalist mode of production [in this context to be understood as meaning "the capitalist socio-economic formation"], is, in fact, historically the oldest free state of existence of capital [*die historisch älteste freie Existenzweise des Kapitals*]'.[13] 'In all previous modes of production [i.e., in all pre-capitalist socio-economic formations] . . . merchant's capital appears to perform the function *par excellence* of capital.'[14] Further on, he adds to this, usurer's capital, or financial capital: 'Interest-bearing capital, or, as we may call it in its antiquated form, usurer's capital, belongs together with its twin brother, merchant's capital, to the antediluvian forms of capital, which long precede the capitalist mode of production [i.e. the capitalist socio-economic forma-

tion] and are to be found in the most diverse economic formations of society [*in den verschiedensten ökonomischen Gesellschafts-
formationen*].'[15] These are at least forms of that pre-capitalist
commercial capital and usurer's capital which theoreticians like
Max Weber regard as 'a capitalism of various forms'. Marx, like
Weber and like Sombart, considers that the capitalist 'socio-
economic formation', to speak like one of them, or modern
capitalism, to use the language of the others, was born out of the
late-mediaeval European forms of commercial capital and financial capital. At first sight, we seem to find similar forms of capital
in the Muslim world of the Middle Ages. It will be important
for us to establish first of all whether these forms really are
essentially similar to those that were known to mediaeval Europe,
for, if this is so, it will have been proved that Islam is not in itself
an obstacle to the initial stages of an evolution that resulted in
Europe in the capitalist socio-economic formation (or, if the
expression be preferred, modern capitalism). Naturally, if the
answer is affirmative, the question must then arise: why were
these initial stages not followed by the same development as
occurred in Europe, and was Islam responsible for this? So as
to facilitate the discussion, I propose to call 'capitalistic' the
whole of the sector covered by merchant capital and financial
capital in these pre-capitalist societies. This is not in fact a
capitalist sector in the sense in which such a sector existed in
Russia under the N.E.P. *That* capitalist sector embraced a
substantial number of small and medium-sized enterprises in
which the capitalist mode of production in the strict sense was
operative, where 'production-capital'[16] fructified by using the
labour-power of free workers. Only the power of the Soviet
state prevented this capital from developing to the point where
it would have controlled all industrial production. Commercial
capital and financial capital were not at all predominant in this
sector, whereas in the Middle Ages this was indeed their role,
production-capital being then reduced to a very limited function.

The existence of a 'capitalistic' sector like this, in particular,
the 'existence and development to a certain level' of commercial
capital are, according to Marx, the necessary condition (but
not at all the sufficient condition, as he emphasizes) for the
development of the capitalist socio-economic formation.[17] On

this point it is probable that all economists would agree, whatever their differences on terminology and whatever their disagreement with Marx on the nature of the supplementary conditions that made possible in Europe the transition to the capitalist socio-economic formation. It is therefore necessary to check whether this sector existed in the Muslim world in the Middle Ages, and if so whether it had an extent and a structure comparable to those that made possible in Europe the subsequent development of the capitalist socio-economic formation.

A problem of the greatest importance arises here. Before the coming of the capitalist socio-economic formation, can all cases of lending money at interest, and of trade (in the widest sense: every exchange of goods), be regarded as being such as to constitute a 'capitalistic' sector, that is, a sector on the basis of which, certain other conditions being given, a capitalist socio-economic formation might, perhaps, be able to develop? Marx tells us that the existence and development of merchant capital to a certain level are conditions necessary for such a development:

(1) as premises for the concentration of money wealth, and (2) because the capitalist mode of production [i.e. the capitalist socio-economic formation] presupposes production for trade, selling on a large scale, and not to the individual customer, hence also a merchant who does not buy to satisfy his personal wants but concentrates the purchases of many buyers in his one purchase. On the other hand, all development of merchant's capital tends to give production more and more the character of production for exchange-value and to turn products more and more into commodities.[18]

Thus, therefore, 'capitalistic' trade must be, at the very least, wholesale trade which uses money so as to develop production for the market.

Max Weber also defines a specific type of economic activity which he calls capitalist, which underlies modern capitalism (what I call the capitalist socio-economic formation) and prepares the way for it, but which is not identical with it. This is indeed the activity of the sector I am here describing as capitalistic. What is meant is an activity 'which rests on the expectation of profit by the utilization of opportunities for exchange, that is, on (formally) peaceful chances of profit'.[19] This activity must be rational, to a certain degree at least,[20] in other words,

the corresponding action is adjusted to calculations in terms of capital . . . The important fact is always that a calculation of capital in terms of money is made, whether by modern book-keeping methods or in any other way, however primitive or crude.[21]

He adds that 'in this sense capitalism and capitalistic enterprises, even with a considerable rationalization of capitalistic calculation, have existed in all civilized countries of the earth . . . In China, India, Babylon, Egypt, Mediterranean Antiquity, and the Middle Ages, as well as in modern times.'[22] Modern Western capitalism is regarded as being distinguished above all by the appearance, alongside the old forms, of 'the rational capitalist organization of (formally) free labour', which is bound up with a legal separation between economic activity and domestic activity, and with a rational system of accounting.[23]

It is easy enough to see that Marx and Weber have in view, with their convergent criteria, the same type of economic sector anterior to the coming of modern capitalism, or the capitalist socio-economic formation. It is by these criteria that I will here judge whether or not such a 'capitalistic' sector existed in the Muslim world. We can perceive, in any case, that at the very least we need to eliminate from the activities to be considered any form of trade that does not offer these characteristics – in particular, barter, and all those forms, about which we know from ethnological writings, of exchange of a ceremonial character or taking the form of a gift, essentially implying prestige values.[24] Similarly, we must eliminate, as regards credit, all non-monetary forms of lending,[25] all those that do not result in 'concentration of large amounts of money capital', 'the formation of moneyed wealth independent of landed property'.[26] *This* – everyone agrees with Marx on the point – is a condition that is necessary, even if not sufficient, for the development of the capitalist socio-economic formation.

Finally, it is clear that we must eliminate from this definition of a 'capitalistic' sector all the economic structures in which a role is played only by capital defined as the totality of objects and resources already at the disposal of an individual or a society and which they can use for production or the simple making available of other resources, whether these be the product of previous labour or the gift of nature. Thus, the digging stick, the most primitive of agricultural implements, is a capital serving for production, just as a bow, a fishing net and even a mere pole are capitals serving for food-collection, for the acquisition of products that are natural in this sense. Actually, such 'capitals' exist in all societies, even the simplest.[27] Their existence and even their importance are only distantly related to the development of the capitalist socio-economic formation. It is of course necessary that a society shall have already at its disposal a large accumulation of 'capital', in this sense, before there can be any question of 'capitalist' development in the Marxist sense, or in Weber's sense. This is the case with the societies we shall be considering here (except, perhaps, some sectors of pre-Islamic Arab societies) and the question will be shifted to a higher level. Similarly, it is not possible to speak of a capitalistic sector in any sense when a community of shepherds look forward to an increase in their flocks, or even to an increase in the population through additions to their own families – despite the view taken by R. Thurnwald, who speaks of capitalism in such a case.[28] As Melville J. Herskovits puts it, 'he is obviously applying concepts to a situation where, in terms of the culture concerned, they have no applicability'.[29] Even if natural increase in flocks may have contributed to develop the idea of interest, as is suggested by some terminologies (especially Greek), there is a long way to go from that, not only to the capitalist socio-economic formation but even to any feature of the capitalist mentality, in, for example, Weber's sense.

I shall therefore adopt the definitions given above – mode of production, sector, economic system, capitalist socio-economic formation, capitalistic sector – for the sake of clarity in discussion. Nevertheless, so as to avoid committing that error of the dogmatic Marxists which I have pointed out above, I shall in my conclusions take account of other definitions, namely, those adopted by the most important non-Marxist writers. It is impossible not to notice, however, that the latter are tending to draw closer to the Marxist definitions. Most of them agree nowadays to describing European society as 'capitalist', from the economic standpoint, since the sixteenth, or at any rate since the eighteenth century. Most of them, nevertheless, consider that the Italian republics so early as, for example, the thirteenth century, 'present us with types of capitalism that are both commercial and financial'.[30] As no one can describe the European economy as a whole in that period, or even the Italian economy as a whole, as capitalist, as no one denies the importance of the differences between it and what Weber, Sombart and others call modern capitalism, this means acknowledging the existence of what I have called a 'capitalistic sector'. Finally, everybody defines, while stressing differently this feature or that, a type of functioning of an enterprise that is essentially the same, and which corresponds to what is here called, in the strict sense, the capitalist mode of production. It seems clear that all the definitions rule out the possibility of a radically isolated enterprise. The capitalist mode of production can function only within a capitalist 'sector' that is relatively extensive.

2 What Islam Prescribes

The most usual way of dealing with the problem under examination is to ask whether what the Muslim religion prescribes has the effect of favouring, hindering or forbidding those practices which make up the capitalist (or some other) mode of production, or whether these prescriptions are neutral in relation to the practices in question. As will become apparent, this is not in my opinion the most important issue. Nevertheless, it is one that arises and that is of some interest in connection with the problem as a whole. I shall therefore take a quick look at it.

The Koran and the Sunnah

The prescriptions of the Muslim religion are codified in one precise and well-defined document called the Koran – God's Word as conveyed to the Prophet Muḥammad – and in a very large and ill-defined number of short texts, called the Sunnah. The latter is the totality of the 'traditions' which record what the Prophet is supposed to have said or done. It is agreed that these words and deeds of the Prophet possess normative value for Muslims, who ought to imitate Muḥammad and carry out his directives. Here one needs to emphasize that these traditions are accepted by historians as truly representing the Prophet's thoughts only in a very limited number of cases. Actually, even today, Muslim writers, including those who are no longer Muslims except in name and by more or less obligatory conformism, and those who have taken up a clearly atheistic, even anti-religious, position, frequently refer to these traditions as though they were authentic historical documents.[1] Now, we know that these traditions were not set down in writing until two or three centuries after the Prophet's time, and that there was a whole period of Muslim history during which such accounts were considered to be of little interest and no value.[2] True, their documentary value is alleged to be supported by the chain (*isnād*) of witnesses which always accompanies them .The last person who reports one of these traditions states that he heard it from someone who, through several intermediaries (all named), had the story, in the last analysis, from a contemporary of Muḥammad's who saw it happen with his own eyes or heard it said with his own ears. However, one cannot rely on these chains of witnesses, for which there is no guarantee of authenticity. Many of the traditions contradict each other, a fact which led Arab writers already in mediaeval times to reject a certain number of them as fictional and to classify others as suspect or dubious, in accordance with various criteria. Modern historical method is a great deal more stringent in its legitimate requirements for evidence of truth. A tradition cannot be accepted as being possibly authentic unless very powerful arguments show it to be such. This applies only to a tiny minority among them, at least where the normative traditions are concerned.[3] But they remain as documents for the epoch at which they may have been invented, and for subsequent epochs. They show what some men thought, what some tendencies tried to get adopted as norms. In so far as they were obeyed, they represent the Muslims' code of behaviour. It must always be remembered, however, that the contradictions between them left a great deal of latitude in practical life – all the more so because there was no centralized authority (as in the case of the Roman Catholic Church) to lay down authoritatively a ruling on the value of any particular tradition or the interpretation thereof.

Let us first look at the Koran, the Word of God, and therefore (although only in principle) a fundamental and irrefutable authority. It is not, of course, a treatise of political economy, and one would seek in it in vain to find approval or condemnation of capitalism as such. But cannot one find, at least, some evaluations of those economic institutions which are regarded as capitalist in character, or as constituting the foundations or the elements of the capitalist socio-economic formation? It is quite clear, in the first place, that the Koran has nothing against private property, since it lays down rules for inheritance, for example. It even advises that inequalities be not challenged,[4] contenting itself with denouncing the habitual impiety of rich men,[5] stressing the uselessness of wealth in face of God's judgement and the temptation to neglect religion that wealth brings.[6] Does it make an exception of property in the means of production? Quite clearly, the notion never even occurred to the author of the Koran. Wage-labour is a natural institution to which there can be no objection. Very many times the Koran speaks of the wages of man in relation to God. In one place it shows us Jethro the Midianite about to hire Moses as a wage-earning shepherd.[7] If a man repairs a wall that is collapsing, he has a right to be paid a wage,[8] and this could have been demanded by one of the prophets and by Muḥammad himself, who nevertheless preached without payment.[9]

There are religions whose sacred texts discourage economic activity in general, counselling their followers to rely on God to provide them with their daily bread, or, more particularly, looking askance at any striving for profit. This is certainly not the case with the Koran, which looks with favour upon commercial activity, confining itself to condemning fraudulent practices and requiring abstention from trade during certain religious festivals.[10] The Koran, as a present-day Muslim apologist honestly sums up the position, 'does not merely say that one must not forget one's portion of this world (28:77), it also says that it is proper to combine the practice of religion and material life, carrying on trade even during pilgrimages, and goes so far as to mention commercial profit under the name of "God's bounty"',[11] (2:193–194/197–198; 62:9–10).

What is most important, though, is that the Koran contains some passages which have been extensively referred to, as will be seen later, condemning a practice which is called in Arabic *ribā*. What *ribā* was, exactly, we do not know for certain. Strictly, the word means 'increase'. It does not appear to signify mere 'interest', in the sense in which we use this word, but rather, the doubling of a sum owed (capital and interest, in money or in kind) when the debtor cannot pay it back at the moment when it falls due. Like most of the Koran's prescriptions (as also those of many other religions), this is perhaps a 'nonce-rule' adopted in order to deal with some temporary circumstance, but which came subsequently to be accorded a universal value, it being thought that God could not have legislated for conditions so limited in time and space. The various passages of the Koran that prohibit *ribā* seem sometimes to be aimed at the Muslims, sometimes at the pagans (this was, it is said, a Meccan practice), and sometimes at the Jews and the Christians. The Jews are also blamed for breaking their own laws forbidding usury. It is possible, some have thought, that it may have been designed, at a time when the little Muslim community, poor and surrounded by enemies in Medina, was trying hard to collect funds from the 'sympathizers', to stigmatize those among the latter who refused to lend money to the Muslims on reasonable conditions. But it is also, from the plain meaning of the passages concerned, a question of getting the Muslims to prefer paying the *zakāt*, alms for the needy distributed through the welfare fund controlled by the Prophet (and which he also used for other purposes), to making more profane, but more profitable use of their resources, by lending at interest.[12]

The Sunnah has, quite obviously, nothing more to say than the Koran on the subject of capitalism. As for private property, it does not challenge this. True, ownership in general is regarded as depending less upon the independent activity of men than upon God's will. True, the use made of whatever is owned is restricted by the prohibition of usury and the legal obligation to give alms. True, and especially, property may exist in undivided form within a family, as well as being private in the strict sense, and this widespread undivided state of ownership is in some respects safeguarded by law. Similarly, there are by custom in the Islamic countries some lands belonging in common to a tribe or a village, which, though not recognized as such by religious law, are nevertheless under its protection. Some kinds of primary product, such as water and grass, are not subject to appropriation. In some ways the Muslim state holds a *dominium eminens* over land.[13] This right of ownership is also limited by certain considerations such as the right of everyone to life. A man dying of hunger is justified in taking (by force, if he can do this in no other way) the minimum of food he needs to keep him alive, at the expense of the 'legitimate' owner.[14] But restrictions of this sort are allowed for by Christian theologians and laid down in a variety of laws, both religious and secular. All this in no way prevents, in practice, the Muslim owner of private property from quite legitimately causing his property to fructify in the capitalist manner, without any more restrictions, whether legal, religious, moral or customary, than the Christian private owner is subject to. There is, of course, no special restriction in religious law upon ownership of the means of production.

Similarly, wage-labour is seen as something perfectly normal. It is a particular case of hiring. One hires a man's labour-power just as one hires a house or a boat. The restrictions laid down are the usual ones that result from moral or religious considerations, or which are derived from other principles of a juridical order.[15] Stress has often been laid upon a special restriction which goes beyond questions of hire, namely, *gharar* (chance). Tradition has, in fact, developed to an enormous degree the prohibition which the Koran lays upon a certain game of chance (*maysir*). Any gain that may result from chance, from undetermined causes, is here prohibited. Thus, it would be wrong to get a workman to skin an animal by promising to give him half the skin as reward, or to get him to grind some grain by promising him the bran separated out by the grinding process, and so on. It is impossible to know for certain whether the skin may not be damaged and lose its value in the course of the work, or to know how much bran will be produced.[16]

Economic activity, the search for profit, trade, and consequently, production for the market, are looked upon with no less favour by Muslim tradition than by the Koran itself. We even find eulogistic formulations about merchants. It is reported that the Prophet said: 'The merchant who is sincere and trustworthy will (at the Judgement Day) be among the prophets, the just and the martyrs',[17] or: 'The trustworthy merchant will sit in the shade of God's throne at the Day of Judgement', or: 'Merchants are the messengers of this world and God's faithful trustees on Earth.'[18] According to holy tradition, trade is a superior way of earning one's livelihood: 'If thou profit by doing what is permitted, thy deed is a *djihād* [that is, is identified with holy war or any vigorous effort undertaken for God's cause] and, if thou usest it for thy family and kindred, this will be a *ṣadaqa* [that is, a pious work of charity]; and, truly, a *dirham* [drachma, silver coin] lawfully gained from trade is worth more than ten *dirhams* gained in any other way.'[19] The taste for business that was characteristic of the Prophet and of the holy Caliphs, his first successors, was reported with tenderness. 'Umar is alleged to have said: 'Death can come upon me nowhere more pleasantly than where I am engaged in business in the market, buying and selling on behalf of my family.' A sort of nostalgia is supposed to have affected these august persons, worthy in this respect of American businessmen, when they thought about the next world. 'If God let the dwellers in Paradise engage in trade', the Prophet is claimed to have said, 'they would trade in fabrics and in spices.' Or, again: 'If there were trading in Paradise, I should choose to trade in fabrics, for Abū Bakr the Sincere was a trader in fabrics.'[20] A Muslim apologist of the present day whom I have already quoted sums up the attitude of the Sunnah in terms worthy of Guizot: 'The Prophet heaps praise upon those who, far from being parasites, enrich themselves so as to be able to help the deprived.'[21] As always, contradictory passages can be found, but, except in isolated instances which perhaps reflect an ascetic tendency, the person criticized is the dishonest merchant, not the trader or trade as such.

Certain commercial practices are, however, forbidden by the Sunnah. These are, in the first place, of course, practices that are in one way or another fraudulent, together with trade in goods regarded by religion as impure: wine, pigs, animals that have died otherwise than by ritual slaughter, or in goods that are considered to be common to everyone: water, grass, fire.[22] Prohibitions directed against various practices have been seen as laying fetters upon the free working of a liberal economy. Thus, any speculation in foodstuffs, and especially the cornering of them, is forbidden. Above all, however, what is involved is prohibition of any selling in which there is an element of uncertainty. For instance, sale by auction, since the seller does not know what price he will get for the object being sold, or any sale in which the merchandise is not precisely, numerically defined (e.g. the fruits growing on a palm-tree) although the price is expressed in definite terms, etc. Attention has been drawn to the prohibition of aleatory contracts, a category to which the examples just quoted may be assigned. Some traditions, however, seem to make of *gharar* (chance) a special case – for instance, the sale of a slave or an animal that has run away, of an animal still in its mother's womb, etc. As usual, there are many disagreements among the learned over details, but the principle is accepted by all. It should be observed that the basis to be found in the Koran for this prohibition is rather slight. It can be linked only with the prohibition of *ribā* and that of the game of chance called *maysir*, so that it has an artificial justification, established *a posteriori*. The origin of this attitude in the Prophet's opinions being extremely doubtful, it is clear that later theories and practices, whose source is open to discussion, have been linked to these verses of the Koran and sanctified by more explicit traditions.

Contrariwise, the prohibition of *ribā* is indeed found in the Koran, as we have seen, and subsequent authorities have endeavoured to interpret and define it by exegesis. What this *ribā* was, exactly, was not known. One tradition even said that the verse of the Koran relating to it was the last to have been revealed, so that the Prophet died before he was able to explain what it meant. The interpretations given to the word and to the precept have been extremely varied. At first, it seems, *ribā* was understood as meaning the exaction of any interest at all when money or foodstuffs were lent. The definition of *ribā* was subsequently made more precise through a complex process of logical deductions and external influences, the course and the motives of which are not well understood. In any case, the results arrived at are, strictly speaking, without any justification in the text of the Koran. They can be legitimized only by alleged statements made by the Prophet which we have no reason to regard as genuine. In general, *ribā* was taken to mean any advantage accruing to one of the contracting parties in the sale or barter of precious metals or foodstuffs. In this sort of transaction, only perfect equivalence between what is supplied by each party is permissible. Jurists refined the definition of this equivalence, sometimes laying down requirements that were quite utopian, and always referring to the authority of so-called traditions of the Companions of the Prophet. Others, on the contrary, were insistent only on the time aspect, forbidding every transaction that was not a cash purchase. The variety of points of view expressed in the traditions is altogether rather wide, and leaves a good deal of latitude to the benefit of the doubt, especially when neither foodstuffs nor gold and silver are involved.[23]

An obstacle to competition might be found in certain scanty traditions which, advocating absolute honesty in trade, prescribe that one should not praise one's merchandise, that any defects in it should be pointed out, and so on.[24]

An ideal of social justice?

The whole question that has just been discussed may be looked at afresh in a more general and universal light. The modern apologists of Islam organize the precepts which have been mentioned, along with some others, into a system which they claim represents justice in social matters.[25] Their assertion is justified, in a way. Every society taken as a whole has, indeed, its own overall conception of social justice, with sometimes also divergent conceptions within it that express the opinions of different social strata, particular groups or even separate individuals. There is no reason to doubt that the social precepts of the Koran represented the social ideal held by Muḥammad and by at least some groups and strata of the society of Mecca and Medina. This ideal was acceptable, at least, in the Arabia of the Prophet's time, since the majority of the Arabs rallied to it without any really irresistible coercion being brought to bear on them.

This ideal does not question the right to own property, whether in consumer goods, objects that can serve for production, land or men. The point has been challenged, as regards ownership of land, by a Pakistani businessman who theorizes about Muslim economics (in opposition to other Pakistani writers, incidentally), one Nāṣir Aḥmed Sheikh.[26] Besides using economic arguments about the hindrance to development that large-scale landownership constitutes, he endeavours to prove by means of textual evidence, in opposition to an important personage, Abū l-Aʿlā Mawdūdī, head of the powerful

Jamāᶜ at-i-Islāmī (the Muslim Society), 'much the most systematic thinker of modern Islam',[27] that Muḥammad and the
Koran were opposed to private ownership of land, at least in so
far as this exceeded the scale of a holding cultivated personally
by the owner. In general, the land ought to be 'nationalized',
and small sections of it periodically allotted to cultivators only.
These two Pakistani Muslims refer each other to traditions that
seem to point in opposite directions. It is a game of no great
significance, for these traditions have no historical value, at any
rate for the Prophet's own time, as has already been said. Moreover, it is clear that (unfortunately) Mawdūdī is the one who is
in the right. The traditions that prohibit one form or another of
leasing land do not in the least mean that large-scale landownership is prohibited as such. They are directed at the element of
uncertainty that is often involved in leasing land in return for a
certain share of the crop, since one does not know in advance
exactly what the yield of the land will be. They thus belong
together with the development by jurists of the prohibition of
ribā (cf. *supra*, p. 18 and *infra*, p. 35). Some, inspired by the
urge to systematize, have gone very far along the road of prohibition. But the more reasonable jurists have restricted themselves to forbidding certain forms in which *ribā* seemed to them
to be especially obvious. They knew very well that the Prophet
himself, his successors and the most venerated of his companions
had themselves leased out their lands in return for dues and
had never contemplated forbidding this practice.[28] The so-called
'nationalization' relates merely to the primitive lack of any clear
distinction between the personal belongings of the head of the
Muslim community and the general resources of this community.
But what was practised on the lands of the leader was certainly
also practised on those of the great men. The last resource of
the advocate of dividing up the land is the Koran, which, indeed,
can alone serve as a serious historical source for the practices of
the Prophet's own time. But the passages in the Koran that he
can bring forward are quite inadequate to prove what he wants
to prove. In the Koran, Moses says to his people, to encourage
them to resist the Egyptians: 'The land belongs to Allah, He
makes whomsoever he willeth of his servants inherit it' (7:
125/128). Elsewhere, reminding his Messenger of his power,

God tells him to proclaim: 'He set up on it [the Earth] [mountain-] peaks above it, and bestowed blessing on it, and decreed in it its [various] foods in four days, equally to those who ask' (41:9/10). This last phrase is understood by some commentators who follow Nāṣir Aḥmed Sheikh as meaning: 'He decreed in it its [various] foods, with equality among those who require [them]'. Even if we accept this meaning it is hard to find in these passages anything but affirmations of God's power.

It is thus clear that the Koran's ideal did not challenge the right of ownership in any form, even if one may think that from certain of the book's principles it would be possible to deduce restriction upon the use and abuse of property in certain cases. This is true of all law-giving. The right to property did not seem to be in any way incompatible with justice. Justice in economic matters consists for the Koran in forbidding a type of gain that was particularly excessive, *ribā*, and in devoting part of the product of the taxes and gifts collected by the head of the community to helping the poor, to hospitality, to the ransoming of prisoners, perhaps to grants or loans to the victims of certain disasters or circumstances of war.[29] It is really a matter of mutual aid organized within the community, with the rich being compelled to participate more or less in proportion to their incomes. It does not affect the differentiation in social conditions, which is conceived as being willed by God, natural and even destined to be perpetuated, doubtless with other criteria, in the next world. 'See how we have given them preference one over the other, but the Hereafter has greater degrees [of honour] and greater preferment' (17:22/21).

This corresponds to an ideal of justice that has been regarded as adequate over many centuries by the majority of mankind including those who suffered by its inadequacies. The history of social ethics consists, however, in the continual appearance of ever new demands. There have always been societies in which part of the population struggled against the privileges of the rest. From the eighteenth century onward, perhaps, this protest against privilege began to become a unified movement, first on the scale of Europe and then on that of the world. It first of all challenged the privileges or deprivations bound up with belonging to a particular 'estate', which conferred a specific status upon a man from birth, such as nobility or slavery. Permanent protest against privileges bound up with belonging to a dominant ethnic group spread ever wider and wider. Eventually, socialist thought put forward an ideal which had in its forefront a struggle against privileges based on the ownership of certain things that confer power over the whole of social life: means of production and sources of materials used for production. It is by no means certain that this evolution has reached its end.

In Muḥammad's time, and in Arabia as throughout the world before the rise of modern capitalism and large-scale industry, ownership of means of production, which was very widespread at the level of the individual workshop (or the workshop with only a few workers), endowed one with no special power in society and could not give rise to protest. Ownership of a large amount of land and movable goods, however, conferred substantial power, especially in certain types of society. Thus, over two centuries before Muḥammad, theoreticians had appeared in Iran who, in connection with a certain system of metaphysics, preached the abolition of this privilege through the collectivization of all goods. Among the possessions that gave the Iranian nobles unacceptable privileges were included the women enclosed in their harems. This doctrine had even been to some extent subjected to the test of power, having been adopted by the Persian ruler Kawādh I (448–531). But Kawādh certainly applied the principles of the communist leader, Mazdak, only in a much less radical form than the latter had preached them.[30] The full right to property was restored by Kawādh's son and successor, Khosrō I, known as Anōsharwān (531–79). It was at the end of his reign that Muḥammad must have been born, and there had undoubtedly been much talk in Arabia about the communistic experiment carried out in the powerful neighbouring empire. Muḥammad, too, rises up, especially at the start of his preaching in Mecca, against riches and the rich. He condemns wealth especially for inspiring men to pride, turning them away from God.[31] His precepts, however, do not attack, as did those of Mazdak and of Zaradusht his master, property as such. The remedy applied to the evils caused by inequality of possessions, taking the form of taxation of the rich, partly in order to support the charitable works of the head of the community, is clearly 'reformist' in type, even for those times. It goes, perhaps, even less far than the precepts adopted by Kawādh, which themselves fell short of the demands of Maz-dakite communism. Since Muḥammad could not but have known about these precepts and this ideology, the fact is not without significance. It was quite mistakenly that, in the work of the great Muslim poet of India, Iqbāl, the *Jāwīd Nāma*, Muḥam-mad's adversaries accused him of being a disciple of the 'non-Arab' doctrine of Mazdak.

Thus, the justice advocated by the ideology of the Koran is not that which socialist thought has established as the ideal of a large section of modern society. Muḥammad was not a socialist, as Grimme thought[32] – and this even though he had, it is true, a not very extreme kind of socialism in mind. There is nothing extraordinary in that. The Koran is not the verbal manifesta-tion of a Supreme Being dictating principles to be applied in every possible form of society, but the work of a man inspired by certain ideals characteristic of the age in which he lived.[33] He was, of course, unable to foresee the power that would one day be put in the hands of some men by their ownership of the means of production. No one can say what his attitude would have been if he had foreseen this.

As for the ideal of justice held in mediaeval Muslim society, so far as we can try to grasp this by means of the Sunnah, it fell somewhat short of the ideal of the Koran. We have, more-over, to distinguish between numerous ideals, which are in part mutually contradictory. Muslim society contained many social and ethnic strata; there were many schools and sects, correspond-ing more or less to the parties of today, expounding their con-flicting theories, all claiming to be based on the 'traditions' which reported the words or deeds of the Prophet, but which were, in the great majority of cases, apocryphal. It is not possible here even to touch upon a study of their various systems. It will suffice to do no more than sketch out a few broad outlines that seem to me beyond controversy.

Some tendencies in Islam contemplated drastic restrictions on the right of ownership, in the form of a limit imposed upon wealth. The source of these conceptions (which are to be found elsewhere than in Islam, and especially in Christianity) is both religious and secular. The religious notion that the good things of this world divert men's hearts from God, that they expose one to the danger of sin, and consequently that the rich and powerful are (very often, at any rate) sinners, is inextricably mixed up with the secular notion that the rich and powerful are unjust and oppressive. We know that these conceptions, familiar to the Prophets of Israel, were developed into some celebrated formulations by Jesus, and subsequently by certain Christian ideologists and sects in the first centuries of our era.[34] They are to be found in the earliest passages of the Koran. They find expression in an attitude of more or less severe hostility towards wealth, in a recommendation to the rich to make worthy use of their possessions, and in a threat to them of punishment by God.

All this, however, can be presented in forms of greater or lesser crudity and emphasis. The extreme form calls upon the rich to abandon all their possessions and give them to the poor, just as Jesus required of the young man of Judaea. It dooms the rich almost inescapably to sin, and threatens them with implacable divine judgement: it is easier for a camel to pass through the eye of a needle than for a rich man to enter into the Kingdom of Heaven. The moderate version is content to require of the rich the payment of reasonable alms and to warn them against the dangers their situation brings for the salvation of their souls, and it does not refuse them hope in God's mercy. The later parts of the Koran clearly lean towards this more moderate line. The latter tends to reduce social problems to equality before God and to dwell upon extra-terrestrial compensations for the inevitable injustices of human society. The extremist attitude usually tends towards an egalitarian vision of the ideal human society. It may be tempted to try and realize this by human means and to think this signifies carrying out God's will. It is difficult when this occurs not to perceive in the tendency in question marks of the frustrations, grievances and social aspirations of individuals and groups. It is not easy to accept the traditional religious and idealist interpretation which sees here merely the conclusion reached by an intellectual process, when it does not discover evil passions lying behind this tendency. The Marxists – now followed by almost all historians – were right, I think, in discerning here an expression of the eternal battle between social groups around the advantages and sources of power.

The extremist tendency found its backing, during the Muslim Middle Ages, in one of the Companions of the Prophet, Abū Dharr al-Ghifārī. Statements were attributed to him according to which, for instance, everyone ought to spend on the service of God, or in charity, the whole of his wealth or income beyond the minimum needed for subsistence. He was said to have shocked people, about ten years after the Prophet's death, by maintaining that the threatening verses in the Koran about rich men unwilling to give alms[35] were applicable to leading members of the Muslim community no less than to the Jewish and Christian clerics aimed at in the preceding verse. He is said to have been banished to a remote locality, as a danger to society.[36] Once again, we cannot separate with certainty what is historical from what is mythical in this portrait of Abū Dharr. It is probable, however, that it has some basis in reality. Whatever the truth may be, Abū Dharr has unexpectedly acquired enormous popularity in the Muslim world of the twentieth century. The socialist and communist Left have seen in him a precursor, or have at least made use of him to prove that socialistic ideas are not alien to the Muslim tradition. Some writers have gone so far as to deduce from his example that communism corresponds to a fundamental requirement of Islam. The Islamic Right wing has no less made use of him to show that Islam was concerned from the very beginning with the social question, and offered a solution to it that transcended the modern systems called capitalism, socialism and communism. It is enough, they say, to go back to the alleged ideas of Abū Dharr, that is, to the redistribution of wealth by way of voluntary alms, of the *zakāt*, etc. – a view that will be discussed later.

What must be kept in mind is this. The semi-mythical Abū Dharr of the Sunnah and of the historians of mediaeval times reflects very well, quite apart from any religious factors, the protest of the disinherited against the frustrations forced upon them by the luxury and oppression of the rich and powerful. This tendency existed both in canalized forms, harmless to the social order, and in activist, revolutionary forms, but it remained without decisive influence. It also ran contrary to Muḥammad's own tendencies towards the end of his life. The doctors of al-Azhar were right in 1948 to bring forward the very clear indications given in the Koran to refute an advocate of the immanence of communism in Islam, who relied for his authority upon Abū Dharr. The Koran does indeed call for a measured degree of generosity, without either miserliness or prodigality (17:31/29; 25:67). The rules it lays down regarding inheritance, for example, assume the stability of acquired wealth, recognized and regulated by God. In a sense, therefore, the *fatwā* (legal opinion) given by the great Muslim university is quite correct in proclaiming with vigour: *lā shūyū ʿiyya fī l-Islām*, 'no communism in Islam'.[37]

Some mediaeval sects adopted this hostile attitude towards the rich, giving it sometimes a more or less ascetic and religious tone, sometimes a more or less activist and revolutionary one, with infinite gradations in between. They had only a limited influence, or else abandoned on their road to power the essentials of their programme regarding this aspect of life. While the Ismaili sect, which held power for many years in several countries, attacked acquired wealth very sharply at the beginning of its career, once it came to power, first in Tunisia and then in Egypt, it did nothing to encroach upon the right to riches. Only what appears to have been a branch of it, the Carmathian movement which came to power in Bahrayn, in Eastern Arabia, established a system of co-operation among free men (the Carmathian republic held many black slaves). This presupposed heavy taxation of the rich in order to finance the state's funds devoted to the relief of the poor. Altogether, it was a sort of 'welfare state', bearing a distant resemblance, *mutatis mutandis*, to those present-day states with well-developed social services, such as Great Britain.

On the whole, the justice which was most sought after by those Muslims who were most anxious to remain faithful to the ideals of the Koran possessed the features mentioned above: a state directed in accordance with the principles revealed by God, treating all believers as equal before the Divine Law, practising within the Muslim community an advanced form of mutual aid, at the expense of the better-off and to the benefit of the poorer sort. This is the ideal that the reforming and revolutionary movements so numerous in Muslim history strove, again and again, to realize. It has been defined as a classless society,[38] a formulation that might be justified if one were to abandon an objective definition of the word 'class' in favour of a subjective one, taking account solely of the felt distinctions between 'horizontal' strata of society which cause some to possess given privileges and others to be deprived of them. The men of the French Revolution, for example, imagined that they were creating a classless society, in the sense that the three 'classes', the previously existing 'estates' (nobility, clergy, third estate) were abolished, and all Frenchmen were thenceforth equal before the law. The distinctions that continued to exist, for example between rich and poor, were regarded by the majority as an irreducible residue of inequality, which was as natural as the distinction between tall and short, strong and weak, but in no way 'pertinent' to the establishment of a 'class' distinction. Similarly, for most of the Muslims of the Middle Ages, equality before the Divine Law, as correctly enforced by the officials and judges charged with this task here below, constituted the ideal. The distinctions between free men and slaves, landowners and tenants, rich and poor, an irreducible residue of inequality, were inevitable and did not encroach, except in cases of 'abuse', upon the only equality that a state could achieve in this world.

There are no grounds for blaming the men of a past age for not realizing an ideal that did not correspond to the conditions of their time. But it is equally absurd to transpose our own age into that past, trying artificially to discover it in that setting. Similarly, to try to reduce the demands of today's consciousness to the demands of an age that is gone is an operation that is, in the strictest sense of the word, reactionary. Neither the justice conceived by the Koran nor that conceived under its influence by the Muslims of the Middle Ages are what the modern ideal calls justice. It is best to be aware of this.

3 Economic Practice in the Muslim World of the Middle Ages

The capitalistic sector

Having set out the theoretical positions of the Koran and the Sunnah, we must now examine how far practice conformed to them, and, more broadly, whether the Muslim world knew the capitalist mode of production, or a capitalistic sector – since it is generally agreed that the capitalist socio-economic formation was never the economic régime in any Muslim country before the present period.

The capitalistic sector was undoubtedly well-developed in a number of aspects, the most obvious being the commercial one. The development of capitalistic trade in the Muslim period is a very well known fact which it will be sufficient to summarize here.

The society in which Islam was born, the society of Mecca, was already a centre of capitalistic trade. The inhabitants of Mecca, belonging to the tribe of Quraysh, caused their capital to fructify through trade and loans at interest in a way that Weber would call rational. By buying and selling commodities they simply sought to increase their capital, which took the form of money. No ceremonial, moral or religious element had much influence in mitigating their zeal to make good use of every opportunity for profit. They are even reproached on this account in the Koran. The traditions of generosity for the sake of prestige, familiar to the leaders of the desert communities, were on their way out. The ritual element was adventitious, aimed only at ensuring divine favour for the rationally-pursued business operations of the Meccan merchants. It was indeed an 'unembedded' economy, to employ Karl Polanyi's terminology, and this to the maximum possible extent. Economic activities were carried out in a framework of economic roles that were grouped in lasting economic organizations, namely, trading companies, and the structure of relations between these companies was in no way 'embedded' in a non-economic context such as the clan.[1] This structure was itself economic, consisting in a market in which prices seem to have fluctuated essentially as a result of supply and demand, so far as internal relations were concerned. When it was a matter of trading relations with the neighbouring states, in connection with the transit trade that was their greatest source of profit, the Meccans had to submit to some extent to the systems of fixed equivalences laid down by these states.[2] However, the non-economic considerations to which these systems might, in part, be subordinate did not come from them but were imposed on them by external societies. To some extent H. Lammens[3] and Martin Hartmann[4] are therefore justified in talking of 'capitalism'. Nevertheless, Mecca was only a small island in the huge peninsula of Arabia which was essentially still at the stage of subsistence economy, with only a very small share of its production directed towards the market. The spice trade that was carried on across Arabia brought income in money, especially to the organizers of transport such as the Qurayshites, and probably also to the leaders of the various tribes through whose territories the caravans passed.[5] This seems to have been enough to disturb the traditional way of life in a certain portion of Arabia. But it was very far from being sufficient to constitute a basis for the development of a really capitalist economy. How could commercial and financial capital have managed to lay hold of productive activity? What form of production would have been involved, and what outlets would it have found?

There then came a transition period when the Arabs made themselves masters of an enormous empire from which they derived substantial profit simply by receiving, directly or indirectly, a share of the tribute levied from the peoples and countries they had conquered. It seems that in this period they preferred to allow their subjects to engage in trade and money-lending, while keeping for themselves the profitable administrative positions, or being content with the fat pensions that the new state provided for all the conquerors. Some Qurayshites, however, continued to carry on the trading activities of their ancestors, as S. D. Goitein has shown: among these was Sa ʿid ibn al-Mosayyab, a man of edifying piety, who also drew a pension and is said to have devoted his leisure to collecting historical and legal traditions.[6]

With the Abbasid revolution of 750, the equality established between ethnic groups, the conversion, now assured, of the majority of the population to Islam, and the Arabization of a large part of the Empire, all caused commercial activity to become widespread among every section of the population, at least to the extent that the natural conditions in which they lived made this possible. The extension of the Empire, embracing regions that formerly had been cut off from each other, afforded an immense field to this activity, bringing new and diverse commodities into a common circuit. Then began the classical period of the economic development of the Muslim Empire and first and foremost its commercial development. This may be seen as broadly continuing (even if there was some lessening of activity) right down to the fourteenth century, inclusive. The merchants of the Muslim Empire conformed perfectly to Weber's criteria for capitalistic activity. They seized any and every opportunity for profit, and calculated their outlays, their encashments and their profits in money terms. Innumerable examples could be given, but it is enough to read the definition of trade given by the great sociologist and historian Ibn Khaldūn, in the fourteenth century. This is unambiguous.

It should be known that commerce means the attempt to make a profit by increasing capital, through buying goods at a low price and selling them at a high price, whether these goods consist of slaves, grain, animals, weapons, or clothing material. The accrued [amount] is called 'profit' [*ribḥ*]. The attempt to make such a profit may be undertaken by storing goods and holding them until the market has fluctuated from low prices to high prices. This will bring a large profit. Or the merchant may transport his goods to another country where they are more in demand than in his own, where he bought them. This [again] will bring a large profit. Therefore, an old merchant said to a person who wanted to find out the

truth about commerce: 'I shall give it to you in two words: Buy
cheap and sell dear. There is commerce for you.' By this, he meant
the same thing that we have just established.[7]

To this quotation should be added what the same writer says
a little later on, commenting, as an aristocrat, upon the shortcomings of merchants. There are few honest men, he says,

among those with whom one deals when engaging in this occupation.
One is obliged to give credit, and many are those who repudiate
their debts. One has to be prepared to face a thousand difficulties
in order to get one's money back, for debtors respect only those
creditors who bear the reputation of being obstinate and litigious.
Those who lack the temperament appropriate to such habits would
do better to refrain from engaging in trade. This is an occupation
in which one necessarily has to make use of cunning, quibbling,
tricks, quarrelsomeness, tactless insistence. Only a few very rare
traders are free from the faults that are implied by a man's accustoming himself to the use of such methods. These few are men who have
become the owners of their initial capital without having been
obliged to acquire it through years of sordid haggling – for example, by inheritance, by a stroke of good luck, etc. This enables
them to entrust to employees the task of causing their capital to
fructify, and to devote themselves mainly to the frequenting of good
society.[8]

It will be seen quite clearly that, for Ibn Khaldūn, who was
able to grasp and penetrate with his sharp eye the whole of the
cultural world around him, the typical merchant is one who
strives, everywhere and all the time, and by any and every
means, to get money. Does he not say that delay in the payment
of debts is harmful to the creditor since, during this period, the
latter is unable to make his capital fructify?[9] This assumes that
the traders concerned do not usually allow their capital to lie
idle. Similarly, a manual of commerce which has been attributed
to the eleventh century defines several types of merchant, who
pursue their activities in an atmosphere wholly in accordance
with Weber's criteria of capitalist economy. There is the bonder
(*khazzān*), who buys goods cheaply and sells them when prices
are on the upturn: he has to be able to foresee price rises and
space out his purchases accordingly. There is the traveller and
exporter (*rakkāḍ*), who needs to possess up-to-date information

on prices in the countries where he disposes of his goods, and on customs duties, so as to be able to calculate correctly his prices and his profit, making allowance for transport charges. He must have a reliable agent in the country concerned, together with a warehouse where he can unload his goods in security. Finally, there is the sleeping partner (*mojahhiz*), who needs to choose a reliable agent. The general advice dispensed by this manual reflects the same setting. For instance, when a man has proved unsuccessful in a particular branch of trade, he is advised to attempt another, following the Prophet's own example; one has to know when to cut one's prices, how to distribute presents wisely, and so on. As has been observed, in this manual price-cutting is recommended as a means of attracting customers, whereas the theological moralist Ghazālī advises that this be done in order to acquire merit with God, to relieve one's co-religionists, and so on.[10]

Regarding the fact that all this activity in search of profit is pursued on a money basis in the civilization he is describing, Ibn Khaldūn is no less clear. 'God', he writes,

created the two mineral 'stones', gold and silver, as the [measure of] value for all capital accumulations. [Gold and silver are what] the inhabitants of the world, by preference, consider treasure and property [to consist of]. Even if, under certain circumstances, other things are acquired, it is only for the purpose of ultimately obtaining [gold and silver]. All other things are subject to market fluctuations, from which [gold and silver] are exempt. They are the basis of profit, property and treasure.[11]

In the purely economic treatises of mediaeval Islam one finds definitions that are perfectly clear, and still valid, of the importance of the precious metals (whether minted or not) as the necessary measure for exchanges between goods and services, as a result of the division of labour. The latter is accounted for by the multiplicity of human needs, both natural and cultural, which has led to the specialization of techniques.[12]

Does all this amount to the constituting of wealth in money distinct from wealth in land, as required by Marx? Certainly the mediaeval Muslim world knew some cases of immense wealth in money and precious metals.[13] True, to be sure, the rich often invested at least part of their wealth in land. It has been suspected that this may perhaps have pointed to development in a non-capitalist direction.[14] But we do not know the relative proportions between investment in land and reinvestment in trade. It certainly depended very largely on time, place and circumstances. Ibn Khaldūn tells us that it is disastrous to invest in land in a period of insecurity. During periods of order and peace, on the contrary, the value of land increases. It never brings in a very large return though. The owner of land cannot rely on the rent he collects to be adequate to support his luxury expenditure, but only to help with his subsistence. It is good to buy land against the eventuality that one may die leaving helpless children, unable to earn their livings. This will enable them to survive. In exceptional cases some men may be able to acquire big fortunes through speculation in land, by buying plots of land that increase greatly in value thanks to their situation. As a general rule, however, the landowner then finds himself despoiled of his property by the military aristocracy.[15] It is clear, from this passage, that in Ibn Khaldūn's view, while landed property might have great political importance, the wealth that mattered was essentially wealth in money, with investment in land constituting only a secondary aspect of wealth.

Similarly, the great development of trade in the Muslim Middle Ages shows that at least part of production was directed towards the market, towards exchange values. True, it has been stressed that a large proportion of this trade was transit trade, which in no way affected the structures of production in the Islamic countries themselves.[16] It is no less the fact that a large proportion of it was internal, consisting of exchange of products between different parts of the Muslim world. This is clearly shown by the local specialization in products both of the crafts and of agriculture. All the geographical writings of the Arab Middle Ages are full of mentions of these specializations, noting them in each section devoted to a town or a district. For example let us take the analyses of Iranian trade between the seventh and eleventh centuries made by B. Spuler. The towns of the North and East, particularly Rayy, Qazwīn and Qomm, exported textiles which often bore the name of the town where they were made and which found their way, in some cases, as far as Europe. Some towns wove silk in various forms: damask, satin, etc., while others worked with cotton, or hides and skins, or made carpets or leather articles. There were even towns and districts that specialized in the exporting of soap, ointments, rose-water and palm-shoots, scent, wax, honey, saffron or indigo. Noted also were many agricultural crops destined for the market: dried fruits, various fresh fruits, especially dates, sugar-cane, spices. Horses and Bactrian camels were bred for the market. The dried fish of the Caspian, the Aral Sea and the Persian Gulf were exported. In certain towns they made weapons, copper pans and pails, scales, articles of furniture, all for export. Furniture was made especially in districts where timber was available: at Pūshang and throughout Afghanistan, in Mazanderan, at Samarkand.[17] Among the foodstuffs that were exported in large quantities – which presupposes the organization of agricultural production in a given district with a view to sale for the market, carried sometimes to the very brink of monoculture – one may mention, in the classical age, the Syrian olive oil which was sent down the Euphrates to Baghdad and district, the dates of Lower Iraq or Arabia, etc.[18] What we know about the prices of certain goods illustrates this orientation towards the market. Big differences in price are to be observed for the same article between the areas where it was produced and those at greater or lesser distances from these areas, or in correlation with greater or lesser ease of transport.[19] Economic and lexicographical treatises contain theoretical discourses on the formation of market prices.[20] Religious jurisprudence condemns practices that might disturb the free play of supply and demand.[21] A tradition allegedly derived from the Prophet himself condemns obligatory price-fixing, that is, the 'maximum', the laying down of price-levels by authority.[22]

Unfortunately we have no quantitative data, and it is quite certain that a subsistence economy prevailed in many sectors throughout the Muslim countries, as also in Europe at the same period. However, the accumulation of data relating to towns and districts certain of whose products were destined to be sold elsewhere shows at least that production for the market was highly developed.[23] Things could not have been otherwise, when we consider how very many towns there were whose means of subsistence could only have come from the countryside, whether near or distant, and how many specialist occupations existed, as we learn from the handbooks of the market police and other documents[24] – a specialization that was carried very far indeed. It is quite obvious that all these numerous craftsmen of many different sorts represented an extremely substantial volume of production destined for exchange.

To this development of commercial capital in a clearly capitalistic direction must be added that of financial capital in the same direction. The practice of lending at interest, with the development of financial capital, was equally well known in the Meccan society[25] in which Islam first appeared, even if Lammens has exaggerated the number and activity of 'bankers' among the Qurayshites.[26] It was undoubtedly practised very extensively in subsequent times, despite the Koran's prohibition of *ribā*. This is what has to be shown here, not for the benefit of Orientalist historians, who are well aware of it, but in opposition to certain popularizers, general economists and jurists who make play with a few impressive words of Arabic. They often try to show that the prohibition of *ribā* prevented any economic activity of the modern type from occurring among the Muslims. They find readers who are dazzled by their erudition, or who are very willing to accept a thesis that appeals to their Arabophobia or their racialism, sometimes disguised in the form of factitious admiration for an idealized traditional civilization disdaining that pursuit of money which is characteristic of the modern world.

It is noteworthy that even modern Muslim apologists like M. Hamidullah do not dare to claim that the prohibition of *ribā* was widely enforced in the classical age. M. Hamidullah, who interprets this prohibition as an attempt at the 'nationalization of credit', with the Muslim State granting interest-free loans, finds evidence for the application of these arrangements only in the reign of Caliph ʿUmar I (634–44).[27] Even this is dubious, given the process of systematic idealization to which the caliphate of ʿUmar has been subjected in Sunni tradition. Even, however, if we accept the historical value of sources belonging to a much later date, what is involved is a period of only ten years in a history covering thirteen centuries.

What indicates clearly that the prohibition of *ribā* had little practical effect is that the doctors of the Law demonstrated great ingenuity in finding ways of getting round the theoretical prohibitions. These methods have a name in Arabic: *ḥiyal*, meaning ruses, or wiles. There are books specially devoted to expounding them, such as those of Abū Bakr Aḥmad al-Khaṣṣāf (d. 874), Abū Ḥātim Maḥmūd al-Qazwīnī (d. about 1050) and Muḥammad Ibn al-Ḥasan ash-Shaybānī (d. 804), which have been published, and in part translated, by J. Schacht.[28] Among the four Sunni schools of law, the Ḥanafite school (to which al-Khaṣṣāf and Shaybānī belonged) was the most tolerant, applying to this case its principle that necessity renders legitimate that which, strictly speaking, is forbidden. It is to be noted that the Hanafite school is followed by the majority of Muslims and that it provided the official legal doctrine of the Ottoman Empire, the greatest Muslim state of modern times, which played a considerable role in history. The Mālikite and Shafiʿite schools are uncompromising, in principle, but they, too, accept some of the *ḥiyal*. Let me quote one as an example. I sell this book which is on my table to X, for 120 francs, to be paid in a year's time, but then I buy it back from him immediately for one hundred francs, payable on the spot. In this way I keep my book, I have given him one hundred francs, and I shall receive 120 francs in a year's time. I have not lent at interest but merely bought and sold! The trick seems a crude one. And yet so widespread was it that it was taken over, along with its Arabic name, by the Western Europeans of the Middle Ages.[29] Pascal, in 1656, in the eighth of his *Lettres provinciales*, can still make fun of the Jesuit who explains to him the advantages of this '*mohatra* contract', in which, says 'the good Father', 'it is only the name that is strange'. In 1679 a decree of the Holy Office was still needed to condemn the 'error' according to which '*contractus "mohatra" licitus est*'.[30] Besides, the ingenuity of casuists confronted with the same problem in societies of similar structure often led them to discover the same stratagems without there being any need to borrow a procedure.

Let me take the example of a treatise on law that is regarded as authoritative among the Shīʿites (those who hold the version of the Muslim faith, regarded as heretical by the others, which has been dominant in Iran since the sixteenth century). After having decreed in principle the prohibition of *ribā* (here translated as 'usury'), it adds:

There is a way of avoiding usury. For example. Zeid sells Emru a bushel of wheat, in exchange for some other commodity, while Emru sells Zeid two bushels of wheat in exchange for something else. The goods handed over in exchange for the wheat being of little value, and being given in payment for the wheat, there is no usury here, since the things exchanged are identical neither in kind nor in weight.[31] It is the same when two values of the same kind but different weight are bartered as reciprocal gifts or borrowings,[32] or when the party handing over a larger amount than he receives surrenders the excess amount as a free gift – always provided that these different transactions are not made the subject of a special agreement aimed at getting round the law.[33]

It is hard not to echo the opinion of the translator, who was the French consul in Tabriz: 'No one could recommend more naïvely a legal way of breaking the law.'[34] What it amounts to is simply the authorizing of loans at interest, provided that some additional formalities are observed.

What do we know about the application of the ban in concrete practice, and about the actual use made of the tricks invented in order to dodge it? To judge properly on these matters one would need to have records available which are in fact very few and have been little studied, or to sift through an enormous number of Arabic, Persian, Turkish and other works of every kind. So far, only a small number of analyses of these texts have been effected. Nevertheless, it is possible to point to some characteristic facts.

A great Islamic scholar said that the prohibition of usury caused the trade in money to be monopolized in the Muslim world, first by the Christians and then by the Jews.[35] It is certainly true that the presence at their side of these numerous non-Muslim communities enabled the Muslims, in any case, to find plenty of potential lenders, as well as persons willing to lend their names for use in transactions that the Muslim religion forbade if one were to obey it strictly.[36] But many facts show that such scruples were frequently scorned, at least in certain places and periods. In most cases, wherever non-Muslim communities were present in considerable number, the Muslims willingly let them fulfil the function of moneylenders operating without any camouflage, practising the trade in credit openly and publicly. This did not, generally speaking, prevent them from competing by means of disguised usurious loans, for, after all, every intermediary gets paid. It will be seen that this was the common situation in Morocco, although the Jews there formed a substantial minority who were very willing to relieve the Muslims of the burden of any sin of that order. This fact did not in the least prevent some Muslims of Morocco from indulging on a wide scale in transactions which in practice brought them in a very high rate of interest, even though, strictly speaking (but only strictly speaking), they were legal from the standpoint of the *shariʿa*. The most that can be granted to those who emphasize the importance of the religious prohibition is that the ease of borrowing from non-Muslim lenders tended to favour specialization in usury by the latter, in a society where many trades tended to become the specialities of particular religious, ethnic or local groups. Thus, usurious loans became the speciality of the Jews in Morocco and elsewhere, of the Greeks and other foreigners in modern Egypt, of Hindu merchants of the *banya* caste in India, just as in mediaeval Europe the Jews and the Lombards fulfilled this role, or as in China the bankers of Shansi held from very ancient times a sort of monopoly in this field. Where, however, communities of this kind existed only in numbers that were too small to be able to provide fully for the social function in question, the Muslims readily took this on themselves. And, above all, let me repeat, even where these specialists were present, many Muslims were never too proud to compete with them in another form, usually only lightly disguised. Here are some examples that leave no doubt on this point.

Let us read Jāḥiẓ, an Arabic writer of Negro origin who lived in the second century AH, the ninth century AD, in Iraq, especially at Baṣra, where he was born. Very intelligent, highly cultivated, witty and shrewd, he left behind him works full of irony, brilliantly coloured, varied and intensely realistic. In his satirical book about misers, he writes of two Baṣra misers who practised usury by using the method, described above, of selling something for payment later, with immediate re-purchase of it for cash. First he mentions a rich landowner who made game of borrowers by hinting that, as he had no heir, they would be able, should he die, to disappoint whoever might find himself holding the claims. Many people went to him for loans on that account. Another miser 'was reckoned among the most important and opulent of usurers'. He 'arranged meetings at which usurers and misers assembled to discuss the principles of saving' (that is, of avarice). This man, when demanding payment from a debtor, stressed that he had asked only a low rate of interest from him because he thought he would be reliable. It emerges from these passages that in Jāḥiẓ's day in Baṣra there were many Muslims who practised the lending of money at interest. One cannot say that the ban on usury was not yet in being at that date, for the Arabic words used in the text to mean 'loan' and 'lenders' are precisely the classical technical terms indicating the device for getting round the rule of which I have already spoken.[37]

Let us now take a quite different period and region. A recent study using legal documents enables us to form some idea of economic life in what is now Tunisia, in the twelfth century especially, but also in the two centuries before that. We see numerous loans and purchases on credit are recorded. The trade of moneychanger and banker was flourishing. The bankers controlled at least a substantial proportion of commerce. The wholesalers, apparently, trading in flax, cotton and oil, butchers, and grain-merchants, had accounts with them (kept in terms of gold currency). They nourished these accounts by paying in part of their takings (in silver currency) and paying their suppliers in bills on the bankers. Let it be noted that to receive (or to have the right to receive) gold coins in exchange for payment of silver ones is already *ribā*, forbidden specifically by the Mālikite school of law which was dominant in the Tunisia of that time. Here, then, there was an everyday practice of violation of the canonical rules regarding *ribā*. It is therefore quite probable that this transgression tainted other commercial operations too of which we have record for this period, and which it would be too naïve to suppose were carried on out of philanthropy and piety. Thus, we learn that, about 1087, at Mahdia, pawnbrokers and craftsmen held many pledges. In the words of the writer of the study I am using, who is not concerned with the questions that are the subject of this book: 'We can imagine what was the nature of certain sales with postponed payment, in conjunction with loans alleged to be interest-free. Some traders specialized in this sort of business, carrying out deals in oil or grain.'[38]

The complaints about usurers that appear here and there in Islamic literature assume, of course, that the lending of money at interest was a prosperous activity. For example, in a Persian poem attributed to the Ismaili propagandist of the eleventh century, Nāṣir-i Khosraw, a chapter is devoted to the 'evil dispositions' of the usurers. They are contemptible creatures, who drink the blood of the poor, and are destined to end up in eternal fire. How can one put any trust in people who are ready to lose their souls in return for a limited gain?[39] It is clear from this last reproach, in particular, that the men referred to are Muslims.

Towards the middle of the seventeenth century, in the Ottoman Empire, in Istanbul itself, the administrators of the property of the smaller mosques, who lacked the extensive estates in mortmain that were held by the big ones, obtained income for the upkeep of these places by lending out at interest the funds at their disposal (from gifts and legacies), at the rate of eighteen per cent, as we learn from a European observer.[40]

The *chevalier* Chardin, an excellent observer who spoke Persian and lived for a long time in Iran in the second half of the seventeenth century, notes that usury 'is especially practised by Indians, among the Gentiles, and by the Jews, who are the country's moneychangers and bankers; but the Mohammedans also engage in it so far as their means allow them'. Interest stands at twelve per cent for dealings between merchants, and at about double that for outsiders. One way of getting round the Law is to testify before witnesses that one is lending a certain sum, whereas in reality the amount paid over is less than this.[41]

Now, here is a very thorough study of the commercial city of Fez, in Morocco, at the beginning of the twentieth century. It should be noted that economic activity was carried on there at that time, just as today, essentially by Muslims, with the Jews playing a very minor role. The author sums up what went on:

It is well-known that the Muslim law, at least as it is interpreted by the Mālekites, strictly forbids the lending of money at interest. It is also well-known that the majority of the Muslim traders, while respecting the letter of this precept, have found a way to ensure that they obtain a proper safeguard against the risks they run by lending money or by selling goods on credit. Fez is no exception to so general a rule: René Leclerc quotes an old commercial custom of this place, by which an insolvent merchant is obliged to pay, when the bill falls due, an annual interest of six per cent, or even more, depending on the conditions of the contract.[42]

The same writer quotes a report by the British vice-consul in Fez, dated 1893:

Interest being forbidden by Muslim law causes usury to be a profitable business, particularly in a capital like this, where country farmers, besides Kaids and Governors, frequently resort and have need of funds wherewith to meet Governmental and other demands upon them. An easy way out of the difficulty has been found by such borrowers. They buy a quantity of staple merchandise, such as sugar or cottons, on a long credit and at an absurdly high price, say thirty to fifty or more per cent over the market value. A notarial document is made for the debt, and the borrower than auctions off the goods or (more often) sells them back to the lender, the loss difference amounting thus to the interest forbidden nominally by the Muslim law. The harmful effects of such transactions are self-evident. Many merchants get eager to buy any staple article which they can get on a long credit; glut in the market and ruinously low prices to legitimate traders result, and when a bad agricultural year occurs the notarial documents are quite impossible to realize and the lenders cannot pay their own obligations. This kind of transaction has been, I am told, more or less prevalent all over Morocco for a long time, but it would appear, for the reason before stated, to be more general here than in other Moorish towns.[43]

Anyone disposed to believe that the precepts of the Law on lending at interest are strictly obeyed by pious Muslims should read in the same book the edifying story reproduced there from an account by the French vice-consul *ad interim* in Fez in 1896, Michaux-Bellaire, an Arabic scholar with many Moroccan friends, to whom we owe some excellent observations regarding the Morocco of those days. Visiting a merchant of Fez who was a pious Muslim, he was present at a sordid and hypocritical scene in which the latter, whom he had found engaged in counting over his hoard and stowing it away in a strongbox, protested his inability to lend any ready money to another merchant who came to ask him for a loan. Eventually, he lent this man some sugar which he claimed to have in his possession but which in fact he sent someone out to buy, and which he put down to the borrower's account at twice the normal price. The borrower had to pay back this alleged value (actually, at 100 per cent interest) in three months' time – that is, he got the loan he asked for, but at a rate of 400 per cent annual interest. A deed was drawn up, with a house belonging to the borrower serving as security. Michaux-Bellaire heard what happened subsequently. The borrower proved unable to pay when the time came round; he was allowed a delay in return for a doubling of the amount owed; when he still could not pay, the creditor took possession of the house given as security and for which he had thus paid hardly a quarter of its price. It should be added that he had contributed to his debtor's inability to pay by making him sell back at a low price the sugar he had obliged him to accept in lieu of cash. All this was accompanied by pious, moral formulas about the service he was rendering and the mutual aid that is proper between Muslims.[44] This slice of life, which must have recurred so many times, will enable the reader to judge correctly any sentimental discourses he may chance to hear about the high moral tone that Muslim precepts cause to prevail in economic relations.

Let me quote again, this time some lines from a good observer and great Islamic scholar who wrote about the current practices of economic life in the Holy City of Mecca during his stay there in 1884–5. The Indian Muslims, he says,

draw a large profit not only from trade, in which they are active, but also from moneylending. The Muslim usury-law is, it is true, very severe, and, in the pictures of the Last Days, lending at fifty per cent is given as a sign of the approaching judgement, but many usurers have no scruple about violating the canon-law, and the interpretation of it gives them every sort of opportunity of getting round it.

The commonest modes of evasion are: (1) a higher sum is mentioned in the bill which is for a fixed date; (2) the lender sells the borrower some article at a high price to be paid at a future date and buys it back from him, as arranged, for a smaller sum to be paid down at once . . . Others have proved apt pupils of the Indians in these matters. I have known born Mekkans who according to the bills in their possession had to get from Javanese alone sums lent of from 50,000 to 80,000 Maria Theresa dollars [M.T. dollar = about 10p], though money-lending was not their main business, but only a subsidiary one. The lenders were in despair over the bad state of things in Java, though the sums really amounted at most to only half of those stated. The lenders belonged mostly to the middle class. These usurious practices should make the Mekkans daily expect the Judgement. The ominous word interest (*ribā*) is, however, carefully avoided, what the Mekkans aim at being described as 'profit' (*merābḥah*). Among the most serious competitors of the Indians in this business are the Hadramis [from the Hadramawt]. These come to Mekka almost invariably without money, but endowed with great adaptability and endless endurance. In Mekka they, in the first place, seek situations as day-labourers in some trade. They thus gain local and technical knowledge of which they as soon as possible make the most on their own account; a fourteen-year-old boy who has earned some twenty-five dollars at once puts twenty of them out at interest, and such small loans often bring in one hundred per cent, even though the time for which the money is lent is only a few months.

And later, discussing the way the Meccans exploit those pilgrims who possess some resources, real 'milch-cows':

Does the pilgrim need money, having seen that in Mekka there are all sorts of pleasures to be enjoyed? His new friend, who in the meantime has found out whether he is of rich family, is ready to lend him money in Mekkan fashion; a good loan (*qarḍah ḥasanah*) it is called here when the debtor signs an acknowledgement for double the real amount lent.

A note explains: 'Properly speaking, these words mean that no interest is paid.'[45]

It is hardly necessary to refer to the abundant literature about the misdeeds of usurers in all the Muslim countries of today.[46] No work dealing to any extent with social questions fails to speak of them, no observer omits to note them. The rates of

interest charged are often enormous. Any *ḥila*, however crude
and transparent, is adequate to keep lender and borrower on
the right side of the religious law. The many measures introduced
to set up agricultural credit institutions in all Muslim countries
all aim, whether avowedly or not, at enabling the peasants to
escape from the clutches of the usurers and provide them with
credit at a reasonable rate. Often the usurers borrow from these
land banks at a low rate of interest and then lend at a higher rate
to the peasants, who are unable to have recourse to such complex institutions. Everywhere one comes upon statements like
the following. In North Africa 'not only is lending at interest
practised on a large scale . . . but even usury has grown to a
degree that makes the mind boggle', and 'the result of these
developments exceeds all imagination',[47] wrote a French
lawyer in Algeria in 1935. In Morocco, 'usury is known to
have become, so to speak, an integral part of economic life',[48]
said E. Michaux-Bellaire, whom I have already quoted above.
He emphasizes:

> It is certain that usurious practices are to such an extent an integral
> part of Moroccan commercial custom that they have acquired the
> status of an institution that cannot be touched, something which the
> *shraᶜ* (the *shariᶜa*, the religious law) itself has not only been obliged
> to adapt itself to but has even had, up to a point, to learn to serve,
> lest interests of too high importance be compromised. Usury is to
> be found everywhere.[49]

The statement of reasons for a French decree on putting down
usury in Algeria (decree of 17 July 1936) notes:

> Increasingly numerous complaints, which have resulted in several
> circulars being issued by the Governor-General's office and by the
> Attorney-General of the Algiers Appeal Court, testify to the increas-
> ingly scandalous conduct of Algerian usurers towards both Euro-
> peans and natives, and also to the skill with which they conceal
> the exorbitant profits they obtain from the money loans they pro-
> vide.[50]

Passages of this kind from official and unofficial sources, could
be multiplied almost *ad infinitum*. I will deliberately conclude
my quotations with the comments made in 1908 by an Algerian
Muslim lawyer:

It is a commonplace that usury constitutes one of the great social evils of Algeria. The victims are above all the natives, and they suffer at the hands of Jews, Europeans and also, alas, their own co-religionists, Kabyles, Mozabites and Arabs . . . The Muslims who become involved in usury have a vague feeling, in many cases at any rate, that what they are doing is illegal, and they always mix up usury with interest on capital. This is probably one of the reasons why one observes among them a certain antipathy – purely formal, to be sure – towards interest as such.[51]

Modernistic Muslims tend to attribute such practices to the influence of colonialism, or, where the Arabs are concerned, to foreign domination. Economists who believe in the rigorousness of the Muslim prohibitions would doubtless rather explain these practices by the influence of modern European economy. We have seen, however, that there is evidence for the existence of this kind of fact in much earlier periods, when these factors played no part. It must also be repeated that legal writings, by their stress upon the *ḥiyal*, upon the conditions in which *ribā* is allowable, and so on, themselves testify that the prohibitions laid down by the law were often evaded.

Now, however, a theoretical question arises which it is impossible to avoid answering. It would have been easy to interpret in very narrow fashion the prohibition of *ribā* that is found in the Koran, the only unchallengeable source of doctrine. Why, then, did mediaeval Muslim society provide itself with ideological precepts that conflicted with its practice? If the Sunnah, as we have seen, actually expresses as norms, attributing them to the Prophet, the ideas of the society that produced it, and if we claim that all ideology is inspired by a social situation, why was it that rules were set up which it became necessary to get round, at once or almost at once?

It could be said that this was the work of theoreticians, themselves not directly involved in the operations in question, who were driven by the logic of their system of thought to develop all its consequences, however disagreeable these might prove to be. It is also not impossible that the ban on usury affected the social group to which they belonged less than it affected others. But there are reasons that go deeper than these. Mediaeval Muslim society, like the Christian society contemporary with it, and like the Israelite society of ancient times (when, and in so far as, it was inspired by the Yahwist tendencies) was an ideological society.[52] It openly proclaimed that its *raison d'être* was to serve God, to prepare the paths of God, to obey God's orders. Now, in Islam especially, God's orders included the temporal organization of the community. This organization might not be egalitarian, in certain fields, but it could not but be just and good in relation to all the members of society. When social evils overwhelm some of its members, a society of this kind cannot keep silent. It must, at the very least, 'deal with the problem'. If it lets such things pass without comment it manifestly betrays its mission in the eyes of the victims: the latter are bound to see this, and that seriously affects the faith of the masses in the ideology that inspires the given society.

The ideologists therefore construct a doctrine regarding the problem in question. This doctrine is usually inspired by the ideology's traditions. In respect of the matter we are concerned with, these may go back to the Old Testament, or to Aristotle; these two authorities both condemned lending at interest. In both cases there were ancient protests against the evils caused by a mercantile economy as it infiltrated into the most intimate structures of traditional society. To this economy was contrasted the ideal of the egalitarian peasant community or the autarkic city, together with that of the ideological concept of brotherhood and religious disdain for riches. The doctrine regarding the phenomenon in question was constructed out of the materials available, and in accordance with an appropriate logic, within the framework of more general doctrines about God, the world and mankind.

The doctrine thus deals with the problem, and no one can claim that it ignores it. But does it solve the problem?

Ideologists do not govern, even in Islam. They merely expound God's opinion. There are revolutionary ideologists who think that God desires the destruction pure and simple of a society that is unjust (and therefore impious) and its replacement by a society that conforms to his will (and thereby to justice). Accordingly, they found dissident movements, sects. Other ideologists, however, consider that they can only say what God's law is and call upon rulers to apply it in the society they govern. Rulers, however pious they may be, take account of the requirements of social life – apart from a few doctrinaire sovereigns who insist on trying to make God really reign upon earth. Such rulers – Akhnaton, Josiah, Asoka, Saint Louis – never last very long. There is soon a return to resignation in face of the blind laws of society and of human nature.

The non-revolutionary ideologists, who are always the majority, can then do no more than exhort the rulers to be inspired as fully as possible by the divine standards, denounce those who contravene them, and (at least implicitly) exhort the masses to resignation and contentment with the consolation drawn from awareness of their piety and just conduct towards God – or, at most, to put forward their demands in respectful fashion. This is the only possible path for them if they do not wish to disturb, and risk upsetting, an order that is bound up with the ideologies they defend. In this sense, all religions, and more than that, all state ideologies, are indeed 'opium of the people'.

If civil society (in its preponderant public opinion) becomes more and more severe towards a certain category of social evils and the social stratum held responsible for them, if revolt against these practices becomes more and more widespread among the masses, then the ideologists, too, will arm themselves with a growing severity. Thus the Catholic Church, having been forced by the social situation to deal with the problem of wage-labour, has, for a hundred years now, shown itself increasingly severe towards the evils caused by the working of the capitalist system and increasingly disposed to blame these evils on the capitalists – without (as yet?) going so far as to condemn the capitalist system. The same has been true of its attitude towards colonialism, and, earlier, towards slavery.

If, however, the preponderant public opinion in civil society shows itself more and more indulgent towards the practices in question, in which it increasingly sees activities that are normal and necessary to its functioning and development, despite the harm they may cause to some persons, then ideologists are increasingly led to allow exceptions in favour of these practices, and the ideological authorities to shut their eyes to violations of

their theory. Thenceforth, as G. Le Bras writes regarding mediaeval Christian society, 'doctrine provides justifications that
seem to respect the fundamental principle while permitting
anomalies'.[53]

The more frequent practices contrary to doctrine become,
the more the ideological authorities (if they want to retain, on
the one hand, some influence over society, and, on the other,
some degree of coherence in their intellectual system) are led to
theorize with finesse and subtlety, to allow for cases, exceptions,
degrees of guilt and of innocence, means of atoning more or less
fully for one's offences, and to work out a graduated scale of
penalties and tolerances. It therefore seems quite in order that,
in mediaeval Christian society as in Muslim society, it was at
the very moment when capitalistic practices implying the need
for interest were developing with the greatest vigour that the
theologians and religious lawyers took the greatest trouble to
theorize about the prohibition of interest, justifying it, explaining
it and allowing for cases and exceptions.

The pressure exerted by ideologists and ideological authorities upon political and legal practice takes a different form depending on where they stand in relation to the state. It always,
however, operates in broadly the same way. An ideal is enun-
ciated and men are called upon to conform to it, while it is
acknowledged from the outset that this ideal is too lofty for
human weakness to attain; it is sought to prevent the abuses
of the powerful by means of remonstrances – sometimes, at
most, when circumstances make this possible, by rare but
exemplary sanctions; the weak are protected (to the extent
necessary for safeguarding the social order and maintaining
their confidence in the dominant ideology) by preventing their
grievances and demands from taking a violent turn, hostile to
the ruling ideology and the society whose soul it is; finally,
theoretical solutions are worked out, in relation to the many
concrete cases in which individuals violate the ideology's directives, mixing condemnation, blame, and indulgence in such
proportions as to enable the ideal to be infringed in practice
while preserving its purity in principle. An ideology cannot seek
to oppose the society from which it emanates and which it
inspires. There is not necessarily any Machiavellianism or im-

posture in this, but rather something profounder, a more or less reticent submission to the exigencies of social life.

It is true that, from time to time, rigoristic reformers arose, who ascribed the woes of their time to the prevailing religious laxity and strove to enforce the law's interdicts, in this respect as in others. Their success, however, was always short-lived, as is shown by the fact that, not long afterward, strict Muslims were to be heard voicing the same complaints, and often yet another reformer would arise. We see here the same succession of fallings-off and corrective reforms that is observed in the history of the Christian monastic orders. To return to the particular subject that concerns us here, examples can be quoted of pious persons who seek salvation by lending without interest to those in need, and there were certainly always a small number of these, but the fact made little difference to the economic functioning of society as a whole. Their relative rarity is clearly apparent from the inability of modern apologists of Islam, who are very anxious to offer historical examples of the phenomenon, to find more than a few cases to exhibit.[54]

It is also true that certain epochs in certain places have been notable for the poverty of the economic techniques employed. These were periods of impoverishment. In such periods one also notes fewer cases of violation of the laws on lending at interest, for that practice was then less necessary. On this we have the remarks of the converted Muslim Leo Africanus, at the beginning of the sixteenth century, about the people of North-West Africa:

> They are utterly unskilfull in trades of merchandize, being destitute of bankers and money-changers: wherefore a merchant can doe nothing among them in his absence, but is himselfe constrained to goe in person, whithersoever his wares are carried.[55]

On the one hand, this is certainly an exaggerated picture.[56] On the other, in so far as it does correspond to something real, it concerns a period when the region in question was beginning to be extremely impoverished. To be convinced of this, one has only to compare it with the situation in the previous period, to which some reference has been made above.

This is perhaps the place to make an important point. The

relation of a landowner to a tenant (in the widest sense) is not at all the relation of a capitalist to a proletarian, whether the piece of land involved be rural or urban, cultivated, covered with buildings, leased out, its subsoil exploited, or whatever. Marx and Engels laid stress on this.[57] It is none the less true that the levying of ground rent in money from rural lands, together with the levying of house-rent from buildings in towns (very commonly also in the form of money) plays an important part in the constitution of large fortunes in money and the development of commodity economy. Where, as is often the case, the landowner to whom the rent is paid is a townsman, this contributes to that exploitation of the countryside by the town which, as it develops, can prepare the way for true capitalism.[58] Broadly, and allowing for contradictory factors, one can say that this levying of rents in money form provides an index to the degree to which the capitalistic sector has developed. It may, in conditions parallel to those that apply to financial capital, contribute to an evolution towards capitalism. Now, while it is not easy to estimate the proportion in which rent for cultivated land was levied in money, the size of capital investments in productive buildings like storehouses, baths, and shops, leaps to the eye. Relations between landowners and tenants are a common theme in classical Arabic literature – focused, of course, upon town life.[59]

Let us now proceed to the capitalist mode of production in the strict sense. There can be no doubt that it was known to the Muslim world of the Middle Ages. We have already seen that legal texts and the holy tradition show awareness of it, which is enough to prove that it existed.

However, attention must be paid to the fact that if the capitalist mode of production as it has been defined above, in the strict sense, be taken in its elementary, so to speak, 'atomic' state (that is as an economic relation between two individuals, one of whom is an owner of means of production and the other not), then it can exist as a mere appendix to the mode of production that the Marxists call 'petty commodity production'.[60] In this mode of production, craftsmen who own their instruments of production produce commodities, that is, objects destined not to be consumed by themselves and their families but to be sold on the market – or, in other words, to be exchanged for other commodities serving consumer needs. It is normal, in societies in which industrial production is largely carried on in this way, for a certain number of petty commodity producers (for simplicity's sake, we will call them craftsmen) to take into their service wage-workers towards whom they behave exactly like capitalists of the classical type. In other words, they pay them for their labour-power and get them to work, usually working alongside them themselves, with instruments of labour that belong to these craftsmen-employers. Since they are paid wages, the wage-workers have no right to the commodities which are produced by means of their labour-power but also with the aid of instruments of production that do not belong to them.

This is the form, of course, in which the capitalist mode of production is to be seen in the Muslim world before the nineteenth century. Petty commodity production is predominant, but quite commonly, craftsmen hire wage-workers, whose customary position varies – they may, for example, in a certain period, themselves become craftsmen, given certain conditions. Certainly in many cases, especially, it seems, before the thirteenth century, the system employed in order to procure help in productive work consisted in contracts of partnership. The partners contributed, in various proportions, their labour-power, instruments of production and raw materials, and the division of gains among them was effected, following complex rules of equivalence, in accordance with the relative amounts of these contributions.[61] This meant that there was an undefined range of cases, in which the wage-worker figured as an extreme case, that of a partner who contributed nothing but his labour-power. It nevertheless remains true that this extreme case is important as a type of relationship that was destined to undergo an enormous expansion. But it also remains true that wage-labour existed even at an epoch when partnerships constituted the most frequent case. It seems to have developed later on, after the thirteenth century, when industrial labour was definitively organized in accordance with the system of guilds. Throughout the Middle Ages, the cases we know best are somewhat marginal to our concerns here: workers in the large manufactories run by the state, such as the sugar refineries in Egypt, or employees of religious foundations. Here and there, however, we find evidence of cases of wage-labour in private industry, in the crafts. Only a few random examples will be quoted: about the middle of the ninth century, a future ruler of Iran, the founder of the Ṣaffārid dynasty, earned fifteen dirhams a month as a coppersmith (ṣaffār), and was known all his life long as 'the coppersmith', a name that he transmitted to his dynasty.[62] A legal opinion given in the first half of the twelfth century in Tunisia lays down that miners working in the lead-mines may receive either a fixed wage for a definite task, or a certain quantity of baskets in return for the extraction of a number of baskets of ore determined in advance.[63] In Egypt throughout the early Middle Ages the large-scale textile industry flourished. At Tinnīs there were 5,000 looms. This industry was often carried on by workers in their own homes, but there were also some big workshops. It was partly a state-owned industry, but there seem also to have been private capitalists employing wage-workers for their own benefit, at very low wages – true, under fairly strict supervision by the state.[64] To be added to these is a type of capitalist enterprise which, though rather special, belonged very clearly to this mode of production, namely, pearl-fishing, about which we are pretty well informed. It was carried on, as today, in the Persian Gulf, the Indian Ocean, etc. Entrepreneurs provided the fishermen with equipment, paid them a wage, and sold the pearls for their own profit alone.[65]

In the period when the organized guilds developed, that is, at least from the thirteenth century onward, the wage-worker has a recognized position in each guild. What the documents tell us about the hierarchy within the guilds differs from case to case, partly owing to differences of time and place. The basic grade is that of *ustā* or *muᶜallim*: 'master-worker'. Under him, and dependent on him, are the apprentice (*mubtadiʾ*, *mutaᶜallim*), who is usually not paid a wage but does get tips. The apprentice can either become a master directly, as soon as his own master decides he is worthy, or else he can pass through the stages of *ṣāniᶜ*, 'worker', and *khalīfa* (Turkish *kalfa*), 'assistant', in which, apparently, he receives a wage. In any case, a man may be helped from the guild's solidarity fund to become a master, a transition which seems to have implied, in certain places, the making of a masterpiece, and, everywhere, a costly initiation ceremony.[66]

The master-craftsman thus worked either on his own, or with unpaid apprentices, or with workers who received wages. In Istanbul in the second half of the seventeenth century there were on the average three or four workers to each workshop.[67] We have more precise information about Egypt at the end of the eighteenth century, thanks to the studies made by members of the French expedition. There were at that time in Cairo 15,000 day-labourers without any means of production, possessing only their labour-power.[68] Pottery workshops, for instance, were run by a moulder who was served by workers whom he paid eight *pāras* a day to prepare the mixture of clay and ashes which he shaped on his wheel. He was also helped by a child or a young boy to whom he gave three *pāras* a day, and, in particular, by a worker who was responsible for the firing of the pots. This man, paid by the piece, received ninety *pāras* for every thousand vessels he put into the furnace.[69] Sugarworks were, apparently, attached to sugar-cane fields, and so must have belonged to landowners. Some landowners, however (Mamelukes), were in partnership with a manufacturer in the province of Girgeh, supplying land and animals and undertaking the construction and upkeep of buildings, and sharing the profits with the man who was responsible for running the manufactory. As a rule, the manufactory employed two camel-drivers to convey the canes to the workshop, two workers to strip and prepare them, two to oversee the working of the mill and collect the juice, two to look after the oxen which turned the press, two stokers to keep up the fire under the boilers, two workers to watch over the baking process and the making of sugar-loaves, and, finally, a foreman to control all these branches of work. The twelve workers were paid six *pāras* a day, in money, or two *raṭl* of molasses.[70] There was also a fairly extensive capitalist domestic industry.[71]

The facts set out above by way of examples are very disparate. They would be strengthened if there were more of them, spread over a larger extent in time and space. Even so, however, they are enough to show that the Muslim world when it lived in the traditional fashion, in the shadow of the Koran and the Sunnah, knew a substantial development of activity by commercial and financial capital, and also knew the capitalist mode of production in its aspect as the fructification of productive capital. None of these economic activities seemed unusual or exceptional in that setting.

We are therefore justified, I think, in speaking of a capitalistic sector. The term 'sector' indicates a certain more or less coherent area of the economy where an activity of broadly the same type prevails, carried on by people subject to similar motives. In the society we are studying here we see before us, without any doubt, a large number of persons who possess wealth in money, this forming at least the main part of their property. They play a certain role in production, as compared with the state, the landowners and those who produce for their own subsistence, through the fact that they own lands or workshops, or at least control these through credit. They play a role that is certainly greater than this in the sphere of circulation by virtue of their taking or purchasing an important share of agricultural or craft production, either from the direct producers, or from the landowners, or from the state. Finally, they play a big role in distribution, by selling to retailers, or direct to consumers, the products they have taken or bought, originating either from the lands and workshops they own or control, or from other lands and workshops.

These owners of wealth in money thus play a substantial role in all the stages of economic activity. Their enterprises are subject to rational calculation; they pursue, by means of these enterprises, the aim of increasing, of 'fructifying' their capital. They transform the largest possible quantity of products into commodities, they direct production, so far as they can, towards exchange-values, they develop production for the market and the area of the economy in which money predominates. We are thus justified in talking of a capitalistic sector when referring to their activities taken as a whole.

Nevertheless, the extent of this sector and the development of these activities are limited. Alongside them, and covering an even greater area, we find production by cultivators for their own subsistence, unrelated to the market; the activity of great landowners who take a share of the goods produced on their estates and do not always sell these goods on the market; and the activity of the state, which figures both as a landowner on whose estates production takes place and as an industrial monopolist carrying on production in its workshops, which takes a share of the goods produced anywhere, and which may also buy a further share, in order to sell them back to consumers or intermediaries or else distribute them free of charge – as, for example, to the army, the officials, or the people in the big towns.[72] The proportions between these different paths of the economy, and so the degree of development of the capitalistic sector, have varied a great deal in time and place, and we are not very well equipped to measure them. In any case, it seems clear that, before the age of modern capitalism, the number of instances in which there was a complete capitalist circuit from production to distribution was limited. It was more frequent for the capitalist to take over at some point or other of the circuit from the landowner or from the state.

We may call these capitalists 'bourgeois', using the terminology that has become traditional in the West. In a thought-provoking article, S. D. Goitein has shown how a mainly commercial bourgeoisie took shape in the Muslim world from the second century AH onward (718–815), attained an important social position, won the respect of the other strata of society as well as their own by causing their activities to be accepted as respectable and praiseworthy, imposing the values that were bound up with these activities, during the third century (815–912), and became a socio-economic factor of the highest importance in the fourth century (912–1009). And yet this bourgeoisie, conscious as it was of itself, of its strength and value, never achieved political power as a class, even though many of its individual members succeeded in occupying the highest appointments in the state. From around the eleventh century AD, domination by castes of slave-soldiers, mostly of Turkish origin, became established throughout the Middle East, with the consequence of reducing the bourgeoisie to an even more secondary role in politics, while the extent of the capitalistic sector began to shrink.[73]

Without proceeding to a thorough investigation, it is possible to note that a capitalistic sector of this kind, coexisting with sectors in which subsistence-production and non-monetary circuits predominate, with intervention at various stages by landowners and the state, is to be found in a number of civilizations: the ancient East, Greece, the Roman world, India, China, Japan, mediaeval Europe. Here, too, the proportions between the sectors vary from period to period and from region to region and protracted research would be needed to determine, if and when this were possible, the structural relationships existing between them. Let me simply say that these civilizations soon got beyond the level of mere transit trade, that slipping of intermediaries into the 'pores' of society that Marx speaks of – the level attained by the Meccan capitalists of the pre-Islamic era who went to seek in South Arabia goods (often originating from a long way off) which they then conveyed to the Byzantine towns of Nabatene and Palestine, or the other way round. In all these civilizations capitalists are found to be intervening, to a greater or less extent, from the production stage itself.[74]

It may even be observed that despite all the uncertainty of our knowledge, a level does seem to have been reached in the Muslim world which is not to be found either elsewhere at the same time, or earlier. The density of commercial relations within the Muslim world constituted a sort of world market (to use a somewhat anachronistic term) of unprecedented dimensions. The development of exchange had made possible regional specialization in industry as well as in agriculture, bringing about relations of economic interdependence that sometimes extended over great distances. A world market of the same type was formed in the Roman Empire, but the Muslim 'common market' was very much bigger. Also, it seems to have been more 'capitalist', in the sense that private capital played a greater part in forming it, as compared with the part played by the state than was the case in the Roman Empire.[75] Not only did the Muslim world know a capitalistic sector, but this sector was apparently the most extensive and highly developed in history before the establishment of the world market created by the Western European bourgeoisie, and this did not outstrip it in importance until the sixteenth century. The extent of the market was simply due to the military victories of Islam, the long duration of the unified Muslim Empire, and the power of the ideological bond that prevented watertight frontiers from being formed between the different parts when it did eventually break up. The fact that merchants' private wealth was from an early stage of considerable importance in organizing the world market in question, without intervention by the state, was doubtless due to the unprecedented accumulation of wealth that the conquest concentrated in the hands of certain classes; the size of the demand thus created; the huge profits that could be realized by satisfying it, especially where luxury goods were concerned, the supply of which was much less than the demand; and perhaps also to the initiative shown at the outset by privileged Arab merchants. The states to which Islam succeeded had, at the time of the conquest, no strong state structure in the economic sphere, and the Muslim rulers who took over the previously existing administrations and made these work for their benefit had no 'statist' temptation to overcome. The reason why such 'statism' became established only to a limited degree and only in certain periods in the Muslim world is something that precise historical investigation, studying both the conjunctures of events and the more or less permanent factors, is alone competent to explain. If the bourgeoisie did not maintain and develop the strength it possessed in the first centuries AH; if the states dominated by a hierarchy of nobles and soldiers prevented it from exercising sufficient weight in relation to political power; if the town did not succeed in acquiring sufficient domination over the countryside; if manufacturing capital did not develop on the same scale as in Europe or Japan; if primitive accumulation of capital never attained the European level – all this was due to factors quite other than the Muslim religion. It is possible to perceive permanent and fundamental factors operative here, such as the relative density of the population, providing a supply of plentiful and cheap labour-power and so giving little incentive to the making of technical innovations. Again, there was the centuries-old tradition of a strong state, required in many Eastern countries for their agricultural production, which largely depends on public works.[76] To be added to these there is also, certainly, the unpredictable succession of historical circumstances, among which the waves of invasion coming out of Central Asia must have played an important part.

Feudalism or Asiatic mode of production?

Minds matured in classical ideological Marxism as it was defined by Engels *ad usum profani vulgi*, and reduced to scholastic formulas by the Social-Democratic educational apparatus and later by the Stalinist administrative machine, will certainly have noticed, doubtless with disapproval, that no allusion has been made to the socio-economic formation within which this bourgeoisie developed. Most of them will no doubt have expected to see it labelled, by a Marxist writer, as being 'feudal'. The *Textbook of Political Economy*, which defines the dogma at present in force in the U.S.S.R. and in those countries and parties that follow Soviet leadership, classifies the classical Muslim world quite clearly as belonging to the 'feudal mode of production',[77] although, it is true, with some special features. An eminent Soviet Arabic scholar recently reproached an American colleague for having spoken of the mediaeval Muslim bourgeoisie without placing it in the framework of feudalism.[78] It is still widely accepted in Marxist circles that feudalism was a necessary stage in human evolution, the only stage in which the primary features of the capitalist formation could emerge.

This reserve on my part where the concept of feudalism is concerned is intentional. The name of capitalist socio-economic formation is given to a society with an economic system in which the capitalist mode of production predominates. It is beyond question that Western Europe and the United States have since the nineteenth century formed a typical society in which many features, both infrastructural and superstructural, are due to this preponderance of the capitalist mode of production. Marx and Engels did not distinguish sharply between 'mode of production' and 'socio-economic formation'. They thought they saw in the Europe of the Middle Ages a formation comparable to capitalism. They perceived clearly the mode of production that underlay it, the relations of production between 'serfs' and landowning lords, but did not demarcate it sharply except from the only other pre-capitalist mode of production that they knew well, namely, the slave-owning order. They constantly mingled with their description of this mode of production the superstructural, and more precisely the political, features that accompanied it in Western Europe. This is especially obvious from the name they used to describe it, which was not strictly their own – the traditional name of 'feudalism' which they simply borrowed from the nomenclature current in their time.[79] It was an unfortunate name, as has been said many times already, since it referred essentially to political superstructures the connection of which with the mode of production is hard to define. This blunder in nomenclature has sometimes provided a reason, or a pretext, for non-Marxist scholars to reject out of hand the entire Marxist problematic of this matter.[80]

It is nevertheless significant that, in the only passage – a draft written for his own use – in which Marx sought to examine closely and to define the pre-capitalist formations,[81] he does not discuss feudalism and hardly utilizes even the word itself.[82] The preconditions of capitalism are for him a set of conditions the formation of which he explains rather inadequately, but which are to be found in existence together as the outcome of an evolutionary process that begins in primitive communities of different forms. These forms gradually dissolve, especially those in which private ownership of the soil exists alongside communal property, even if it be restricted by the circumstance that one owns land only by virtue of being a member of the community. The agent of this process of dissolution seems to be, first and foremost, the development of this private property, which tends towards independence with regard to the community, especially under the influence of exchange and of the wars that increase the volume of exchange, causing man himself to enter the domain of goods subject to appropriation, in the form of a serf (*Leibeigen*) or a slave. It is to be observed that these two types of men appropriated by others are put on the same plane. This appropriation of men has to wither away and give place to the free worker, who is one of the essential preconditions of capitalism. There is no question of a stage in which serfdom is particularly dominant succeeding one in which slavery is particularly dominant; what we see is a multiform evolution starting from types that are themselves already different. The term 'feudalism' comes in only incidentally, in order to indicate, for purposes of comparison, the whole political system of mediaeval Europe, with its ties of vassalage, or the historical period of the European Middle Ages.

I would not hesitate to abandon Marx's views if they seemed ill-founded, and indeed I shall abandon them where some points are concerned. But it seems to me that his conception of the role of slavery and serfdom, as it is set forth in these pages, is entirely justified. What we have here are particular modes of production which enter, more or less partially, more or less predominantly, into a variety of economic systems, from the time when exploitation of man by man becomes economically possible, that is, as soon as technical progress has created the possibility of producing a regular surplus (broadly, with the Neolithic 'revolution'), and so long as the capitalist system has not been introduced, presupposing as it does the existence of a mass of free workers. Everyone knows that serfdom, in a very broad sense, was the dominant mode of production (as regards the reproduction of society as a whole) in mediaeval Europe, in which ties of vassalage were also dominant – in other words, the socio-political structure properly called feudal. It remains to be studied how far this mode of production conditioned this socio-political structure.[83] But it is firmly established that serfdom appeared in many other societies besides mediaeval Europe, and apparently in societies which it is hard to classify, from the standpoint of their socio-political superstructure, as belonging to the feudal type.

The conception of dogmatic and institutionalized Marxism, according to which 'feudalism', defined essentially as being based on serfdom as the fundamental mode of production, is a world-wide socio-economic formation, succeeding the slave-owning form of society and preparing the way for capitalism, is thus a conception that is both alien to Marx and contrary to historical facts. The same is true of its conception of this 'feudalism' as evolving in a specific, unilinear way, based on a succession, always in the same order, of the three forms of ground-rent (in labour, in kind, and in money) analysed by Marx in Volume III of *Capital*.

It is therefore perfectly futile to try and classify the socio-economic structure of Muslim society in the Middle Ages as belonging to this formation, even if one renders such a classification more plausible by attributing 'peculiarities' to Oriental 'feudalism', as compared with classical, typical 'feudalism', which is said to be that of Western Europe, as the Soviet *Textbook* does.

Some other Marxist writers have hoped to stay closer to the facts and to Marx's thought by substituting for Oriental feudalism an 'Asiatic mode of production' of which Marx wrote on a number of occasions and which was formally cast out from dogma by institutionalized Marxism in 1931. In the draft mentioned above, Marx saw in this 'Asiatic mode of production' one of the several forms of the primitive community – the one least susceptible to evolution. It was characterized by collective ownership of the soil by the community, without the individual having any right to more than a precarious appropriation, a mere 'possession' (*Besitzung*) of part of the community's land, which possession might or might not be hereditary. The community is '*durchaus* self-sustaining',[84] as Marx writes in his private Anglo-Franco-German jargon, in other words, wholly autarkic, its members making for themselves all the objects they need, over and above their agricultural work.

It was the Indian commune that provided Marx with this model. Noteworthy is the fact that he writes of it, throughout his draft, as an independent unit. Elsewhere, he explained how this commune had, over the ages, formed the basis of the empires that succeeded each other in India. These empires hardly affected its structure, resting content with levying a tribute from it and, in exchange, undertaking the hydraulic works necessary for agricultural production in that country. In other words, here the 'Oriental' mode of production seems to be integrated (in Marx's thought) in a large-scale economic system, a real 'socio-economic formation'.

M. Godelier[85] has tried to promote this formation (he does not distinguish, any more than Marx does *in his terminology*, between 'mode of production', in the strict sense, and 'socio-economic formation') to the rank of a universal, or quasi-universal, stage in the evolution of mankind. He sees it as, in fact, the first form of class society, derived from the primitive community, and with the other formations in turn derived from it.

This notion seems to me to be a thoroughly mistaken one.

The mode of production defined by Marx as the autarkic community is indeed found on the world scale, and there can be no doubt that it is the most primitive form of production (preceded by similarly communal forms of 'collection', at the stage of food gathering, hunting and fishing), dictated by a low technical level and the primitive separateness of human groups. There is no reason why it should be called, as Marx calls it, 'Oriental' or 'Asiatic'. He was thinking more particularly, to be sure, of the primitive *agricultural* community, the Indian form of which he knew. But there have existed everywhere in the world egalitarian agricultural communities of this type. This mode of production might be called, say, the 'primitive communal mode of production'.[86]

On the other hand, when especially in his writings other than the draft on pre-capitalist forms of production, Marx seems to be conceiving an entire socio-economic formation under the same name of 'Asiatic mode of production', it is not possible to go along with him. The essence of this formation is seen as being the levying of a share of the production-surplus of these communities by a 'higher community', a state, which in return intervenes in the conditions of production by organizing large-scale works that are useful, or even indispensable, to this production. Godelier proposes that this concept be extended to the numerous cases in which the state, or higher community, intervenes not in the conditions of production, but in other functions, for example the control of inter-tribal trade.

It would indeed be possible to define in this way a very widespread type of social relations. However, to see in this the *only* relatively primitive type of formation of the structure of exploitation would be erroneous. In the first place, the primitive communal *mode of production* is not the only type of community liable to be exploited by a higher community. Marx indicates this in his draft. He distinguishes other modes of production fundamentally lacking in *internal* exploitation, and names those known to him: the 'antique' mode (defined according to its Roman form, but which he assumes to have been also that of the primitive Greeks and, *nota bene*, the Jews) and the 'Germanic' mode. But he also writes, in passing, of the 'Slavonic' mode, and the list is obviously not a closed one, so far as he is concerned. He sees in these various modes, in which, in contrast to the 'Oriental' mode, private ownership of the soil plays a certain role, a development from the 'Oriental' mode – 'developed to the point of contradiction in classical antiquity and Germanic property, though still the hidden, if antagonistic, foundation'.[87] But

these different forms of relationship of communal tribal members to the tribal land – to the earth upon which it has settled – depend partly on the natural character [*Naturanlagen*] of the tribe, partly on the economic conditions in which the tribe really exercises its ownership of the land, i.e. appropriates its fruits by means of labour. And this in turn will depend on the climate, the physical properties of the soil, the physically conditioned mode of its utilization, the relationship to hostile or neighbouring tribes, and such modifications as are introduced by migrations, historical events, etc.[88]

It is an excellent formulation, and one which I see no reason to try and improve upon. To be further noted is the point that Marx also writes about the special forms of relation between a community of nomadic shepherds and the land.[89]

The community [*Gemeinwesen*] itself appears as the first great force of production; special kinds of conditions of production (e.g. animal husbandry, agriculture) lead to the evolution of a special mode of production and special forces of production, both objective and subjective, the latter appearing as qualities of individuals.[90]

If this is correct, if the primitive modes of production, including those in which private property in land is partly present, are indeed only so many conditioned variants of the *logically* most primitive mode of production, then it is not the transition to another socio-economic formation that *necessarily* conditions the formation of these particular modes of production. They may all equally be exploited by a higher community with a more or less state-like structure, whether or not this community intervenes in the conditions of production.

Modern ethnology and history confirm the views contained in Marx's draft and discredit any conception based on the succession of socio-economic formations allegedly distinguished by different primitive modes of production. Actually, private ownership of land, more or less well defined, appears in primitive communities and there is no correlation between this type of appropriation and the exploitation of the community by a higher community.[91] The first states whose structure we can get to know through history or archaeology, and the simplest of the types of state existing in our own time which are known to us through ethnological observation, are based on exploitation of the surplus of communities in which private appropriation is combined in infinitely varied ways with the rights of the community. The pure concept of private property as an absolute right to use and abuse, as it was defined in Roman law, is rarely if ever encountered. Everywhere there is a hierarchy, a variety of multiple rights of the various communities, families, lineages, religious and political authorities, etc., over the land and its fruits.

If one were to try to classify the modes of production thus observed, the result would be an infinite variety. It would not be possible to correlate with each and every mode of production, if one adopted the scale of a totality defined by the superimposition of a co-ordinating and exploiting state, an economic system and a socio-economic formation the essential features of which would be precisely determined by the predominant mode of production, as is the case with capitalism. Perhaps this would only be the case where the slave-owning mode of production or the serf mode of production was predominant – where production was essentially carried out in slave-owning 'enterprises', by slaves (a very rare case), or in 'enterprises' based on serfdom, as seems to have been the case in mediaeval Western Europe and in Japan. It has to be noted, moreover, that this predominance is hard to define; that it may be challenged in certain regions and certain periods; that, while slavery can be defined fairly clearly, serfdom is a rather vague notion which contains an infinite range of gradations and variations around the exploitation of a peasant enjoying variable legal rights, in particular over the land that he cultivates, by a landowner who also enjoys variable rights, which are never absolute, over this peasant and his land; that it is possible to move imperceptibly from the status of a slave, or that of a free contracting party (farmer, share-cropper, etc.), to serfdom.[92] Furthermore, as will be considered later, exploitation by the landowner, the lord, is in many cases hard to distinguish from exploitation by the state.

Before the age of capitalism, if one seeks to take a 'world' view of the matter, it is possible at most to distinguish a primitive communal mode of production which, by hypothesis, was the only one in existence in the beginnings of mankind. Then came an infinite variety of modes of production with a structure of exploitation, in which one community might exploit another while allowing the latter to retain its independent existence, coherence and autarky, or in which individuals were exploited as individuals by members of the higher 'class' or community, or by this community functioning as a whole. In this domain there were slaves and serfs, public and private. If, in a given region, connections were formed that imply a certain coherence, then one may speak of an economic system existing on the scale of that region. It seems that, in general, these systems imply juxtaposition or articulation of various modes of production, combined in different ways and different proportions. It is to be supposed that these economic systems would be very hard to classify.[93] If we want to speak of socio-economic formations corresponding to the various systems, we shall have to see them as formations that are valid only on the regional scale, which is often a very limited one. Their characteristics will doubtless have some points in common, but only at a level of generalization that is very lofty, and therefore not very specific. Only the striking predominance of a mode of production in a particular system, as happened with slavery in classical Greece (and this assertion calls for some qualifications), or with serfdom in mediaeval Western Europe, would confer on this system and the corresponding socio-economic formation a highly characterized specificity. Even then it would be necessary to take account, at the level of the system and at the level of the formation, of secondary economic features (such as, for example, the development of trade), as regards the former, and cultural features, as regards the latter, which, even if not absolutely fundamental, may be of great importance and modify to a very notable extent the structure and appearance of the whole.

If labels are needed, I would suggest the following terms: 'modes of production in which there is exploitation', adding, as appropriate, the adjective 'communal' or 'individual'. The corresponding economic systems could be called, in general, 'pre-capitalist systems of exploitation', and categories could be distinguished among them, if need be, by means of expressions such as: predominantly communal (or individual), predominantly agrarian (or pastoral), etc. For the particular cases mentioned above it would be wiser to speak of 'systems with a predominant slave-owning (or serf) element' rather than of 'slave-owning society' or 'feudalism'. The corresponding socio-economic formations would all enter into the category of pre-capitalist formations with a basis of exploitation, and here, too, it would be possible to make serious distinctions only by using geographical adjectives, or descriptive terms referring to the predominance of certain elements, among which would have to be included the greater or lesser role played by town life and trade.

The economic system on which the Muslim society of the Middle Ages was based varied between periods and regions. One can say that it consisted in a co-ordination of different modes of production. In the countryside we find village communities exploited from outside by individuals or by the state, in accordance with Marx's schema of the Indian communities, the model for the so-called 'Asiatic mode of production'. On the one hand, however, far from being in every case survivals of primitive communities, there is evidence to suggest that many of them, at least, are of relatively recent formation. On the other hand, they have coexisted, in proportions varying by period and region, with ownership or usufruct of a small plot of land allowed to the individual peasant. Exploitation then occurs through the taking of the surplus by a landowner, by the state or by some other holders of rights (sometimes a collectivity), authorized by miscellaneous forms of legal status. The respective rights of the peasant cultivator and those who hold rights to exploit him have also been very varied, often involving attachment of the peasant to the soil, and thus serfdom, but often also, especially on certain kinds of lands such as gardens, vineyards, etc., with a conception of property relatively close to the Roman one. It will be seen that one cannot classify this system sweepingly either as 'Asiatic' or as 'feudal'. Some lands at some periods were also worked by slaves, as in the case of Lower Iraq in the eighth and ninth centuries, the background of the famous revolt of the Zanj, a slave war which shook the Caliphate between 868 and 883; but this was an exceptional case.[94] Agricultural wage-labour always existed, but the establishment of capitalist agricultural enterprises employing wage-workers only was certainly a very rare case, if indeed it ever occurred. It was in the relations of the holders of exploiting rights among themselves or with the state that structures appeared which at some moments resembled those of European 'feudalism'.[95] These, however, were superstructural phenomena, very interesting, to be sure, but with little effect on the modes of production themselves. The fact that sometimes the state and at other times a 'feudalist' received the dues paid by the peasant (a variation which Soviet writers in general – though an opposition that points out the real facts of the matter is now making itself felt[96] – have turned into an important distinction that is to be fitted into a unilinear evolution, and which Godelier too wants to use as a criterion of demarcation between the 'Asiatic mode of production' and 'feudalism') does not seem to have possessed in reality any major significance. This is all the more so because the line of demarcation is frequently very hard to draw, the 'feudalist' often appearing, in the East, as the representative of the state, or himself constituting the state.

To these agrarian modes of production must be added the urban modes of production that have been mentioned above.

This digression has been a long one, and I beg the reader's pardon for it. It was needed, I think, in order to clarify some questions that are still very confused in Marxist writings. What I have tried to show is that the origins of capitalism cannot be explained, as Marxist dogma considered (contrary to Marx's own ideas), by means of a unilinear evolution of agrarian relations of production. It is from an essentially urban development that one needs to start – the accumulation of substantial wealth in money and the orientation of production (above all, industrial production) towards the market. True, if this urban development is to lead to a capitalist economic system (that is, to a system in which the already existing capitalist mode of production is *dominant*), it must find confronting it a substantial

number of free workers whom it can employ in the capitalist
way, by exploiting their labour power. 'The relationship of
labour to capital . . . presupposes an historical process which
dissolves the different forms in which the labourer is an owner
and the owner labours.'[97] It is therefore above all necessary,
Marx adds, that the relationship of possession between the
worker and the land, the instrument of production, and the consumer goods produced, shall be dissolved: that relationship by
which the worker is placed as a whole (him and not just his
labour-power) among the objective conditions of production,
and can therefore be appropriated as a serf or a slave.[98] This
abundance of labour-power 'freed' from all bonds of this kind
was put at the disposal of the capitalists of Europe at the end of
the feudal epoch, for example, in England towards the end of the
fifteenth century and in the first half of the sixteenth.[99] This was
due to the social, political and incidental conjuncture of Europe
in that period – a conjuncture that has been as yet insufficiently
analysed. Nobody, however, has proved that it could occur only
because the economic system of Europe was based on the mode
of production called 'later feudal' by Marxist dogma, that is,
the exploitation of the peasant by a landowner holding rights
over him, through the exaction of a rent in money. Still less can
it be proved that, as Godelier supposes, the tendency towards
this mode of production goes back to the Greco-Roman option
in favour of a mode of production with private ownership of
land. Nobody has proved, above all, that the predominance of
this mode of production alongside substantial moneyed wealth
in the hands of capitalists was alone capable of bringing about
the development of the capitalist economic system. It is therefore not certain that the existence in the Islamic world of the
various economic systems I have mentioned, with the variety of
agrarian modes of production which they imply in general,
constituted an obstacle to the appearance of capitalism in this
region.

A just society?

Was the mediaeval Muslim economy a 'just' economy? The
wildest apologists for Islam find it hard to maintain this view,

though some particularly ignorant innocents and some unscru-
pulous popularizers and politicians try to do so, and though
few have the courage to refute the mythical ideas that are so
widespread among the masses on this subject.[100] The latter see
in mediaeval Muslim society a regrettable distortion of the
Koranic ideal. Those of a more religious turn of mind ascribe
this distortion to that deplorable *penchant* of human nature
towards evil which religion can explain only by Satan's extraordinary power over this world. Those of a more nationalistic
mentality, among the Arabs at any rate, often see it as a result
of Turkish domination. Has the Muslim ideal never, then, been
put into practice? In order to avoid accepting this conclusion,
a quasi-ideal period is located at the very beginning of Islam,
in the twenty-nine years between the Prophet's death and the
victory of the Omayyad dynasty, the period when the community
was governed by companions of the Prophet – his fathers-in-law
and his sons-in-law, the four Caliphs called *Rāshidūn*, 'those
who walk in the right path'. Since long ago this epoch has been
idealized, at least among the Sunni. The idealization is effected
as a rule by means of anecdotes that are witnessed to for the first
time at least two centuries after the event. These belong to the
category of 'traditions' such as those mentioned above that
circulate concerning the Prophet, the authenticity of which there
are very good reasons to doubt. They are too closely related to
currents of thought and socio-political and religious attitudes in
subsequent centuries which are well known to us. This warning
is necessary, because popularizers, journalists, religious and
politicians in the Muslim countries very often make use of these
anecdotes as arguments. The serious historians of these countries do not dare, for social reasons, to question their authenticity publicly, even when privately they doubt it. Western
writers who are not Islamic specialists often tend to accept them
as historical on the word of books that are published in Muslim
circles.

Having said this, it must be observed straight away that,
according to the Muslim apologists themselves, these twenty-
nine ideal years were not without their dark side. The Shīʿites
naturally see in them only abomination, until the accession of
ʿAlī in 656, thus reducing the period to the five years in which

the latter reigned, under very difficult conditions. The Sunni are obliged to admit that the charges brought against 'Uthmān (644–56) and which resulted in his assassination were at least partly justified, in that his weakness had led to a certain favouritism. Under 'Alī (656–61) the intense struggle between the parties also encouraged iniquities. Thus the ideal epoch contracts to the twelve years of the reigns of Abū Bakr and 'Umar.

On the other hand, there is doubtless an element of truth in this view that is defended with such highly debatable arguments. The Muslim community then consisted of a relatively small group of compatriots, bound together by a common faith and common interests, who had set out to conquer the world. Among them there undoubtedly prevailed the (comparatively) egalitarian ideal of the Beduin tribe and the Koranic ideal of equality before God and well-developed mutual aid, required, and even imposed, between the members of the community. The little group of conquerors had at their disposal immense wealth taken from the conquered countries, so that a considerable share could be given to the least of the soldiers. A system of pensions had been worked out, which put a premium on seniority in party membership, if we may employ these modern terms, but which was reasonably adequate. The leaders were dependent on their troops, whom they had to satisfy if they were to be obeyed. The army was still filled with the anarchic and turbulent spirit of the Beduin tribes. All these circumstances dictated a certain equity in the policy followed in relation to the community which was then identified with the Arab conquerors.

This equity, however, was wholly relative. The policy followed by the leaders already at that time aroused protests, revolts and intense conflicts between 'tendencies', which led in 657 to the first 'schism', that of the Khārijites, the 'goers-out'. And it could obviously not go on like that. The community increased enormously in size with the conversion of the conquered peoples. The inequality existing between Arabs and non-Arabs moved from outside the community to within it. It was largely abolished by the Abbasid revolution in 750; but the inequalities between those who had been lavishly endowed with landed property and the rest, and then between rich and poor in general, continued to grow. As a result of the conversions there were Muslim slaves. The state was, as always, particularly sensitive to the interests of the privileged social and ethnic strata.

This situation was so much out of accord with the aspirations of the masses that revolutionary movements started regularly appearing in the Muslim world. These protest movements can be classified, like all such movements that arise within an ideology, into reformist and revisionist. The former assume that all the trouble results from abandonment of the original principles, and all that is needed is to go back to them; they denounce the shamefaced revisionism of the rulers, who are alleged to have surreptitiously modified the principles of the faith. The latter, the revisionist movements, themselves propose additions or modifications to the principles.

The traditional conception of Muslim history sees the cause of these movements in ideological divergences, related more specifically to religious doctrines. This is not the place to criticize this conception. It will be enough, for the line of argument I am following here, to note that we know, where the majority of these movements were concerned, that their ideological criticism, which was often at a high level of abstraction, was accompanied by denunciation of the way of life of the circles that formed and supported the ruling power. This way of life was generally denounced as being immoral and opposed to the true precepts of religion. It will hardly be denied that, at least among the mass of simpler-minded adherents of these movements, it was this critique of the persons in power that caused them to take part and show enthusiasm, rather than considerations regarding the sources of legal arguments or the relations between the higher intelligences. For some of these movements, such as the Ismailis, we have definite evidence that preachings on social matters accompanied their religious doctrine.[101]

But we find no trace of any movement that radically modified the Koranic ideal of the just society. At most, it was a question of the equality of all before God and before the religious law, of the mutual aid that there should be between members of the community of true Muslims, reduced to the members of a sect, a party. More vigorous measures can be taken to promote this mutual aid; the rulers can, for a certain period, set an example of frugality and simplicity in their way of life. With rare exceptions, there is no question of encroaching on the principle of private property, nor even on that of the hereditary status of slaves and free men. Thenceforth the same causes continually reproduce the same effects. There are property owners and persons without property, rich and poor, and, again, slaves and free men. The state power is, as a rule, in the hands of the property owners and the rich, and normally tends to favour them. Wealth makes possible a degree of luxury that, no less normally, prompts a lax attitude towards morality and the precepts of religion. The ruling authority usually tends to take steps, sometimes immoral and sometimes contrary to the religious law, with a view to strengthening itself and increasing the wealth of those who wield power. In all this there is nothing that is not deplorably commonplace in human history. Islam offers no originality in this regard. Like every body of moral and religious doctrines, it can do no more than, at best, limit, among a certain number of the rich and powerful, the tendency to abuse the power and wealth they possess. It may be that one can establish degrees in the capacity of different ideologies to bridle such behaviour. Familiarity with Islamic history suggests only that Islam's capacity is of the same order of magnitude as that of its rival ideologies, in other words, a very weak one.

But, at least, was Islamic doctrine obeyed in the limited field in which it recommended a certain economic attitude? It is important to answer this question, since the modern apologists of Islam assure us that these precepts should ensure the functioning of an economically just society. Let it be recalled that these precepts amount essentially to prohibition of loans at interest and of all aleatory contracts, together with obligation to pay over a substantial share of one's goods to the state, as manager of the welfare fund of the community. The state has the duty of distributing all of this fund that exceeds what it requires for its own functioning.[102] It also has the duty (M. Hamidullah considers, interpreting in this way the prohibition of loans at interest) to lend to the needy, so that there is, in fact, nationalization of credit.

No one, even among the most fervent apologists of Islam,

will deny that reality has usually fallen far short of this ideal. It is commonplace among Islamic scholars to define the *shari'a,* the religious law, as an ideal of life that Muslims have always resigned themselves to recognizing as a standard well beyond what happens in real life. True, the Muslim state has always felt obliged (like the Christian state and the Buddhist state) to finance welfare activities, such as hospitals, public drinking-fountains, schools with grants for poor pupils, public distribution of foodstuffs, and so on. But this expenditure has never accounted for more than a small part of the state's budget. It is, alas, quite certain that few Muslim rulers have given up much of their lavish spending on luxury, prestige and war, in order to enlarge their expenditure on welfare. There have been some exceptions, perhaps: a few very pious sovereigns, dynasties carried to power by a revolutionary movement (at first), and so on. But these have been only exceptions. On the whole, the traditional Muslim states offer throughout history the spectacle of a poignant contrast between the astonishing luxury that prevails at the courts and among the rich, and the most abject misery in which the mass of the people are sunk.

What is much more important than recording this obvious fact is stressing that it could not have been otherwise. The social surplus of production, meaning that part of the social product that exceeded the amount strictly needed in order to keep the members of society alive, was too slight to allow for both luxury among the dominant elements of society *and* a comfortable life for the poor. One must also note that the division of the social product was effected, here, too, not in accordance with the precepts or suggestions of a divinely revealed morality, but in accordance with the 'natural' human tendency of each group to maximize the advantages that its situation could bring. Whatever moral and ideological precepts may exist, in every state the rights and interests of any social category are fully respected in the share-out of the social product only if this category is represented in the state and possesses sufficient strength to compel such respect. Neither of these conditions was fulfilled in the traditional Muslim state. The welfare activities of government and individuals did no more than mitigate for a minority the disastrous effects of such a situation.

Thus, the practice of the traditional Muslim world was not, broadly speaking, unfaithful to the theoretical precepts of the Koran. The latter were, moreover, not of such a nature as either to prescribe or to prohibit any particular economic activity. The calls to justice and charity found in the sacred writings of Islam were listened to neither more nor less than in the case of other religions. They were adequate to give rise to a substantial number of acts of beneficence, both public and private, but inadequate to make the ruling *élite* feel obliged to try and ensure a decent standard of living for the majority of the people even at the expense of their own comfort. It was inevitable that this should be so, since the divine precepts imposed neither effective political control over the minority by the majority, nor a weakening or abolishment of the foundation of the minority's power by questioning the right to property. As ever, God's good counsel proved powerless unless backed by institutions that gave power to those human beings whose interest it was to cause this counsel to become reality. It must be emphasized, in passing, that during the period of history being examined here there was no lack of doctrines which (with the inevitable assurance that these precepts were divinely inspired) proposed measures of the kind indicated – measures that would, in principle, have established greater equality in society. The advocates of these doctrines were in every case defeated. It is impossible not to think that there must have been permanent reasons for these constant defeats. The economic and social conditions of the time did not, apparently, allow them to triumph.

The relations between practice and the Sunnah are somewhat more complex. The Sunnah was more precise than the Koran. It did not go any further as regards limitation of property rights, or popular control over rulers. In these matters it reflected the social situation of the time and the general opinion of the privileged strata. But it did present in theoretical form a prohibition that was a nuisance for many of these privileged ones – even if, almost immediately, it provided them with means of escape from this. We have seen, above, what causes may be found for this fact. In any case, in so far as there was conflict between doctrine and practice, it was practice that, broadly speaking, got the best of the argument. The bans were strictly enforced only in limited regions during brief periods. The development of the theory of the *ḥiyal* contributed very soon, and throughout a very extensive area, to the formation of a theory justifying a more easy-going practice. Even where it was not so greatly favoured, such practice was the most current, in wide sectors at least. Thus, religious theorizing had only a limited effect on practice. In any case, it did not challenge the fundamentals of economic activity in the age in question. Let me stress once again that those doctrines which did go so far as to challenge these foundations were eliminated by a sort of natural selection process.

4 The Influence of Muslim Ideology Generally in the Economic Field

We have up to now been considering the economic teachings of Islam, expressed in the Koran and in the Sunnah. We have seen that these teachings did not condemn in principle, or hinder in practice, the development of what has here been called the capitalistic sector of the economy. Now we must proceed further. In fact, a capitalistic sector of the same type existed in Western Europe in the Middle Ages. It developed in such a way as to produce what is variously described as 'modern capitalism' or 'the capitalist socio-economic formation'. However, a development like this did *not* occur in the Muslim world, or at least not before the nineteenth century, and there are reasons to think that it was then due to external influences. Is the cause of this unevenness of development to be found, perhaps, in the nature of the Muslim religion or, more broadly, in the ideology of the Muslim world in the Middle Ages, which may have been less favourable than the ideology of Christian Europe to an evolution of this kind?

A very widespread popular view holds this to be so. Particularly accused of responsibility in this connection is the alleged 'listlessness' of Muslims, based on a fatalism that their ideology is said to foster. This fatalistic indifference of theirs is contrasted with the spirit of initiative said to be characteristic of Europeans, whether this spirit be regarded as an hereditary feature of the latter or as something developed in them by Christianity in general or by some particular form of Christian ideology. Again, it was Max Weber who did more than anyone else to systematize, transform into a theory and base upon learned arguments a view tending this way.

Here we must emphasize the obvious fact that the realm of Islam is not the only part of the world that failed to follow the same path as Europe. As has been mentioned above, the ancient East, Greece, the Roman world, India, China, Japan also had a capitalistic sector of apparently the same sort as the Muslim world's, and also failed to follow Europe's path. Any explanation, therefore, must be applicable to all of these civilizations no less than to the Muslim world. This is the case with Max Weber's thesis.

For Weber, the collective mentality of Europe is marked by a superior degree of rationality. He hesitates to define the cause of this phenomenon, timidly putting forward the hypothesis that it may be due to biological, in other words racial, factors, but without venturing any further on this slippery ground.[1] He lists the manifestations of this rationality. Apparently, it is in Europe and only in Europe that one finds a rational state based on a body of specialized officials and a highly rational system of law, Roman law, which created 'formalistic legal thinking' (*das formal-juristische Denken*), in contrast to law founded on 'material' principles such as utility and equity. It is in Europe, he claims, that the adversaries of capitalist development were least in evidence: the tendency to think in terms of magic, certain material interests, and an ideology of the traditionalist type, based on religion or morality.[2]

It must be pointed out at once that Weber's approach is itself contradictory, like that of most of those who follow a line more or less similar to his. He considers that Europe produced modern capitalism because it was more rationalistic than the other regions of civilization – yet most of the examples of this European rationalism that he cites are from later than the period in which Western Europe took its decisive steps along the path of modern capitalism. Logically one could retort to Weber that there is a vicious circle here – these features of rationality might just as well be due to economic development along the capitalist path, or else correlative with this development, being effects, like it, of some common cause. We know that the same argument has been levelled, and convincingly, against Weber's special thesis according to which the origin of modern capitalism lies in the Protestant ethic. Since the ethic in question makes its appearance precisely at the moment when the economy is becoming capitalist in the modern sense, it is not in the least proved that it does not itself depend on this economic orientation, and there is even some evidence to suggest that this is indeed the case.[3]

Whatever the truth of the matter, these views make it unavoidable for anyone who deals with the subject to look closely and see whether the Muslim ideology is unfavourable to a rational orientation of thought, whether it favours 'magical' thinking or fatalistic indifference, whether it constitutes a stronger obstacle than mediaeval Christian ideology to capitalist development in the modern sense. It seems clear, as will be seen, that one needs to study Muslim ideology, from this standpoint, at two different levels: the ideology of the Koran, and mediaeval post-Koranic ideology. Only the main lines will, of course, be examined.

The ideology of the Koran

The Koran is a holy book in which rationality plays a big part. In it, Allah is continually arguing and reasoning. In a very characteristic way, the Revelation entrusted by God to the various prophets down through the ages, and eventually to Muhammad, the most irrational phenomenon there is in a religion, is itself regarded as essentially an instrument of proof. It is said again and again that the prophets have brought 'the evidences' (*al-bayyināt*)[4]. What is it that guarantees the conclusive character of these 'evidences', it will be asked? It seems that for Muhammad the criteria were internal coherence and substantial agreement between revelations received at different dates by different peoples and through the medium of different prophets. His own Revelation is guaranteed authentic by the fact that it is substantially identical with previous revelations, which in turn seem to him guaranteed by history.[5] He challenges his opponents to 'produce a discourse like it' (52:34; 28:49; 10:39/38), meaning one with the same divine features of form and content. Let them 'bring then a book from Allah which gives better guidance' than that of Moses or that of Muhammad! (28:49). Should one not accept these criteria, however, then recourse may be had to another argument, identical with Pascal's famous wager. This is the argument used in favour of Moses by 'a man of the family of Pharaoh, believing but concealing his faith', a crypto-Muslim:[6]

Will ye kill a man because he says: 'My Lord is Allah' and has come to you with the Evidences from your Lord? If he is speaking falsely, his falsehood is upon his own head, but if he is speaking the truth (and you do not listen) some of what he promises you will fall upon you (40:29/28).[7]

The Koran continually expounds the rational proofs of Allah's omnipotence: the wonders of creation, such as the gestation of animals, the movements of the heavenly bodies, atmospheric phenomena, the variety of animal and vegetable life so marvellously well adapted to men's needs.[8] All those things 'are signs (*āyāt*) for those of insight'[9] (3:187/190).

A typical example is provided by the polemic against the Christian dogma of the Trinity. The Koran refutes this by reference to what Muḥammad believed to be historical fact, namely, that which Jesus himself is reported to have said, rejecting divine status. Also, however, the Christians are called upon not to exaggerate – 'do not go beyond bounds (*lā taghlū*)', exceeding what is reasonable (4:169/171; 5:81/77). How could Allah have a child? Why should the Almighty, who fills the whole world with his presence, have need of a paredrus? Jesus was a 'messiah' (*masīḥ*), a prophet of a higher order, his mother was a saint, great miracles were accomplished in their favour or through their action. But they 'ate food' (5:79/75). This testifies that they were subject to man's estate, to generation and corruption, and that, consequently, Allah could cause them to die (5:19/17).

Repeated about fifty times in the Koran is the verb *ʿaqala*, which means 'connect ideas together, reason, understand an intellectual argument'. Thirteen times we come upon the refrain, after a piece of reasoning: *ʾa fa-lā taʿqilūn*, 'have ye then no sense?' (2:41/44, etc.) The infidels, those who remain insensible to Muḥammad's preaching, are stigmatized as 'a people of no intelligence', persons incapable of the intellectual effort needed to cast off routine thinking (5:63/58, 102/103; 10:43/42; 22:45/46; 59:14). In this respect they are like cattle (2:166/171;

25:46/44). As H. Lammens says, quite rightly, Muḥammad 'is not far from considering unbelief as an infirmity of the human mind'.[10] Like conservatives in every age, the unbelievers say that it is good enough for them to follow the customs of their forefathers, and like all innovators, Muḥammad is exasperated by this argument. Did their forefathers never reason, then, he demands, when they initiated what has become custom? (2: 165/170; 5:103/104). Allah particularly detests those who are unwilling to subject their fundamental ideas to re-examination: such people are the worst of all in his eyes (8:23, cf. 10:100). If Allah places in his creation, sending them as indications of his presence and his will, 'signs' of which the most important are the words and phrases that he dictates to his Messenger, Muḥammad, this is in order that they may serve as grounds for reasoning, whereby they may be assimilated and understood (16:69/67; 29:34/35; 45:3/4, etc.). After an argument that seems especially convincing, the Divine Author concludes: 'Thus do We make the signs [that is, Our Revelations] distinct for a people who understand' (30:27/28). All that Allah can do, given the existence of human free will, is to set down these signs, which are conclusive pointers to the truth, if only men will set to work their senses and their faculty of reasoning.[11] Perhaps men will draw from these signs the deductions that should be drawn (24:61; 57:16/17). If so, then they will be 'those who have knowledge' (29:42/43). They will share in the knowledge (*ʿilm*) that God has communicated to his Prophet (2:114/120, 140/145; 3:54/61; cf. 17:108/107), and which is contrasted with the state of ignorance of natural man before the Revelation (5:55/50; 25:64/63; 28:55; 39:64; 7:198/199) – the knowledge that brings the Truth (*ḥaqq* 39:2, 42/41, etc.; *ṣidq* 39:33/32).[12] Those who will not believe are wilfully ignorant men, who 'dispute about Allah without knowledge or guidance or light-giving Book' (31:19/20); one must say to them: 'Have ye any [revealed] knowledge? Bring it forth for us then; ye follow nothing but opinion, and ye are only conjecturing' (6:149/148). In order to make easier the task of those who belong to the Arab people, Allah has taken the trouble to send them preaching in their own tongue; perhaps thereby they will understand (24:61; 57:16/17).

Intellectual grasp of the truth is not sufficient. For example, the Jews of Medina understood the Preaching perfectly, but then 'perverted it knowingly' (2:70/75). One must proceed from pure reason to practical reason, appreciate that it is to one's interest to apply the precepts dictated by Allah and join the community founded at his command by his Messenger. In order to inculcate this idea of the need for active piety, and later of militant partisanship, Muḥammad has recourse to arguments of a commercial order, such as would be particularly easy to understand for the Meccans, a tribe of merchants, and for the men of Medina, who were familiar with trading activity. They came quite naturally to a man who had always lived in a mercantile atmosphere and whose discourses were spontaneously studded with commercial expressions, as was shown in detail in 1892 by Charles C. Torrey,[13] when elaborating a hint given by August Müller. It will suffice here to give Torrey's summary of the practical theology of the Koran, which concludes his precise study of its vocabulary and concepts:

The mutual relations between God and man are of a strictly commercial nature. Allah is the ideal merchant. He includes all the universe in his reckoning. All is counted, everything measured. The book and the balances are his institution, and he has made himself the pattern of honest dealing. Life is a business, for gain or loss. He who does a good or an evil work ('earns' good or evil), receives his pay for it, even in this life. Some debts are forgiven, for Allah is not a hard creditor. The Muslim makes a loan to Allah; pays in advance for paradise; sells his own soul to him, a bargain that prospers. The unbeliever has sold the divine truth for a paltry price, and is bankrupt. Every soul is held as security for the debt it has contracted. At the resurrection, Allah holds a final reckoning with all men. Their actions are read from the account-book, weighed in the balances; each is paid his exact due, no one is defrauded. Believer and unbeliever receive their wages. The Muslim (who has been given *manifold* payment for each of his good deeds) receives moreover his special reward.

As Torrey concludes: 'A more simply mathematical "body of divinity" than this is difficult to imagine.'[14] When one says mathematics, one says rationality. This does not mean, of course, that, according to the ideology of the Koran, *everything* is accessible to reason. On the contrary, many things are outside its reach. This is even one of the proofs of God's transcendent power and knowledge. Of these things that cannot be known by the mere power of human reason, God reveals a part to men through the agency of his Prophets. Other things remain hidden for ever.[15] The role of reason is to understand the plausibility, the verisimilitude, the validity of the messages about the unknowable that are brought by the Prophets, and also to understand the advantage of conforming oneself to what these messages prescribe.

To be sure, faith, an irrational notion, does make its appearance here: but faith is indispensable to any religion, and perhaps to any ideology. What has to be explained is why, faced with the same phenomena, men apparently endowed with the same faculties and placed in the same situation adopt different attitudes. Some join and others do not, some become fervent adherents while others remain slack in their zeal. If one is to fight against those who do not believe, then it is necessary, in order to be able to denounce them and threaten them with punishment, to attribute to them a certain measure of responsibility for their unbelief. In religions this clashes with the dogma of divine omnipotence, putting one in the insuperable dilemma where a choice has to be made between the two ideas, alike intolerable, of the (at least relative) helplessness of God and of his wickedness.

'The Koranic conception of faith is limited to a tenacious holding on, by means of a vigorous act of will, to this faith which is freely given by God.'[16]

Faith, however, is in direct relation with rational conviction. The proof of this is that it is said of unbelievers who waited too long, and against whom God had to loose arguments of a catastrophic character, that *then* they believed, *then* they had faith (*īmān*) – but it was too late, and they were none the less doomed to the Supreme Punishment (40:85; 6:159/158). These two passages show very well the identity between faith and conviction achieved through seeing a proof. God's intervention is confined to 'permitting' objective argument to have its convincing effect; it is significant that, in the same phrase, aimed at justifying toleration, in which this permission is mentioned, there is also mention of rational conviction:

If thy Lord so willed, all those in the land would believe in a body; wilt thou then put constraint upon the people that they may be believers? It is not for any person to believe except by the permission of Allah, and He layeth the abomination upon those who do not show understanding (10:99–100).

It cannot be denied that Koranic faith is *also* something *more than* intellectual conviction and assent to the truths revealed by the Prophet. This conviction gives rise to an attitude that commits the whole man. Faith brings peace to the soul, releases one from fear (while developing the fear of God!), gives patience, endurance, resignation to the insults and ill-treatment suffered in God's cause, humility, and the will to risk all for God and to carry out good works.[17] But this does not imply irrationality in the mechanism whereby this faith is acquired. The important point is that it is never a question of faith that comes gratuitously, through intuitive enlightenment, without reasoning. True, the Revelation came to Muḥammad in the course of mystical trances, but the Tradition which describes these assures us that the Prophet was at first plunged into doubt about what their origin might be. He asked himself whether he was perhaps the prey to some inspiration from the Devil. He had to discuss his experiences with 'specialists' on matters of Revelation, like Waraqa ibn Nawfal, his wife's cousin, a monotheist seeking God,[18] to receive encouragement from his family, to talk with the Archangel and even to subject the latter to tests,[19] before he became convinced that what he had been given really was a message from God. These data from the Tradition are not particularly convincing in themselves, any more than anything else from that source, but here they are corroborated by the Koran, a source of incontestable authenticity. In the Koran, Allah is said to reply to those who saw in the Revelation an intuition of dubious origin and unverifiable accuracy. It is most remarkable that this objection is acknowledged as being a valid one. However, the objection is groundless in the given circumstances. Muḥammad did not suffer an attack of illness. He received, during his trances, clear messages that were transmitted to him by a personality supernatural but real, precise and worthy of respect, and this happened in exactly defined circumstances and in well-known places.

Your comrade has not gone astray, nor has he erred; nor does he speak of [his own] inclination. It is nothing but a suggestion suggested, taught by One strong in power, forceful . . . (53:1–6).

It is verily the speech of a noble messenger, powerful, beside Him of the Throne established, obeyed there and trustworthy. Your comrade is not mad, he saw him on the clear horizon . . . (81:19–23).

Whatever Y. Moubarac may say, there is a difference between this faith based on a reasonable message, transmitted, under conditions that guarantee its genuineness, by a personality who, though supernatural, makes himself accessible to certain men, and a gratuitous, intuitive faith, based on some intimate, inexpressible feeling of certainty.[20]

It would carry us too far if we were to compare, thoroughly and in detail, these conceptions with those of other religions, and especially with those contained in the Old and New Testaments. We must be content with only a few notes. If the Koran reasons in support of the Revelation, this is because it considers the latter to consist of reasonable propositions, accessible to human reason, or at least not in conflict with it. True, the messages of the Prophets contain points that man would not have been able to discover by himself. But rational arguments show that faith should be accorded to these messages in the same way that we accept as correct, for example, the information brought us by reliable travellers about distant countries. Other very rational arguments show that it is to our interest to follow out the prescriptions transmitted through the Prophets.

In contrast to this, the Old Testament emphasizes to a much greater extent the mysterious and inaccessible character of the divine plans. To be sure, Jehovah reveals to some degree his intentions, his will, and something of his nature, to the patriarchs, the prophets and others. He even gives signs of the genuineness of the message brought by his true messengers, such as, for example, the miracle on Mount Carmel that was vouchsafed to Elijah. But what is appealed to in order to bring about conviction and decision in men is, in addition to fear of God, also, complementing this, faith in God. This faith is not needed in order to demonstrate Jehovah's existence or to accept the intellectual premises implicit in the content of his revelations. One is at a pre-critical stage where none of that is subject to doubt. This faith is simply confidence in the profound, mysterious and unfathomable intentions of Jehovah, Israel's supernatural leader. It is the confidence shown by Abraham, whom Jehovah calls upon to sacrifice his son, a confidence held up as a model to all. One must not discuss the directives from the leader as transmitted by his spokesmen, the prophets. It is on this practical, political plane that the problem is set. Against the 'false prophets', meaning those whose tendency was opposed to the one that triumphed after the Exile, and whose works have unfortunately not come down to us, the practical argument is simply raised, that their predictions failed to come true. In the age of the Prophets there appeared, too, the theme of antagonism between human wisdom and divine wisdom, which at first served the purpose of refuting the rational political calculations of the counsellors of the Kings of Judah, the advocates of resistance to Assyrian expansionism: 'Woe unto them that are wise in their own eyes . . .' (*Isaiah*, 5:21). (The Lord said) 'the wisdom of their wise men shall perish, and the understanding of their prudent men shall be hid' (*Isaiah*, 29:14). A certain rationalism (G. von Rad goes so far as to speak of *Aufklärung*) developed from the very start of the period of the Kings, in order to study the mechanism of Jehovah's action upon nature.[21] In the age of the calamities, however, on the plane of politics Isaiah was one of the first to call for unconditional faith in Jehovah, which implies rejection of the calculations of the wise men, not as operations of the reason but as signs of lack of confidence in the supernatural leader.

This theme was to be developed in the 'Wisdom' writings and in the Psalms. Human wisdom was apparently developing among the Israelites and starting to establish a field in which it thought itself able to judge of the things of this world with its own powers, since the Biblical writers thought it necessary to combat this state of mind – not the use of the reason as such, but that pride which might lead to the use of the reason being extended too far. They set limits to the realm of the reason.

Wisdom is a gift from Jehovah, 'the form in which Jehovah's will is made present to men';[22] the wisdom of Jehovah is alone perfect; blind faith in Jehovah[23] fills up the gaps in human wisdom, which is unable to direct unaided the day-to-day conduct of Everyman, just as (the poem of *Job*, 28 shows us this) it is unable to discover on its own the hidden mystery of the divine plan, the divine wisdom that is concealed in nature: 'Trust in the Lord with all thine heart; and lean not unto thine own understanding ... Be not wise in thine own eyes: fear the Lord and depart from evil' (*Proverbs*, 3:5, 7). 'He that trusteth in his own heart is a fool' (*Proverbs*, 28:26). There are two knowledges, two wisdoms, and only one of these is genuine. The only true wisdom is obtained from Jehovah, through first having faith in him – the opposite of what the Koran tells us. 'Teach me good judgment and knowledge: for I have believed thy commandments' (*Psalms*, 119:66).

Contact with Hellenic rationalism, that striving to find a secular explanation of the universe, which was strong in the prestige and penetrating power of Greek civilization, set some quite new problems. The 'wisdom of this world' meant no longer the ramblings of elderly sages, or the always questionable divagations of politicians, but a body of truths that were rationally demonstrable on the basis of premises accepted by everyone. The Bible's Revelation thenceforth took on a new character: it was a collection of statements that could not be proved, or which, at least, had been transmitted without any concern for proof. Evidence became prejudice, accepted ideas stood exposed as arbitrary. Those who nevertheless held to these ideas, and especially to the direction that the latter gave to their lives, and also to the national significance of these ideas, were obliged to theorize about them in the Greek manner. We know that the great man in this theorizing was Philo of Alexandria. He occupied himself – and this was something that was wholly new – with justifying the Revelation, finding proofs of its truth.[24] An enlightened man, he allowed a place to philosophy, accepted secular reasoning as a secondary and subordinate source of knowledge, as the servant of the Revelation, in the image of Hagar's relationship with Sarah.[25] He was the first to raise, in all its fullness, the problem of the relations between faith and reason which was so greatly to preoccupy the next two thousand years.

Jewish pietism in Palestine itself certainly went less far than the great doctor of Alexandria in making concessions to Hellenism. And popular feeling could not but burst forth, strong in the backing of the late Old Testament passages quoted above, against the wisdom of this world, bound up with impiety, wealth and betrayal of national values. This is what is expressed most fully by the primitive Christian kerygma which was rooted in this soil. True, the word of Jesus often takes the form of discussion and argument. His miracles are signs, arguments aimed to convince. But all this only sets an enigma for John the Baptist (*Matthew*, 11:2 et seq.) and obliges the Pharisees and priests, amazed but incredulous, to take up a hypocritical attitude (e.g. *Matthew*, 21:23–27 and parallel passages). The activity and personality of Jesus are causes of scandal – that is, their apparently contradictory and irrational character is a stumbling-block.[26] The only way of escape is through unconditional and unreasoning faith. Everyone will think of the famous words addressed by the risen Jesus to Thomas: 'Because thou hast seen me, thou hast believed: blessed are they that have not seen, and yet have believed' (*John*, 20:29). But Jesus had already been shocked by the need men have for proofs: 'Except ye see signs and wonders, ye will not believe' (*John*, 4:48). Paul was to carry to extremes this emphasis that was especially characteristic of St John's Gospel. He refers to the Old Testament passages: 'For it is written, I will destroy the wisdom of the wise, and will bring to nothing the understanding of the prudent. Where is the wise? where is the scribe? . . .' (*Isaiah*, 29:14; *Psalms*, 33:10; *Isaiah*, 33:18; *Isaiah*, 19:12 – more or less telescoped together and quoted according to the Septuagint). And he goes on:

Where is the disputer of this world? Hath not God made foolish the wisdom of this world? . . . But we preach Christ crucified, unto the Jews a stumbling-block, and unto the Greeks foolishness . . . Because the foolishness of God is wiser than men . . . And I, brethren, when I came to you, came not with excellency of speech or of wisdom . . . And my speech and my preaching was not with enticing words of man's wisdom but in demonstration of the spirit and of the power: that your faith should not stand in the wisdom of men, but in the power of God (*I Corinthians*, 1:19–20, 23, 25; 2:1, 4–5).

It has been maintained that, in relation to the Old and New Testaments, which express a distinctively Hebrew anthropology, it is inappropriate to apply the categories of Greek anthropology which inspired Gnosticism and modern philosophy. In particular, it is said, faith was not distinguished from intelligence, any more than the latter was distinguished from action and life. This was *an* intelligence, *a* knowledge, and not, as with Plato, one of the lower forms of knowledge, namely, belief.[27] There is doubtless some truth in this view. But it remains the fact that in the New Testament, and in at least one current of thought that runs through the Old Testament, human reasoning is seen as radically inadequate for approaching the profound reality of the world, in other words, for approaching God. It is contrasted fundamentally with the intuition of the divine which is given in an intimate experience that procures immediately and inexpressibly, in a way that is prior or exterior to any argument, the feeling of close contact with the being and will of God.

Starting in the second half of the second century AD, the Christian doctors were to take up Philo's problematic, introduce Hellenic philosophy into the framework of Christian ideology, and develop Philo's ideas on the relations between faith in the Revelation and rational proof of it. Some of them – Tertullian providing the model of these – were to reject any suggestion of a rational proof of the revealed truth.

Wretched Aristotle! who hath taught them [the heretics] the dialectic art, cunning in building up and pulling down, using many shifts in sentences, making forced guesses at truth, stiff in arguments . . . what then had Athens to do with Jerusalem? What the Academy with the Church? . . . Away with those who have brought forward a Stoic, and a Platonic, and a Dialectic Christianity. To us there is no need of curious questioning now that we have Christ Jesus, nor of enquiry now that we have the Gospel. In that we believe this, we desire to believe nothing besides.[28]

The Son of God died: it is immediately credible – because it is silly. He was buried, and rose again: it is certain – because it is impossible.[29]

Most of the Christian theologians, however, would think that reason ought to come into the matter in one way or another. It can bring out truths that have not been revealed, and provide subsidiary proof of the content of the Revelation. The idea that faith is reasonable was destined to triumph. As regards that which is not rationally demonstrable in what is revealed, it is reasonable to trust in the messengers of the Revelation. This is what Augustine was to explain, long before Muḥammad. In ordinary knowledge and even in philosophy one accepts the truth of propositions that cannot be verified and have not been absolutely proved. One trusts certain transmitters of truth just as we trust travellers who tell us about towns and countries we have never seen. In contrast to the suspect sources of knowledge that the Manichees draw upon, the Christians can base themselves on the Gospel and the Old Testament, which are well-founded historically and worthy of confidence.[30] On the whole it was the rationalistic current that came to predominate in the Christianity of the first centuries. We see this well in Syria, among the great doctors of the fourth and fifth centuries, Aphraates, Ephraim, and Philoxenus of Mabbog, whose indirect influence on the Koran was shown long ago by Tor Andrae.[31] In their writings we find already that same rationalist and intellectualist conception of faith[32] which seems fundamental in Muḥammad.

But the primacy of faith, the natural view of popular piety in the tradition of Tertullian, the implicit theology of humble people, who through their very position feel distrustful towards even the well-intentioned reasonings of scholars and thinkers, was to be reinforced in unexpected fashion on the plane of intellectual dignity itself, by the mystical theology of neo-Platonic inspiration, a tendency still surviving across the centuries, even though somewhat crushed, and handed down in a form of questionable purity, and which was developed extensively for the first time in the East at the beginning of the sixth century by the Pseudo-Dionysius the Areopagite. Faith, loyal confidence in God, or willing assent to the truths discovered by reason, becomes a 'theopathic' state to which one attains by mystical contemplation, during which one *experiences* God and arrives at transcendent knowledge which is incommensurable with the knowledge that other methods can procure.[33] The idea of the primacy of unreasoning faith was to turn up in the writings of many Christian doctors, whether derived from this source or due to other influences – e.g. in John of Damascus at the beginning of the eighth century, in then-recently-Arabized Syria.[34] The Latins worked out a whole problematic of the relations between reason and faith, in which reason was entrusted with the subordinate task of partly elucidating the mysteries accepted by faith, while the latter held priority on all levels.[35] Thus, in Anselm of Canterbury, at the end of the eleventh century,[36] and, finally, in Thomas Aquinas who, in the thirteenth century, canonized this view, so to speak, thanks to his immense authority:

> *Invisibilia Dei altiori modo, quantum ad plura, percipit fides quam ratio naturalis ex creaturis in Deum procedens.*[37]
>
> *Puta cum quis aut non haberet voluntatem, aut non haberet promptam voluntatem ad credendum, nisi ratio humana induceretur. Et sic ratio humana inducta diminuit meritum fidei.*[38]

In contrast to this, the rationalism of the Koran seems rock-like. This calls for further explanation. It does not appear to be related directly and unilaterally to Hellenic rationalism. Rather does it belong to the attitude of mind that was common to the men of Mecca. The merchants of Quraysh whom Muḥammad combated were also rationalists. They, however, held to a naïve, down-to-earth rationalism without any prestige to it, which was not put forward as a body of doctrine comparable to Hellenic philosophy. For reasons that will have to be elucidated one day, if this can be done, the society to which they belonged was poor in myths and rites. They assumed, of course (though some of them sceptically, it seems), the existence of supernatural beings, but these were only a sort of invisible men, with powers a little greater than our own. This belief altered but little the picture of man subject to the laws of nature but able to work upon the conflicts between these laws, and the gaps in them. In this kind of 'tribal humanism', as Montgomery Watt calls it, of the desert, which the life of the merchant town of Mecca seems to have accentuated, man took the exact measure of his strength and of his weakness.[39] He was not disposed to believe in anything of which he could not observe the effects and evaluate the power and significance.

Muḥammad set up the authority of the monotheistic Revelation, which for him was reasonable, rational and unassailable, enjoying, moreover, the prestige of its association with the great civilized states, with the world of culture, writings, books and scholars. He took up again, in order to defend it, the apologia of Judaism and Christianity, the themes of which, as developed by learned writers, reached him by way of oral tradition. He naturally adopted the language of his opponents and their way of thinking (a sphere from which, indeed, he never completely escaped) in order to show them the rationality and efficiency of the Message he brought – namely, in essentials, the power of Allah, his one-ness, and the validity of Muḥammad's own Revelation as the prophet of the Arabs. Against the barbaric rationality of the Meccans he set up his own, civilized form of rationality. The conflict latent within the Judeo-Christian problematic which he had taken over escaped his notice entirely. In any case, the intellectualism of the Christian thought of the Syrian Church, the one nearest to him – as also, doubtless, that of the Judaism with which he was in contact – blurred for Muḥammad the latency of this conflict. No one any longer was raising against the triumphant Church, or the defeated but still intellectually powerful Synagogue, the banner of pure Aristotelianism, which later centuries were to see revived. Both Church and Synagogue had assimilated all the rationalism they could digest, and employed it to present themselves as not only the depositories of the divine message but also the representatives of Reason and Knowledge. Philosophy, a servant chained to the chariot of her mistress, had the task of enhancing the latter's beauty. It is not surprising if our Meccan merchant, not very learned, but disgusted by the intellectual crudity of those around him, and dazzled by the prestige of the Scriptures that came from the world of civilized men and scholars, should have seen no contradiction in this common message of Civilization, but should have offered it to his compatriots as the only reasonable and rational alternative to their ignorance.

We see, then, that the Koran accords a much larger place to reason than do the sacred books of Judaism and Christianity.

There has also been sought (not by Weber, of course, for obvious reasons, when one thinks of his theory of the Calvinist origins of European capitalism) an explanation for the allegedly unfavourable climate provided by Islam for the development of capitalism, in which the finger is pointed at the Koranic doctrine of predestination. It is true that, alongside sentences stressing man's freedom, in the earliest of the Ṣūras, there are also later passages which set forth the thesis of predestination – sometimes modified by the endowment of man with tendencies that may deflect the direction taken by divine grace, but sometimes extremely crude. In reality, Muḥammad was reacting in his own way against the fatalism of pre-Islamic ideology, the view current among the Arabs of the dominance of blind laws of fate imposed upon men as upon the gods, a prefiguring of the determinism of the idea of natural laws. He replaced the omnipotence of fate by that of a personal will, the will of Allah, whom one could at least invoke, pray to and supplicate.[40] What we find here are evidently ideas that Muḥammad conceived independently of each other, without perceiving the contradictions between them. It was necessary at one and the same time to encourage conversion; explain why men apparently honest and intelligent were hardened in incredulity; inspire everyone with fear of and reverence for God; promise rewards to the faithful; and threaten adversaries with the worst of punishments. Muḥammad's thinking moved between a few simple and powerful 'evidences', which he could not reject.[41] He was no subtle theologian, trained in the dialectics of reason, but a deeply religious man, convinced of God's omnipotence, and in addition a man of action. When he thought about the problem he must, as Grimme has well perceived, have seen 'events on earth as resulting from the concurrent influence of the activities of God and of man'.[42] To analyse any further was not possible for him, probably inconceivable, and certainly would have seemed to him quite pointless. While the tradition is certainly false which describes how he went red in the face with anger when he heard men in the mosque of Medina discussing predestination and free will,[43] it is quite possible that he would have reacted rather like that if the question had actually been raised.

What is important for my present argument is to show that this thesis of predestination – more or less modified, and contradicted by other maxims – did not in the least exclude incitements to action from the ideology of the Koran. If the latter exhorts the believer to such virtues as impartiality, respect for oaths, continence, straightforwardness, etc., to pious works, to charity towards the poor, towards kinsfolk, neighbours and travellers, it is clear that a certain freedom, at least in appearance, to act or not to act, is acknowledged to be possessed by man. Furthermore, social activities which are not in themselves pious or beneficent, are, if not recommended to man, at least permitted and treated as normal modes of existence. Thus, honest trade is quite frequently mentioned as a normal activity. For example: 'O ye who have believed, do not consume your property among you in vanity, except there be trading by mutual consent on your part' (*Koran*, 4:33/29). If earthly sustenance, in the strict sense, is so frequently praised as a boon from God, especially fruit, and the pastures where the flocks and herds graze (e.g. 80:24 et seq.), it necessarily follows that agriculturists, horticulturists and stockbreeders are encouraged to carry on their work, which contributes (powerfully!) to make actual these divine gifts. Are not the calls to holy war an incitement to yet another sort of activity? Does not the Koran commend courage and steadfastness in face of the enemy, and stubbornness in battle? 'So do not grow faint and call for peace, seeing ye have the upper hand' (47:37/35). Divine help is promised, it is certain, it is an essential factor in victory, but it is in no way a substitute for human struggle with human means. Thus, God helps David, the blacksmith prophet, in his work: 'We made iron tractable for him: "make ample [coats of mail] and weave them closely"' (34:1010–11).

There is nothing in all this that can be seen as an incitement to wait passively for Allah's help. It is true that many verses of the Koran bring out the vanity, fragility and deceptiveness of the things of this world.[44] Later mystics saw in these an incitement to asceticism, to holding aloof from the affairs of this world in order to devote oneself wholly to the seeking of God.[45] It is not impossible that contemporaries of the Prophet themselves already drew such conclusions, or that these texts served to reinforce their previous inclinations that way. It is certain, however, that for Muḥammad they did not at all signify an encouragement to such an attitude. To show that God is all-powerful, that the things of this world are secondary, is to exhort the faithful to put active devotion to the community above concern for personal success, to persuade them of the certainty of the victory that benefits from such help, to urge unbelievers to rally to an irresistible current. The extremely active life led by the Prophet shows clearly that for him, even if he doubtless sometimes was tempted to abandon himself like a wisp of straw to the powerful breath of Allah, this temptation was quickly overcome.[46] In the Koran, Allah himself orders action on the part of his faithful servant: 'Recite . . .', 'Say . . .', that is, proclaim, catechize, stir up men's minds. He commands Muḥammad to say to the infidels: 'O my people, act as ye are doing; I am going to act [in my way]' (39:40/39; cf. 11:122/121). He calls on him to fight them: 'O prophet, strive against the unbelievers and the hypocrites; and be rough with them' (66:9). If Muḥammad is often also told to have confidence in Allah, to leave to him the success of his undertakings, this clearly does not imply that his implacable master will let the servant rest inactive.[47]

If one wanted to agree that the verses on predestination inevitably led the Muslims into fatalism, one would logically have to say the same about Judaism and Christianity. Let me rapidly quote a few passages. 'And the Lord had respect unto Abel and to his offering. But unto Cain and his offering he had not respect' (*Genesis*, 4:4–5). (The Lord said) 'I . . . will be gracious to whom I will be gracious, and will show mercy on whom I will show mercy' (*Exodus*, 33:19). 'And the Lord hardened the heart of Pharaoh, and he hearkened not unto them; as the Lord had spoken unto Moses' (*Exodus*, 9:12; cf. 10:1, 20, 27; 11:10). Here are passages which logically ought to offer little encouragement to effort in order to acquire merit in the eyes of God by doing good works. More generally, on the plane of labour in and for this world, and of the omnipotence of Jehovah, the Psalmist draws, in a very beautiful and famous poem, the conclusion that all human striving is in vain:

Except the Lord build the house, they labour in vain that build it; except the Lord keep the city, the watchman waketh but in vain. It is vain for you to rise up early, to sit up late, to eat the bread of sorrows: for so he giveth his beloved sleep (*Psalms*, 127:1–2).[48]

Jesus, similarly, talking about salvation, speaks of God's *elect*, 'affirming thus the personal nature and sovereignty of this choice'[49] (cf. *Mark*, 13:20). It is well known how strongly Paul emphasized this theme of predestination:

For whom he did foreknow, he also did predestinate to be conformed to the image of his Son . . . Moreover whom he did predestinate, them he also called . . . (*Romans*, 8:29–30).

And, in connexion with Jacob and Esau:

For the children being not yet born, neither having done any good or evil, that the purpose of God according to election might stand, not of works but of him that calleth; it was said unto her [i.e. Rebecca, their mother], The elder shall serve the younger. As it is written, Jacob have I loved, but Esau have I hated (*Romans*, 9:11–13, referring to *Genesis*, 25:23 and *Malachi*, 1:2–3).

As for labour in and for the world here below, it is enough to recall a famous passage, the moving poetic and personal quality of which rings in all our memories:

Take no thought for your life, what ye shall eat, or what ye shall drink; nor yet for your body, what ye shall put on . . . Behold the fowls of the air: for they sow not, neither do they reap, nor gather into barns; yet your heavenly Father feedeth them. Are ye not much better than they? . . . And why take ye thought for raiment? Consider the lilies of the field, how they grow; they toil not, neither do they spin: and yet I say unto you that even Solomon in all his glory was not arrayed like one of these (*Matthew*, 6:25–30, cf. *Luke*, 12:22–27).

I do not mean to claim that absolute determinism is dominant in either Judaism or Christianity – only that these few quotations suffice to show that any possible development of a tendency to fatalism and inaction could have found in the sacred writings of these religions just as much, if not more, to justify that attitude than can be found in Islam.

Might we not, however, discover in the ideology of the Koran that other enemy of the economic rationality characteristic of capitalism, or which leads towards capitalism, namely, magic? Magic is certainly mentioned in the Koran.[50] Muḥammad accepted the reality of magical operations. In this, however, he merely shared the general view of the age in which he lived. His opponents, the polytheists of Mecca, accused him of being a magician, a sorcerer, interpreting in this way the trances in which he received messages from the other world. All previous prophets had similarly been accused of witchcraft – in particular Moses and Jesus,[51] on account of the miracles they performed, which were a great deal more impressive than the deeds of Muḥammad. If, therefore, the latter had, in his turn, been endowed with real power to work miracles, as doubters required, they would only have seen in this yet another manifestation of magic.

It is necessary to observe that this signified a *rationalistic* interpretation on the part of Muḥammad's opponents. For them, magic was a science or a technique that produced extraordinary effects, and which only certain men could practice who were possessed of exceptional knowledge, but it was nothing more than that. Perhaps it was practised with the help of the djinns, that is, of a category of persons who were invisible but whose existence was doubted by no one and who made themselves tangibly known to mankind. Classifying Muḥammad's Revelation, and the miracles of earlier 'messengers', among operations of a magical character, meant attributing them to natural, or quasi-natural, causes and bringing them down to the level of the powers, whether normal or exceptional, possessed by certain men and by certain creatures which, though somewhat superior to men, were subject like them to the laws of nature and of destiny.

Muḥammad evidently shares this interpretation. This is why he strives to show, or else forcibly asserts, that his Revelation and that of the previous 'messengers', together with the wonders they performed, were all sent from Allah, or at least were only accomplished with Allah's permission. Solomon, who was a powerful magician, commanding the winds and having djinns under his authority, possessed these powers, and the knowledge for which he was famous, only by the grace of Allah.

Magicians who work independently of Allah are doomed to failure (20:72/69), and doubtless to damnation (2:96/102), overcome by the magic that Allah permits (7:115/118, etc.); their magic is reduced to naught by Allah (10:81; 26:44/45 et seq.). The Prophet himself, who seems to be afraid of the spells directed against him, is instructed by Allah to seek refuge with Him (Sūra 113). As we see, Muḥammad does not deny the role of magic, but subordinates it to the will of Allah.

This is important. Why, indeed, did Max Weber regard magic as inimical to capitalism? In so far as magic is used in trial by ordeal, it obstructs the rationalization of law. We shall come back to this problem. Further, it implies a stereotyping of technique and of the economy. In China the geomancers opposed the building of factories and railway lines on certain mountains, woods, rivers, and hills that were used as cemeteries, because they would disturb the repose of the spirits. Similarly, in India, the 'impurity' of the different castes in relation to each other may prevent workers belonging to different castes from working together in the same workshop.[52] Let us, for the moment, accept this idea, even if the examples given are perhaps not wholly concerned with magic, and even if we may suspect that the relations between magic and economic rationality are more complex than Weber supposed. Magical considerations obviously may in some cases operate as a hindrance to the development of a 'rational' economy. But, this being so, who can fail to see that the subordination of magic (acknowledged as real by everyone) to religion is a step forward? One can always pray to Allah, the Almighty, to frustrate magical snares, no less than to overcome technical difficulties. We must therefore reject Weber's assertion that, 'apart from Judaism and Christianity, and two or three oriental sects (one of which is in Japan), there is no religion with the character of outspoken hostility to magic'.[53] He forgot Islam.

For the 'outspoken hostility' to magic of the Judeo-Christian scriptures is only of the same type as that of the Koran. It is a recognition of the validity and effectiveness of magical techniques and the principle underlying them, limited only by the omnipotence of God. The latter may or may not allow a magical operation to succeed – he acts in just the same way as in relation to any technical operation. Adapting the Psalm already quoted, one might say: Except the Lord change the rod into a serpent, the magicians labour in vain . . .

According to *Exodus*, the Egyptian magicians really did change their rods into serpents, but the serpent that had been Aaron's rod proved, with Jehovah's permission, to be stronger than them, and swallowed up the anti-Israelite serpents (*Exodus*, 7:8–12). It is possible to say with truth to Balaam: 'I wot that he whom thou blessest is blessed, and he whom thou cursest is cursed' (*Numbers*, 22:6). And Jehovah cannot make such a curse ineffective. All he can do is to stop Balaam from pronouncing his curse, and oblige him to bless Israel instead (*Numbers*, 22–24). A blessing is automatic and ineffaceable in its effect: Isaac blessed Jacob, who had succeeded in passing for Esau, his brother, taking advantage of the blindness and senility of their father. When Esau returns from hunting, succeeds in making his father recognize him, and protests at what has happened, Isaac answers that he can do nothing more for him, and that it is henceforth his fate to serve his brother. It is, in part at least, upon this act of deception that Israel's status as the Chosen People is based[54] (*Genesis*, 27). Ezekiel rages in Jehovah's name against the witches who 'hunt the souls of my people'. Jehovah promises to 'tear' the 'pillows' and 'kerchiefs' that they use for their incantations, and to 'deliver' the souls they have captured. This implies that the magical operations in question have been effective (*Ezekiel*, 13:17 et seq.). If Jehovah several times forbids the consultation of wizards and necromancers (e.g. *Deuteronomy*, 18:10 et seq.), and even orders that they be put to death (*Exodus*, 22:18; *Leviticus*, 20:27), this is because their powers are maleficent, which means they are real, effective. It is significant that their operations are called *'amal*, the general Semitic word for 'labour'.[55]

The Gospels assume the reality of demons and their activities. Jesus alludes to those who are able to 'cast out devils' (*Matthew*, 12:27; *Luke*, 11:19). *The Acts of the Apostles* speak of two practising magicians, Simon in Samaria (8:9 et seq.) and Elymas Bar-Jesus, who exercised his talents in Cyprus, 'with the deputy of the country, Sergius Paulus' (13:6 et seq.). They in no way dismiss the powers of these men as fictitious, any more than does the *2nd Epistle to Timothy*, which denounces the evil-doings of enchanters who 'creep into houses' to cast spells upon women (3:6 et seq.). This is why *The Revelation of St John the Divine* threatens eternal punishment to sorcerers at the end of time (21:8; 22:15). The underlying idea is, clearly, that magical powers really exist, but are subordinate, like the powers of any technician (which they closely resemble), to God's permission. Moreover, they are usually maleficent. The magician, conscious of the limited nature of his powers, could have said, reversing Ambroise Paré's phrase but keeping the same implication: 'I bewitched him, but God slew him.'

The ideology of the Koran is thus seen to accord a greater role to reasoning and rationality than is found in the ideologies that are reflected in the Old and New Testaments; to invoke the idea of predestination more or less to the same degree as we find in those scriptures, while clearly exorting men to be active in their individual and social lives; and, finally, to subordinate the technique of magic to the divine will exactly as in the two other books of revealed truth, thereby safeguarding men's ability to frustrate this technique, however cleverly it may have been employed.

Post-Koranic Muslim ideology

If, then, the ideology of the Koran cannot in any way have set Islam on an economic path that was inimical to the development of capitalism, or was even radically different from the path followed by the societies that are regarded as having been inspired by the Old and New Testaments, may one not, never-theless, shift the problem to a later stage? May it not be claimed that it was the *post-Koranic* development of Muslim ideology that gave Islam this orientation?

There is an invalidating objection to this way of looking at the problem. Post-Koranic Muslim ideology is not expressed in a closed body of doctrine with well-defined limits which, like the Koran, imposes its authority upon society from outside, so to speak. The texts in which it is expressed were conceived and written down during a long period of history and an extended phase of social evolution. For the non-Muslim who is unable to believe them to have been divinely inspired, they emanate from the social consciousness of their time[56] to no less an extent than they impose themselves upon it. They cannot therefore provide in themselves an explanation of this social consciousness. At most they may have given extra strength to some tendencies within the latter. And it is these tendencies that need to be explained. We have already seen what there was in them that might have been derived from the Koran, and could therefore be claimed to be of strictly Muslim origin. We have seen that these Koranic elements could not provide any explanation of the economic tendencies in question. What is not Koranic can be regarded as typically Muslim only *a posteriori*, through having been developed in a society which regarded the Koran as its holy book. To take an example, if we assume, as some do, that fatalism is characteristic of this post-Koranic Muslim ideology, there is nothing to prove that it was fatalistic because it was Muslim. I have shown that this ideology could have found (and did in fact find) in the Koran just as many sentences tending to favour a fatalistic attitude as others tending to foster the opposite one. I have also shown that the same coexistence of assertions pointing in opposite directions is to be found in the scriptures of Judaism and of Christianity. If, therefore, it be assumed that one of these ideologies was deeply marked by fatalism while the others were not, it seems clear that Islam as a religion can have nothing to do with the matter.

An epoch arrived, however, when a certain body of doctrine, formed in the previous epoch, *had* become 'closed', and thereby had acquired that exteriority to society which I have mentioned: from then on it could, consequently, influence social evolution, to some degree, from without. The Tradition, the Sunnah, codified in authorized compilations in the third century AH (the tenth century AD),[57] acquired sacred validity and came to be looked upon as divine revelation on the same footing as the Koran.[58] It would therefore be possible to accuse the ideology shaped during the second and third centuries AH (the ninth and tenth centuries AD) of having affected in one direction or another the evolution of society in subsequent centuries. Once again, this ideology itself cannot be considered purely and simply as something specifically and essentially Muslim. Even, however, the thesis of a decisive influence exercised by the ideology underlying the Tradition needs to be tempered, at least, by a number of qualifications.

In the first place, the *corpus* of the Tradition reflects and conveys tendencies that are as numerous as they are contradictory. Passages can frequently be found in it which favour conflicting views. There is no lack of such contradictions throughout the history of the Muslim world. This diversity has caused the process of interpretation to become very extensive. The doctors have reasoned about these passages and have drawn from them a great variety of conclusions, forming divergent schools which have fought against each other more or less violently. Islam has never had a supreme dogmatic authority such as Christendom possessed in the Councils, the Synods and the Papacy, able to give definitively a ruling that was accepted as authoritative everywhere (or even merely over a fairly wide area) on a given point of doctrine or practice. In the fourth century AH (the eleventh AD) the door of free interpretation (in matters of practice, especially) and independent reasoning was shut, in principle, and Muslims were thenceforth to be content with the doctrine set out in the manuals.[59] Nevertheless, discussion of problems of dogma continued, and even where problems of practice were concerned there was a certain amount of development, dictated by the evolution of ways of behaviour and of social life generally. Above all, there were always several different schools in existence at the same time, to which one could adhere or refer. Even the numerous sects that were regarded as heterodox were usually tolerated. Muslim society was eminently pluralistic. The public authorities supported now one school and now another, sometimes persecuting those extreme tendencies which seemed to them excessively dangerous and heterodox, or else merely hindering their propaganda. In general, however, they upheld to a very large degree the pluralism I have spoken of. And the political fragmentation of the Muslim world meant that, with different choices being made by different governments, the tendencies that were most strongly combated in certain areas could always find a place of refuge somewhere.

While the Koran offers a rather narrow choice of opinions (even though this can always be broadened by the process of exegesis), the Tradition forms a huge mass of propositions, among which the most antagonistic tendencies can easily find what they need and justify the choice they have made – and all the more so because the interested parties do not omit to increase the possibilities open to them, here too, as in the case of the Koran itself, by exegesis and interpretation. Consequently, it can be said that no tendency discernible among Muslims is to be explained by the constraint exercised by a body of sacred writing existing previously and acting as a force from outside to shape men's minds. If a particular passage is invoked, this is because someone has chosen this rather than another one. Essentially, therefore, post-Koranic ideology is not an external force moulding society, but an expression of tendencies emanating from social life as a whole.

This does not, of course, rule out, in Muslim society any more than in others, a certain gap, a certain 'distancing', between the ideology and the society that is contemporary with it. The ideology is transmitted by tradition. A condensation of the social life of preceding ages, it does indeed appear, if we study the matter in terms of chronological periods shorter than we have so far been assuming, in the more or less deceptive aspect of an external force. There are delicate and difficult problems involved here which can hardly be touched upon, and even less solved, in this book. Interpretation, unconsciously inspired by contemporary life, reduces the 'distancing' without doing away with it altogether. Certain earlier texts which have acquired a sacred character are resistant to an interpretation that harmonizes with the new setting. These may be forgotten, or concealed. Traditionalists may make use of them to try and impose the old moulds upon the new society. Backward-looking reformers may brandish other texts in order to call for a return to an alleged primitive purity which often conceals adaptation to new requirements. Despite what has been said above, it is not possible to brush aside the problem of the influence of ideology. What needs to be emphasized most strongly, however, is that this ideology is derived only to a very slight degree from sources that are specifically Muslim. All that we can regard as such are the Koran; a few traditions which it is very hard to single out from among those of quite different origins; and perhaps certain tendencies which are implied structurally by the Mohammedan ideology, which may have continued to operate in relatively independent form, and which alone may deserve the famous description of 'invariants' of Islam. It seems to me very doubtful, however, that these tendencies, in so far as they did operate, were not so greatly distorted by contemporary circumstances as to lose much of their initial aspect. They are, therefore, more susceptible of explanation by the social, cultural and ideological context of the age in which they operated than by their Muslim origin.

If Max Weber was right, and capitalism did not develop in the Islamic world because the ideology prevailing there was inimical to the rationalism needed for such a development, the cause would therefore seem to have lain not in Islam itself, the Muslim religion, but in all the factors that underlay this ideology – the social life of the Muslim world in all its aspects, and the previously existing ideologies, including Christianity in its Eastern form.

Nevertheless, it is perhaps worth taking the trouble to show, briefly, even if only to combat certain excessively sweeping ideas which are all too widely held, that post-Koranic Muslim ideology did not, in the Middle Ages, present that sharp contrast with the ideology of the Christian world which might, even though merely partially and superficially, seem to give support to Weber's thesis. One can show, too, that, in so far as there was a difference, it did not always point in the direction that Weber supposed. When ideological evolution does begin to seem to justify Weber's thesis, this is an epoch when, in any case, the chips are down, and the paths taken by the two economies have already diverged. Consequently, the new face presented by ideology cannot account for a separation that had begun earlier.

The rationalistic character of mediaeval Muslim culture is in reality very marked, to at least the same extent as that of Western culture in the same period. True, what was involved was an ultra-analytical form of reasoning, and it may be considered that this was a tool inadequately adapted to a thorough comprehension or a transformation of the world. It is true, too, that the rational activity carried on maintained respect for premises that had nothing in common with it, religious ones especially, from which this rational activity was content interminably to deduce consequences. But the situation was exactly the same in Western society in the same period. One cannot but be filled with respect and admiration for the immense effort of reasoning made by thousands of Muslim intellectuals of the Middle Ages to develop a de-ontological and juridical doctrine that would foresee all possible cases (and sometimes impossible ones as well), on the basis of a small number of premises. This they did with impeccable logic, taking up, thinking over afresh and completing Aristotle's philosophy and the whole heritage of Greek science, and developing a body of historical writing that filled thousands of volumes and was based on a critical foundation, the confrontation of different pieces of evidence, even if the criticism of these pieces of evidence themselves was not thorough enough. Even the art of the mediaeval Muslim world was highly intellectual, a rationally inspired creation whose multiple forms always seem to be deduced one from another by rationalizing reflection rather than inspired by the requirements of sensibility.

The problem of the State is more complex. Weber speaks of a 'rational' Western state *for the modern period*.[60] But as it exists *then*, it is without any explanatory significance, for one may suppose that, being contemporary with modern capitalism, it has emerged from the latter or is due to the same causes. Earlier on, he tells us that the *Ständestaat*, the state of the *rex et regnum*, in which the king rules in order to conserve and protect the orders and corporations of society, settling as arbiter the conflicts between them, is specific to Western Europe.[61] Perhaps this is so. But we know that the type of state he means arose at the *end* of the Middle Ages, being born of the decomposition of the classical feudal structure – that it appeared, that is, when Europe was well on the road to capitalism, so that it cannot serve to explain this orientation, with which it is apparently correlated.[62] Weber also gives a rational form of law as an essential element in the rational state. He shows with subtlety how the modern national state found support in the jurists who transmitted the eminently rational Roman law. He admits that 'all the characteristic institutions of modern capitalism have other origins than Roman law'. But the reception of Roman law was decisive in so far as (and only in so far as) it forged 'formal juristic thinking' (*das formal juristische Denken*), at the expense of law oriented upon 'material' principles such as utility and equity, the law typical of theocratic and absolutist régimes, of which the jurisdiction of the Muslim *qāḍī* provides an example. The connection between the modern state and the lawyers who upheld formalistic jurisprudence was favourable to capitalism, because the capitalists need a kind of law that safeguards their rights without any intervention from magic, morality, religion or personal arbitrariness.[63]

It is certainly true that the development of capitalism (and, before that, of capitalistic sectors) was favoured by a coherent, authoritative and relatively fixed system of codified rules. It is possible that the fact of having the impressive corpus of Roman law at its disposal favoured the development of capitalism in Europe. It may be that the importance of the personal factor in judgments, despite the imposing volume of the corpus of rules to which he had to refer, in the Muslim system of the jurisdiction of the *qāḍī*, had a tendency to discourage an evolution parallel to what occurred in Europe. But it is difficult to see in this a *decisive* factor. Even if we keep strictly to the data given by Weber, without trying to subject them to the critical examination they certainly need, we observe that the Europe of the Middle Ages in which capitalism took root was far from being dominated by Roman law. This was only one factor in a mixture of practices and systems of miscellaneous origin. The 'reception', and in the first place the recovery of knowledge of Roman law, which had almost been forgotten, took place gradually from the eleventh century onward, intensifying in the twelfth. As Paul Koschaker has well shown, these processes were closely connected with the 'Twelfth-Century Renaissance', that renewal of contact with the classical sources, through Byzantium and the Arabs – connected, consequently, with the renewal of trade and the flourishing of the merchant cities.[64] It is therefore permissible to see in the recovery and reception of Roman law an effect, or at least a correlative phenomenon, rather than a cause. Furthermore, this belated 'reception' was slow and partial in character. Weber himself notes that 'England, the home of capitalism, never accepted the Roman law'.[65] It should be added that in France too, for example, resistance to Roman law was very strong. It was customary law that prevailed and provided the basis for French law right down to the Revolution of 1789. Although at first accepted as being established practice in their southern provinces, Roman law was combated by the Kings of France, as favouring the claims of the Holy Roman Empire to world power. It is well known that Philip Augustus obtained from Honorius III the decretal *Super specula* of 1219, forbidding the teaching of Roman law in the University of Paris. It was accepted in the north of France only in so far as it could suggest solutions to problems on which custom was silent. In the sixteenth century the writing down of custom checked its progress. The adage 'custom grows into law' became established, and where local custom gave no guidance men preferred to refer to the general spirit of customary law, with a tendency for customs to become unified, preparing the way for the Civil Code.[66] Broadly speaking, it would seem that the European judge of the Middle Ages, whether guided (in no imperative fashion) by custom that was at first oral and later written, or by Roman law that evolved and was interpreted and adapted, was not so very much more closely restricted by hard-and-fast rules, or so much less free to give rein to his own views of right and wrong, than the *qāḍī* of the Muslim world, who was himself guided, in principle, by the huge corpus of the *fiqh*, which was much more thoroughly systematized, unified and rationalized than was Western custom.

As for the other element of the rational state according to Weber, a body of specialized officials, here too, very generally, it can be said that the mediaeval Muslim state possessed an administration of the same order of density as that of the Western states of the later Middle Ages,[67] and a great deal more substantial than that which existed before the development of Europe's capitalistic sector, in the early Middle Ages.

Among the great foes of capitalist development, Weber puts magic in the forefront, as we have seen. It can be said that the conceptions prevalent in the Muslim world offered no obstacle of this kind. Notions of magic exist in Islam, of course. Certain religious rites have come to be regarded as being endowed with magical effect; and in everyday life Muslims have always had recourse – perhaps to an increasing extent – to magical methods for ensuring the success of their actions, those of an economic character no less, doubtless, than others.[68] But there is nothing to show that the 'coefficient' of magic was any higher in the Muslim world than in the European society of the Middle Ages. It is known, for example, that, in the latter setting, magical notions obtained for a long time in the domain of law, with practices like trial by combat, 'the judgment of God', and the various forms of ordeal. Nothing of this kind ever existed in Islam.

It must be added here that magic never diverted men from activity in the technical sphere, in the Muslim world any more than elsewhere. An orientation towards magic certainly may cause attention to be focused upon investigations and practices of an illusory kind, to the detriment of the pursuit of technical innovation, and the latter is indeed the necessary basis, if not perhaps of capitalism, then, at any rate, of industrial civilization. Yet the development of magic in mediaeval Europe did not prevent the latter from adopting or discovering new techniques which provided the basis for development towards the Industrial Revolution, as has often been shown. And we have just seen that magic was at least as well developed in the Christian West as in the Muslim East. At all events, if, from a certain period onward, technique in the Eastern world was at a lower level than in Europe, the reason for this cannot have lain in the Muslim religion. This is clear, first and foremost, because in the previous epoch the technical superiority of the Muslim East over Europe was strikingly obvious, as is shown in particular by the numerous borrowings made by the latter from the former in this sphere.[69] It is clear, secondly, because nothing can be found in Muslim doctrine that could have served as an obstacle to technical activity. This has been demonstrated by an authority in the field, Louis Gardet, and I shall be content to refer to his brief but solid study,[70] which concludes thus: 'In fact, it is impossible to see how study of the practical sciences and the developing of technical equipment can be contrary to Muslim dogma'.

As for ideological resistance to the constant striving for profit, the driving force of capitalism, a resistance to which Weber attributes great weight, there was certainly less of this in the Islamic world than in the Christian West. A full comparative study needs to be made of Christian ethics and Muslim ethics in the Middle Ages: this would be a lengthy and delicate undertaking that cannot be attempted here. Of course the theologians on both sides condemned 'lucre', excessive appetite for wealth, preoccupation with the goods of this world at the expense of the search for God. But subtle and significant divergences soon made themselves apparent. For the Christian theology of the Middle Ages, the sin of avarice consists in endeavouring to acquire, or desiring to retain, goods in excess of what is necessary:

> *Homo secundum aliquam mensuram quaerit habere exteriores divitias, prout sunt necessaria ad vitam eius secundum suam conditionem. Et ideo in excessu huius mensurae consistit peccatum: dum scilicet aliquis supra debitum modum vult eas vel acquirere vel retinere.*[71]

For Islam the stress is laid rather upon the good use to be made of one's possessions, the merit that lies in expending them intelligently and distributing them with generosity[72] – an attitude more favourable to economic expansion than that of the Christian theologians.

It is similar with the 'charitable character' of Islam, which C. H. Becker regards as an obstacle to this expansion – the fact that the receiving of alms is for Muslims a right recognized by the religious law, that the beggar is justified and encouraged by popular opinion, which 'must' have the effect of keeping many persons away from productive work.[73] Without going deeply into this latter conception, so typical of liberal capitalism, it is surely enough to recall the exaltation of the poor man and the beggar in mediaeval Christian ideology, the constitution of the mendicant orders, etc. Here, too, we are not faced with a feature that is distinctive of Islam.

Finally, there has been talk of a deficiency in the Muslim East of the spirit of enterprise, and to mediaeval Islam has been attributed an indifferent fatalism that relies on God to furnish man with the goods he needs in order to live, if God should judge this to be worth while. This view is, as is well known, one of the most widespread held about Islam in Europe, and has even acquired the status of an established truth, a dogma for the European collective mind, well expressed in Leibniz's expression *fatum mahumetanum*. It was developed by innumerable European writers in the eighteenth and nineteenth centuries, who were able to point to the spectacle offered by the stagnation to which the Ottoman Empire, Morocco and Iran were all then subject. It is still frequently repeated in our own time.[74] And yet it is highly questionable. 'It must be very seriously considered', wrote C. H. Becker, 'whether Oriental fatalism, which is indeed widespread, should not be ascribed much more to political declassing and economic distress than to religious precepts.'[75] It is not possible here to go into the complicated windings of Muslim theology. As in other religions, the problem of the relation between God's omnipotence and foreknowledge, on the one hand, and man's freedom and responsibility, on the other, has greatly preoccupied the theoreticians, and schools of thought have taken shape which offer rival solutions to it and struggle with one another. What has predominated is undoubtedly a stress upon the divine omnipotence, God's total freedom, which to human eyes presents the aspect of something arbitrary: God's inscrutable transcendence, the incomprehensibility of the choices He makes, of His own free will. Man thus appears as practically a negligible factor, and he is accordingly impelled to take up an attitude of submission (*islām*) and trusting surrender (*tawakkul*) to this will which is greater than himself. It is impossible that God's will should not have known and determined in advance all human actions and their consequences, including their ultimate retribution. This emphasis has undoubtedly entered deeply into popular consciousness. 'A man kills another man: *maqdūr*! it was decreed by God. The people will say: *maktūb*! it was written in the "hidden tablet".'[76]

Nevertheless, whether these ideas be logically in contradiction or whether a reconciliation between them be feasible, in the domain of reason, historical Islam has always, continuing the line taken by its founder, exhorted its adherents to action in this world. At least, this is true of the dominant tendencies in Islam; and all the more so because the distinction between the temporal and spiritual spheres was, if not unknown, at any rate seen quite differently from the way Christians saw it. Islam 'takes responsibility for the temporal sphere in order to organize it on the temporal level itself, and allows its adherents to find in this sphere, in conformity with God's laws, reasonable sufficiency and enjoyment'.[77] The Muslim community, owing to the historical circumstances in which it began its existence, was essentially a state, and not, like the Christian Church, an organization that successively expected to be tolerated by the state, then to influence it, to exercise control over it, and to dominate it, but that hardly ever *identified itself with* the state. It was the religious duty of the leaders of the Muslim community to conquer, to defend, to administer, and that of the members of this community to help them in these tasks. All this meant action – rational action, calculation and foresight, organization of resources for the pursuit of a purpose that was earthly, even though gratifying to the Divine Will.

Religious duty itself, therefore, hurled men into action, or, rather, authorized and sanctified action. The 'holy war' (*djihād*) is a duty obligatory upon the Muslim community when circumstances require it, and, of course, everything must be done to ensure that it results in a victorious outcome, to the greater glory of God. It has often been observed that the biggest efforts along the line of technical advance were devoted, in the Muslim world as elsewhere, to the technique of war, even when this was directed against brothers in Islam![78] It is also a duty laid upon the rulers to ensure the economic prosperity of the community and, given the framework of an unplanned economy, it was difficult to prohibit in any fundamental way the use for personal advantage of the privileges and gains that were obtained by the community.

Everything comes from God and goes back to him. Since, however, God entrusts to his servants the good things of this world, is it not their duty to utilize them for the best, in a reasonable way, without becoming enslaved to them – thanking God when there is plenty and submitting without complaint in times of trial?[79]

Does not a contemporary Muslim apologist explain that, in Islam, the duty of taxpaying is a religious one, on the same footing as, for example, prayer? And this is strictly true, at least as regards taxes that are legal in the sense of conforming to the religious law.[80] The Muslim state is therefore prosperous to the extent that the Muslims living in it are prosperous.

The latter feel that they are authorized, or even obliged, to earn their livings, to make profits, especially through that activity which the theoreticians of the classical epoch treat with particular respect, namely, trade. A theologian, Bājūrī, who in the nineteenth century brought to perfection the provisional solutions to problems that were available up to then, concluded that surrender to the will of God was better for some, and activity for others, depending on individual temperament. Since, moreover, action itself emanates from God,

it is enough for a man who is engaged, for example, in commercial transactions, to be aware from speculative knowledge that he counts for nothing in what he does. Let him thereafter profit as he pleases from that feeling and appearance of freedom which have been implanted in him by God.[81]

'It is believed', said the great Ghazālī, much earlier,

that what *tawakkul* means is abandoning *kasb* [the will to make one's own acts that are in reality performed by God] in one's body, abandoning in one's heart the capacity to organize, and letting oneself drop to the ground like a rag that is thrown away or like meat on a butcher's stall. This is what the ignorant believe, but it is forbidden [*harām*] by the religious law.[82]

It is even recorded, says an eighteenth-century commentator on Ghazālī, that Ibrāhīm an-Nakhāʿī, a pious authority of the first century AH, was asked which he preferred: an honest merchant or a man who has given up all forms of work so as to devote himself wholly to the service of God. He is said to have replied:

The honest merchant is dearer to me, for he is in the position of one waging a holy war. Satan approaches him through measures and scales, in the course of commercial transactions, and so he fights a holy war against Satan.[83]

This was, moreover, the more usual attitude. 'People are of three kinds,' says Ghazālī in another place:

those whose activity in making a living diverts them from the future life, and they are doomed to perdition; those whose concern with the future life diverts them from the activity needed to make a living, and they are the gainers; and those, finally, nearer to the happy medium, whose activity in making a living leads them towards the future life, and they are the average run of people.[84]

Using a parable, Ghazālī advises those who trust in God not to put forth excessive efforts to drag from him more than he intends to give them, in the manner of poor men clinging to the servants of a King who have been given the task of distributing loaves among them, in the hope of getting more than their share. But what happens in practice? 90 per cent of people, this theologian estimates, cling to these servants with a view to getting as much as they can, and this proportion seems even to have increased in recent times.[85]

In brief, the theoreticians counselled men to join trust in God with a reasonable degree of activity, neither too avid nor too listless. This was how the matter was understood by those men who wanted to live a pious and honest life.[86] The majority, however, had the usual attitude of most men under conditions when there was no special fever of ideological excitement, that is, they tried to maximize their privileges and gains by every legal means open to them. Islam sought to regulate these 'natural' tendencies and keep them within limits compatible with good social order. Its theories on divine omnipotence, whatever their origin, were harmonized with reasonable forms of activity, especially the activity of traders. We have already seen how the Muslim traders were animated by an indefatigable activity in search of profit, and constituted a sort of capitalistic sector. If Islam in no way hindered this activity and did not prevent them from reaching that stage of development, it is hard to see how it could have stopped them or their fellow-Muslims from carrying on activities, strictly of the same kind from the standpoint of religious morality, that would have led farther along the line of development of modern capitalism. And we know that the Calvinist dogma of predestination was reconciled, to say the least, with the giving of a blessing to the pioneers of capitalism in Europe. If it be reduced to this observation, Weber's thesis on the connection between Protestantism and capitalism is irrefutable.[87]

The examples of 'Muslim fatalism' that have probably been most often quoted by European writers were taken above all from the under-developed rural areas of the Islamic world. G. Destanne de Bernis has shown in a very scholarly way, using mathematical methods and with a close and deep knowledge of Tunisian country life, that, if the peasants of the Muslim countries are indeed fatalistic, this is not at all an irrational attitude on their part, but represents a just estimation of the enormous, and discouraging, weight of the chancy factors that condition the success of their efforts. 'Anyone so placed would be fatalistic, at the very least,' this writer comments with justification, and he adds that 'every traditional rural civilization, if by this we mean one that has not been altered by the impact of technical progress, is sunk in fatalism.' He shows that mediaeval Christendom knew the same mentality for the same reasons.[88] One cannot but agree with his conclusions, while stressing, however, that there are degrees of fatalism. Some social conditions, in the West and in the East, in certain regions and certain periods, have further accentuated the chanciness – already great owing to natural conditions – of the return that the peasant can expect for his labours. I refer to the deductions from his crops that he was obliged to make in favour of landlords and the state. These deductions were often so substantial, and determined in such an arbitrary way, that they radically discouraged all effort in labour, and especially all effort to bring about improvements that the peasant knew would only benefit others. Once again, there is nothing here that is attributable to the Muslim religion.

True, I have not yet said anything about mysticism, that tendency which gradually developed in Islam, eventually acquiring great strength, and inspired confraternities which recruited their members from the ranks of the common people, spreading among the masses their characteristic conceptions and practices. It must be emphasized, however, that in Islam as in Christianity the dominant tendency integrated the mystical experience in a synthesis in which it was accorded an eminent, but limited, position alongside the activity of reason. Rational knowledge, prophetic revelation, and the special illumination (*ilhām*) which gives inner certainty to the initiated of a rank lower than the prophets, are so many different modes of knowledge which are hierarchically ordered in accordance with their respective values, but which since, if they are authentic, they lead to the same results, taking account of the same truths, cannot be in contradiction with one another. These are the conceptions held by Ghazālī (1058–1112), whose influence was considerable.[89] In general, a large place was allotted to reason not only in theological theory but also, and especially, in the actual intellectual activity of educated Muslims. The mystical confraternities themselves did not turn any large number of persons wholly away from the world's affairs. The mystics regarded themselves as an élite which, fortunately, could not be joined by everyone, so that their maintenance required of necessity the profane labours of peasants and craftsmen, the organizing activity of statesmen, the military activity of soldiers, and so on. Moreover, many of them considered that their life in the world should not be abandoned but only transfigured, acquiring a different significance through their inner illumination. They became active in spreading Islam through missionary work, or in defending or extending its domain by force of arms, and they often devoted themselves to welfare work.[90] The adepts of many confraternities work in the world while also participating in mystical exercises: in all the confraternities at least one category of adepts do this. In some Eastern monasteries of the mystical confraternities, manual labour is held in honour.[91] Turkish historians have shown that certain confraternities played, on their own initiative, a big part in the economic development of the Ottoman Empire in the sixteenth century.[92] The degeneration of mysticism, however blameworthy from the moral standpoint, resulting as it did in the exploitation of the mass of the adepts for the benefit of one family or of a narrow circle of rulers of the confraternities, has tended to reinforce productive and social activity. The Eastern monasteries are often owners of land and live on the income from their land: in other words, on the labour of the peasants who cultivate it.[93] In Black Africa some new confraternities have emphasized so strongly the sanctifying virtue of manual labour that they have become very sizeable enterprises, exploiting the poorly paid labour of thousands of adepts.[94]

C. H. Becker has defined more clearly than anyone else a phenomenon that many have felt and have described more or less explicitly. In the traditional Muslim world the individual feels a special respect for the *shariʿa*, the religious law, even if he does not know what it is. He thus conceives the whole of his life as being encompassed by a network of religious obligations, as regulated by religion. This leads him to accord a sacred character to existing institutions, even if these are not at all Islamic in origin. Hence comes a conservatism that hinders the individual's innovatory initiative,[95] a misoneism, a '*Nicht Progressivismus*' as A. Rühl puts it. In the Middle Ages the idea of progress was not very widely held, and it was rather the idea of the superiority of the past that was preponderant.[96] This description is certainly true to a large extent. But it is enough to point out that it is equally applicable to the Christian world of the Middle Ages. Yet the mentality in question did not prevent the Christians of Europe from taking the road to capitalism, which led to the decay of this mode of thinking. It ought not to have been able to prevent the Muslims from doing the same.

A very clear proof that Islam was not inherently opposed to the development of an ethic and a mentality favourable to capitalism is given by the Mozabites, among others. The inhabitants of Mzab, a group of oases in the South of Algeria, belong to the Muslim sect of the Abāḍites or Ibāḍites. All who have studied them have been struck by their resemblance in many ways to the Calvinists whom Weber places at the origin of capitalism. It has become commonplace to call them 'the Puritans of Islam'. The Mozabites labour with untiring zeal to maintain palmgroves in a desert region, something that calls for ceaseless effort. But they are above all traders who, throughout Algeria and beyond, amass fortunes that are often very substantial, through steady application to trade and to lending money at interest. It must be stressed, in contradiction to what has sometimes been said, that the religious dogma held by these typical capitalists presents hardly any marked originality as compared with Islam in general, on the relevant points that might serve to explain the nature of their activity. One can convince oneself of this by reading, for example, the somewhat mnemonic poem published by Z. Smogorzewski on the differences between the Abāḍites and the Mālikites, that is, the adherents of the juridico-theological school which is overwhelmingly preponderant in North Africa.[97] In particular, the Abāḍite position on the problem of predestination is no different from that of other Muslims. From the standpoint of the religious law as it affects the economy, though they lend at interest, they do this by utilizing *ḥiyal* that are well known in the other tendencies of Islam.[98] The secret of their special economic dynamism is to be found only in their situation as an ideological minority, their will to maintain a particularism based on a very strong cohesion. This will to cohesion leads to special importance being accorded among them to the clergy, the experts in religious law, who closely watch over the moral conduct of their flocks, ˜their austerity in morals, and so forth, and this ensures that they will not let themselves be drawn into indolence, dissipation or extravagance. Here we see a phenomenon which, characteristic of ideological minorities, is found elsewhere in Islam for example, among the Ismailis, not to speak of what happens in other religions. Schumpeter has stressed the role played by 'creative minorities'. Living under conditions different from those of their Algerian brethren, the Ibāḍites of Oman, in South-Eastern Arabia, 'have shown', says an American economist, 'little predilection for enterprise other than tweaking the tail of the British lion'.[99] It is not in ideas that the initial cause of the attitude in question is to be found, but in the social situation of the group. And this shows that the ideas of Islam on economic life, or on the conduct of man in general, are not in the least opposed to an orientation of activity in the direction of capitalism.

Thus it would appear that Weber's thesis attributing to the specific rationality of the European the development of modern capitalism in Europe and in Europe alone is without foundation, if we examine the obvious corollary that the other civilizations, including that of Islam, in which capitalism did not develop, showed a lower degree of rationality. Besides, Weber's whole procedure, and that of those who more or less share his tendency, is contradictory in itself, as I have tried to show.[100] Weber describes substantial features of higher rationality existing in Europe only in the modern age, the age when modern capitalism was already predominant, so that it is impossible to prove that these features were not created by the economic régime they accompany. The question of their origin remains exactly where it was.

Accordingly, there is nothing to indicate in a compelling way that the Muslim religion prevented the Muslim world from developing along the road to modern capitalism, any more than there is anything to indicate that Christianity directed the Western European world along that road. Islam did not prescribe to or impose upon the people, the civilization, the states that adopted its teaching any specific economic road. The economic structure of the mediaeval Muslim world was broadly comparable to that of Europe in the same period, as also, no doubt, to that of China, Japan and India before the impact of Europe upon them. The development that followed in Europe was different from that of the Muslim world and of the other civilizations just mentioned. Discussion is going on about the reasons for this divergence; without wishing, here at least, to join in this discussion, it will be enough for my present purpose to note that the causes of the divergence cannot be sought in men's adherence to some pre-established doctrine. In particular, the divergence cannot be seen as resulting from the influence of a concern for justice that may be alleged to have animated a certain doctrine as compared with others.

5 Islam and Capitalism in the Muslim Countries Today

We have seen that there was always a capitalistic sector in the countries of Islam, and that this was even very extensive in certain periods. One cannot, however, speak of a capitalist socio-economic formation existing in the Middle Ages. Such a formation presupposes a capitalist economic system as its basis – that is, a system in which the capitalist sector plays a predominant role, influencing the other sectors without being influenced by them to any important extent.[1] This was far from being the case in the Muslim Middle Ages.

At the present time, however, in many of the countries of the Muslim world this question really does arise. The capitalist sector has at least begun to play a predominant role. An American economist estimated, a few years ago, that it accounted for 20 per cent of annual investment in Iraq and Iran, 50 per cent in Turkey, and 80 per cent in Syria and the Lebanon.[2] It is possible to foresee the possibility that it may extend to the point where it predominates completely. This process may in some countries have been halted, or crowned, by the establishment of another economic system in which the state sector is predominant. In such cases, however, this break has either occurred in a situation where a tendency towards extension of the capitalist sector in the way indicated was already very pronounced, as in the Asiatic part of the Russian Empire at the time of the October Revolution, or it has consisted essentially in the statization of existing capitalist enterprises, as in Egypt, so that the term '*state capitalism*', put forward to describe this economic system, is justified from this point of view at least.

It is naturally difficult to point to a precise moment when the capitalist sector becomes predominant. The realities of Europe, North America and Japan, even taken as a whole, show us, nevertheless, that for this to be so it is necessary that a capitalism of *production* – in other words, industrial enterprises organized in accordance with the capitalist mode of production – shall exist and shall have attained a certain level of development. We know that this predominance of the capitalist mode of production is found only when factory industry is actually present, with machine production in place of craft enterprises connected with petty commodity production, or even of manufactures.

Now, the most superficial survey is enough to show us that industry has only started to develop very recently in the Muslim countries. To give some definiteness to general notions, I am going to set out some figures, none of which are wholly reliable, but which will serve to indicate orders of magnitude. So as to eliminate the difficulties connected with defining such concepts as 'occupied population' and the like, I shall simply put the number of workers employed in industry in relation to the total population. In this way it is possible to compile the table below, which has no claim to scientific exactness.

However imprecise the figures given, or disparate the criteria on which they are based, they none the less suffice to bring out one fact clearly. The Muslim countries, with the (partial) exception of those that had been colonized, were still in 1952–9, despite some progress observable in the preceding half-century, far from having attained the level of industrialization of France in the first half of the nineteenth century.[3] In 1914 industrial capitalism was as yet at an extremely low level of development in all these countries. Nevertheless, already at that time this phenomenon was accorded decisive importance. 'All Asia is being permeated with modern industry and present-day mechanical progress', wrote an American observer in 1914.[4] Since then great efforts have been put forward to expand this sector, with results that on the whole are proportionately significant.

In the setting of the very wide problem that I am examining here, the questions that need to be asked seem to me to be the following:

(1) Is this extension of the capitalist sector in the Muslim

Country	Date	Total population (in thousands)	Population employed in industry (in thousands)	Percentage
Afghanistan	1958	13,000 (a)	—	—
Afghanistan	1959	—	13 (b)	0·1
Iran	1958	19,680 (a)	208·5 (b)	1·05
Iraq	1952	4,871 (a)	—	—
Iraq	1954	—	163 (b)	3·32
Lebanon	1958	1,550 (a)	21·2 (b)	1·36
Ottoman Empire	1913	23,000 (c)	17 (d)	0·07
Turkey	1957	25,500 (a)	613 (b)	2·40
Egypt	1917	12,750 (e)	201 (f)	1·57
Egypt	1937	15,500 (e)	273 (f)	1·76
Egypt	1958	24,600 (e)	280 (g)	1·13
Israel	1958	{ Total 2,032 (h) Jews, 1,810 (h)	{ 142 (i) 135 (i)	{ 6·98 7·45
Tunisia	1956	3,800 (a)	265 (b)	6·97
Algeria	1954	9,529 (a)	322 (b)	3·37
France	1815	29,380 (j)	1,600 (k)	5·44
France	1866	38,080 (j)	3,800 (k)	9·97
France	1906	39,270 (j)	4,000 (k)	10·18

Sources
(a) United Nations Annual Statistics of Population.
(b) Table VI (compiled from a variety of sources) in *Aziya i Afrika 1950–1960 gg., statistichesky sbornik*, Moscow, 1964, p. 18.
(c) J. Birot, *Statistique annuelle de géographie humaine comparée, 1913*, Paris, Hachette, 1913, p. 7.
(d) *Statistique industrielle des années 1913 et 1915*, Istanbul, Ministry of Trade and Agriculture, 1917, quoted in O. Conker and E. Witmeur, *Redressement économique et industrialisation de la nouvelle Turquie*, Paris, Recueil Sirey, 1937, p. 58.
(e) Hassan Riad, *L'Egypte nassérienne*, Paris, Éd. de Minuit, 1964, pp. 135, 137.
(f) L. A. Fridman, *Kapitalisticheskoye razvitiye Egipta (1882–1930)*, Moscow, 1963, p. 167.

(g) H. Riad, op. cit., p. 62.

(h) *Statistical Abstract of Israel, 1958–1959*, Jerusalem, Table I, p. 7, quoted in Sh. Sitton, *Israël, émigration et croissance*, Paris, Éd. Cujas, 1963, p. 106.

(i) Sitton, op. cit., pp. 200, 219.

(j) *Annuaire statistique de la France, Rétrospectif*, Paris, I.N.S.E.E., 1961, pp. 32, 34.

(k) E. Mossé, *Marx et le Problème de la croissance dans une économie capitaliste*, Paris, A. Colin, 1956, p. 153.

countries external or internal in origin: in other words, can it be regarded as having been brought about by an impetus from outside or as the result of a spontaneous development?

(2) Has the Muslim religion hindered or favoured this development of capitalism in the present period, and to what extent?

(3) Has contemporary capitalism taken a specific road in the Muslim countries? If so, is the cause to be found in the Muslim religion?

Origination from within or from without?

Though this question has been made unnecessarily complicated it is easy enough to answer. A few distinctions do need to be made, however.

Let us take the case of Egypt. Industry was introduced there under Mehemet Ali (1805–49), but as state-owned industry, from 1816 onward. It was the state that constructed the new industrial buildings, made all the investments, paid the workers' wages and sold the goods produced. The state monopoly of industry extended to the craft workshops as well, which also worked for the Pasha. The workers in his service must have numbered over 70,000[5] (or, perhaps, 2·3 per cent of the population of that time). This industrial monopoly of state capitalism was abolished after Mehemet Ali's death – in what circumstances we shall see later. Economic liberalism led to the resurgence of the privately owned crafts, and the closing down of most of the large-scale Egyptian enterprises, in face of competition from European goods. In 1873 all that remained were a few workshops employing about 7,000 workers in the iron and steel industry, and a textile and clothing industry with a workforce of 28,000.[6] The British occupation (1882) reinforced and accelerated this process. Developing industry was wholly in the hands of foreign capital, mainly British and French.[7] Egyptian capital was invested to an overwhelming degree in large-scale landed property. In 1917 a 'committee for trade and industry' gave attention to creating Egyptian-owned industry. 'For the new bourgeoisie of the towns – traders, businessmen and members of the liberal professions, especially lawyers and engineers – it was a question of providing the modernistic wing of the big landowners with a field of operation and investment for their idle capital', writes A. Abdel-Malek.[8] In 1920 Tal'at Harb founded the Banque Misr (Bank of Egypt), with the aim of financing this new Egyptian national industry. In the struggle for political independence the bourgeois leaders of the struggle called upon Egyptians to contribute to the financing of this bank and to give preference to the products of the enterprises it controlled. This was the start of the slow process of forming a really modern Egyptian capitalist sector – which, however, had many links with foreign capitalism.[9] It was this sector that was to be, in large part, progressively nationalized after 1952, and managed by the military bureaucracy of Nasser's régime, along with the Muslim section of the old capitalists and also with new capitalists, some of whom became officials and some of whom retained interests in the private capitalist sector, which was in any case placed in a subordinate position.

For the Ottoman Empire in general, apart from Egypt, one cannot speak before the nineteenth century of capitalist industrial enterprises in the true sense. There were some privately owned manufactories, though not, apparently, very many. In any case, the techniques used were 'not very advanced, and were essentially based on manual work. There were few machines or none, even in the factories and the large workshops, where production methods were still at the craft stage.'[10] The large enterprises (where technique was hardly more advanced) were state-owned. In the nineteenth century, when the impact of Europe became quite threatening, the Ottoman rulers did not try to react, as Mehemet Ali did, by creating large-scale state industry. Though some of them may have entertained the idea, political circumstances and the disastrous financial situation prevented them from even beginning to put it into practice. Worse than that, they collaborated effectively, under British influence in the main, in destroying the work of Mehemet Ali. The Anglo-Ottoman commercial treaty of 1818, completed by the *firmān* of 1820, restricted taxes on imports to 3 per cent *ad valorem*. It was replaced by the treaty of 1838, which abolished the monopolies in the name of sacrosanct 'freedom of trade', and, in exchange for this fundamental measure, raised the import tax to 5 per cent *ad valorem*, while exports were taxed at 12 per cent.

As the worthy interpreter Belin naïvely put it, this meant taking a line 'more favourable to foreign interests than to native ones'.[11] In fact this treaty (usually regarded by Orientalist historians as not worth mentioning), which was extended in the same year to all the European powers, nipped in the bud any attempt that might have been made to build an Ottoman industry.[12] Between 1812 and 1841 the number of silk-weaving looms at Scutari and at Tirnovo fell from 2,000 to 200; the total production of silk fabrics of all kinds in Anatolia was in the first half of the nineteenth century only one tenth of what it had been in the previous half-century; during the same period the value of the cotton and silk fabrics produced at Aleppo fell from one hundred million piastres to less than eight million.[13] Application of the treaty of 1838 was imposed upon Egypt by Palmerston and the British fleet in 1840, and a repentant Mehemet Ali had to make an act of contrition to the religion of Free Trade.

I recognize that the advantages of free trade are consecrated by the existing treaties – striking proofs witness to the benefits they bring, and I cannot deny what is now obvious to me. Imperative circumstances alone forced me to establish and uphold the monopoly.[14]

Despite some unsuccessful attempts to resist (notably the treaties of 1861, which raised import duties to 8 per cent, and 1907, which raised them to 11 per cent, a level still not high enough to constitute effective protection), the Ottoman Empire rolled rapidly down the slope of subordination to foreign capital. The decree of Muḥarram (20 December 1881) gave European organizations – the Ottoman Imperial Bank and the Ottoman

Public Debt – complete control over the country's economy. Foreign enterprises were safeguarded from all taxes except the tax on buildings. The result was obvious. What capitalist enterprises there were in the Ottoman Empire were mostly foreign-owned. Those that were nominally Ottoman operated with European capital, or, to a large extent, with capital belonging to minority groups that were closely linked with Europe. In 1913 there were 269 industrial enterprises in the Ottoman Empire, 242 of which were actually functioning. Of their capital, 10 per cent was held by foreigners, 50 per cent by Greeks, 20 per cent by Armenians, 5 per cent by Jews and only 15 per cent by Muslim Turks.[15]

The situation can be studied in rather more detail in the Syrian region, for example. In the Lebanon, at the beginning of the nineteenth century, there was still a silk-producing craft industry, which had formerly enjoyed greater prosperity but which the conditions prevailing in the Ottoman epoch had caused to decline.[16] The peasants each reared a few cocoons and the silk was spun on primitive lathes that were either owned in common by the villages or belonged to the emirs. The spinning industry was brought up to date in 1840, on a capitalist basis, by a Frenchman, Nicolas Portalis, who, bringing with him some forty spinning-women from the Drôme, founded a silk factory at Bteter. By 1850 five new spinning mills had been set up, three of which were French. This example, and the autonomous organic statute granted to the Lebanon in 1864 by the Ottoman government, encouraged Lebanese to invest capital in similar enterprises. In 1885 there were 105, of which only five were French,[17] but all of these spinning-mills were dependent on French capital, mainly raised in Lyons. Half of the capital devoted to the purchase of cocoons (the biggest item of expense) was borrowed in Lyons, at a rate which in practice came to 10 per cent. As against this, nearly all the silk made in the Lebanon went to supply the Lyons market.[18]

In Syria as a whole around the period of the First World War a good observer who was working for the Zionist movement, taking a general view, noted that the whole of large-scale industry was in the hands of Europeans, with the natives retaining for themselves only craft production and domestic industry. He estimated at fewer than a hundred the factories where more than fifty workers were employed, and at hardly a dozen those with more than one hundred. None of them had more than 300 workers.[19]

In Iran before 1921 the number of factories was extremely small. Exceptions were a match factory (the only one of its kind) founded in 1891, and a sugar works founded in 1895 at Kahrīzak on the initiative of a statesman, Ṣanīʿ od-Dowle, with the co-operation of a Belgian firm. The latter was soon closed, either because of superstitious rumours or because of competition from imported sugar,[20] and thirty years had to pass before other such factories were opened. In any case, industry was negligible before the war of 1914 and even long afterward, if we leave out of account the extraction of petroleum by the Anglo-Iranian Oil Company. There can be no doubt that we must include, among the principal factors, at least, hindering industrialization, the commercial agreements made with foreign powers after the treaty of Turkmanchai (1828), which was imposed by Russia after a military defeat suffered by Persia. This treaty established a uniform customs duty of 5 per cent on all the imports and exports exchanged by the two countries concerned – an example that was followed by the other powers. This removed any possibility of ensuring tariff protection to a nascent industry that might have need of it. Persia imported from Britain in 1828, 11·5 million yards of printed cotton goods, and in 1834, 28·6 million yards.[21] The effect of foreign competition was greatly increased by the concessions that were granted to foreigners by virtue of their political predominance, while, in turn, the country's state of economic underdevelopment caused it to be politically helpless in relation to the West. 'Through granting one concession after another, Persia will soon be wholly in the hands of foreigners,' wrote the French physician Feuvrier in April 1890.[22] Between 1885 and 1900 'capitulations' were signed to the advantage of fifteen different countries. Nothing might be done that would be harmful to European interests. In 1905 the geographer Élisée Reclus could write: 'Russia and Britain are now the two rival overlords whose desires and caprices the government of Persia has to be careful constantly to study, courting their favours, avoiding their anger, and anticipating their wishes.'[23] The first great demonstration of popular reaction was directed against an act of economic submission, the granting of the tobacco monopoly (covering production, sale and export) to the British capitalist G. F. Talbot in March 1890. The Persian revolution of 1905–11 was crushed, however, thanks above all to Russian intervention. It was unable to prevent the Anglo-Russian agreement of 31 August 1907, by which the two powers divided Iran into zones of influence – taking the trouble to inform the Iranian Government of this only a whole month later. No attempt at independent industrialization was possible under these conditions.[24]

Since 1920 the problem that interests us here has presented no difficulty and can give rise to no doubts. In a clear and open way, in all the independent Muslim countries, including those more or less colonial ones where the native bourgeoisie retained some possibilities of economic initiative, the striving to build capitalist (or state) industry was undertaken in imitation of European and North American capitalism. Ṭalᶜat Ḥarb, an Egyptian capitalist who fought zealously and effectively for the creation of a modern Egyptian industry, wrote in a discussion with a French journalist:

We want to follow your example ... Our requirements are modest. We merely desire a place in the sun, *to live like other people*, producing and increasing our production, exporting what we produce, consuming and increasing our consumption. In order to reach this goal we are working in accordance with your example. And we are grateful to you for having shown us this path.[25]

Similarly, in 1923, the Turkish sociologist Ziya Gökalp, one of the clearest-headed ideologists of modern Turkey, and one of the most influential in Kemal's time, wrote:

The modern state is founded upon large-scale industry. If the new Turkey is to be a modern state it must above all develop a national industry. The new Turkey, which must introduce the most up-to-date and advanced techniques from Europe, cannot afford the luxury of waiting for its industrialization upon the spontaneous development of a spirit of enterprise among individuals. Just as we have done in the field of military technique, so in industry we must reach

European levels by an effort undertaken on the national scale.[26]

This same Ziya Gökalp put forward the slogan: 'Belong to the Turkish nation, the Muslim religion and European civilization.'[27] Kemal's entire team was guided by the will to Europeanize. '"We are Europeans" is the unanimous assertion of all of us,' wrote one of the group in 1929. 'This phrase on our tongue is like the chorus of a very stirring martial song. All of us, poor and rich, young and old, have this phrase on our lips . . . To be European is our ideal . . .'[28] 'The Turkish nation,' declared the Minister of Justice, Mahmud Esad, presenting the new Code of Civil Law in 1926, 'has decided to accept modern civilization and its living principles without any condition or reservation.'[29] This modern civilization which, as Mustafa Kemal Atatürk himself had exclaimed lyrically in the previous year, 'pierces the mountains, flies across the heavens, sees everything, even to stars that are invisible to the naked eye, this science that illuminates and investigates', this civilization 'to whose seething torrent it is vain to offer resistance',[30] is European civilization. It is with this model in view that industrialization is undertaken – that is, the introduction of state enterprise and private capitalist enterprise, the latter being duly encouraged and aided in every way, despite the proclaimed principle of statism. The law on aid to industry which was adopted in 1927 soon produced important effects. The number of industrial enterprises was already 1,400 by 1933, as compared with 242 in 1913, and this on a much smaller territory. The number of industrial workers, which, in 1923 was 16–17,000, had grown ten years later to more than 62,000 and by 1939 to about 90,000.[31]

Matters are no less clear in the case of Iran. To be brief, let me confine myself to quoting the memoirs of the present Shah, on the motives of his father, Riẓā Shāh:

My father admired Persia's great past, and he wanted to keep those of our ancient ways of living which were not incompatible with modern progress. But he was convinced that Persia's national integrity, as well as the welfare of her people, demanded rapid modernization. Although his travels abroad were so limited, my father was always filled with visions of modern factories, power plants,

dams, irrigation systems, railways, highways, cities and armies. Just
how he did it I don't know, but he always seemed to know of the
latest industrial, economic and military advances abroad.[32]

It was in accordance with this vision that the ruler of Iran
devoted all his efforts from 1930 onward to the industrializing
of his country.[33]

If, in Turkey and Iran, the drive for industrialization was
expressed, especially at the start, in the creation of industrial
enterprises that belonged to the state, and if in Turkey this was
even canonized under the name of 'state socialism', or 'statism',
as one of the six principles of the Kemalist movement, it was not
at all with the aim of avoiding the path taken by the capitalist
West, or in conformity with some imaginary tradition. It was due
to necessity, as Ziya Gökalp explains in the passage quoted
above. Let me quote a Turkish lawyer, the Dean of the Law
Faculty of Istanbul:

> Given the inadequacy of initiatives and possibilities on the part of
> private enterprise, and the weak development of economic education
> and of the spirit of social co-operation, it fell quite naturally to the
> lot of the state, as bearer of the national ideal, to take upon itself the
> accomplishment of this huge task . . . This is the meaning of statism
> in Turkey. It is thus out of national necessity and not through any
> doctrinal fantasy that the Republic has adopted statism as a principle
> of action.[34]

'Statism, as defined by the most authoritative personages,
begins where private enterprise stops,' we read in a book
written in collaboration by a Turkish economist and a Belgian
professor, who add that Turkish statism 'is neither anti-
capitalist on principle, nor anti-foreign'.[35] The programme of the
People's Republican Party, which ruled Turkey on its own until
1950, stipulated straightforwardly:

> Although considering private work and activity a basic idea, it is one
> of our main principles to interest the state actively in matters where
> the general and vital interests of the nation are in question, especially
> in the economic field, in order to lead the nation and the country to
> prosperity in as short a time as possible. The interest of the State in
> economic matters is to be an actual builder, as well as to encourage

private enterprises, and also to regulate and control the work that is being done.[36]

The Shah of Iran is equally clear:

Because of the shortage of technicians and managers and because private investors were timid about entering the industrial field, the Government had to do much of the pioneering. This was true in my father's time, and in some fields it is still the case today. For example, only the Government can launch Iran's new steel industry . . .

. . . It is our policy gradually to hand over the Government's existing factories to private concerns. Accordingly, we have employed an American management consulting firm to study the factories, suggest all necessary improvements in efficiency, and advise on preparing them for sale to private interests.[37]

In short, in these countries the ideal so far as the rulers are concerned is the private capitalist enterprise. However, they have found themselves up against the low propensity of native private capital to invest in modern industry, because no model is available to it for such activity; because the attitudes of modern capitalism have not developed spontaneously, as we have seen; and because it was in fact a question of importing, by a conscious decision from above, structures that were foreign to these countries, alien to them in origin. Furthermore, in this case as always, those basic investments that were most useful for the economic transformation of the country were the least profitable ones. The state has thus played, on the one hand, a 'pedagogic' role (as already in the Egypt of Mehemet Ali) in order to teach by example the native owners of capital how best to invest their capital, and, on the other, a role of assistant to private capitalism, helping the latter to invest profitably by making itself responsible for unprofitable investments, and in particular for the laying down of the infrastructure essential to a modern economy.

In the light of the summary just given of how industry has evolved in the principal Muslim countries that have remained more or less independent, and despite the fragmentary nature of the facts adduced, it is clear that industrial capitalism appeared in the Muslim East as an imitation of the West. The place

where industry had been developed farthest before the last
forty years was the Egypt of Mehemet Ali, through the establishment of state-owned industry. And if this path was chosen by
Mehemet Ali, it was precisely because it seemed to him vain
(and to a certain extent he was right in this) to count upon a
spontaneous development of native industrial capitalism. The
Pasha of Egypt was intensely aware of this fact. He expressed it
plainly in 1833 to Baron de Boislecomte:

> I have taken over everything, but I have done this so as to make
> everything fruitful. Who but I could do this? Who would have
> provided the advances that were needed? Who could have shown the
> methods to be adopted, the new crops? Do you suppose anyone
> would ever have thought of introducing cotton, silk, the mulberry-
> tree into this country?[38]

The role of Mehemet Ali was not at all, as the Soviet historian
F. M. Atsamba[39] feels obliged to say, to accelerate processes that
were already under way in Egypt, but, on the contrary, to break
with existing conditions in order to start up a new process,
inspired by the European model. Everywhere the example of
European strength showed native governments how desirable
industrialization was from the national standpoint. None of them,
however, before the years following 1920, either wished or
was able to imitate Mehemet Ali. What was needed was intelligence, clearsightedness, vigour, and the help of circumstances.
When a clear awareness of the advantages of industrialization
was forced upon all concerned, it was usually too late. The
military and economic strength of the Western imperialisms
made it extremely difficult, if not impossible, to follow the
example of Egypt.

Besides, the Egyptian experiment had been able to develop
during a quarter of a century only thanks to the rivalry between
Britain and France. The European unity that was recovered,
more or less under constraint, in 1840 put a check to it. Europe's
supremacy dictated penetration by European capital, and it was
the latter that began to industrialize the Muslim East. Native
industrial capitalism began to develop only in accordance with
the European model, imitating it, and generally speaking, under
its domination. The preponderance of Europe made this development very difficult, especially owing to the lead that European

technique had acquired, the lack of protection, free trade imposed by force, and the subjection of those states that had remained independent, through the mechanism of the public debt and owing to their economic and military weakness. There was no reason why a native industrial capitalism should not have developed (as it did develop in Japan) if this European supremacy had not existed. It is clear, however, that, since Europe's lead was a well-established fact by 1800 and even earlier, such a development could take place only under the inspiration of the European model. In Mehemet Ali's time we see no sign of any private attempt, or even any private project, to create an industrial enterprise of any kind. And the industrial enterprises established by the state were frankly imitated from Europe.

As regards one sector of the economy, however, there has been talk of the development of an essentially native large-scale capitalism in the modern period. The reference is to agrarian capitalism in Egypt. A. Abdel-Malek sees as being formed in Egypt between the last years of Mehemet Ali (who died in 1849) and the revolution of 1952 a 'capitalism of a colonial type, backward, predominantly agrarian, heavily tinged with practices inherited from the feudal past'.[40] Indeed, after 1880 and the British occupation, with the intensification of cotton-growing, which tended to become a monoculture, there did develop the exploitation of landed estates by means of wage-workers. According to the census of 1907, 36·6 per cent of the occupied rural population was already made up of agricultural workers.[41] In 1958–9 the number of landless peasants amounted to 74 per cent of the rural population. These were potential wage-workers, having practically no other way of life open to them, but out of the fourteen million persons represented by this percentage, of whom ten million were able-bodied, only three million were regularly employed for wages. To them must be added the owners of dwarf holdings who could live only by hiring themselves out to the better-off landowners: these amounted to 215,000 heads of families, representing 1,075,000 peasants altogether, or 5 per cent of the rural population.[42] At the same date it was estimated that the proportion of the area of the large estates (more than twenty feddans) that was not leased out but was directly exploited by the owner (that is, in practice, by employing wage-workers) came to 56 per cent.[43]

Capitalist relations thus do play a very important role in the Egyptian countryside. But does it follow that they are predominant on the scale of society as a whole? A. Abdel-Malek mentions the development of bank capital (mainly foreign), which dominates agriculture through its credits. All this is bound up with the commercialization, to a very large extent, of the produce of agriculture, which consists above all of the cotton that is put on the world market. It remains true, nevertheless, as Hassan Riad has pointed out, that the factor of production which is scarcest and therefore most important in Egypt is not capital but land. It is not enough to possess a lot of capital to be able to take one's place among the landed aristocracy, even if the latter does operate primarily by using capitalist relations. This means that capital does *not* dominate the countryside, where, moreover, non-capitalist relations continue to be important.[44] And agrarian capitalism, whether on its own or in connection with a substantial development of commercial or bank capital, is incapable of transforming society in the direction of a capitalist socio-economic formation. Capitalist forms of exploitation of the land existed in Antiquity[45] and also, as we have seen, in the Muslim world of the Middle Ages.[46] The commercialization of agricultural production and its linking-up with a world market dominated by commercial or bank capital do not necessarily lead in that direction. A situation of that kind existed under the Roman Empire;[47] and it is also known how the linking-up of the agriculture of Eastern Europe with a Western Europe that was well on the way to capitalist development had as its first consequence, in the regions east of the Elbe, the appearance of the 'second serfdom'.

What is clear is that an agrarian capitalistic sector developed in Egypt after 1880. What matters here is that this development took place as a result of the impact of Europe. Hassan Riad sees it as mainly the effect of population pressure. Here, however, as elsewhere, the pressure of population is itself, in one way or another, a result of entry into relations with the European capitalist world. That there is a connection with the mass commercialization of agricultural produce is undoubted. That commercialization would develop was necessary in any case, Hassan Riad considers. But the production of foodstuffs need not have been wholly commercialized. Cotton is inevitably a commercial crop, and the development of cotton monoculture obviously took place in connection with the world market. It is known that it was intensified especially on account of the American Civil War, which deprived Europe of its usual source of cotton.[48]

Some Soviet writers, inspired by a highly praiseworthy desire not to acknowledge any inferiority on the part of the non-European peoples, have endeavoured to establish that the East was in any case about to arrive at the capitalist socio-economic formation at the moment when the impact of Europe was felt. The late V. B. Lutsky declared in June 1960 that 'the level of socio-economic development reached by the Eastern countries before they were transformed into colonies or semi-colonies is a subject of controversy, for Marxist historians occupy on this matter an advanced front line of struggle with Western orientalists'.[49]

A pugnacious declaration like this, taken up with enthusiasm, of course, by many intellectuals in the non-European countries, is a clear manifestation of that ideological totalitarianism,[50] a constant temptation for every ideology, and especially virulent in our time. I shall refrain from criticizing it on the moral plane, since I was myself markedly affected by this virus for many years, and contributed with zeal to the propagating of it. It is idle to suppose that a tendency that is so strong, so deeply rooted in the nature of man at grips with social demands, can ever be overcome. It is even perhaps not desirable that it should be, if the mobilization of masses of men for noble tasks necessitates this tendency. However, reason and clarity of thought also have their rights. And the abandonment of clear thinking, to a certain degree, at certain moments and under certain conditions, is also a practical error that may prove costly.

Having no other aim here but to search for truth, I shall restrict myself to observing to the ideological extremists, as I have already done elsewhere,[51] that the human value of the non-European peoples is not at issue. No scientific proof has been found up to now for the theses of racialism, and it will be seen that a large part of what I have written is expressly opposed to them – not because they are harmful but because, in the present state of our knowledge, they are erroneous. If the extra-European peoples have not developed a capitalist socio-economic formation, and if the European peoples have achieved such a structure, which is *in a sense* superior, this is not due to the 'shortcomings' of the former or the 'qualities' of the latter. The non-Europeans do not deserve to be punished, nor the Europeans to be rewarded. The former do not need to feel inferior nor the latter to feel proud. Profound social and historical factors, for or against which men could do little, were working in that direction. This does not mean that the role played by human decisions was not very important. But these decisions related to particular projects the significance of which in this general evolution could not be appreciated by anyone, with few exceptions, at least before a certain stage had been reached. And when that time came, the world was so far advanced in the mesh of factors and events that no human will was capable of effectively reversing the course of things – not on account of the sovereign will of some deified History, but because of the objective strength of the social mechanisms that had been set going.

The arguments brought forward by the Soviet writers – in clear contradiction, let it be said (not without irony, but also without drawing any conclusions for or against), to the theses of Marx and Engels – are anything but convincing. Lutsky and others point to the development of manufactories, in Egypt, for example. But manufacture (state-owned as well as privately owned) is a phenomenon that has appeared since Antiquity in a variety of societies which had a fairly well-developed capitalistic sector that nevertheless did not develop into a capitalist socio-economic formation. 'Sporadically', Marx observed,

manufacture may develop locally in a framework belonging to quite a different period, as in the Italian cities *side by side with* the guilds. But if capital is to be the generally dominant form, its conditions must be developed not merely locally but on a large scale. This is compatible with the possibility that during the dissolution of the guilds individual guild-masters may turn into industrial capitalists; however, in the nature of the phenomenon, this happens rarely. All in all, the entire guild system – both master and journeyman – dies out, where the capitalist and the [wage] labourer emerge.[52]

It is the same with the other features that are put forward as signs of preparation for capitalism: urban development, evolution of ground-rent, development of private ownership of land . . . These phenomena are (at most) conditions necessary for a possible transition to the capitalist formation. They can be elements in a social structure with an economic system that includes an important capitalistic sector. It was on the basis of a social structure like this that in Europe, given a certain number of structural and circumstantial conditions, the capitalist socio-economic formation was able to develop. But nothing at all proves that this structure must inevitably give birth to the capitalist formation. We can therefore perceive the ambiguity of the vivid formulation employed by V. B. Lutsky: 'In one way or another the majority of the feudal states of the East were pregnant with capitalism.'[53] To stay with the same meta-phor, it would be better to say of these societies that they were nubile. And nobody can deduce from the fact that a woman is nubile that she is necessarily pregnant. Some women are barren, and there are others who either refuse or are refused the act that can make them pregnant.

It is the same with societies. The implicit notion behind Lutsky's approach and that of many others is an ideological conception with regard to which Marx's thinking was hesitant and contradictory, but which became strongly implanted in ideological Marxism owing to its development amid the evolu-tionist ideology of the nineteenth century. It postulates that all social forms follow the same evolution, with merely a difference of speed. This is a postulate that the facts rebel against, even if the ideological requirements of present-day progressive move-ments force them to maintain it. There have been developments that have come to a dead end. This is not a question of some sort of backwardness such as can be made a matter of reproach to certain peoples, which is the view that Lutsky attributes to his opponents. The interpretation that makes of the non-development of modern capitalism a matter for reproach, a blemish, is indeed to be combated, as I have said earlier. But this should not lead us to see everywhere in the world a capitalism on the point of bursting into flower.

To come back to my central argument, it is not possible to prove, in the present state of knowledge, that, if the colonial conquests had never occurred, the Muslim socieities would have engendered a capitalist formation of the European–American type. Nor can it be proved that they were incapable of engendering such a formation. On the contrary, everything seems to point to their possessing the essential structures which, if certain developments had taken place, could, given certain circumstances, have led to something of the kind. The fact is, simply, that these developments, these circumstances, were not there at the time of the European impact. Consequently, the development of capitalism occurred in these countries as something external in origin, an implantation from or an imitation of Europe. European capitalism represented, in a visible, tangible way, a superior formation to which one had to submit or to adapt oneself, which had to be imitated or before which one had to bow. But adaptation was difficult for reasons of internal structure, and because the conditions in which it had to be effected, in the threatening shadow of the overwhelming superiority of Europe, were unfavourable to independent decision-taking by the peoples concerned. Many native rulers and élites endeavoured for a long time to avoid this disagreeable choice, with disastrous consequences. Ideologists strove vainly to escape from it by constructing unrealistic models of a third path, a mythical Koranic economy, which could find belief only in mystical minds with a fantastic picture of social reality, or among some European economists who were also in search of a salutary myth. The attempt to keep control of the process that was made by Mehemet Ali with his 'pedagogical'[54] statism, destined to prepare the way for capitalism, the attempt that was later made by Mustafa Kemal Atatürk, led to very unimpressive results. A third path was not really opened until the socialist model, first presented by the experience of the U.S.S.R., became available. This could apparently enable the results offered by capitalism to be attained, along with a higher stage of society – even higher, perhaps, than capitalism

– while putting an end to certain structural difficulties and at the same time not incurring the risk of losing the power of independent decision. It was not free from difficulties and dangers, either; but that is another question.

Influence of the Muslim religion?

I have shown at some length in previous pages that the Muslim religion never raised any objection to the capitalist mode of production, and that its precepts constituted no obstacle to the development of this mode of production in the direction of establishing a capitalist socio-economic formation.

What is valid for the Middle Ages is fully valid for the modern and present periods too. We have seen that 'capitalism of production' was known in the Middle Ages, in the form of workshops and manufactories. It has developed in our own day in the form of the factory. The fundamental production-relations between capitalists and wage-workers are the same in all these cases: what changes is the scale, the lay-out and, above all, the techniques used. There is no reason why these relations, traditionally accepted, should suddenly have seemed unacceptable, since no scriptural text condemned them.

What may have been condemned by religious opinion here and there in Muslim countries was the making of certain goods, or certain forms of exploitation which conflicted not so much with the scriptures as with canonized tradition, to which centuries of stagnation had given religious validity. Thus, the making of alcoholic drinks (with good religious references going back to the Middle Ages), or the employment of women as productive workers. Conservatively minded people used against the introduction of certain techniques the theoretical condemnation of *bidʿah*, or 'innovation'. Since the Middle Ages, however, the habit of condemning absolutely every practice that did not go back to the time of the Prophet had been given up. A distinction had been drawn between *bidʿah* that was good, or praiseworthy, and *bidʿah* that was blameworthy, or bad.[55] All important innovations in ways of life were in their day condemned as *bidʿah* – the use of coffee and of tobacco, for example.

But this never stopped them from spreading and, in general, after a short time ministers of religion were found who gave formal endorsement to what their predecessors had condemned. Opponents and supporters of the new ways were never short of texts or arguments to back up their mutually contradictory decisions.

The Wahhābī 'sect', which arose in Central Arabia and which provides the official ideology of Saudi Arabia (having conquered most of Arabia since 1924), is distinguished by the severity with which it condemns *bidᶜah*. Its ministers of religion endeavoured at first to prohibit certain modern techniques. However, the political rulers, and first and foremost King ᶜAbd al-ᶜAzīz Ibn Saᶜūd, himself a sincere Wahhābite, soon overcame this opposition to, for example, the telegraph, the telephone and broadcasting.[56] It is enough to recall that Saudi Arabia derives much of its national income (and a quarter of the state revenue) from the oil industry,[57] as also do several Muslim states of the Persian Gulf coast; this implies the presence on the soil of these states of installations of the most up-to-date kind, on a considerable scale, working for an American capitalist firm, with the employment of numerous manual workers and office-workers drawn from the native population as wage-earners in the service of this firm.

The way in which the Muslim religion seems most often to have influenced in a negative manner the evolution of the economy in a capitalist direction is through the ban on lending at interest and on aleatory contracts, about which I have written at some length above. I will quote at random, from among a hundred possible sources, the words of Lothrop Stoddard, written in 1921:

> We can then realize the utter lack of capital for investment purposes in the East of a hundred years ago, especially when we remember that political insecurity and religious prohibitions of the lending of money at interest stood in the way of such far-sighted individuals as might have been inclined to employ their hoarded wealth for productive purposes.

Very significantly, though with artless illogicality, he at once adds:

There was, indeed, one outlet for financial activity – usury, and therein virtually all the scant fluid capital of the old Orient was employed.[58]

The factor constituted by the religious ban on lending at interest and on aleatory contracts certainly played a part, but this was much less considerable than has often been alleged. Why was it that the religious law was got around, constantly and on an enormous scale, in favour of loans for consumption rather than in favour of loans for investment, for example? The repugnance of capital in the Muslim countries, in the nineteenth century and at the beginning of the twentieth, to seek investment in industry, and to use for investment the technique of the joint-stock company, is an established fact – but the commandments of the *shariʿa* had little to do with this fact. They served mainly to sanctify, to canonize, certain attitudes which were imposed by the entire social structure of the age.

Clear proof of this is given by the fact that certain societies that were not Muslim in the least, but which had a social structure similar to that of the Muslim countries, presented the same phenomenon. Let us take the example of China and Japan, where the Koran's prohibition was certainly without effect.

A Chinese economist wrote in 1935:

Private fortunes acquired by the Chinese merchants, militarists and government officials are not directed into industry, but are largely in the forms of real estate and bank deposits. These people lack ability and knowledge for entering the field of industrial administration.[59]

Again, on the eve of the victory of the socialist revolution in China, another economist wrote:

What is most lacking in China is industrial capital . . . It is a pity that the capital accumulated by the modern banks has not been made available to industries, except in the form of short-term loans. Investment banking has not yet developed, and that is one line of activity which is absolutely necessary to the industrialization of the country.[60]

As for joint-stock companies, these were established only with difficulty. 'Even today,' wrote S. R. Wagel in 1915, the Chinese have not grasped the principle of joint-stock business . . . Thus practically all business, including banking, is owned and is under the control of particular individuals.[61]

Similarly in Japan, despite the vigorous effort at modernization undertaken since the Meiji era, that is, since 1868, it was still possible to say of the period 1914–27:

> The number of persons prepared to invest directly in industrial securities remained very small. The vast majority still preferred to entrust their savings to banks, savings banks, or the post office, and much of the capital for industry was provided by these institutions or by the official Industrial and Hypothec Banks which raised money on debenture increases for this purpose.[62]

At the start of industrialization, even the great families, the 'financial magnates', who possessed very large sums of money,

> showed hesitation in risking their capital in enterprises which demanded at the very outset such an immense outlay of capital, and before there was any clear indication of the profitability of such undertakings . . . Thus, early Japanese capitalism may be described as a hothouse variety, growing under the shelter of state protection and subsidy. Big private capital preferred to remain in trade, banking and credit operations, particularly in the safe and lucrative field of government loans, while small capital had no inducement to leave the countryside where trade, usury and, above all, high rent . . . prevented capital invested in agriculture from flowing into industrial channels.[63]

As for joint-stock companies, in the period between the two world wars, while they dominated large-scale industry and large-scale commerce, they 'had yet to take over major sectors of the Japanese economy'.[64]

All these descriptions could be applied, with only a few words altered, to the Islamic countries. It will be seen that the reasons for this situation common to a whole group of societies has nothing to do with a dogmatic prohibition which was got around for centuries with such facility, which affected no less the Christian Europe of the Middle Ages, and which did not prevent the latter from developing towards capitalism. Clearly, this situation has nothing to do with 'the essence of Islam', but is due in the main to economic causes.

Unwillingness to invest in industry is normal so long as the profit to be expected from an industrial investment is less than that which can be hoped for from making some other use of one's savings. Less, it must be understood, not only in gross amount, in 'profit' in the strict sense, but in advantages of every kind, both on the economic plane (for example, 'liquidity', as emphasized by Keynes) and on the social plane, especially as regards prestige. In a certain type of society the 'liquidity' of land may be no less than that of money.[65] With reference to Japan, W. W. Lockwood shows the greater advantages of investment in land, or of hoarding, in a formulation which is, I think, unassailable, even if one does not wholly agree with its ties with Keynesian doctrine:

In a densely settled agrarian economy of the pre-industrial variety, land rent is sustained at a high level by the pressure of population and the weak bargaining position of the small tenant. It is not easily reduced by increasing the supply of land. As compared with other producer goods, land affords still other advantages to its owner: high political and social prestige attaching to the landed class; a relatively safe and stable return; ease of disposal (liquidity) if necessity arises; and related opportunities for gain through combining the functions of landlord, tax-collector, moneylender, etc. The same values are found in varying degrees in hoards of precious metals and treasures of art. The resulting preference for landholding (or money hoards) sets a high standard of yield which funds must return if they are to be invested in producing new capital assets for industrial and commercial enterprise. But opportunities of sufficient attractiveness in such a society are apt to be severely restricted by the limitation of the market, by a stagnant technology, and by the lack of security and status in non-agricultural pursuits. By the time all the costs and risks of new business ventures are reckoned under such conditions, the anticipated net return is apt to be too meagre to bring forth any large amount of investment funds. New investment is therefore discouraged except where high profits can be anticipated over a short period, as in the quick turnover of certain types of trading ventures.[66]

It was the same, moreover, in Europe, at the dawn of capitalism, in the period of the primitive accumulation of capital. 'The conditions for profitable investment in industry', writes Maurice Dobb, were not fully matured in earlier centuries [of the capitalist epoch]. Other investments were preferable to the difficulties and the hazards and the smaller liquidity of capital devoted to industrial enterprise. The crucial conditions necessary to make investment in industry attractive on any considerable scale could not be present until the concentration-process had progressed sufficiently to bring about an actual dispossession of previous owners and the creation of a substantial class of the dispossessed.[67]

Before the end of the eighteenth century,

the state of industry was not such as to provide an attractive field for capital investment on any extensive scale. Usury and trade, especially if it was privileged trade, as was generally the case in those days, held the attraction of higher profits even when account was taken of the possibly greater hazards involved.[68]

The conditions in Western Europe at the time of the beginnings of capitalism were, of course, different in a number of ways from those in the Muslim East of today. But certain common factors, and certain convergent specific factors, make investment in industry as little attractive in that region as it was in the Europe of three centuries ago. Hence the important role played by the state both in Europe in the age of mercantilism and in Turkey, Iran, Egypt and Japan at the start of their industrialization.[69]

Furthermore, when the tendency to modernization began in the Muslim states – in other words, their penetration by European values – it does not appear that the canonical ban on usury and aleatory contracts was often mentioned to justify resistance to this tendency, or even as an obstacle that would have to be got round somehow. In practice it seemed to worry active and responsible Muslims very little. As one of the best authorities on modern Muslim law puts it,

although . . . the Sharīʿa was in theory all-inclusive, it was never in fact applied in its purity and entirely throughout every sphere of life . . . [This was true] of the field of commercial law; for here the doctrinaire prohibition of 'usury' and of speculative contracts made demands that the merchants found intolerably severe in the life of the markets. As a result, various rival jurisdictions began to appear at a very early date – such as the Court of Complaints, the police, and the inspector of markets, or such as informal courts of mercantile arbitration.[70]

In that state which in the nineteenth century was still the centre and bastion of Islam, which grouped under its authority the great majority of those Muslims who were not colonial subjects, and which was also the first Muslim state to take decisive steps towards Europeanization, namely, the Ottoman Empire, legal measures were adopted very early on that implied absolute disavowal of these religious regulations. Thus, in 1268 AH (1851–2) an Imperial *fermān* aimed at regulating the rate of interest made no allusion, either in the preamble or in the actual clauses, to the religious ban on interest:

> In order to protect the interests of all the population in general and those of the landowners and agriculturists in particular, who are obliged to borrow money from provincial capitalists, either at exorbitant rates or on the ruinous condition of accepting repayment at compound interest, it had been decided [previously] that all these debts would be examined, so as to secure a reduction of interest to a uniform level of 8 per cent. Fermans issued to this effect prescribed that this system be applied throughout the Empire.[71]

In face of the practical difficulties, modifications were introduced. It was specified in the *fermān* of 1268 that the measure was to apply to 'licensed traders, whether Ottoman or otherwise', no less than to foreigners. It was even said that the interest on 'advances made from the funds belonging to orphans and to the *evkaf*', that is, to pious foundations or estates in mortmain (Arabic *waqf*, plural *awqāf*; in the Maghreb, *ḥābūs*), was to be 'fixed, as in the past,' at 15 per cent.[72] In 1863 the Code of Maritime Trade adopted by the Empire dealt in the same way with the bottomry bond, in conformity with the Dutch and French codes, speaking of 'interest agreed at a rate even higher than that fixed by law' as constituting 'maritime profit' (art. 151), and of repayments of capital 'with the legal interest' (art. 158, cf. 155 and 159).[73] The same code dealt with insurance, in its section XI, adapting the various European codes[74] without troubling about the general ban on insurance, which was allowed only in very exceptional cases by certain religious jurists of the Ḥanafite school.[75] The second great charter of the Europeanizing reformism of the Ottoman Empire, the *khatt-i humāyūn* of 18 February 1856, assigned to the state, in its article 24, the task of 'creating banks and other similar institutions',[76] and, eleven years later, a circular from the Ministry of Foreign Affairs to the Ottoman ambassadors in the European capitals, intended to inform opinion abroad about the application of this programme, declared: 'The Imperial Government has encouraged to the utmost of its power the establishment of the great credit institutions needed for developing the country's trade and industry . . . It is not the Imperial Government's fault if the numbers of such institutions are not greater, and the benefits from them more extensive.'[77] Among the banks established was the Agricultural Bank, set up in 1888, the constitution of which explained that it was founded: '(1) to lend . . . money to cultivators; (2) to receive interest-bearing funds', (art. 2), that it 'pays 4 per cent interest on all the money deposited with it', (art. 8), and that it 'charges 6 per cent interest on all sums that it lends', (art. 29).[78]

Since long before this, however, the Ottoman state, in its financial distress, had been having recourse to interest-bearing loans. In 1840, for the first time, it issued a sort of Treasury Bonds which served as paper-money and bore interest at 8 per cent.[79] These were the famous *Qāʾime*, which constituted a floating debt that the Empire strove desperately to shake off by means of foreign borrowing and consolidation. The consolidated debt was made up of government bonds issued from 1857 onward, and which were no less productive of interest. It must be mentioned that when financial insolvency obliged the Ottoman Empire to meet only 50 per cent of its obligations under the public debt, and then, after 1876, to default on them altogether, Sultan ʿAbdul-ʿAzīz, Commander of the Faithful, excepted himself from the law that applied to everyone else, and continued to draw all the interest due on the eight million bonds that he held. Such, at any rate, was the allegation made in the manifesto issued by the Muslim reformers led by Midḥat Pāshā, who were to depose him a few months later.[80]

So far we have been considering interest in its open and undisguised form. If, however, we were to examine all the roundabout ways whereby a rent (and usually a very high one) could be obtained for money, a very much more impressive picture would obviously emerge. Thus, a good French observer of the Ottoman Empire, describing in 1861 the operations whereby the *waqfs*, or pious foundations in mortmain, were leased out, shows that in practice these often amounted to the collection of a rent at very high interest in favour of the administrations of the mosques and other religious institutions. The latter 'bought' (in a way that was barely within the law) a piece of land from its owner in return for a small sum amounting to about one-tenth of its value. The ex-owner was then allowed to remain as tenant for an unlimited period (with right of alienation and of transmission to his immediate heirs), which safeguarded him against any spoliation, and in return the purchaser drew a rent that was often extremely high – representing interest on the money that had been invested in purchasing the land. M. B. C. Collas then quotes the verses of the Koran dealing with usury, and waxes indignant: 'The ministers of religion, forgetting these precepts, have transformed God into Shylock.'[81]

In short, it seems clear that, so far as legal documents were concerned, the Koran's ban on interest had, in the Ottoman Empire of the nineteenth century and the early twentieth, mainly a negative influence: it explains why, in the *Mejelle*, the Ottoman 'Civil Code', the attempt at standardizing Muslim law which was promulgated between 1869 and 1876, there was no mention of loans at interest. This shamefaced silence alone speaks volumes. But the *Mejelle* constituted only part of Ottoman law.[82] Thirty-six years had to pass before a new law introduced into the texts dealing with the legal rate of interest a regulation in which the Koran's legislation found some slight reflection. The law of 9 Rajab 1304 (3 April 1887) fixed the conventional rate of interest at 9 per cent, but also stipulated that the total amount paid must not exceed the principal of the debt.[83] This was an evocation of that verse of the Koran which alone gives a certain (enigmatic) precision to the ban on usury: 'Live not by usury duobled twice over' (3:125/130). A convenient, though questionable, interpretation underlay this law. It enabled one inexpensively to claim to have taken the sacred text into consideration. But the same law did not dare to go even so far as to forbid capitalization of the interest on a loan, that is, the practice of charging compound interest, which Justinian had already forbidden, in the name of Christian morality, less than a century before Muḥammad, and which we may well presume the latter would have condemned. The Ottoman law allows it in three specific cases (in commercial dealings, by virtue of an agreement between the parties valid for not more than three years, etc.), which are quite adequate to provide the necessary loop-holes for whoever might wish to use them.

Thus, what was involved was not, as is often claimed, transition from an economic practice of credit that was interest-free (apart from exceptional cases) to one in which money lent produced a rent, but replacement of a practice of credit paid for in accordance with complicated procedures by a practice in which the rent for money, which was usually less than before, was open, public, declared and regulated, and in which institutions employing modern techniques (banks) had as their recognized function the granting of credit in return for payment, with the purpose of channelling through their procedures all transactions that implied such credit. Scruples came later. Prolonged, extensive and difficult research would be needed to find out just how they arose. They were certainly voiced by men of strict religious views. If, however, we look a little more closely, the suspicion arises that they were also inspired by usurers of the old-fashioned sort, anxious about possible encroachment by the banks upon their domain.[84]

The example of Morocco is instructive. In 1908 the notables and religious authorities of Fez proclaimed the deposition of Sultan ʿAbd al-ʿAzīz. The grievances against this ruler were numerous and largely justified. Essentially, it was his frivolity and love of pleasure that had enabled European financiers to get control of his Empire, preparing the way for the political conquest that was to be carried out by France.[85] He had been obliged, at Algeciras in 1906, to agree to set up a state bank that was virtually under foreign management. In a much more useful innovation he had, at the very beginning of his reign, in 1901, sought to replace the traditional taxes (partly based on the Koran), which weighed unequally upon the taxpayers, and were uncertain in their return,[86] by the *tartīb*, a uniform and universal tax to be collected in a rational manner. All these facts taken together – acts of submission to European finance along with salutary efforts at innovation – stirred up violent opposition among the Moroccans, some being moved by national feeling and others by concern for their material interests: many by a combination of these impulses that is hard to break down into its components. This is well reflected in the complaint of the ʿ*ulamā* of Fez, testifying that

the present emir Mūlāy ʿAbd al-ʿAzīz has been guilty of acts contrary to the *shra*ᶜ [the religious law] and to reason . . ., that he has replaced the *zakāt* . . . by the *tartīb* and the Bank that produces interest on money, which is the worst sin it is possible to commit.[87]

What a splendid mixture of patriotic indignation, religious fervour and bourgeois hypocrisy! Doubtless there was not a single signatory of this document who had not been involved in some usurious transaction, either as an active participant or by providing it with cover drawn from the authority of the *shra*ᶜ! If the reader will refer to what I have written earlier, and to the details given by E. Michaux-Bellaire on the practice of usury in Morocco and the way it was covered up by the religious authorities, he will be duly edified.

The development of a modern banking system, imposed by Europe or by modernistic native rulers in imitation of Europe,[88] was nevertheless to subject even devout Muslims to ever greater temptation. While many cared nothing for the Koran and the *fiqh*, and others were satisfied with crude *ḥilas*, and appeals to what was required for the nation's welfare as justification for using them, some sought excuses that were better-founded from the religious standpoint. A thorough study of the collections of *fatwās* (consultations on religious law) and of the records, where these exist and have been preserved, would be needed to constitute a chronology of the consultations and opinions given, and perhaps to discern the motives and the groups concerned. I will restrict myself to a few easily accessible references.

The Turkish *fatwās* which were usually required to sanction the acts of the Ottoman government mentioned above seem never to have attracted much interest. Several writers mention them, on trust, so to speak,[89] though nobody seems ever to have actually seen them. 'However,' said one of these writers, ʿAbd al-ʿAzīz Shāwish, giving an address in Cairo in 1907, 'one cannot suppose that the orthodox Muslim Ottoman government could for one moment contemplate deliberately violating the provisions of the Holy Book'[90] – an assumption about which one may feel free to be sceptical.

Muhammad ʿAbdūh, the celebrated reforming sheikh who, despite his liberalism, held the office of Grand Mufti of Egypt from 1899 until his death in 1905, published (apparently in 1903) a legal consultation which legitimized the deposits of money in the savings banks where, of course, they earned interest. It seems that he distinguished between usurious interest, which was to be condemned, and participation in the profits of a business that was legitimate in character, and he identified with the second category the interest paid by the banks.[91] Although Father Jomier has not been able to discover the precise reference and text of this *fatwā*,[92] there is no reason to doubt its existence. An echo of it is heard in an obituary of the sheikh which mentions 'the discussions and disputes that arose between the deceased and his enemies' on this subject,[93] in a thesis published three years after his death.[94] The Khedivial decree of 14 February 1904 which authorized the postal administration to set up savings banks was supposed to have got round the Koranic ban, with the aid of Muhammad ʿAbdūh's consultation, by describing the interest that the savings banks were to pay as 'dividend', with a ceiling of 2·5 per cent. Given this purely verbal transmutation, the decree ruled that the depositor could set his conscience at rest by signing an authority that empowered the administration to 'employ the funds paid in . . . in accordance with all procedures allowed by the religious law, avoiding any form of usury'. This was wonderfully contradictory, since the very operation that the decree was concerned to organize involved what the religious law unquestionably called 'usury'.[95] However, what men's consciences usually require is verbal reassurance rather than real conformity to the Law they are supposed to have chosen to accept.

In 1908 the Muslim (Urdu-language) daily paper *Paisa Akhbār*, published in Lahore, put to an assembly of eighteen *ʿulamāʾ*, presided over by Ahmad ʿAli Muhaddis, the following questions: May a Muslim deposit money in a bank for a certain time, without drawing interest on it? May he legally send money from one place to another by cheque, accepting a commission for this? The reply given was affirmative on both points. It is true that the money deposited in the bank may serve the purposes of usury, that is, it may attract interest. But the believer's aim has been the security of his property and not the obtaining of interest, so that he has committed no sin. Similarly, the commission received is a remuneration, a wage, and not interest, and so it may legitimately be taken.[96]

What needs to be emphasized here is that the *fatwās* in question played an extremely secondary role in the economic process. If we think about the matter we can perceive the theoretical importance of this fact. According to an idealistic conception of history – or, so as not to use so equivocal a term, a conception that assumes a dynamic contrary to that proposed by Marxism – we should expect that the Muslims, faithful in the main, with inevitable exceptions, to the prohibition laid down in their sacred writings, would feel free from it only after their religious leaders had so decided. Undoubtedly, however, it was in the contrary order that events occurred. The *fatwās* in favour of lending at interest may sometimes (it is not certain) have accompanied the laws concerning the latter, but they never preceded or determined them. At best they represented a formality that was obtained without difficulty from accommodating theologians, in order to put in the clear with religious opinion rulers who had already decided to adopt a certain measure for reasons that were strictly economic and political. These documents passed unnoticed to such a degree that it is now very difficult to find any trace of them. When a man who looked on these problems with greater seriousness and sincerity, Muḥammad ʿAbdūh, resolved to issue a *fatwā* in the same sense, he may have assuaged some troubled consciences, he may even have decided some who were hesitating to yield to the current, and he certainly aroused protests from hard-liners. But all that was of little significance in relation to the overall economic life of the nation. The best proof of this is that he himself and his faithful disciple Rashīd Riḍāʾ entertained no illusions about the real importance of the religious consultation. They knew well that practice had run ahead of it. The disciple wrote thus, reporting his master's thoughts:

> Many people of modern education . . . think that the Muslims have become poor and have seen their wealth pass into the hands of foreigners owing to the ban on lending at interest. When they needed money, it is thought, Muslims borrowed it from foreigners, paying them interest . . . This is an error which thorough study of these matters could have enabled us to avoid. The Muslims no longer take account of religion in most of their actions. If it were otherwise they would have been plunged into debt through usury, the only result of which is their ruin.[97]

He lists some of the usurious procedures, roughly disguised, that were in use in Egypt.[98] While indulging in some illusions about the Middle Ages, he sets forth in a disenchanted way a general rule that can be accepted as valid, apart from the chronological restriction he proposes:

> The principle of usury has been forbidden by all religions, but nevertheless the peoples practise it, though to an unequal extent . . . The Muslims abstained from it for a long time, but eventually they imitated the rest. For half a century now, lending at interest has been allowed in all the Muslim countries. In reality it was practised earlier, under the cover of a *ḥila* that was called 'legal' [*shar ʿiyya*] and several legal authorities recognized it, for instance, for the investment of capital belonging to an orphan under age, or to a full-time student.[99]

Although in some regions, such as the Indian subcontinent, the traditional specialization of certain groups in the trade in money kept Muslims out of it, the development of modern transactions in our own day has broken through this barrier, before any *fatwā*, for or against, could be pronounced. In the Punjab in the first quarter of this century,

> Even the Muhammadan agriculturist is beginning to square the precepts of religion with the claims of business, and there are well over a thousand who have bowed the knee to Mammon. They are drawn from all tribes and include even Seyyeds [i.e. descendants of the Prophet], and charge anything from 12 to 50 per cent. At such rates, the temptation to lend is great.[100]

This relates to traditional forms of lending. But the development of modern banking has also drawn the Muslims in. A Muslim who is a fervent advocate of a return to the supposed norms of primitive Islam states that this is so, and we may believe him. He lists the banks in India that were already large-scale

affairs before the Second World War and were directed by
Muslims with Muslim capital: the Habib Bank of Bombay,
'which is now prospering in Pakistan', the Hyderabad Bank,
and several others in Madras and elsewhere. He adds, with some
bitterness: 'Of course, these were on Western models, indulging
in interest.'[101] A little later he generalizes, and here again we
have before us a competent appreciation by an expert who would
prefer to find more examples of the contrary tendency: 'It is
certainly a deplorable fact, from an Islamic point of view, that
practically all the Muslim countries of the world are actually
according official toleration to interest.'[102]

In the Indian subcontinent, interest-free lending, says the
same Muḥammad Hamidullah, is 'not wanting, though in
more modest proportions'.[103] This relates to a relatively recent
development, a belated awareness of and reaction to the *de
facto* situation created by the sudden discordance that has been
revealed between the religious ideal and the revisionist practice,
implicit but constant, of the adherents of Islam, caused by the
pressure of underlying social forces. It must be added that this
acknowledgement of the requirements of the religious ideal has
come about only as a result of the pressure of other social forces,
among which an important place must be given to the spread of
Marxism. The great religions of today provide excellent examples of the truth of Hegel's famous phrase about Minerva's
owl taking wing only at dusk. Just as the Christian churches
have suddenly discovered in recent decades that some, at least,
of the consequences of capitalism are contrary to the Christian
ideal, similarly pious Muslims have suddenly become terrified
by the behaviour of their co-religionists. To be fair, it should be
added that in a non-religious ideological movement like the
Communist movement, implacable pressure by phenomena
from outside the field of ideology was at least as much needed
in order to compel the ideologists and leaders to perceive the
gap that had insensibly grown between the ideal foundations of
the movement and its reality.

The triumphalism that the Roman Catholic Church has
recently discovered in its past, and has set about denouncing, is
not a disease peculiar to that body. Every ideological movement
that arrives at a position when it can control a temporal authority

usually succumbs to this, so long as the authority in question is
not seriously challenged. After the initial enthusiasm has ebbed,
believers settle down into a cosy conformism which confines the
original impulse within the bounds that are appropriate to an
ideal and a consolation for idle hours. Safety-valves of a socially
harmless sort are provided for the benefit of ardent spirits. Under
these conditions the activists of the movement tend to allow their
ideology to bend gently before the suggestions that arise from
the needs of underlying social life and of human nature.
Compromise flourishes, and people congratulate themselves on
their capacity for adaptation. A challenge has to be serious
before men are ready to tear themselves away from this pleasant
torpor.

The Ottoman legal authorities were probably pale hack-
ideologists, mere 'court bishops'. Muḥammad ʿAbdūh, a man
of quite different stature, was a modernist, convinced of the
power and of the overall beneficial character of evolution in the
European direction, which he regarded as being compatible with
the basic principles of Islam. It was, he thought, merely a
matter of adapting the traditional interpretations of these principles to the foundations of the new order of things. Others
took a different attitude. They saw, on the contrary, a contradiction between the principles of Islam and modern civilization,
and this state of mind was reinforced when critiques of capitalist
society, the dominant economic form of this civilization until
recently, became widely known. In the clash between Islam
and the European world, the latter was in the wrong and must
be the one to yield. Islam had anticipated by centuries (and how
cheering this must have been for the pride in his own community that is hidden in every man's heart) these criticisms
that were now being levelled by Europe's own children at the
system under which Europe lived. Islam had put forward
its solutions, which its own followers had failed to recognize,
and these solutions were right, because they came from God –
for many, perhaps, these solutions were right above all because
they came from their own community. All that was necessary
was to revive these solutions.

Thus a whole movement was launched, to establish credit
institutions that would grant interest-free loans. An entire

theory was worked out to demonstrate the virtues of this system, as a real remedy for all the troubles of the world of today. Actually, it has above all the virtue of enabling one to enjoy a good conscience as a Muslim and a human being, contributing to the apologia for the *umma*, while giving one a heroic feeling of struggle against the ills of our time, without having to renounce the charms of a comfortable existence.

This movement, which was at first perhaps one of those rare endeavours that in every age are made by a few pious and mystical souls to win salvation through helping the poor without themselves profiting thereby, has up to now achieved only limited success. M. Hamidullah tells how it developed in India from the end of the nineteenth century onward, and later took the form (under the influence, as he acknowledges, of the European co-operative movement) of co-operative loan societies 'with affairs running yearly in some cases into six figures'. He stresses the fact that the members were not exclusively Muslim, which seems to him to prove that Muslim solutions are valid for everybody. One of these societies, in Hyderabad, Deccan, has even, since the abolition by India of the Nizam's government, been re-started by a non-Muslim.[104] However, all this has remained something of 'modest proportions', as M. Hamidullah himself says, in comparison with the institutions that operate in the usual way, with interest. And this relates only to the Indian subcontinent, where some attention has been given to the problem.

To claim, however, that the Muslim countries 'are in a transitory stage, and are struggling as best they can to get rid of [interest]', as M. Hamidullah does (seeming to ascribe the diffusion of the present-day practice of interest to ignorance of the Muslim law on the part of economists and ignorance of economics on the part of the *ʿulamāʾ*!)[105] is to offer an example of naïve utopianism and, in an extreme form, of that 'idealistic' conception of history which I am here seeking to combat. What do we find in Pakistan, the state that has shown most resolution in introducing Koranic legislation into real life? The draft constitution provided for elimination of interest, as one of the guiding principles that should preside over the evolution of the new state that proudly proclaimed itself, from the outset, a

Muslim state. While the draft was being discussed, a meeting of the Indo-Pakistan Islam League Convention at Hyderabad, Sind (in West Pakistan), asked that this provision, among others, be inscribed in the constitution not just as a principle but as an applicable clause, to be enforced. No notice was taken of this resolution when the constitution was voted on (29 February 1956)[106] and the final text merely refers to the rapid elimination of *ribā* as one of the aims toward which the state should strive – along with, for example, the welfare of the people.[107] Since then the situation can be adequately summed up in these words which I read in a weekly paper while I am writing these lines: 'Regularly, the National Assembly of Pakistan discusses a motion aimed at abolishing all interest rates, on the ground that they violate the law of the Koran. So far, commercial considerations have carried the day against it.'[108] Meanwhile, the state bank of Pakistan raises and lowers its rate of interest just like all other such banks. And the agrarian reform of January 1959 stipulates that landowners who are expropriated shall be compensated with bonds bearing interest at 4 per cent.[109]

It seems that there is one Muslim state of the present day that has had the courage to introduce – not into practice, to be sure, but at least into the text of its laws – the prohibition of interest. This is, as one might have expected, one of the most backward states from the economic and cultural standpoint, namely, Saudi Arabia. We know that this state, by its very formation, is inspired by a diehard and backward-looking ideology, Wahhābism, which preaches a return to the pure Islam of the early days and rages against other Muslims who are seen as having abandoned themselves since long ago to the most unbridled laxity, which nowadays takes the form of a Europeanizing modernism. Saudi Arabia's relative isolation, and the archaic way of life of most of its inhabitants, have allowed it hitherto to maintain its backward-looking policy, with such reforms as the application of the penalty of cutting off the hands for theft. Fidelity to the Wahhabite ideology, and, something that is more embarrassing, the need that is the corollary of this, to avoid directly offending its representatives, the Wahhābite *'ulamā'* of Nejd, have so far succeeded in slowing down very effectively the more or less modernizing tendencies of the political leaders of the country and the new strata of its society. It is therefore not surprising that the commercial code of the kingdom, which is elsewhere inspired by the Ottoman commercial code of 1850, and through that by the French code of 1808, remains eloquently silent on the matter of interest. Positively, the commissions set up 'to provide for good and to suppress evil' in the towns of Saudi Arabia have forbidden all forms of *ribā* in the regulations they have decreed.[110] In 1950 a loan granted by Saudi Arabia to Syria was expressly defined as being free of interest.[111]

The moment has come to conclude. The factual survey, incomplete but substantial enough, which has occupied the last few pages seems to me to provide solid grounds for the following opinion. The alleged fundamental opposition of Islam to capitalism is a myth, whether this view be put forward with good intentions or bad. On the theoretical plane, the Muslim religion presents no objection to the capitalist mode of production. In the Middle Ages, to be sure, a theoretical prohibition by the religious law was developed, aimed at certain special economic practices which are indispensable for the formation of the modern capitalist economic system, and this already constituted more or less of a hindrance to the development of a capitalistic sector. But this prohibition was, from the start, got round in practice to such a degree that the capitalistic sector experienced an incomparable efflorescence in the Middle Ages. In this period and subsequently, the only practical consequence of the prohibition was, in certain regions, to bring about specialization by certain minority elements – religious or ethnic – in the openly-practised trade in money, a specialization that seems to be a law of societies of this type: and also to sanctify the unwillingness to invest in industry which is common to these societies, and applies in a number of them that are not Muslim. It was with the obstacle constituted by this generalized repugnance to invest in industry that the development of a native industrial capitalism in the modern Muslim world, and in China and Japan in modern times, came into conflict, as had happened during the rise of modern Europe: the religious backing for this repugnance was invoked only very rarely, at the beginning of the process of industrialization.

The latter has gone forward thanks to the intervention of the

(Muslim) state, and above all, to the preponderant influence of Europe, in ways the main aspects of which have been explained in the previous section. The native capitalists eventually followed the European model, little by little, without appearing to be at all worried by the prohibitions of the previous period; or at most, in the case of specially scrupulous consciences, sheltering behind modernizing religious authorities, applying the stratagems canonized since the Middle Ages, or renouncing accessory profits (as with those who refuse to draw the interest on their bank balances).

Only belatedly has a hard-line reaction become manifest, which flatly and comprehensively refuses to resort to these facilities, but without challenging the actual foundations of the capitalist mode of production. This movement has succeeded, however, only in creating a few co-operatives of limited economic importance in the Indian subcontinent, restricting the operation of the capitalist sector of the economy as little as the co-operative movement has managed to do in Europe and America – a movement, incidentally, inspired by a somewhat similar, even though secular, ideology. The state that is theoretically most determined to conform to the prescriptions of Islam, namely, Pakistan, has been unable, despite its gestures in this direction, to resolve to sanction juridically the theses of the movement. Only one of the economically most backward of the Muslim states has had the comparative courage to inscribe the traditional bans in its law-books, under pressure from a demanding, diehard ideology. It is not very likely, in view of what is happening in the more advanced Muslim states, that these bans will remain in force (if they ever have actually been in force), legally or practically, should Saudi Arabia eventually follow the same line of development as the others. It is possible, at most, that ideological developments resulting from political circumstances may cause some of these others to introduce similar legislation. It is extremely probable that, should that happen, such legislation will provide for exceptions and escape-clauses (ideologists are already preparing schemes for these[112]), and that it will be applied in practice in inverse proportion to its severity – unless the question of the rate of interest loses much of its importance through the going-over of these states to socialist, or at least statist, types of economy, under the influence of causes of a totally non-religious nature. What is most likely is that, once again, the religious authorities will follow the movement of society, and will supply their governments with ideological justifications in strict conformity with the requirements of the economic policy these governments will have chosen.

The facts of history are thus fully in accordance with the theses of Marxism. Ideology shows itself to be a great deal less powerful, in the long run, than the requirements of the social situation, the struggle of societies and social groups for maximum power and maximizing of the advantages and privileges of every kind that they enjoy. In addition, and in order to reply to some fashionable views, let us note that the world of symbols and significances plays, at best, only a secondary, and relatively not very independent, role as compared with the factors that have just been mentioned – at least on the scale of overall evolution.

A Muslim path for capitalism?

We have seen that the introduction into the Muslim countries of a modern capitalist sector, similar to that which gives direction to the entire economy in those countries where the capitalist socio-economic formation is dominant, was a process that originated from outside the Muslim world. We have seen, too, that the precepts of the Muslim religion, in the form that they had assumed in the previous period, were incapable of preventing the adoption of new economic practices in consonance with the operational requirements of this sector, or the development of this sector towards predominance in the total economic system of each country, as in the West.

Has this modern capitalist sector – by definition structurally identical in its general outline with that which is dominant in the Western countries – any special features in the Muslim countries? If so, are these special features due to the Muslim religion? These are the questions that now call for an answer.

That in each national community the functioning of the modern capitalist system presents special features seems to be a fact that is generally acknowledged by practical economists, and that the theoreticians endorse without, as a rule, being able to give it precision and scientific form. I will quote the highly-condensed formulation provided by François Perroux:

While the techniques of modern capitalism have quickly become widespread and have established striking similarities between different national economies, each of the latter has its own distinctive organization, and the persons who participate in the economic activities of each of them have certain distinctive mental tendencies in common. Without in the least yielding to the worn-out fantasies of the old-style 'psychology of nations', and indeed reacting vigorously against their hasty generalizations and excessive claims, modern science has begun to observe that certain characteristics are indeed held in common by the classes or groups of classes shaped by the history of a particular nation. The businessman with interests all over the world is well aware of the differences, even if he cannot define them exactly, between the businessmen, engineers, office-workers, manual workers and farmers of one nation as compared with another . . . Property, contracts, the state – in others words, the institutions that form the framework of production and exchange – receive a certain imprint from the tradition and way of life of each nation. The economist who seeks to go beyond these general and vague observations will try to determine the proportions and relations characteristic of a particular national capitalism, and draw up a structural survey of the latter . . . We are not concerned only with imports and exports by British and American individuals, the supply and demand of individual citizens of these nations. We have the right and duty to consider the imports and exports of Britain and of the U.S.A., their total supply and total demand, as nations. Economically, the nation is a group of enterprises and households which are co-ordinated and regulated by a centre which possesses the monopoly of public power: that is, by a state. Among the component parts of the nation special relations are established which render them complementary to each other.[113]

There is point in recalling here that this was already Marx's view as well, at least as regards differences in the level of comparative productivity between capitalist countries:

An industrial nation achieves its highest productivity when it is altogether at the height of its historical development. In fact a nation is at the height of its industrial development so long as, not the gain, but gaining remains its principal aim. In this respect the Yankees are superior to the English . . . Certain races, formations, climates, natural circumstances . . . are more conducive to production than others.[114]

And more generally:

Apart from the degree of development, more or less, in the form of social production, the productiveness of labour is fettered by physical conditions. These are all referable to the constitution of man himself (race, etc.) and to surrounding nature.[115]

These assertions need to be qualified, of course. What they attribute, in accordance with the science of their time, to 'race',[116] we should rather attribute to the cultural tradition of a certain ethnic group – which was, moreover, what was meant, in part at least, by the term 'race' as it was used in the epoch of Marx and Taine. They also need to be widened, to be made to extend beyond the domain of productivity alone. Nevertheless, they imply a clear awareness of the possible diversity of national styles that may be assumed by one and the same socio-economic formation or mode of production.

If this special style, these specific features of capitalism do really exist, then it is quite possible that something of the sort may be found in the Muslim countries. However, in the Muslim world we are confronted with communities of the national type which are in general rather different from the nations of Europe. The frontiers separating them are not always fixed, and in some of them, first and foremost in the Arabic-speaking communities, there is a national consciousness that exists at two different levels (in the case mentioned, the general 'Arab' level and, for example, the 'Tunisian' level). In many of them the cultural tradition which has contributed to the forming of this national consciousness has included the Muslim religion as an important factor of identification. Consequently, a national style of economic behaviour needs to be explained at several levels, by the various factors in the cultural history of the given country. In principle, it could be that the Muslim religion figures among these factors in some or all of the countries where it has been predominant.

Studies of economic psychology need to be consulted here.

The Marxist attitude to the role played by the economy in social life is not incompatible with taking account of this factor, as is often supposed by both its supporters and its opponents. The theses of Marxism do indeed assume that the general laws of overall economic structures, the major changes that these undergo, the transition that takes place from one to another, do not depend on differential psychological structures that are characteristic of some human groups in contrast to others, or on changes in these psychological structures that are independent of the evolution of the social structure. But this attitude is in no way hostile to the idea that the functioning of economic systems can be affected by the psychology of individuals and groups, even though it is the structure of these economic systems that plays a great part, at least, in determining the broad characteristics of this psychology.

So far, economic psychology does not seem to have produced interesting results regarding the differential behaviour of particular ethnic communities in economic matters. It is, generally speaking, limited to observations on the economic behaviour of very large categories of people, such as, for example, all the peoples of the underdeveloped or semi-developed countries taken as a whole, or to scattered notes (usually not very well backed by scientific proof) on the general tendencies of businessmen, bankers, etc., in the societies of Europe and North America.[117] There is no need to do more than mention in passing the ethnographers whose usual method is to analyse the behaviour of members of societies in which the economic function seems to them to be closely bound up with other social functions. Their approach appears to me to be often highly questionable. In any case, however, societies of the kind they deal with are to be found in the Muslim countries only in relatively isolated rural communities, which are, moreover, caught up in the general movement of the national economy. The functioning of the capitalist sector clearly proceeds independently of the special problems peculiar to this type of economy.

The writers who have tried to bring out the specific features of capitalism in the Muslim countries mainly consist of a few economists who know little about Islam, and that little only at second hand. To them must be added those Muslim ideologists who are determined to find, wherever they can, features of Muslim distinctiveness, preferably flattering in character. Greater prudence has been shown by Western and Near-Eastern sociologists and social historians, who have a better knowledge of the facts and are less inclined to draw bold conclusions. If one hunts around, it is possible to compile a little collection of these peculiarities of Muslim capitalism. But this result proves on examination to be disappointing and far from specific.

Given that 'the traditional mentality of Islam has not favoured the development of capitalism', writes the young economist J. Austruy, who has ventured boldly into the *terra incognita* of Islamology and written books and articles about it in a very forthright style, capitalist forms have penetrated but little into the industry and commerce of the Muslim countries, 'most of the enterprises of major importance being the work of foreigners', while the Muslims' own capitalist enterprises have shown only 'feeble dynamism'.[118] He admits in a note, to be sure, that his ideas on this point have been somewhat modified as a result of reading J. Berque, who has composed a picture showing the penetration of modern economy into the Arab world. The fact is, Austruy thinks, that the Arab world has changed, and he is taking account of this change.[119] Actually, the pages in which he states that he is taking the new developments into consideration are confined to tracing a picture, chimerical and remote from any reality, of what is supposed to be a 'Muslim economy' obedient to the alleged 'economic vocation of Islam'. I shall come back later to these utopias, which illustrate very well the danger of an 'idealistic' way of looking at these problems.

Elements of this way of seeing the question are found, though much less crudely expressed, in works a great deal more competent than those of Austruy. The American sociologist Morroe Berger, in a work of synthesis on the Arab world of today which is remarkably well-informed, intelligently written and showing considered judgment, asks himself whether the traditional Islamic suspicion with regard to 'risk' may have something to do with the preference displayed by Arab businessmen, and mentioned by many observers, for substantial profit-margins derived from investments that give a quick return, such as investments in cultivable land or in building plots in the towns. He quotes the Egyptian economist El-Gritly, who has noted that even the law textbooks used in Egypt 'unduly exaggerated' the advantages of bonds over stocks from the standpoint of security.[120] Berger himself, however, suggests that 'very likely the general political and economic insecurity in the Near East has also been at work in the creation of these attitudes toward risk'. He adds the pertinent comment that those Arabs, especially the ones of Syrian and Lebanese origin, who have emigrated to the United States give proof in this new environment of a more enterprising spirit. These are, it is true, mostly Christian Arabs, but there are also Muslims among them.[121] The same can be said of the Arab diaspora, mostly of Syro-Lebanese origin, in Latin America and Black Africa. And it is striking to observe that these Christian Arabs largely share, so long as they remain in the East, the characteristics of their Muslim compatriots in the sphere of economic activity. Furthermore, the most recent observers note an increasingly marked participation by Muslims in capitalist economic activity in the Middle East, once they have caught up on the lead that socio-historical conditions gave to their Jewish and Christian compatriots.[122]

Several writers thus refer to the desire for easy, certain and quick gains that is found among Middle-Eastern entrepreneurs. The latter dislike investments that tie up a lot of capital and are slow in bringing a return. They tend to engage in too many activities, organizing a variety of enterprises, none of which is highly specialized in character. They are said to want to do everything themselves, having little appreciation of the need for technical advice and the advantage to be gained by investing money in research. They are individualists. They have the mentality of go-betweens rather than of leaders. They manage their factories in an amateurish way. The consequences of these tendencies of theirs are inconsistent successes resulting from disordered and often unlucky investments.[123] Frequently, alongside better-grounded diagnoses, we find set out a list of the alleged causes of the attitude described: the Muslim ban on usury and aleatory contracts, fatalism, and so forth, together with (and this has greater validity) the confusion brought into the environment of the enterprise by the change going on in mental and social structures. All this is said to dry up at source the motives and stimuli of capitalism.[124] To these tendencies are attributed (in part at least) the fashion for economic planning, in which the risks are assumed on the scale of the entire nation, by the country's political leader.[125]

J. Berque, in his talented essay on the phenomenology of the Arab world of today, develops the same theme synthetically, with fairly plentiful examples drawn from recent Arab economic publications. On every side there is talk of 'distrust of slowly-maturing investments'.[126] 'Always the same complaint was heard: the available capital is absorbed by land, building and luxury.'[127] Berque refers, after analysing the behaviour of the capitalists of Iraq, to 'the old horror of risk', which has its 'roots in ethics'.[128] Elsewhere, however, he notes more correctly that the dogmatic ban on aleatory contracts is no longer anything but 'a theoretical obstacle; it no longer in the majority of cases evokes any conflict of conscience'.[129] Similarly, in the 'Oriental' characteristics of fatalism, indifference and inconsistency which are so often denounced not only by Europeans but also by Muslims,

public opinion sees features derived from a past that must be swept away. In fact, these realities, for they are realities, are becoming less and less important every day in their actual social and moral significance. They constitute, for more and more of the groups which are evolving, that very thing which they have to rebel against, and despite which they have to act.[130]

These last comments by a good observer are conclusive. They accord with what we learn from those writers who are the shrewdest and best aware of contemporary realities. They may also be applied elsewhere, to the non-Arab nations of the Muslim world. A general economic evolution is in all these countries causing at least a substantial section of those individuals who play a leading role in the economy to engage in economic behaviour similar to that which is regarded as normal in the European capitalist world. In the works of Berque in particular, close analyses of this evolution will be found devoted to this process, on all planes, and especially on that of underlying psychology: attitudes towards things, towards quantity, etc. It has been documented in detail through the sociological inquiries that Daniel Lerner has directed and analysed so intelligently. The economist A. J. Meyer and the Middle-Eastern sociologists Charles Issawi and Yusif A. Sayigh, have described it in relation to a number of sectors, and at first hand. It is to be observed that this evolution clearly does not result from a *religious* development, but from an economic and technical change.

Thus, the features that the analyses I have been able to bring together regard as specific to at least some national capitalist groups in the Muslim world are transitory features on the way to disappearance. But it is necessary to go further. Contrary to what is claimed – with the more caution shown the more competent they are – by many of the writers I have mentioned, and by others, these features are not specifically *Muslim*. Everything that has been said in this book testifies to the truth of that, and in particular the comparison I have made with the facts of Chinese and Japanese experience. What is involved here is behaviour that is bound up with the economic and social structures of the past, canonized by Islam during a whole period of history, and tending to disappear or to become transformed in proportion as the economic and social structure is transformed, though not without a certain time-lag. It may be that there are national styles in capitalist enterprise in the Muslim countries, just as there are national styles in capitalist enterprise in the Christian countries. If serious scientific research succeeds in defining what these are (which has not been done up to now), a certain kinship will *perhaps* be discovered to exist between these styles, due to the presence of a common heritage of ways of thought and conduct. This common heritage arises from a cultural history that is in some degree common to the countries concerned. This common cultural history embraces, along with many other elements, features shaped by the few constant tendencies of the Muslim religion, the rare 'invariants' of Islam. It is therefore not absolutely impossible that 'Muslim' characteristics may be discovered in the capitalist styles of the Muslim countries. For the moment, however, so far as I know, nothing of the kind has been discovered that will stand up to critical analysis.

If the theses which, explicitly or implicitly, assume that a religious doctrine exercises an important influence on the economic behaviour of its adherents were sound, there is one point on which one would be interested to see what Islam's effect had been. If Islam preaches justice towards the humble and compassion towards human suffering – although, in general, this compassion is counterbalanced, to a greater extent than in the Christian scriptures, by invocation of what is required for the functioning of society and the state – then we should in theory expect to find that Muslim capitalists are solicitous not to impose on their wage-workers either excessive toil or excessive privations. The reality of social relations is so strongly felt by all (even by those who proclaim, in theory, their conviction that ideal or religious values prevail) that nobody expects to find that Muslim capitalists have ever felt that the way the system works gave them a share of the return from the work they financed, and also a degree of power, that was out of proportion to the contribution they made. Without, however, going so far as that (although there would be grounds for expecting religion to go so far), it is significant that nobody has dared even to claim that Muslim capitalists have shown any special humanity towards the wage-workers whom, in Marxist terminology, 'they exploited'.

It is therefore hardly necessary to dwell upon this point. In order, however, to be fairly complete in my treatment of the subject, and to leave no doubt in the minds of those of my readers most disposed to contamination by apologetico-nationalist ideology, I will briefly review some facts which will serve as examples, and refer to writings that discuss the subject.

In the period when the Muslim East was being industrialized we find more or less the same excesses committed that marked the industrialization of Europe and were so vigorously denounced by Marx: exhausting labour imposed on the worker, up to the very limits of his strength and beyond, dreadful privations to which he was reduced by a very low wage that was cut still further by fines, deductions, etc., a prison-like discipline weighing down on him, absence of any legal or extra-legal means of defence, living conditions that were sordid and unhealthy – in a word, inhuman – and so on. No more than the humane principles of Christianity prevented the most pious European capitalists from resorting to such methods, or than the Christian religious organizations saw fit to blame them for this, no more did the humane principles of Islam restrain the Muslim capitalists from following this line, or the Muslim religious authorities utter the slightest protest or reservation regarding such conduct.

One of the practices that has proved most repugnant to the humanitarian conscience of Europe, very belatedly awakened and made tender (not at all, however, by any action on the part of ministers of religion, whose role this should, ideally, have been), is child labour. Now, child labour has also been a characteristic feature of capitalist enterprises in the Muslim countries, whether the owners of these enterprises were Muslim or not. This occurred, moreover, despite the fact that the influence of the European model caused social legislation to be adopted in these countries a great deal sooner after the industrialization process began than had been the case in Europe. The working class of the Muslim countries benefited, in theory at least, from the time-lag and from the victories dearly bought in earlier times by the European working class, which had obliged the capitalists to give consideration to its needs and to its dignity. The example of the West, and especially fear of the development of a powerful labour movement on the Western model, leading to violent strikes and even revolution, played a highly salutary role. For the privileged classes, fear is the beginning of wisdom.

Thus, child labour flourished under Muslim capitalism no less than under the Christian variety. I will confine myself to the case of Egypt, which will serve as a typical example. Here is a dry and succinct résumé of the question, taken from the brief introduction to a sober Egyptian collection of legal documents on labour legislation:

In 1909 the Egyptian government made the first efforts in modern history to draw up legislation to protect the worker. It issued the law on the regulation of children under thirteen years old in cotton-

ginning establishments; later, this law was extended to cover ciga-
rette factories (in 1926), spinning and weaving mills (in 1927), and
cotton-presses. In no case, however, was the law adequately applied:
these factories were inspected by officials belonging to the Ministry of
the Interior who did not take their work seriously enough, the information given by the employer was never subjected to criticism, and
violations were taken up only when, during inspection, it was observed that the labour-contractor was using physical violence
against the children.[131]

In February and March 1931, the deputy-director of the
International Labour Office, Harold B. Butler, carried out an
official investigation of labour conditions in Egypt at the request
of the Egyptian Government. His official report, published by
the Egyptian Ministry of the Interior, contains the following
observations:

Perhaps the most striking difference between the general appearance
of factories and workshops in Egypt and those in European countries is to be found in the large number of children employed. It was
estimated in 1927 that 15 per cent of the total staff engaged in industrial establishments were children. In the course of my tour I have
frequently seen boys and girls under the age of ten not only in native
workshops, but in some up-to-date modern factories . . . They
receive very low wages . . .[132]

As a result of this report, the law of 25 December 1933 (8
Ramadan 1352) forbade the employment in industry of children
less than twelve years of age. However, it also provided for an
exception. Children of nine to twelve could be employed in
spinning, weaving and knitting mills, as well as in other work
that might contribute to their vocational training. They were
not to work more than seven hours a day, whereas adolescents of
thirteen to fifteen could work up to nine hours. The conditions
of hygiene, security, etc., added to these regulations make
interesting reading.[133] Anyone who has been a wage-worker
knows how helpless people in this position are as regards
ensuring that such conditions are respected, even in a country
like France. It can be imagined what the situation could be in
Egypt, where all trade-union activity was suspect *a priori*, and
enjoyed only marginal legality (freedom to form trade unions
was not formally recognized until the law of 1942), and where

the corps of labour inspectors was inadequate in numbers, poorly trained and badly paid, like all the other officials, and consequently not difficult for the employers to corrupt. It is clear that child-labour continued to flourish extensively even after the law in question was promulgated. To quote an Egyptian economist: 'The Under-Secretary for Social Affairs in the 1944 report states, with disarming candour, that the law was not strictly observed, and that children were still working in unhealthy establishments.'[134]

From all this one might draw conclusions once again about the relative ineffectiveness of ideologies and the vanity of claims made for religions. But I will content myself with an observation more directly related to the line of my argument: the Muslim religion has influenced significantly neither the structure nor the functioning of the capitalist sector in the countries of Islam, even in that field where naïve people might have supposed that a religion would have had something to say, namely, the field of humane treatment of workers.

If this was indeed so (and I do not think it can be seriously denied), then was this religion totally without effect on the ambience in which the capitalist sector was placed – did it not at least contribute to restricting the role played by this sector in relation to other modes of production that were allegedly more in accordance with that phantom entity which some call the economic vocation of Islam, and better adapted, perhaps, to that other elusive factor which Austruy calls the 'inner rhythm of Islam'? It is in this fashion, I think, that one may try to translate into assertions of a scientific type the vague and woolly suggestions that are made by a whole group of writers belonging to very different levels.

The relatively weak development of the capitalist sector in the Islamic countries, its equally weak dynamism, the important role played by the state in the economy from the very outset, and the trend towards more pronounced forms of state-managed economy and straightforwardly socialist structures, are all attributed by these writers to the influence exercised by Islam.

Looking at the facts from a distance, they have formed the impression that there was a sort of gap between the modern economy imported into the Muslim countries and the already existing structures. This impression was correct. It was made stronger by the circumstance that these writers were most familiar, where Muslim countries were concerned, with French North Africa, a region especially backward as regards ways of life, never having known that sort of cultural synthesis between the Muslim East and Europe (especially Central Europe) that was attempted in the Middle East under the auspices of the Ottoman Empire, roughly between 1850 and 1914. Austruy and others, however, have wrongly interpreted this impression – correct in the main for a certain sector of the Muslim world – by identifying these backward structures with the 'inner rhythm of Islam'.

It is indeed true that there was a gap between the new economy and the inner rhythm of the Muslim world as it was at the moment when the former was imposed upon the latter. In the first place, however, what the latter signified was not a *permanent* characteristic of the Muslim world. On this point I will merely recall to the reader what I have written above, and the references given concerning the dynamism of the mediaeval economy. In the second place, although this 'rhythm' may well have been canonized by Islam, and ministers of religion may well have sometimes brandished the charge of impiety against those who broke it, it remains none the less true that this 'rhythm' was in no way intrinsically bound up with the Muslim religion. This is what I have endeavoured to show in the preceding pages. I do not deny that there may be 'invariants' that are of the essence of the Muslim faith. These must be sought for, however, elsewhere than in the characteristics of an age of stagnation. Resignation, renunciation of effort, *tawakkul*, leaving one's affairs in the hands of God, are neither specific to Islam nor intrinsic to it. These writers have mixed up the reactions of a transitional phase, when a society at a certain stage in its evolution finds itself suddenly confronted with quite new techniques, structures and values coming from abroad, and often forced upon it by foreigners, with the reactions that would result from the confrontation of two cultures that were fundamentally impenetrable and eternally alien to each other by their very natures. Observation or discovery of the rapid developments of recent years, made especially clear through the descriptions given by Berque, have not succeeded in modifying false notions that have struck deep roots. The authority accorded to someone like E. F. Gautier, the painter, talented but reckless, of an apparently stagnant society, who was led by his position as a colonialist to give theoretical form and a permanent character to the characteristics of a society of this kind, or to popularizers who were largely incompetent and whose outlook was also distorted by the colonial situation, like R. Charles and A. Pellegrin, served to reinforce these radically mistaken conceptions.

The view taken of the former situation as being a kind of theological state is no less mistaken. Here too we must be careful not to confuse different phenomena. True, Muslim society in the age of stagnation that preceded the European penetration did impose upon its members a strict religious conformism, an outward piety, that was manifested, for example, in very frequent invocations of the name of Allah, ostentatious observations of ritual obligations, etc. It should be noted, however, that this habit had the effect of depriving these words and practices of much of their strictly religious significance, turning them into patterns of automatic behaviour that essentially expressed men's adherence to the values of their society. Hypocrisy and pharisaism were no less characteristic of this attitude than was sincere piety. Besides, this religious conformism varied, to a large degree, between social strata, sections with different ways of life, ethnic groups, sects. As it has been described, and wrongly expanded into an eternal characteristic of the Muslim religion, it was above all a feature of the urban bourgeoisie. The number of 'deviators' was none the less considerable, as can be appreciated from a glance at the moral and religious vituperations with which the literature of this period is filled.

Above all, however, the existence of this state of mind does not mean at all that one is entitled to deduce automatically the habitual behaviour of these conformists from the precepts of the Koran, or even from those of the Sunnah, any more than one can deduce the behaviour of Christians, even in the ages of profoundest faith, from the precepts of the Gospel! In the one case as in the other, accommodating interpretations were easily obtained, consciences were elastic, theólogians obliging. Let the reader look back over the pages in which I have given examples of shameless violations of the ban on *ribā*, under cover of obviously false interpretations of the sacred texts. And that went on in a milieu that was particularly proud of its piety, the world of the Moroccan bourgeoisie! I think one cannot but accept the truth of this picture if one has the slightest familiarity, whether derived from books or from real life, with this traditional world of Islam. But the consequences are less often perceived on the theoretical plane. The fact is that it is clearly vain to seek the basis for social conduct in this world mainly in the Koran and the Sunnah. The basis lies elsewhere. The Koran and the Sunnah serve essentially to provide a conformist and religious veneer to behaviour that is basically responsive to pressures of quite another kind.

If the dynamism of Muslim entrepreneurs was for a long time only slight, if many Muslims remained for a long time unwilling to commit themselves to the path of modern industrial enterprise, Islam is thus in no way responsible. Islam did not prevent anyone from taking up, out of self-interest, an attitude that was directly contrary to its precepts on the question of *ribā*. Besides, we have seen that the same aversions were found in Japan and China. It was a normal reaction for an age of transition in face of the sudden introduction from abroad of radically new and strange forms of economic conduct into the network of traditional social relations, along with the attitudes and behaviour that were correlative with these.[135] It would be fitting, moreover, to keep in mind, first and foremost perhaps, the hindrances that were laid upon native enterprise from the very moment that it might have had the chance to take off. Some details have been given above about the commercial treaties imposed by Europe upon the Ottoman Empire and Iran.[136] Elsewhere, colonization brought with it fetters that were even more effective. In addition to all these difficulties, the technical lead that Europe had won constituted, in the background, that major obstacle of which all the others were so many indirect manifestations, but which also made itself felt directly, at several levels. As Y. Sayigh points out, enterprise is not the primary and sole driving force of development. It becomes an important strategic factor only when a favourable institutional framework is present.[137]

The same writers, and some others as well, readily quote as tendencies that are intrinsic to Islam, in which the gap in question is expressed (and by which, consequently and logically, it is bound to be prolonged if society in these countries continues to adhere to Islam), the restriction on the right of ownership and the practice of mutual aid within the community. Some writers even draw optimistic conclusions, considering that these tendencies may serve to guide the Muslim world along the road to socialism.

I have already spoken above about property rights under Muslim law. Perhaps this point should be emphasized again, in view of the errors that are current on this subject and the importance of the mistaken conclusions that have been drawn from them. Here too the distinctiveness of Muslim law has been exaggerated. Historians of law are well aware that, even where Roman law is concerned, that classical domain of absolute ownership, the famous definition in the *Digest*, '*dominium est jus utendi, fruendi, abutendi re sua quatenus juris ratio patitur*', has to be taken with some reservations, which are indeed already indicated in the second part of the definition, which is not usually quoted. 'Property is the right to use, to enjoy, to dispose fully of [and not exactly to "misuse"] whatever belongs to one, *in so far as this is in conformity with the system of law*.'[138] Restrictions on this right existed from the time of the Law of the Twelve Tables, to safeguard the interests of neighbours. Other limitations were added to safeguard the interests of society, and for reasons of equity, humanity or clarity. Many obligations were attached to the ownership of real estate. During the decadence of the Roman Empire, the owners of agricultural domains were threatened with forfeiture of their property if they neglected to cultivate it, and a man was allowed to exploit a mine that he had discovered, regardless of whether the owner of the land gave his consent, and with only one-tenth of the product due to be paid to this owner. Expropriations 'for the public good' were numerous. A theory of the misuse of property rights was worked out, and, where slaves were concerned, their masters found themselves subjected, from the first century onward, to serious restrictions on their rights of ownership, which were imposed in the interests of humanity.[139] Christian theology, constructing a general theory of the rights and duties of man in the shadow of God, accorded to property rights only a relative and conditional validity, somewhat similar to the theorizing of Muslim theology and law on this subject. The classical formulations of St Thomas Aquinas on the matter are well known. It was possible for the Roman Church to revive them, from Leo XIII's Papacy onward, when it became necessary to show that this Church was not indifferent to the social evils which the socialist movement laid at the door of the right of property in its absolute form.[140]

The Islamic concept of landed property was profoundly influenced by the circumstances of the Arab conquest. The latter put immense areas of cultivable land at the disposal of the conquerors. It was indispensable that this land be exploited, so as to fill the conquerors' common treasury (*Bayt al-Māl*), which was controlled by the Caliph, in the first place mainly with a view to redistributing these funds among those who had the right to receive payment, a proportion being kept back to meet the costs of the machinery of state, to provide help for the needy and so on, as prescribed in the Koran. Increasingly, as was natural, the share taken by the sovereign for his own purposes grew larger, but this only made it the more necessary to ensure that revenue was regular and substantial. In this type of society, revenue came in the main from agricultural production. For this reason, conditions being similar to those in the Roman Empire, but on a more extensive scale than there because a large part of the land was regarded as conquered territory, property rights were somewhat precarious. It has been said, with some exaggeration, and generalizing wrongly from what applied above all to landed property, that

the idea of property is . . . intimately bound up, in Muslim theory, with the idea of the development, the fructification of what one possesses. The right of ownership has to be deserved. Although . . . the right someone has acquired to a piece of land is not lost merely through non-use, it vanishes if someone else brings this land under cultivation.[141]

This, however, is only lawyers' theorizing, and I have already stressed the purely theoretical character of Muslim canonical law. Application of the law has been infinitely varied as between different times and places. There have not been many studies devoted to this point. Broadly, one can only say that, if the enjoyment of private property was noticeably more disturbed in the East than in the West, this was not because Muslim legal theory made it more precarious, but owing to political and conjunctural circumstances: wars, invasions and conquests, the frequently absolutist character of the ruling authority. Let it not be forgotten that, under the absolute monarchy in France,

property was not untouchable, either. No doubt the property-owner who was expropriated for reasons of public utility received reasonable compensation. But taxation, which is the practical way for a ruler to encroach on subjects' property, was ultimately at the King's discretion . . . His subjects were his, 'body and goods alike'.[142]

The idea of misuse, which calls in question the right of ownership, is thus neither so specific to Muslim law nor so well applied in practice in Islamic countries as G. Destanne de Bernis thinks.[143] And to speak, as Austruy does, of the 'non-adaptation of Islam to the type of exclusive private property which arises from Western capitalism'[144] is totally unjustified. This means confusing the theological ideal with practical social relations. One could just as well say, invoking Aquinas, that Christianity is unadapted to exclusive private property. In reality, it seems that the Muslim law of property has never prevented a factory being installed, or capital being made to fructify, by any capitalist, Muslim or non-Muslim. Furthermore, from the nineteenth century onward, the chief independent Muslim countries have purely and simply taken over Western land law, and have done this without encountering any resistance at all, while in the countries subjected to European colonial rule the agrarian régime was largely altered for the benefit of the colonial power.[145] Here, too, the writers concerned are mixing up theory, or one aspect of theory, with the structure of real facts, while in other places they take the real state of things in the recent past, which may still be true of a whole sector in the present, to be an immutable structure permanently associated with the *entire* past (and the entire future) of a certain group of societies.

It is quite true, as Austruy emphasizes, following A. Piettre and François Perroux,[146] that the concept of property in capitalist society tends to evolve, becoming functional, and its absolute character being encroached upon by the considerations of social need to which it is expected to correspond. This is due partly to the requirements of modern industrial societies and partly to the power of the socialist challenge, in ideas as in facts, through the competition, externally, of the socialist countries, and, internally, the powerful pressure of the wage-workers within the capitalist world. It needs to be observed in passing that the latter is still very far from having arrived at the socialist conception of property, despite the apparent convergence of the formulations.[147] But the notion that it is possible to use the traditional concept of property found in the Sunnah, and the relative restrictions it imposes, in order to advocate and promote a move by Muslim societies towards socialist structures, or even towards those vaguely defined forms of social control of economic life which are recommended by 'advanced' economists, is utterly fantastic. The classical *fiqh* is as dead in the consciousness of the masses as is scholasticism in the West. All that is possible, given the fidelity of the masses to the traditional religion, due to factors of national identification, is demagogic use (demagogic in the strict sense) of the slogans and prestige of Islam as a banner to be raised above more or less socialistic decisions that have originated elsewhere than from religious sources. They could have done as well for almost anything else.

This Machiavellianism which tempts so many political leaders in the Muslim world comes up against just one practical objection (if we leave aside the moral considerations). Reactionary Muslims can equally well make use of the arsenal provided by the Koran and the Sunnah in order to combat the solutions thus proposed. They even hold certain advantages over those who interpret the same sources in a progressive sense. In the first place, whatever may be said, the texts do favour their side, since they belong to an epoch in which the right of property was not seriously challenged, and the limitations imposed upon it were far from having the very great significance that it is now proposed to give them. We have seen this already in connection with the controversy in Pakistan about large landed property. In the second place, and much more dangerously, the reactionary interpreters of the scriptures enjoy the benefit of the whole heritage of the past, the weight of centuries of interpretation in the traditional sense, the prestige of these interpretations, the established habit of relating them to the generally accepted religion, for reasons that are not at all religious in character. Finally, and perhaps this is most important, the ministers of religion, whose authority is reinforced by this superficial but mass-scale adherence to the doctrines whose guardians they are, are often (though, to be sure, not always) inclined to support the traditionalist interpretation.[148] These factors could be eliminated only after a radical *aggiornamento* of the Muslim religion. It is easy enough to see the difficulties that such an evolution is encountering in the Catholic world. In the Muslim world the obstacles are even bigger, and the process of evolution less advanced, for a variety of reasons which I cannot go into here.

The same considerations have to be applied to the tendencies to solidarity, mutual aid, and a communal way of life, that the same writers and others (in particular, certain Muslim ideologists and politicians) proclaim to be inherent in Islam. In this connexion, phenomena of very different orders are mixed up together. Some emphasize the traditions of mutual aid in the rural community.[149] What is meant here is facts that can be found in all societies of this type, including those remote from Islam and having nothing to do with the Muslim religion – facts that have disappeared, or are tending to disappear, everywhere with the introduction of those relations characteristic of industrial life. We know the rebuffs that were suffered by those who in Russia hoped in the same way to base social evolution on exactly comparable traditions. This does not mean that in certain circumstances and certain places, with the taking of many precautions, something may not be done with these communal practices. There is talk of the spirit of solidarity of the *umma* (the Muslim community), the paralysing constraint that this sense of community develops: but also of the positive values that can be drawn from it. More cautiously than others, J. Poirier writes:

> Technical and economic progress heralds proletarianization, the degradation of the old values and the appearance of *individual* miseries . . . In other words, this progress seems to foster a frenzied egoism which, as regards relations between persons, leaves man indifferent to man. If Islam, in becoming industrialized, were to retain the substance of the Koran's precepts of fraternity and solidarity, if it were successful merely in keeping differences in standard of living within acceptable proportions, it would give the world a resounding lesson.[150]

Views like these have been expounded in a much farther-reaching way by some contemporary Muslim ideologists. Thus, the Syrian Muṣṭafā as-Sibāʿī, an outstanding member of the Muslim Brotherhood, in his book *The Socialism of Islam*, which is a best-seller in the Arab world, devotes numerous pages to this question. In the fantastical view of human history common to all these diehard ideologists, Islam discovered nearly fourteen centuries ago those principles the value of which is only just being recognized by a Europe at last become somewhat aware of the disastrous situation to which its own principles of life have led her. What is involved first and foremost is the 'principle of social solidarity' proclaimed by the Koran and the Sunnah.

> The verses [of the Koran] that I have quoted show clearly that God prescribed co-operation and solidarity in all the forms indicated by the different meanings of the words *birr* [broadly, 'pious kindness'] and *taqwā* [broadly, 'piety']. The *ḥadīths* I have quoted show that the Prophet established the institution of social solidarity in its full and broad sense. This is why it is expressed in a variety of ways in Muslim socialism.[151]

He then lists succinctly 'the most important and most indispensable to the good of society', from among these ways, quoting *ḥadīths* to back them: moral solidarity, solidarity in knowledge (one must enable others to profit from one's learning), political solidarity, solidarity in defence of the community, solidarity in compensating the victims of a crime, solidarity in maintaining sound morality in the community, economic solidarity, ritual solidarity, cultural solidarity, 'alimentary' solidarity aimed at ensuring for every member of the community at least a decent level of subsistence.[152] He ends with this conclusion, which can be heard throughout the Muslim East, in one form or another (and in the West too!):

> The principle of social solidarity in Muslim socialism is one of the features that distinguish this humanistic and moral socialism from every other kind of socialism known today. If it were applied in our society, the latter would be ideal, and no other society would come anywhere near its lofty grandeur.[153]

Indeed, this is not to be doubted. The only question is: how can this magnificent principle find application, when more than thirteen centuries of faith have to so large an extent overlooked it?

Contrary to what may be thought by Muṣṭafā as-Sibāʿī, J. Austruy and other such writers, in their sovereign contempt for real history, these principles (which are really to be found in the scriptures) have had no more and no less influence on this history than the equally admirable precepts of Prophetic and Rabbinical Judaism, of Christianity, of Buddhism, etc. – not to speak of secular moralities. Austruy, following E. F. Gautier and others, believes that (negative) traces of such influence can be seen in the conformism of traditional Muslim society.

> In all ages and all countries, even if there is no physical coercion, every Muslim feels that he is under the gaze of the others, and the silent pressure of universal reprobation is extraordinarily effective.[154]

Austruy adds:

> Consider the success, incomprehensible to a Latin [*sic*], of the boycott of foreign goods, and the way Muslims, even after long residence in Europe and despite their showing much religious scepticism when with us, prove afraid to break the laws of the Koran in the presence of their co-religionists.[155]

The power of social constraint is not to be denied, in traditional Muslim society any more than in other societies of the same type, or in ideological movements. This is not a feature special to the East, as Gautier supposes, or to Islam, as Austruy supposes. The Muslim world has in its time been pluralistic and liberal. 'Latin' France has known centuries when attendance at mass on Sundays was obligatory, and it was dangerous to stay away. At the moment when the constraints of traditional society were weakening in the Muslim world, they were succeeded by the exigencies of an ideological movement on the offensive. Nationalism, expressing general aspirations to which the lukewarm and sceptical themselves had to pretend to give full support, naturally adopted among its symbols the rites of the native religion, despised and combated by the alien rulers. So the support given by a whole people is beyond the comprehension of a 'Latin'? What Frenchman would have dared, between 1914 and 1918, to give a lecture in which he voiced his admiration for German music? And, among the 'Latin' masses of the *pieds-noirs* of Algeria, who dared to stay away from the great collective demonstrations that expressed the fears and hatreds of a community threatened in those privileges that seemed to it to constitute its very *raison d'être*? Even at the heart of French society – 'Latin', liberal and pluralist – the adherents of an ideological movement, the Communist Party, in the days when this movement was vigorous, forced themselves, whether voluntarily and joyfully, or else by making an effort of self-mastery, to manifest their support for the values of the movement in the practices of daily life.

The Koran's exhortations to fraternity, to co-operation among Muslims, are the normal expressions of an ideological movement in its early stages, the cohesion of its adherents being a necessary condition for the movement's success. The later exhortations of the Sunnah and of the religious writings of the Middle Ages are to be explained above all, I think, by the efforts of the ideologists to make the privileged sections of Muslim society realize the need to show at least some little solidarity in action with the frustrated who belonged to the same movement. This was one of the foundations on which the whole of society was based – the trusting support of the masses for an ideology that guided men towards God and built on earth the least evil of societies, in submission to God's directives. The moral and religious conformism shown by the élites expressed the ideological conviction that their privileged place in society was deserved, good, just, willed by God. This is the usual attitude of traditional societies. The modern attachment to everything that shows one's adhesion to Islam – participation in Muslim values, practices and professions of faith – is a nationalistic assertion that one belongs to a community that is being attacked and threatened in its identity. This is, I think, how one can analyse that 'unitary vocation' of the Arab world (though this can be applied, more or less, to the whole of the Muslim world) which Berque thinks *this* world has not had time to lose, owing to 'the suddenness of its contemporary history', which has enabled it to 'leap over our bourgeois centuries'.[156] That is a simplified formulation which conceals an altered significance, and could mislead one into falsely presuming that there has been no change.

All these principles, all these expressions of support, have been unable to modify the process of incorporation of the Muslim world in the capitalist world, any more than they could affect the process of implantation of a capitalist sector in a Muslim country. The Muslim capitalists have made their capital fructify just as the Christian ones have done. Doubtless one can find among the former, as among the latter, individuals who, taking seriously the ideology to which they adhere, have tried to bend certain rules of the system so as to palliate some of its humanly harmful consequences. But it is impossible to perceive any important modification of the general functioning of the system on the national scale. As an American economist who has observed them closely has written,

> Not by the wildest stretch of imagination could the commercial communities of any Middle Eastern city be labelled as 'spiritually oriented' or as holdouts from the chase after Mammon. Indeed, to employ Fritz Redlich's phrase, they are every bit as 'daimonic' and as much tacit believers in social Darwinism as American and British businessmen of an earlier era.[157]

It is not clear why that Muslim solidarity which did not prevent the landlords from sucking the blood of the peasants, the owners of houses from bleeding their tenants white, the usurers from reducing their debtors to poverty, should prevent the owners of capital from applying to their wage-workers the (often gentler) laws of capitalist exploitation.

To base oneself on the principles in question, as Poirier does, in order to bring about a minimization of differences between the classes, or, as Muṣṭafā as-Sibāʿī does, to build an ideal society, is an expression of gratuitous idealistic utopianism. These principles have not prevented, but on the contrary have camouflaged, to the greater profit of the beneficiaries, the coexistence of a class of privileged persons living in unheard-of luxury with great masses of people sunk in the most abject wretchedness – alms serving merely to give the rich a good conscience, for the price of a small number of poor persons saved from the worst consequences of their poverty. It is hard to see by what process these principles could have served any other purpose. The world knows only one certain means whereby the unprivileged sections of a society can ensure that their human rights are respected, and that is to give them at least a share in the control of political power, and, at best, to abolish as many privileges as possible, safeguarding these conquests by establishing adequate and solid institutions. The latter may be decorated, if one so wishes, with the phraseology of Muslim, Christian, Jewish, Buddhist, Stoic, Kantian or any other precepts. To do this would even do justice, in a certain sense, to these precepts. But the precepts without the institutions are nothing but hot air, and shameful camouflage for fundamental evils. This is true even of the precepts of Marxism if, in practice, they serve as a cover for exploitation and subjection. Marx has at least given us the means of understanding and exposing this mechanism.

The partial orientation of Muslim societies towards socialism has nothing to do with the precepts of Islam, except to the extent that *all* religions have given expression to certain fundamental human demands. But these demands could not enter, even if only to a partial extent, into practice unless they were to transcend the problematic of religion. The importance of Islam in the history of human liberation is, precisely, that it *has* partly transcended this problematic. It has not merely recommended, it has legislated. But this legislation, conceived for a small, embryonic community, for a nascent ideological community that immediately turned itself into a state, was content to organize mutual aid within this community, ensuring a minimum of protection to the weak and poor among its members. No institution was provided that went beyond the institutional horizon of the Arab tribes, none that might prevent or even hinder the formation or perpetuation of privileged strata, any more than the 'natural' tendency they showed to concentrate in their hands the maximum amount of power and of wealth, at the expense of the rest of the people. Popular protests in the Muslim world of the Middle Ages resulted only within a few sects in the transcending of this stage, with the conception, at least, of a structure of property free from privileges stabilized by institutions. These sects either failed or betrayed their own programme, and doubtless it could not have been otherwise. The only result of such protest was to inspire ideologists to press counsels of moderation upon the privileged, backing these with references to the scriptures. And, with the help of their material strength, the privileged took but slight account of these counsels, whatever their piety, whether pretended or sincere.

The principles of the institutional mechanisms that could prevent the creation of privileges and the domination of society by the privileged were always known in the East, no less well than in the West: participation by all citizens in political power, and control by this democratic political power over the economic sources of privilege. For these principles to be translated, however, into institutions applicable to the vast societies of which the empires of Antiquity furnished the first examples, complex societies made up of many elementary units, which were often specialized, brought together by the state and by an active commercial life, it was necessary to await the coming of the ideologists of modern Europe who were to proclaim them and to begin shaping them into precise theoretical form. Only with the American and French Revolutions was the theory of political control of power by the masses put into effect on a large scale. Only with modern European socialism was theoretical form given to the abolition of economic privileges in a society on the road to industrialization – and only with the Russian Revolution of October 1917 was a first attempt made to apply this theory. That God, or the Human Ideal, demands this twofold control of the privileges of power and wealth had been proclaimed long since, but that fact was of secondary importance compared with the giving of theoretical form to the institutional mechanisms that could ensure such control.

Into the Muslim world of the late eighteenth century and the nineteenth, resigned to the political and economic domination of the privileged, convinced by its religious leaders, through the more or less valid interpretation they gave of the religious ideology, as well as by the hard experience of centuries, that things could not be otherwise, the French Revolution and its consequences brought back the idea that a democratic state was possible and viable;[158] and the Russian Revolution brought the idea that a state without privileged classes could be established – however widely the states born of these revolutions may have deviated from the principles on which they were originally based. The rapid economic development of the capitalist states, in the first place, and of the Marxist states later, caused these models to be particularly attractive to the élites who wanted to make themselves independent through economic progress, and to the masses, hungry for freedom and happiness, who now learnt that freedom and happiness were to be had. The model came from outside, Islam having no responsibility for its formation. At most one can admit that the low degree of development of the capitalist sector and the slight extent to which it had struck root (its recent character) had not allowed individualistic traditions to take shape as fully in the Muslim world as they had done in Western societies. The Muslim world 'leapt over our bourgeois centuries', as Berque puts it. The class that is attached to liberal economics and benefits from the functioning of that system has been much weaker there, and that has certainly reduced mental resistance to the attraction offered by the socialist model. But this has nothing to do with the precepts specific to Islam. It was only the normal nationalistic pride of the peoples concerned that later caused justifications and precedents to be sought for the choices towards which they were irresistibly moving.

The Muslim principles of solidarity, like the Christian and Buddhist principle of compassion for all suffering, may indeed serve to give a religious blessing to a society without privileges, if such a society is possible, and in any case to the movement directed towards creating and defending it, the movement combating all forms of political and economic privilege. But these same principles have up to now most often served to justify societies based upon privilege, and this has inevitably weakened their power to mobilize men in the direction indicated. In any case, this circumstance shows that it is vain to count upon these principles alone to transform the world. Secular theorization of the mechanisms of an egalitarian society is essential, and cannot be effected solely by way of recourse to religious and moral precepts, even if these may give legitimacy to the society in question: any more than – as President Nasser put it, familiarly but very justly – exhortations to win a football match for all sorts of 'moral' or religious reasons can take the place of the necessary training for the game, a preparation in which only technical factors play a part, without any moral reference. It is certainly essential to try and find factors that can serve to mobilize men's energies, as I should be the last to deny, having particularly concerned myself with studying the power of ideologies. But it is not possible to count for this mobilization exclusively upon precepts that are too broad, open to many interpretations, and integrated historically in ideologies that are opposed to the effort envisaged. In any case, and this is what particularly interests us here, these precepts have hitherto played no role in orienting countries towards socialism or state economy. They have played no role in checking or modifying penetration by capitalist economy. There has been no special Muslim road for capitalism. It may be that there will in the future prove to be Moroccan, Algerian, Egyptian, Arabian, Turkish and Iranian roads to socialism. It is highly unlikely, however, that their chief characteristics will owe very much to the Muslim religion.

6 Conclusions and Prospects

Correlations and priorities

The conclusions that emerge from the preceding pages may well seem sadly negative. They certainly run counter to current notions. Islam as a religion strikes imaginations by its inimitable, incomparable originality. Its hold on the souls of its adherents has seemed unquestionably firm. Is it conceivable that Islam can have had so little influence on their economic life? Could this conclusion of mine have been due to a dogmatic prejudgement of the issue which took no account of reality? On the plane of research, may I not have brushed aside rather too easily some suggestions and lines of study that could prove fruitful?

Actually, I do not claim to have brushed anything aside. Saying that a phenomenon is not the origin of everything else, or that it has not evolved independently, does not mean denying its importance, which may sometimes be considerable, nor does it mean advocating the abandonment of investigations that relate to it. Furthermore, I do not pretend that in examining the facts I have not been guided by a certain underlying attitude – though I do deny that other investigators who have applied themselves to the same problem have worked *without* any previously determined attitude, even if this was implicit or subconscious. I have, however, endeavoured to assemble the essential facts relevant to the subject, and to interrogate them honestly. Nobody is exempt from the risk of making a mistake in his choice of material or his reasoning. But one can at least strive to the best of one's ability to be well-informed and rigorous in argument, not letting oneself be influenced by extra-scientific considerations – neither by the desire to prove a thesis nor by the desire to please, or to shine. Some may find this book absurd, and specialists may perhaps discover serious gaps in the information on which it is based. I have tried to ensure, however, that it cannot be faulted for dishonesty.

The correlation between Islam and any particular economic system has emerged as being very largely inconclusive, at least on the plane of fundamental structures. For example, it was not the precepts of Islam that created the propensity to commercial activity that is to be observed in many Muslim societies. The leaders of the Muslim expansion were traders even before their conversion, and they conquered societies in which trade was very highly developed already before the conquest. The precepts of Islam have not seriously hindered the capitalist orientation taken by the Muslim world during the last hundred years, and nothing in them is really opposed to a socialist orientation, either. If Muslim merchants have sometimes caused their mode of activity to be adopted by societies into which they have moved, this is an influence of their overall behaviour that cannot be seen as a strict application of imperious directives of their religion. While the latter may view the trader kindly, it does not command anyone to become a trader. Similarly, the precepts of Islam have nowhere created a social or economic structure that was radically new. The adoption of Islam, concomitant with a conquest, with the integration of small communities into a great total community which had this religion as its ideology, often entailed integration into the economic and social system constituting the structure of this great Muslim community. This is a total phenomenon in which it is hard to see quite simply the influence of the ideology on the socio-economic structure, even if ideological factors did play a role in causing the adhesion of communities that were not initially Muslim to the community that was already Muslim. It is quite clear to whoever studies the facts without prejudice that the expansion of Islam was to an infinitely greater degree a function of sociological and purely circumstantial factors (of a political, military, etc., kind) than of ideological convictions. The fact is less obvious in the case of the expansion of religions that engage in vigorous missionary activity, like Christianity and Buddhism. But one cannot cut man up into slices. Every change in ideological convictions, every conversion, takes place *partly* under the influence of sociological factors. This is so clearly seen nowadays that a whole school of Catholic sociologists of religion lays particular emphasis upon it and is investigating it in detail. I may be accused of charging at open doors. Nevertheless, there is still in existence a whole body of writing that expresses those views, implying a mutilation of the human personality, which absolutely dominated the historiography of former times, and against which the school to which I belong rose up in protest. Whether implicitly or explicitly this kind of writing argues as though every ideological change took place as a result of conscious deliberations or impulses of feeling, bringing into play exclusively what, for simplicity's sake, may be called the spirit.

In the other direction, on the contrary, there was an influence that was extremely clear-cut, although it is important to perceive its limits and appreciate its nature. The changes in social structures in Arabia in the sixth and seventh centuries produced a state of dissatisfaction in certain strata of Arab society. These changes inclined the strata in question to pay attention to the preaching of a Prophet whose thought was conditioned by his personal history, by the previously formed ideologies of which he had knowledge, and by the same social conditions that affected his hearers. His actions, and the solutions to temporal problems that he put forward, depended to a large extent on these social conditions, given the great capacity for adaptation that ensured his success and his greatness. It was these social conditions that provided the essential stimulus to the great Muslim invasions, and it was the political and socio-economic situation in the invaded countries that provided the condition for the Muslim victory. Later, the economic and social situation in the Muslim world influenced in noticeable ways certain details of the thematic of Muslim ideology – for example, the apologia for commerce and the glorification of the merchant.

But it would be ridiculous in many cases, and pointless in others, to relate particular points in the thematic of Muslim ideology to corresponding elements in the economic system. This is an approach that has tempted many Marxists, with results that are, in the best instances, thought-provoking but incapable of proof. It has rather often provided a target for justified criticism, most recently by my late friend the young pan-structuralist philosopher Lucien Sebag, whose correct insistence on scrupulous rigour in deductions of this sort led him to give up Marxism altogether. He showed, for example, the unwarrantedness of a correlation attempted by R. Garaudy between the heavenly hierarchy of angels and other supernatural beings in mediaeval Christian theology, on the one hand, and the structure of feudal society, on the other. Although this is a suggestion that is doubtless not to be brushed aside completely, and in favour of which there may be some presumptions, at least, it is not approaches of this kind that furnish essential explanations of the influence of an economic and social system upon an ideology. One cannot deduce directly and automatically from the former the elements of the thematic of the latter, such as, for example, the dogma of predestination, or that of the Last Judgement, any more than the rites of pilgrimage or prayer. On the contrary, it is quite certain that the thematic of ideology is endowed with a great deal of independence. It is the way in which this thematic is conceived, interpreted, animated, mobilized and experienced that is influenced to the highest degree by fluctuations in the social basis. 'Ideology-in-itself' becomes manifest in a series of 'ideologies-for-society' which are constantly changing.

In the specific case we are studying here, that of Islam, we can clearly see, if we consider the main mass of the Muslim community, that the foundation of dogmas and rites that constitutes the heart of the Muslim religion has changed little or not at all since it was first created. The development of its theological interpretation during the Middle Ages bears principally the mark of the impact of a certain system of ideas, namely, Hellenic philosophy. The theologians, philosophers and mystics carried on their reflections around themes that were emphasized by the Koran, by Greek thought, and to a smaller extent by Hindu thought, and were subjected to other influences as well, in the domain of ideas. They dealt with the great eternal problems of man's place in the world in accordance with the particular tendencies of their own minds. It is clear, nevertheless, that these problems were also considered in terms dictated by man's particular situation in mediaeval Muslim society, and that the thinkers' mental tendencies had themselves been formed in this same setting. Some problems they pondered on were those problems of a most general kind that arise for men everywhere and always, the same that concern us today, while others, which possessed validity only during a certain period of history, were the same as those that had interested the Greeks. They thought about these problems with the mental equipment of their age, as this had been constituted by history. I tried on an earlier occasion, in connection with Avicenna, to show (in too summary a fashion) how a philosophico-religious problematic could be built up on these foundations.[1] But the activity of pure thought cannot explain everything, as H. Corbin, for example, has recently asserted in a challenging way.[2] The ideological choices made were taken, too, in the course of an extremely hard and vigorous struggle, violent and non-violent, among politico-religious parties and philosophical tendencies, a struggle that found expression in an astonishing swarm of what are described as Muslim sects. The complexity of this process does not seem to allow of such simplistic correlations as gave delight to vulgar Marxists – as also to their opponents, so easy are they to demolish. Nevertheless, it is clear that Islam as it was understood in the tenth century was not exactly the Islam of the Koran, that the Islam of the eighteenth century was not that of the tenth, and so on, and that this is not without some connections with social evolution. For the present time, which we are able to know in greater detail, and in which social transformations have been more radical and more massive, the facts are obvious. While the basis of dogmas and rites which has been mentioned has hardly been modified, we can see that modern conditions have already greatly altered the way in which this basis is understood by the mass of Muslims, the way in which this religion is interpreted and lived. Secondary dogmas have been questioned, or interpreted in very different fashion, rites have been virtually abandoned, transformed, cut down, etc.

There is thus no point-by-point correlation as supposed by the view that the pan-structuralists denounce. Their attempt to carry out structural analyses (to be formalized, if possible, in mathematical fashion) of the various systems of relations that go to make up social life – but which do not constitute the totality of social life, as H. Lefèbvre has rightly emphasized – is interesting and may help a great deal towards the understanding of social life. But their assumption, in practice, of equivalence between these systems, and their conception of these systems on the pattern of language, are unacceptable. Nor is it true that any judgement as to priorities must be postponed until after these formalizations have been completed.

Our knowledge of the mechanisms of human society is doubtless inadequate. It is indeed true that this knowledge can and must be improved. But the experience accumulated by the known history of societies allows us to make hypotheses the overall validity of which can be tested both by more thorough study of past history and by the course of contemporary history and trans-historical sociological analysis. The hypotheses set out by Marx, on the basis of the historical experience accumulated down to his time, seem to me to have been broadly confirmed by subsequent studies, and the mistakes in formulation (gross, it must be admitted) made by the majority of Marxists, and by Marx himself, do not justify their being called in question.

The relations that give structure to the production and distribution of goods still seem, no less than in Marx's time, to be of fundamental importance in all known societies. 'Economic relations are no less products of the mind than theories are,' Lucien Sebag boldly wrote,[3] synthesizing the views of contemporary pan-structuralists – and, so far as this point is concerned, those of many other writers. Yes, of course, since every human activity passes through men's minds. But basic economic relations constitute the structure of the primordial task of every society. They form a system, but they are not a language and, consequently, it is highly improbable that the structure of this system will prove to be fundamentally similar to that of a language. A society is not built around 'significances' but around the essential *tasks* without which it cannot continue to exist. And, like the individual, society seeks first and foremost to survive, to perpetuate its existence (rather than its essence). It then strives (and this could be described as constituting its essential tasks of the second degree) to maximize (through competition and, it may be, through struggle) the advantages enjoyed by its members, and particularly, where the society is hierarchical, the advantages enjoyed by its most privileged members. The relations that are organized around these tasks (and not the consciousness or theorization of these relations) have a repercussion on the whole of social life. All the other forms of relations and consciousness are obliged to adapt themselves to *these* relations, whereas the converse does not apply. The organization and consciousness of society must, at the very least, not hinder fulfilment of the primary essential tasks (or of the secondary essential tasks, either, in many cases). A process that has nothing abstract about it, and which breaks down into manifold pressures from 'the nature of things', tends to eliminate those forms of organization and consciousness that, through their own evolution, might have become a hindrance to the fulfilment of these tasks. A process of the same order will 'naturally' *tend* to cause the adoption of forms of organization or consciousness that are favourable to the fulfilment of the essential tasks, especially the primary ones – but not without difficulties, conflicts and 'smudges', not without tension between the will of certain groups to perpetuate themselves and maximize their advantages and the need of society as a whole to pursue the same purpose for itself.

As regards ideology, which is our particular concern here, the relations of production are primary quite simply because they constitute the structure of society's primordial function, whereas ideologies, religion, philosophy and the rest *think about* production and reproduction, their structures, society and many other things. This thinking about man's world, in its social and natural aspects, is undoubtedly structured in accordance with 'codes' which it is of the highest interest to study. And it is indeed true that several codes are always available or possible and that the type of situation does not always predetermine the code employed or – completely – the way it is employed. But it is also absurd to suppose that studying the code does away with the need to study the text that is being coded, replacing this and rendering it superfluous, as an entire school is nowadays tending to convince a dazzled public. Society has to live and functioning can be subordinated to the requirements of 'signification' only by way of exception and momentarily. It is hard, too, to suppose that the screens which the message passes through are so opaque as to allow nothing to show through of the situation that the message translates.

The problem is not in the main a problem of correlations but one of the action, and influence, of systems of relations upon each other. It is very interesting to study comparatively the codes in accordance with which various human activities are organized, and by which the ways of carrying on these activities acquire significant value. In this way it may be possible to arrive at a reconstruction of the collective imagination of a society (R. Barthes[4]), and, more broadly, at a general semeiology and a theory of the structure of the human intellect,[5] which is of very great anthropological importance. However, while structural analysis is a very useful thing, the pan-structuralist vision of society as an aggregate of systems which ideally are deducible from this structure of the human mind needs to be fought against with all the strength at our command. The human mind does not impose its law, it proposes this law to something that is resistant to it. There is no coexistence of 'man feeding himself' with 'man clothing himself', 'man producing', 'man thinking', etc., with each activity proceeding in accordance with the rules of isomorphic codes. One and the same man is engaged in all those activities. It cannot be that in this total man these different activities of the same subject do not affect each other. 'Man thinking' thinks *also* as man engaged (in one way or another, in one place or another) in production.

The converse is true, of course. 'Man producing' is also 'man thinking'. And his thought influences the way in which he engages in production. But this cannot, except with difficulty and rarely – under favourable conditions, and respecting strict rules of action that are always subject to a natural and social datum which it can do nothing to alter in the short run – bring about any change in the relations of production, whereas the relations of production, which are always there, exert permanent pressure on ideology, and all the more strongly because this pressure is not exerted in the sphere of consciousness. If it is desired to appeal to the model provided by language, as is done by the pan-structuralists (the more readily in proportion to their ignorance of the subject), one might compare (with many precautions) the result of changes in production with that of those unconscious phonetic changes whose effect, wrote F. de Saussure, is 'unlimited and incalculable i.e. we cannot foresee where they will stop', and which bring about 'a profound disturbance in the grammatical organism'.[6] We know that, contrariwise, changes in the 'grammatical organism' themselves bring no changes into the phonic structure, apart from very rare and secondary instances. I shall come back to this analogy.

This, of course, leaves unaffected the importance of consciousness, the supremacy which in one sense it wields, its incomparable value, or even the validity of its operations. In the same way, a phonetic evolution may have led to the formation of a grammatical structure that can be judged, quite independently of the causes that have led to its appearance, in relation to its efficiency, its adaptation to the needs of communication at a given stage, or even its aesthetic value. But the question that arises here is not that of knowing, for example, whether religion is more important for the individual or for society than the economy is. A Buddhist monk may, out of conviction, commit suicide, totally destroying the complex network of physiological relations which has made up his life, and breaking through the no less complex network of social relations which has governed it. He was none the less dependent upon both sets of relations, not excluding the moment when he performed the deed by which he put an end to himself. The question here is to know *what* acts upon social evolution and the history of mankind, and *how* it acts.

The question is of fundamental importance for political action, among other things. This is why, if data are available that enable one, even if only broadly and roughly, to approach an answer to this question, it is wrong to leave free play to empiricism, and await before taking action in any direction the slow accumulation of detailed knowledge of the most delicate (and often the least relevant) mechanisms that go to make up the mechanism of society. This amounts to a shameful capitulation to unconsciousness and the most noxious factors in the life of societies. It is extremely important to know and to proclaim, first and foremost, that societies are not to be changed *solely* by working to change their consciousness, that they cannot be changed *at will*. It is not possible to rule over society any more than over nature except by submitting to its laws. In order to change societies one has to act upon the social forces they include, to create institutions that will give some of these forces the power to act, to set up the elements of a new way of functioning, and to do all this while yielding to the constraints of the natural and social *datum*, so as the better to be able to dominate them. Everything else is empty preaching and, at best, fine writing. The Prophet crieth in the wilderness. His voice becomes a force only when it encounters men who are ready to hearken to his message, to his directives for practical action: Prepare ye the way of the Lord, make straight in the desert a highway for our God.

Illusions and mystifications

Many writers, including some very intelligent ones like Raymond Aron, pronounce without much interest a general judgement ('in the last analysis') on long-term priorities such as the conclusions I have just set out are an attempt to formulate, and which in this book I have tried to base upon a specific case. That interweaving of relations with which the historian, the sociologist and the politician have to deal in their practice is in no way clarified by such broad and general considerations.

This way of thinking is very widespread, and the dogmatic schematism of many Marxists has contributed greatly to favouring its diffusion. It seems to me quite unfounded. The fundamental agnosticism that it implies (like the methodological agnosticism of the pan-structuralists) is an obstacle both to our knowledge of the dynamic of reality and to our striving to get a practical hold on reality.

This agnosticism presents itself (literarily, one might say) in two main forms: exaltation of the role of 'man' and exaltation of the eminent value of ideas and consciousness, which opens the way to proclamation (this time not at all agnostic) of their preponderant role. In both cases the resonances that are evoked appeal strongly to the romanticism that slumbers (lightly) in everyone's heart. Besides, the concrete, individual, practical advantages of this position are great, through the impression of many-sided understanding and depth of thinking that it conveys, and the facilities it offers for brilliant literary excursions, while allowing one to evade taking up embarrassing stands on anything at all. There is no call to be surprised at the predominance of this position, without even bringing in class factors, which are less relevant here than 'institutional' Marxists have claimed. I should like to look a little more closely at these themes, for the benefit of the serious reader. Everyone is free to make his own choice. One may, for instance, prefer the poetry of dreams to the cold analysis of reality. I shall at least be acknowledged to have made the opposite choice, reserving poetical enjoyment, so far as I myself am concerned, to other uses than elucidation of the springs of human history. I am addressing myself here only to those who have made the same choice, provisionally at least.

Of course man is the subject of history. We see him making this history in two different ways. On the one hand the great men who overturn established frameworks and seem to bend groups, states and societies to their will. On the other, the groups and masses whose sentiments and aspirations permanently influence the course of events.

The historical function of Marxism has been to show the limitations imposed on the action of great men by the social milieu in which they live. It has often done this to excess, and, as a rule, crude and vulgarizing formulations have been most widely employed at the level of the diffusion of ideas. These have attracted most notice and have been most combated. Yet it was easy to see that the principles of Marxist sociology did not necessarily dictate these crude simplifications, and that in their own descriptive and analytical historical writings the founders of Marxism showed themselves much more subtle. Sartre has recently held forth on the necessary coexistence of psychological explanation of the individual with sociological explanation at the level of history. Intelligent Marxists have never doubted this. One cannot understand any individual if one leaves out of account his particular temperament, his physiological and psychological tendencies as a person, his individual history, which implies his relations with his family and the micro-milieu in which he has developed.[7] And, naturally, it is not merely justified but indispensable to use the most modern methods, if these are scientifically valid, in order to undertake this analysis. But it cannot be overlooked, either, that, however great this man may be, he acts in given settings, his ideas are variations (sometimes important ones, to be sure) on the conceptions held generally in his milieu and his age, the problems he tries to solve are those that have been set him by the conditions of the time in which he lives. He can act only if he finds more or less extensive groups to accept his ideas and his leadership, that is, to recognize the value of these in relation to their own concerns. The role for which his individual history has prepared him must be acceptable to and accepted by the groups to whom he proposes that he be allowed to play it. History is a perpetual race between personages in search of a role: but also a perpetual sorting out by social groups and by events of the roles that are offered to them. On the bridge at Arcola Bonaparte's life depended on the marksmanship of a few obscure Austrian soldiers. Hoche, whose prestige might have altered the face of things, died of an illness. Here were events in which only a mystical conviction indifferent to proof can see the hand of God, or of a Providence that can be decorated at will with the most pleasing names, even the most 'materialist' ones. But it is also true that Bonaparte presented himself with ideas, intentions, an implicit or explicit programme that made him acceptable to and caused him to be welcomed by the French society of his time. He was acutely conscious of this fact, moreover, and had adapted himself accordingly. Had he remained faithful to the opinions that had led Augustin Robespierre to esteem him, he would have enjoyed, at best, the melancholy glory and posthumous influence of a Babeuf. It is necessary to distinguish between planes. The fact that it was Bonaparte who survived and succeeded, and not Hoche, for example, certainly changed a great many things. Contrary to what some Marxists have thought, it is not at all certain that the French bourgeoisie would have been able to find another Bonaparte. But certain fundamental structures could not have been changed by any individual, however great. It is not a matter of the implacable march of a deified History, as the eternal tendency of the metaphysical type of thought to go beyond its limits tends to represent it. More prosaically, the established structures make their pressure felt upon men and facts through thousands of little everyday events. These pressures allow certain acts and prevent others. The leash allowed to a great man is much longer than that of others, but if he pulls too hard on it, it strangles him.

The controversy about the role of great men is somewhat out of fashion. Nowadays the Marxist insistence on the effectiveness of social structures is more frequently countered, demagogically ('anthropogogically' would be more precise), by 'man', including under this term the psychology of the different strata, categories and social groups. The infinite variety of the mental tendencies that can be observed here, the subtle nuances that are discovered, can enable some writers to deploy their exactitude of observation and their literary talent so as to communicate to their readers an intimate understanding of these mentalities in all their tasty diversity. Others, on the contrary, can apply in their studies those complicated techniques of evaluation and measurement the precision and the zealously mathematical form of which make an extremely 'scientific' impression. All this is far from being pointless. But the descriptive stage of the investigation – however important it may be, however agreeable its literary form to the reader and for human understanding between the nations, however satisfying to the serious mind it may be in its 'scientific' form – must and can be transcended. Collective mentalities are resultants. They are the aspect in which are manifested all these forces, general and particular, that shape man – general characteristics valid for the entire human race, and also social characteristics, since we are concerned not with individuals but with socially delimited groups. The resultant changes whenever one of its components changes. Now, nothing is more baneful than to regard these collective mentalities as independent *data*, relatively permanent. The writers in question are sometimes (though not always) innocent of this way of seeing the facts, but the line taken by their research suggests (at the very least) this point of view.

The practical conclusion, which obviously affects the Marxists especially, and towards which one is so irresistibly urged, is that any social change has to be preceded by a change in these mentalities. It is true that they can be modified more or less seriously by direct interventions of the psychological type, such as education. All historical experience shows, however, that radical changes can be achieved only through action upon the social components of these mental dispositions. True, the social situation never changes completely, certain general factors always remain at work, and consequently the mentalities in question are never completely transformed. But certain social changes, often very abrupt in character, give rise to fundamental transformations that are much more thorough than those produced by decades and centuries of superficial pressure by purely psychological means. Thus, it is clear that agrarian reforms, when these have been far-reaching, have profoundly altered the mentality of the peasants who were affected by them. The French peasant who had become a perfectly independent small proprietor was no longer the mediaeval serf or even the tenant burdened with many obligations towards a feudal landlord. Industrialization has everywhere, despite its recent date in some cases, brought about radical changes in the mentality of the groups affected by it. And yet there is, on the surface, no phenomenon that is less 'psychological'. The Lebanese and Syrians, the Jews, the Italians, the Ukrainians transplanted to America, although frequently retaining a certain cohesion in each case, acquired tendencies of which they had shown no trace in their activities in their countries of origin. Examples of this kind could be multiplied endlessly.

The point is that, despite the claim made by many of the writers of this type to be getting down to the very innermost essence of man (and when they are more modest than this the public takes no notice of them), in reality they describe only the surface, and cheerfully ignore factors of major importance. The method proposed by the Marxist orientation is very often badly applied and slips easily into an inept schematism that can easily be stigmatized and ridiculed. Potentially, however, it enables us to attain the total man. To define it by a thesis of the predominant influence of the economic factor, as is done by both supporters and opponents, is, at the very least, equivocal. It would be fitting, moreover, to define what the economic factor consists in. It seems to me that the profound design of Marxism is much rather to oppose *fragmentary* conceptions of man. Those resultants, group consciousness and individual consciousness, have as an essential component the situation in which the group or the individual is placed by the role assigned to it in social production and in the redistribution of the fruits of this production. For these are, together with the biological reproduction of mankind, the essential, primordial tasks that are first of all imposed upon any and every society. Any investigation that ignores this situation or minimizes its significance is doomed to invalidity. And it is those who ignore it that mutilate man, and not the Marxist – not, at any rate, the ideal Marxist.

The role of the spirit, of ideas, is no less frequently set in opposition to the Marxist approach. Here too, in order to understand the complex intermeshing of individual and social factors, one must not allow oneself to be led astray by sonorous phrases about the supremacy and freedom of the spirit, but must carry the analysis deeper. Demagogically, Marxism is accused of making the intrinsic value of ideas depend upon their social conditioning. Yet this is not a necessary deduction from the theses of Marxism. The planes are different.

It may well be that the perfection of the rules of Aristotelian logic could only be worked out in the social atmosphere of ancient Greece. It may well be that the rules of Chinese logic, say, more or less parallel to Aristotle's, could only be deduced in a social situation distantly akin to that of Greece. This in no way prevents us from appreciating and utilizing the relatively universal value of these rules. One can equally well, in the twentieth century, derive pleasure from looking at a work of art, such as a picture by Botticelli, which it is nevertheless impossible to conceive as having been produced by any society other than that of fifteenth-century Florence. Considerations of general aesthetics can be drawn from this. But the field of vision of the present book is a different one. It is that of the historian or the politician concerned to establish the main lines of the dynamic of events. It is centred less upon 'ideas in themselves' than upon 'ideas for society', ideas in their capacity to mobilize the drives and aspirations latent in thousands or millions of men.

From this standpoint (and only from this standpoint) ideas

can be of two kinds, which enter easily enough into Mannheim's classification. On the one hand, there are 'ideological' ideas in the restricted sense of the word, that is, ideas that express and sanctify the existing situation, the interests and values of the group. They constitute the formulation of a certain *esprit de corps* (*'aṣabiyya* was the Arabic word used by Ibn Khaldūn) which arouses many-sided loyalties, particularly effective for defence of the group, for struggle against other groups, etc. On the other hand, there are the 'Utopian' ideas that go beyond the existing situation and outline a programme for transcending or overthrowing established conditions and accepted values. They too may be valid for the whole of a group – for example, in the world of today, the programme of an independence movement aiming to liberate and advance the national group. On the other hand, they may propose the break-up of the group, to create new groups on new foundations, as a universalistic religion often does at its beginning.

One has often been struck, and with justification, by the amount of devotion that has been placed at the service of these ideas, involving sacrifices that are admirable in the transcendence of individual egoism that they imply, even though this frequently occurs in the service of group egoism and causes of most questionable, even very harmful kinds. Proof has been seen in all this that it is ideas that lead the world. And yet it is quite clear that the ideas (both 'ideological' and 'Utopian') that preach the defence or the advancement of the group as it exists emanate from the situation of the group itself. British patriotism in the Kipling style served Great Britain, a society with aspirations that were defined primarily by its industrial power. The Zionists who worked to create the state of Israel defended one of the possible programmes for solving the problems posed by the situation of the Jews in Europe, and worked for the interests – as they saw them – of the Jewish group which was partly already in being and partly still to be formed. In the case of 'Utopian' ideas that aim to create new groups at the expense of existing ones, these can have mobilizing effect only if they answer to widespread aspirations that transcend the existing groups. Marxism had for a certain time the effect of dividing society in several European countries by causing the values of the international group of the proletariat to take precedence over those of the national groups. Furthermore, like primitive Christianity, it integrated into a new group, of a new type, numerous individuals who were dissatisfied with the values that their society offered them. Here the supporters of the supremacy of ideas can enjoy an advantage. It is indeed true that the individuals who join these new groups (apart from those who do so mainly as a result of their social position, like the proletarians who join the Communist movement) are impelled by motives that are often highly individual, due to unpredictable circumstances made up of the tendencies of their personal characters, their history as individuals, and the events that have affected their own particular micro-milieu. If, however, the new group succeeds in reaching substantial dimensions, and if, consequently, it acquires historical significance, this is because factors operating on a large scale – social factors, therefore – have caused to move in the same direction these numerous individual aspirations that might have been dispersed in a thousand different and conflicting directions. Hardly is it formed, moreover, than the new group, however 'ideal' its original principles, finds itself caught in the network of the relations, aspirations and interests of the society in which it is established. Willy-nilly, it has to take up a position in relation to these other groups and total societies, to lay down a programme that cannot avoid having temporal implications. Many of its new members will no longer be those who have 'left their father and their mother', and 'let the dead bury their dead', to follow the call of the Lord, or of the Idea. On the contrary, they will be persons who are Christians, Communists, etc., because they submissively follow the ideas of their parents, and they will bury their dead within the movement, with the rites that the latter prescribes. They will have the ideas of the group in which they were born, will share its values and strive to serve its interests and aspirations, even if in doing this they sacrifice themselves as individuals.

This rapid sketch of the mobilizing power of ideas leaves on one side the question of their intrinsic value. Once again, it is not my intention to deny this, and I think no intelligent Marxist ever has denied it. There are ideas that have no mobilizing power on the plane of social action, and the mobilizing ideas themselves can be looked at from a quite different angle. The ideas without mobilizing power (or which are without this in any *immediate* way) may be the most important ones culturally; thus, for example, ideas on art, on man, on nature, on whatever may be sensed or imagined to exist beyond and above nature. The value of such ideas can be appreciated regardless of their social roots and also regardless of the social role they may play, in the framework of aesthetic, anthropological, scientific, philosophical or religious theories. One may take pleasure in them, savour them, study them, enrich one's mind and heart with them without being concerned with their origin or the functions they fulfil. But this cannot serve as a reason for ignoring these roots or these functions, or for reducing this role to an epiphenomenon of no importance.

The ideas that are most remote from social practice, whatever their intrinsic value, whatever their place in an ideal system, thus cannot be without social roots. It is impossible not to accept this fact if one is not to adopt the unprovable conviction that these ideas come from somewhere beyond our world. Even in that case, moreover, it must be agreed that the supernatural power from which they emanated has taken care to adapt them to the requirements of society and of human nature. This is the theme which is being increasingly developed by open-minded religious ideologists, and they use it as a means of excusing those characteristics (past, or even present) of religious organizations and their laws which are excessively unworthy of their supposed supernatural origin.

It is open to some to interest themselves only in metahistory. Those, however, who are interested in human history will study with particular attention the points at which ideas, regardless for the moment of what their origin may be, play a part in this history, and will examine the social function they perform. Those ideas which by their nature are not in themselves capable of mobilizing people may nevertheless sometimes exert an influence on history conceived as competition and struggle between groups of men. Scientific and technical ideas, for instance, may modify the relative strength of existing groups. They will have all the greater effect in proportion as their social implications are at first unobserved and therefore do not come up against strong resistance from the established structures and the groups served by them.[8] Even, however, ideas that have no direct influence on history, understood in this sense, do enter into a system and help to form a social consciousness which determines the overall attitude of a given society towards the problems that arise in its social existence.

Ethnographers, ethnologists or anthropologists, whatever they may choose to call themselves, have stressed the *originality* of types of social consciousness. Fascinated by those which they have discovered, they are impelled to conclude that the dynamic of human history as it was deduced, apparently, from European experience by Marx and by European historians was not applicable to other societies. Could the continual struggle for power and its advantages serve, for example, to explain societies in which religious or aesthetic contemplation, or a general attitude of pacific quietism were accorded a value higher than acquisitive or predatory activity? Could the unfolding of events of the 'political' or 'economic' variety be given first place in our understanding of societies that were 'sunk in endless repetition'? The myth, the category of 'that which is sacred', dominates many societies: would it not be appropriate to envisage for these societies – and perhaps, in transposed forms, the same might apply to all societies? – a causality determining their attitudes that is founded on this domain of 'the sacred' rather than on 'interests' of a temporal, 'material' order? Some specialists in the study of great civilizations have followed this line of thought. Was it not reading Sseu Ma-tsien, the Chinese historian, that led Lucien Lévy-Bruhl to the concept of primitive mentality, one of his conceptual models that has most often been rejected and even spurned, although it marks, historically, one of the first formulations of this idea? A Belgian ethnographer wrote not long ago: 'Political science belongs to the comparative history of religions.'[9] Recently Louis Dumont, the Indologist, in a sort of manifesto, rejected in the same way the application of Western, and especially Marxist, categories to the history of India.[10] A large number of specialists in religious phenomenology, among whom Mircea Eliade is outstanding for talent and learning, have also tried to confine the very idea of history within the conceptual fields derived from Judaism (with many variants).[11] In the history of Muslim thought, Henry Corbin subordinates history to meta-history.[12] Intellectuals belonging to the peoples who descend from these great civilizations, and also those from less advanced cultures, are divided between the desire to reconstitute for themselves a history on the European model and the desire to be able to boast of something fundamentally specific and original to which the categories worked out for Europe cannot be applied. Idealization of their past, a consequence of nationalist ideology, often leads them to exclude from it those sordid mechanisms that have obviously provided the motive power of European history. It cannot be said that Europe's intellectuals (or at least those belonging to the essay-writing category, who are the only ones read by the general public), allured as they are by the social attractions of personal originality, give them very much help in seeing their problems clearly.

It is quite true that certain cultures offer no encouragement to the individual to make efforts to acquire personal possessions and maximize the advantages he enjoys, as happens in our society. Often the individual is in these cultures not even recognized as a social subject. The close imbrication of the sacred and the profane in all spheres of social life in these cultures cannot be denied. But we must note that social groups everywhere show the same tendency to defend and maximize whatever they collectively possess, whenever this is possible, by the methods of competition and, in some cases, of physical battle. The most peaceful and contemplative strive above all, by methods both sacred and profane, to maintain and perpetuate a world order which always begins with the order of their own society, even if this be seen as something sacred. Where more or less virulent competition is ruled out at the level of small groups, it often reappears at the level of the larger groups that include them. If some groups, finding themselves in a hostile environment (and it is highly improbable that at some moment or other the environment will *not* become hostile[13]), should show a propensity to collective suicide, either by action or by refusal to act, they are eliminated by a kind of social selection. Similarly, those religious groups that have adopted such ideas as refusal to reproduce, and which have applied these ideas in practice, have disappeared from the earth. The history of Christianity, with its scriptures favouring inaction and chastity, illustrates very well the continuous elimination (at least as an historical factor of any importance) of sects that endeavour to live according to these views, in favour of those that adapt themselves to the 'normal' social dynamic. At the same time, one must not confuse (as is frequently done in the study of Muslim societies) resignation to a state of submission or poverty that experience has shown to be unchangeable with a tendency to be unaware of struggles for well-being and freedom. When a break occurs in the clouds and a model of a better society, or of action to make life better, is put before them, we see that, little by little, the 'stagnating' people straighten their bent backs, become used to putting forward demands, and then to fighting for them, and insist more and more emphatically upon getting their share of bread and sunshine.

Despite all the brilliant and pretentious plays on words that bring cheap glory to their authors, there is no society without politics, that is, in the ordinary meaning of the words, without a history.[14] And history or politics treated as sacred are still history and politics. It is quite certain that acts of a political order (struggles, contests, truces) have been and will continue to be carried out for purely ideological motives, even though what is usual is an inextricable mixture of ideology and 'rational' interest – in archaic societies, of sacred and profane. It is too easy (and I quite agree that Marxist popularizers and ideologists should show a livelier awareness of this) to make of ideological motivations always a transposition, a 'reflection', of 'rational' ones. Among the most serious gaps in Marxism as it has generally been practised is inadequate appreciation of ideological levels or stages. I shall return to this point. But it is no less unjustifiable to regard this level as a primary and independent *datum*. Ideology, as has been said, cannot develop in a way that would bring it permanently into conflict with the essential requirements of the social life of the group on which it is imposed. Indeed, historical experience often shows us how more or less secondary requirements make themselves felt through ideological sublimation.

The holy war waged by the eleven tribes of Israel against the city of Gibeah, collectively guilty of a sexual crime, of 'lewdness and folly in Israel', and against the tribe of Benjamin that had identified itself with this (*Judges*, 19–21), is obviously an ideological war. The Israelites were led into it by religious duty. The regrets they subsequently express, and their efforts to restore the tribe of Benjamin by getting round their own oaths, even show that this act was in a way contrary to their feelings and interests. In another aspect, however, it was a corollary of the amphictyonic alliance that gave the people cohesion against their enemies.[15] The 'holy wars' resolved upon by another amphictyony, the pan-Hellenic council of Delphi, had political undertones that have never been obscure to anyone, and to contemporaries less than anyone else. Nothing allows us to suppose that those considerable coalitions of Greek cities which opposed the council's decisions, thus making themselves accessory to the sacrilege being denounced, contained fewer worshippers of Apollo than the states which supported the amphictyony for obvious political reasons, such as Philip of Macedon in 354 and 339.

According to Mircea Eliade, to take a different example, when the Scandinavian settlers took possession of Iceland they performed a rite. Bringing the island under cultivation was not a 'human and profane task' but a repetition of the primordial act transforming Chaos into Cosmos – of the Creation in fact. According to him, the rite was not the consecration of the practical deed but its explanation.[16] We may agree that the newcomers attached great importance to the ritual of colonizing this new land. If, however, they had come there and had not remained content to serve their various gods in their native Scandinavia, it is hard to separate this fact from the general causes of Viking expansion, for which it is idle to seek religious reasons. Snorre Sturlason himself ascribes the emigration to Iceland and the Faroes to the discontent of the Norwegians when Harald Haarfager unified the country and 'seized on the lands of Norway' (*Heimskringla*, III, 20).

The Crusades are a classical instance of political acts (wars) carried out with ideological motivation. There can be no doubt that for many, at least, of the Crusaders the force that impelled them to undertake these distant expeditions was the desire to obey God's will, this being mixed more or less, depending on the individual, with more down-to-earth motives. At the social level, however, collective and not individual, the initiative for the expeditions was taken at particular dates as a result of projects, plans and calculations that took account of extra-religious factors. Already at the time of the First Crusade the Genoese who offered their services for transporting the Crusaders to the Holy Land were thinking of the rights they would acquire in this way in the lands to be conquered. The first unorganized Crusaders spent a great deal of energy on plundering the Christian towns they passed through, and did not shrink from sacking Byzantine churches. The barons clearly gave much thought to the lands and riches they would win, and were open about this. The scandal of the Fourth Crusade, which turned aside to seize Christian lands, Constantinople and the Byzantine Empire, is a striking case. The Christian states established in Syria and Palestine conducted a policy in relation to their Muslim neighbours which aimed at retaining and increasing their territorial and other advantages through a game of inter-changeable political alliances which often disregarded religious obstacles. 'But these incessant wars', writes an authority on the history of the Crusades,

were not in the least religious wars. The annals of any feudal state of Western Europe are just as full of petty wars as are those of the crusader states. The issue was the political control of Syria . . . There were certainly as many wars between conflicting Muslim states as there were between Muslim and Christian; there were probably as many civil disputes among the Christian princes as there were wars with the infidels. Furthermore, neither religion hesitated to ally itself with men of the opposite faith against their own co-religionists. Unholy alliances of Christians and Muslims characterized the history of the Latin colonies in Syria.[17]

This writer, John L. La Monte, concludes his study with these words:

In the twelfth and thirteenth centuries, in the age of the crusades and of the *jihāds*, religion played the same role that political ideology does today; neither Christian nor Muslim, with a few notable exceptions, invoked religion save as a cloak for secular political ends, but it was the ideological banner under which men fought and for which men can always be counted on to die. Religious fanaticism, in the age of the crusades, was an important and valuable stimulant; it was seldom a prime cause or dominant motive.[18]

If we find this appreciation too sweeping, and suspect its author of prejudice, though he is a competent specialist on the period, it is enough to reflect upon a fact that is more patent and plain to everyone. Why were reiterated calls for a Crusade unsuccessful *after* the thirteenth century? There is nothing to suggest that faith was less widespread or profound then than in the eleventh and twelfth centuries. The simple fact was that the religious motives for a Crusade, which were always present, could no longer be integrated in political projects in consonance with the needs of European society in *this* period.

Were matters any different in India on account of the values peculiar to Indian civilization, as Louis Dumont claims? If so, then the examples I have given would serve only as manifestations of that famous specifically-European rationality of which Max Weber and others speak, and which would thus be seen as showing itself even under the cover of attachment to the Christian religion. For Louis Dumont, in India, 'the politico-economic sphere, cut off from values by the initial secularization of the monarchical function, remained subordinate to religion'. This is said to explain the political fragmentation and instability characteristic of Indian history, which contrasts with the country's social and religious unity.[19] It is hard to see the point of such an explanation. Many societies belonging to one and the same civilization, that is, having broadly similar social structures and institutions and religious and non-religious beliefs in common, have remained divided for long periods. It is enough to mention ancient Greece, the Sumerian world, feudal Europe, ancient Gaul, the Arab tribes before Islam, the Maya cities, and even, on a larger scale, in accordance with technical progress, the nations of present-day Europe. The reason for this is clearly to be sought in the balance of political and military forces at a certain level.

In any case it cannot be reduced to factors that are specific to India. The history of that sub-continent is obviously made up, as elsewhere, of political struggles for power between various centres, victories of the strongest followed by unification on a more or less extensive scale, then break-ups due to centrifugal forces, in which we see at work local aspirations to power which seize as soon as they can the opportunity of winning advantageous independence. This was even given theoretical form in the Arthashāstra, Kauṭilya's political treatise, which is emphasized by Louis Dumont himself. 'If', he writes, 'we try to deduce from the Arthashāstra a definition of politics, we find something like: the exertion of force in pursuit of interest and the maintenance of order.'[20] An excellent definition, provided we add that the maintenance of order also forms part of the pursuit of interest.

Very well: but this wholly secular and non-sacred political activity was subject as a whole to religion. What does that mean? All societies acknowledge the supremacy of religious and, in the modern period, ideological values. The Kshatriyas of India ideally recognized the supremacy of the Brahmins, just as the Kings and lords of Europe recognized that the clergy were nearer to God than they were. This did not prevent them from engaging in conflict on the temporal plane with certain priests. In India, writes Dumont, 'the King often appears . . . as a sort of policeman charged with maintaining public order and receiving a share of the crops in return for his services – almost as a servant'. And he recalls the ideal distribution of the harvest, on the threshing floor, 'where the King stands next to the servants'.[21] If we refer to Dumont's own description of this share-out we learn that the King first receives his share, amounting to one-sixth or one-third, then, in some cases, the 'proprietor', and that 'the servants or helpers who serve the household . . . each have the right to a certain number of measures of grain: the Brahmin, the laundryman or the barber, along with the smith, the cartwright and the rest'.[22] It must strike the simple-minded reader of Dumont's book that the Brahmin is more closely associated with the servants than the Kshatriya is. 'Standing next to' the servants turns out to signify taking a strikingly larger share of the surplus than theirs.

Of course the Brahmin regards the King as an inferior personage. The Brahmins and Mandarins of Europe, in their professorial chairs or at their café tables, are perfectly free to hold the same opinion about their own politicians. But this does not alter the fact that, in India as in Europe, it is the politicians who administer the communities, deciding between war and peace and making the organizational decisions that give structure to their social life and bring about changes therein. These decisions are, of course, influenced by their ideology and their total culture. No less obviously, they take account first and foremost, always and everywhere, of the relations of strength between power-centres, and tend to protect and maximize the advantages and privileges of the society represented – of its leading stratum in the first place, and of its head in absolutely first place. And these decisions which have profound repercussions in the total life of the groups concerned cannot but have an influence, in the short or the long run, upon ideologists and even upon ideologies. It is precisely because they do not *immediately* affect the ideological domain, because their consequences remain unperceived, that these decisions can be made. Everyone agrees that the religion of an agricultural people possesses features different from those of a people who live by food gathering or by hunting. And yet the adoption of agricultural pursuits by food-gatherers or hunters was a decision in which ideology played no part. The ideological consequences became apparent only later.

Social consciousness may thus assume many different forms. It can exercise, in the most ideal forms, a powerful influence over the decisions taken by whole societies and by groups. It can give a specific orientation to their attitude towards the problems that confront them. On the one hand, however, one cannot deny its roots in social reality, while, on the other, among the decisions that *must* be taken there figure in the front rank those that concern the survival of the group or of the society, through its activity or its passivity in relation to other groups or other societies outside, and in relation to its essential internal activity. The latter means, in the case of whole societies, the production and reproduction of their social existence; for the privileged functional groups organized around production and distribution, it means perpetuating the situation that brings them these advantages. The decisions taken may be judicious or stupid, pregnant with consequences, either good or bad, sometimes even self-destructive. In any case they cannot be understood except in relation, first of all, to these essential tasks of any and every human society. These tasks can indeed be left out of consideration in order to think only of man's ideal or aesthetic activity in itself, for example. Not, however, if we are trying to grasp the dynamic of historical events. And this dynamic, reacting upon the total fate of individuals and groups, cannot be overlooked if we are to understand the evolution of systems of ideas themselves. Archimedes may despise the soldier who interrupts him, and prefer to go on pursuing the solution of his theorem. The soldier kills him, all the same, and puts back by a thousand years, perhaps, mankind's solving of this theorem. That is perhaps of no interest to the pure mathematician of today, who finds this theorem already solved. It *is*, however, of interest in relation to the history of mathematics, and thereby, to the general history of mankind.

The harmful nature of the conceptions I have been attacking, for our comprehension of the dynamic of history, both on the plane of knowledge and on that of action, is particularly well seen in the sphere that concerns me here, that is, the current history of the Muslim world. It is doubtless not good manners to mention this fact. I shall do so nevertheless. Only fifteen years ago, the great majority of Islamic scholars, followed by all those who were impressed by their competence as specialists, judged of the future of the Muslim world from the phenomenology of *homo islamicus* or the dogmas of Islam. It was therefore supposed that the Muslim, attached as he was to values of a sacred character, thinking in categories that were not those of the European, being unaware, for example, of the 'teleological-historical' conception of time (an expression I borrow from C. A. O. Van Nieuwenhuijze),[23] could not be attracted by socialistic ideologies, such as Marxism in its institutional form of Communism. Were not these ideologies derived from the European mentality, putting in the forefront the redistribution of material goods? After fifteen years we can record that the views of future development held by the most schematic and most grossly dogmatic of Marxists (of whom I was one), an insignificant and despised group, have turned out to be a great deal closer to the real evolution of events than those held by the 'idealists' in question. We have seen the socialist ideology lay hold, in various ways, of nearly all the countries that are called 'Muslim'. Communism itself has found many supporters in some of these countries. The measures taken against it themselves show that the political rulers (the best experts in this matter) have no confidence in the supposed inaccessibility of their peoples to the propaganda of this movement. It may be said that the Muslim peoples have borrowed from socialism what it suited them to borrow; I have indeed myself said this. But what they have taken from it, what they have seen in it, is not, for example, that which corresponded to an alleged specific way of perceiving time and space – it is above all that which answered to their concrete aspirations to shake off domination, exploitation and oppression and to maximize their well-being and their power to manage their own lives in their own way. It is those political leaders who have based themselves on these tendencies in the most consistent and convincing way that have won the support of the masses. J. Berque says that it is the boldest hypothesis, the most stirring idea, the most striking symbol, representing more things than any other, that carries the day.[24] This may be true, but only within definite limits. The sign that triumphs is the one that signifies *certain* things, and not just any things, with the greatest force, and which is wielded by organizations that employ the most adequate means, and so on. The struggle is not waged in the empyrean of 'significant systems', but on earth, through men who fall for *certain* slogans only. It is highly important to be clear about this.

Man is a totality, and it is true that, if we are to understand history, nothing in man, no aspect of his being or of his behaviour must be overlooked. It is no less true that he makes up his mind on the basis of ideas, forms of consciousness, conceptions of the world that are frequently expressed through signs, symbols and slogans. The general springs of human and even animal psychology make themselves felt in everything that he does. Cultural tradition strongly influences all his attitudes. But it is extremely harmful to mix up all these different planes, and proclaim or suggest that 'everything is operative in everything else', with nothing discernible but partial structures that are related to each other only by formal analogy. The contribution made by Marxism, where historico-sociological analysis is concerned, has been to start (rather crudely, to be sure) bringing a little order among all these levels. This contribution needs to be made more precise, refined and perfected: it should not be rejected out of hand. Marxist schematism, which has so often been condemned, is a necessary stage. Many shades of meaning are sacrificed in this first stage, and it is bad that a lot of people get stuck at this stage. On the other hand, however, to try and keep everything on the same plane, though it may enable one to compose brilliant descriptions, is not helping knowledge to progress.

Here, once more, the model of language, with which contemporary sociologists are so infatuated, tells, if anything, against them. Within the total system of a language, as has been already mentioned in passing, the various partial systems do not all play the same role, with the same effect or influence. The phonic system, the necessary building material of every language, has its own evolution: the causality of this has not yet been very well elucidated, but we know that it acts on everything else in a way that is as formidable as it is unconscious. No language can do without a grammatical system. *This*, however, has only a very limited effect on the phonic system. It is more than likely that, within the total system of society, each of the partial systems also has its own specific effect, role and influence. The system of relations of production and reproduction also evolves through a succession of changes of which we are hardly, or even not at all, aware – changes that are often inevitable, and the formidable consequences of which are in any case rarely foreseen. It can be totally and consciously changed only through a revolutionary decision of the catastrophic type, just as when a people goes over from one language to another (and consequently to another phonic system); not without, in this case too, unforeseen consequences and an unforeseeable influence from the substratum that has been abandoned. This revolutionary decision can itself be understood, moreover, only as the outcome of a previous total evolution in which spontaneous modifications effected in the old system of production played a major role. Man's stature and the eminent value of man's consciousness gain nothing, but quite the contrary, from wilful refusal to see the factors that condition them. The desire to transcend does not rule out clear thinking, and the ethics of transcendence demands this.

Islam and socialism

The states of the Muslim world are today at precisely one of those decisive moments when it is open to them to choose the path they will take. General decolonization, abandonment by the Western imperialisms of methods of direct domination, and competition between the two great economic systems of industrial society have brought about a revolutionary situation in which it is possible to break with the past, to some extent, and start again on a fresh footing. Everywhere the ruling groups are in a position to choose – within certain limits and under certain conditions.

They must respond to the aspirations of the masses they are supposed to be leading, the aspirations that are responsible for the social ebullition that has brought these groups to power. What I have just said can easily be verified. These masses, in many cases resigned for centuries, or even for thousands of years, to oppression and want, have suddenly discovered the existence of models of societies that enjoy greater well-being and freedom than they do, and that furthermore claim to be advancing along a road that is continually bringing increase in these eminently desirable values. The masses are demanding ever more loudly to see at least a movement in this direction, and it is no longer possible to ignore their cry.

The most obvious and palpable kind of freedom, the ending of direct foreign domination, has been secured more or less everywhere. The forms of subjection that survive, both externally and internally, are more subtle, and almost invisible. In any case, their weight is not felt as too great a burden after the immense relief brought by national liberation. The conquest of relative well-being is now everywhere at the top of the agenda. This aspiration is linked, moreover, with the desire for freedom. In face of the power of expansion and attraction shown by the European–Soviet–American models of industrial society it is becoming plain to everyone that the other societies in the world are confronted with a choice that cannot be evaded: either to let themselves be dominated economically by the industrial societies (and economic subordination inevitably entails political subordination, whether disguised or open, despite all the verbal protests that may be made against neo-colonialism) or to become industrial societies themselves.

If the latter choice is made (and everything impels them towards it, even when the objective conditions are not at all favourable), they are again confronted with two fundamentally different possibilities. Contrary to what is thought by European economists who would like to escape from the dilemma of 'capitalism or socialism', and by so many Third-World ideologists who would like to give a 'national' colouring to their economic programmes, there is no third way.

The possible number of economic structures, if we confine ourselves to their essential features, is not unlimited. In the pre-capitalist stages, many more or less different modes of production could be juxtaposed or articulated over an area that varied as regards territory covered or sectors involved. The power of capitalist economy has reduced the other modes of production to secondary roles within definitely limited sectors. None can stand up to the competition of capitalist economy, inside a capitalist socio-economic formation, unless protected by special circumstances, and it is the capitalist sector, even when this is limited so far as volume of production is concerned, that tends to give direction to the entire economic and social life of such a community. Every extensive society where production-capitalism establishes itself (and which refuses to be a mere external appendix to a foreign capitalist zone) tends to evolve into a capitalist socio-economic formation if the socialist choice is not made at a certain moment, so as to halt this evolution.

Industrialization will be carried out either by groups of free capitalists or by the state, or under the latter's control. When industrialization is well advanced, the main economic choices will be made either by the free capitalists or by the state, or else, under the state's protection and under its necessary supervision (for a long period, at least), by groups of individuals who possess no capital of their own. Infinite variation is possible in the proportion of capitalist enterprises, state enterprises and non-capitalist enterprises protected by the state (they cannot develop to any considerable level without this protection). Infinite variation is possible, too, in the limits imposed by the state upon the free activity of the capitalist and non-capitalist enterprises. First of all, however, the essential question governing the evolution of the economy as a whole is the extent to which the free capitalists, in so far as they exist, are able to impose their will, their principal economic choices, upon the state. After that, the functioning of the overall economic system depends above all on the proportions of the society's economic activity provided by these sectors and, especially, on their influence over the ruling authority.

Every other variable is secondary so far as the general orientation of the given society is concerned. Domination by private capitalists or by the state (whether itself managing the enterprises or entrusting them to non-capitalists) entails enormous consequences for the whole of social life. Political factors, influenced by social life and consciousness, may impel the society in question to choose one road rather than the other. Once the choice has been made, however, it is not possible to avoid the consequences that follow from it.

There is thus no economy that is Muslim or Christian, Catholic or Protestant, French or German, Arab or Turkish, Dionysian or Apollonian. All that sort of thing can, at most, amount to superficial colouring given to the fundamental economic choices. National characteristics may contribute interesting variations to the way in which the systems operate: they cannot, however, on their own transform essential foundations of these systems.

The capitalist choice usually has no need of a mobilizing ideology that puts before a whole people a programme to be carried through. The profit motive is indispensable – but it is also sufficient so far as the capitalists are concerned. The masses are not asked for their opinion. Doubtless the orientation of a part of society towards the hunt for profit presupposes a certain state of mind, a mentality that does not appear inevitably in *every* society. The capitalist spirit is a fact. It presents rather different aspects, to be sure; but among the merchants of

Genoa or Venice in the Middle Ages, the shipowners and bankers of Amsterdam during the Renaissance, the pioneer industrialists of the Industrial Revolution in eighteenth-century Britain, the financial magnates of the imperialist era, and the American businessmen of today, we find the same feverish chase after profit, the same quasi-ascetic dedication of their lives to this pursuit, and numerous other common features that are more or less derivative from it. The same demon has taken possession of them all. And certainly it is not enough, in a country and among people who do not know this fever, to set up banks, factories and counting-houses, and cry out, trumpet-voiced: 'Get rich!', in order to develop this spirit.

Yet this spirit is not born of nothing, nor is it born, as Max Weber thought, of another spirit. The capitalist spirit existed among a small nucleus of individuals. It was social, political and economic conditions that enabled it to develop and, at a certain moment, to take over the whole of society in Europe and North America. The Europeans, who complained (not without hypocrisy) of the absence of the spirit of enterprise among capital-owners in the countries they descended upon and in some cases colonized, failed to see, or chose not to see, that conditions in these countries were such as to break in advance all the springs of the capitalist impulse, and that, furthermore, their own presence and the laws they imposed, although they removed some obstacles, were quick to install others, which were often more effective. If the conditions are provided for a capitalist enterprise to be able to make an interesting profit, for the capitalist to keep this profit and to make it multiply with a certain degree of security, for competition from foreign capitalism to be sustained with a certain minimum degree of likelihood from the start that the native capitalist will not be crushed by it – then we see the social obstacles constituted by the traditional mentality and the religious and moral bans gradually fading away, the laws themselves being got around, the success of the first pioneers of the foreign models encouraging others to emulate them, the demon of capitalist profit invincibly laying hold of ever wider sections, and the grip of the system becoming, through its incomparable dynamism, ever more extensive and powerful. This is what we have seen happen in Japan, China and India, and begin to happen in the Muslim world, despite the bigger obstacles introduced there by a stronger European competition, safeguarded by commercial and other treaties imposed by force, rather as in Latin America.

Did the previously existing mentality or consciousness play, then, no part at all in this choice? That is not what I am saying. In India, it is true that the Hindus threw themselves with more ardour and earlier than the Muslims into the adventure of capitalism, as in Europe the Protestants before the Catholics. But it was not religious precepts in the pure state that were involved here. The choice made between religions by the peoples of Europe in the sixteenth century did not result simply from convictions produced by comparative study of the Gospels, Papal bulls, and the writings of Luther and Calvin. Profound social factors and even the fortunes of war played a much bigger part. The confessional division corresponded to a large extent to different social situations. In India, where choice hardly entered into the matter, Hindu and Muslim societies were different on many other planes besides that of religious belief. The resistance opposed to development of the capitalist spirit by the pre-existing mentality of a society, inextricably bound up with the conditions of its social life, is in varying degrees strong and effective. But the establishment within it, or on its borders, of capitalist economy, with the legal and economic conditions that enable the latter to develop, exercises upon this society a pressure that proves eventually to be irresistible. God and the gods, rules for living, sacred or semi-sacred moralities, all in turn bow down and in the end prostrate themselves before triumphant Mammon.

Capitalist structures fighting to strike root in a non-capitalist milieu may develop ideologies that are 'utopian' in the sense of Mannheim's classification. But these are not *economic* ideologies, they are *political* ones. The call is not made to struggle for an extension of a profit-making economy or of the economic conditions for its development. Either, as in Europe in the eighteenth or nineteenth centuries, what is called for is a fight for political structures favourable to this development, but which imply political and extra-political values that are universal: liberty and equality, following a dynamic that Marx explained in masterly fashion, notably in his *On the Jewish Question*. Or else, it is a question of a nationalist ideology in which capitalist development figures as one element, as in the European imperialist ideologies of the nineteenth century and in Kemalist Turkey in the twentieth.

The economic ideology of capitalist society is an 'ideological' ideology in the strict sense, according to the same classification made by Mannheim. It idealizes and transposes reality. It can evoke a certain resonance in the industrial societies of the present time in Europe and North America. It can persuade those who actually gain from this economy that their privileged situation is good, just and in conformity with the nature of things. It can also persuade a numerous stratum which is produced by these societies in a developed phase, enjoying comparative plenty, that they live in the best of all possible social structures and that the opportunities of social advancement for its members are better than they could be in any other type of society. Even the unlucky ones may be convinced of this, if their material advantages are sufficient and if the rival models that exist are generally unattractive.

In the Third World, however, these factors do not apply except to a narrow stratum of society which is the only one gratified by the capitalist economy. For the great majority of the peoples, including those strata that correspond broadly to the middle and petty bourgeoisie of capitalist societies, the fundamental aspiration on the economic plane is to acquire the standard of living of industrial society, a highly attractive model which is always being put before them through a host of media: films, newspapers, radio, the presence of prosperous, well-dressed foreigners who possess means of life that seem fabulous. The political ideology of internal liberty and equality becomes of secondary interest to the hungry masses and the officials or office-workers whose lives are miserable in comparison with the splendours, real or supposed, of the industrial societies. The nationalist ideology soon loses its capacity to arouse enthusiasm when there are no longer any external enemies and the privileges of one's own compatriots, the profiteers of capitalism, become ostentatious.

The poor mobilizing power of capitalist ideologies has been

well seen in countries such as Turkey, Iran, and monarchical
Iraq previous to July 1958, where the rulers thought they could
go forward along the road of a regular economic progress that
would, in the end, increase the general welfare through the
free working of liberal capitalism encouraged by the state itself,
as we have seen above. Later they endeavoured to regularize
this evolution by means of non-coercive planning – of the
French type, for instance – leaving great freedom of decision to
the private capitalists. They were helped in this by the Western
capitalist powers, especially by the United States. They thought
they could do without ideology and were even extremely distrustful of it, or still are, even in Turkey, where the Kemalist
ideology had originally brought about a general mobilization
on a mainly nationalist basis. Any ideological stirring-up of
the masses, even in a reactionary way, seemed, correctly
enough, to the ruling classes to involve dangers to their continued domination. In Iraq this led to the revolution of 14 July
1958 and the consequent collapse of the plans – far from negligible from the strictly economic standpoint – of the Development Board.[25] Elsewhere, the groups that have taken over
dream seriously of a new start for radical economic reforms that
would imply the mobilization of the masses, and consequently
construct ideologies suitable for securing this mobilization.
They have observed that pronounced economic progress
demands participation by the whole people in a vigorous effort,
involving substantial individual sacrifices. This seems to them,
very rightly, to require a new share-out of the benefits of this
progress, and, in so far as this would not be felt very much at
the start, the stirring up of the people by means of a mobilizing
ideology that exalts the effort called for and its results, promising
a radical reform of the social structure at the expense of established privileges. Here arises the problem of the choice of this
ideology. It is clear to everyone now (except to some European
and American economists and sociologists) that the ideology to
be adopted cannot ignore the essential consideration of an
increase in the people's well-being.

   This is how it comes about – naturally, so to speak, impelled
by the force of circumstance – that the second, the socialist
choice, is the one dictated. This choice, let it be emphasized,

owes nothing or almost nothing to the pre-existent spirit, the specific mentality, of the people who make it. In some countries there was a revolt of the masses against a régime bound up with the capitalist economy that oppressed them, and this revolt was canalized by élites professing the socialist creed, under the influence of the Marxist ideology that the Communist movement has spread throughout the world. In other countries the rulers, seeking to liberate their country and advance it, have seen that, in the specific political social conditions in which they found themselves, attachment to the capitalist system jeopardized this liberation and did not allow progress to go forward far or fast enough.

In contrast to the capitalist choice, the socialist choice has need, as has been shown, on the economic plane, of a 'utopian', mobilizing ideology. Capitalist economy spreads step by step, automatically, so to speak, once the necessary conditions are provided. Individuals apply themselves to it one after another when the prospects of profit are sufficiently attractive to them, and their propensity to take advantage of these prospects has overcome any mental obstacles that may have stood in the way. With the socialist, or statist, economy it is not like this. Such an economy has to be organized socially, collectively. The advantages that the individual is to obtain from it are not always obvious. In the first phase they are frequently non-existent, and can be conceived only at the level of collective interest and over a fairly long period of time. Consequently, the mobilization of individuals calls for the combined influence of an ideology and of material incentives. The latter can always, or almost always, be relied on to achieve their object. This needs to be stressed. But receptivity to ideology varies in degree depending on the pre-existent type of social consciousness, which one can, of course, strive to modify, though with varying facility, and a diversity of precautions and intermediate stages. As for the other component, the amount of the immediate advantages allowed has to be bigger or smaller in inverse proportion, broadly speaking, to the power of mobilization that the ideology itself possesses, so far as a given people is concerned.

No one denies the need for an ideology if socialist construction is to be undertaken. This ideology must imply the necessity

of this construction, but must go beyond that. It is possible, if
need be, to arouse the people to make a big effort during a
limited period, so as to carry out a 'great leap forward' from
which the people will gain, without adding motives of an ideal
order to this prospect. Even so, it is important that the effort
demanded shall not be excessive, and that those who make it may
reasonably hope that there is some likelihood of their benefiting
from it themselves. This case is a rare one, however, and even if
it occurs, people may prefer a wretched but calm way of life to
an inordinate effort the results of which are speculative. The
usual rule is, in spite of everything, to set up ideal aims (often
disproportionately high) for every collective effort. We see this
happening in wars, even in those with the most sordid motives.
Moreover, the ideologies with the greatest mobilizing power
have been ideologies of struggle, or at least of competition. Man
is so made – at any rate, man as we know him, the man with whom
we are dealing – that he is ready to exert himself above all in
order to crush his enemies, or outstrip his rivals.

The ideal aims to which the ideologies we know have related
themselves are broadly of three types: the greatness of the
'national' groups, the greatness of God, the greatness of mankind. In practice, of course, the two latter motives are often
reduced to the greatness of the group (national or other) which
is regarded as the only one that is really fighting for God and for
mankind. In principle one can appeal in the name of these aims
for sacrifice in struggle and for sacrifice in everyday life – but
the latter is especially feasible if everyday life is presented as
being a struggle. Economic construction can be related to one
or other of these three aims; but only on certain conditions.

If economic construction proceeds according to the accepted
norms of a given society, without any intention of overthrowing
the old-established structures, there is no reason why it cannot
be conceived as bound up with the three types of aim mentioned
above, namely, the nationalist ideology, the religious ideology or
the universalist-humanist ideology – or even more than one of
these at once. In that event, however, the behaviour required
will be of the conformist type. Conformism has less mobilizing
power than revolt, at least when no external struggle comes in to
give it virulence. Its drive is easily checked by realization that

there are privileged persons, profiteers of the ideology, hypocrites who use it as a mask for pursuit of their own individual egoistic aims. Moreover, each of these ideologies goes beyond economic construction. It is possible to choose to serve the nation, God or man, by other means. It is hard for the individual to find other means of serving the nation if no struggle looms on the horizon, and if the role he has chosen to play in society is not outside the field of economic construction. But one may prefer to serve God, for example, by mystical contemplation and mankind by charitable activity, as a monk or a doctor. This is why the nationalistic ideology is, broadly speaking, that which is best adapted to an economic development of this type.

If economic construction is conceived as overturning the accepted norms, then the ideology, implying as it does a struggle, is more virulent, more attractive, through the element of unexpectedness that it contributes; in short it has greater mobilizing power. The privileged ones, the profiteers, the hypocrites (there are always some) can more easily be despised as so much unavoidable rubbish, the blots and smudges around a great deed. They will be transcended by history as it moves onward to fulfilment; a later stage will see them condemned and swept away. A project like this, however, implies resistance from groups and individuals whom the new structure that is envisaged dooms to loss of their established position, their privileges, or even simply of their habitual way of life, their material and moral comfort. These individuals or groups nevertheless form part of the national or religious community and may outwardly show devotion to the nation or to God. It is, of course, possible to denounce them as objectively betraying these values; but more difficult. On the other hand, it is easy to denounce them as traitors to the cause of mankind, as deserters from the struggle to build a society more favourable to the free development of the potentialities of all its members, and of mankind in general, as foes of liberty and equality. This is why a universalist-humanist ideology is the one best adapted to *this* type of economic construction, which does, after all, imply a class struggle. The 'reactionary' can easily claim to be a good Frenchman, Chinese or Arab, Christian or Muslim. It is not so easy to refute him on this plane. But, by definition, he cannot be a good 'revolutionary'.

This is indeed what we see more concretely, in the facts, when we examine the claim put forward by some to make a religion, Islam, the banner of socialist economic construction in the Muslim countries. The Muslim religion seems poorly fitted to play this role.

Mobilization of the masses, by means of ideologies, for economic ends of a new type is a modern phenomenon. In former times no one thought of carrying out a radical transformation of economic structures. If the masses of a given society were called upon to work for its improvement in its existing form, this work was conceived either as carrying on with their normal activities, but at a more rapid pace, or as conquering new lands, to be exploited in the same way as the old, or the subjection of other populations, whose activity would be directed to the service of this society. If some small groups did rise up in revolt within a total society, this they did in order to obtain a bigger share of the social product, or the advantages resulting from participation in power, and not in order to transform the society's mode of activity. If new groups did appear that were called upon to organize themselves in a way that broke through the established frameworks, their aim was to create a limited society specializing in a cult required by the will of supernatural powers, or else to transform the whole of existing society in accordance with this divine will. It was very unusual, however, for the latter to require a radical transformation of the established modes of production and reproduction.

Islam has not in the past sought to mobilize the masses for economic ends. It first called upon certain Arabs to break with their tribal ties and enter into a new community destined to serve God. And God required of his followers that they lead a pious and virtuous life, without any alteration in their habitual and normal economic activity. He asked no more when, soon afterward, entire tribes, and then individuals not tied to tribal life, entered the community. If the community's economic life changed, this happened as an effect of temporal events: conquests, and specialization of production within a 'common market' of world dimensions. In these new circumstances a pious and virtuous life required the fulfilment of new duties. These were defined in accordance with the new economic structures, and they were, of course, sanctified as having been laid down by God and his Prophet. Thenceforth Islam became an ideology that demanded a certain form of conduct from the individual. On the collective plane it preached the perpetuation of social life in the form that it had already assumed, merely insisting that it function in accordance with morality. This had the usual degree of success and failure met with by demands of that sort; in other words, failure preponderated heavily over success. On the collective plane in its *external* aspect, Islam became an ideology of the nationalist type, mobilizing the Muslim communities for defence against the non-Muslims, and in some cases, when circumstances were favourable, for aggression against the latter. The sectarian forms of Islam reproduced on a smaller scale the evolution of the Muslim movement as a whole, often with revolutionary demands, but in general without any other programme of economic transformation beyond the strict observance of morality and piety in the carrying on of everyday activities, and so without any radical transformation of structures. Finally, those Muslims who travelled into non-Muslim countries, spreading Muslim values by example rather than by preaching (for the infrequency of missionary effort in the ordinary sense is one of the characteristic features of this religion), often induced new adherents to adopt their way of economic life, which was capitalistic trade. Nowhere do we find any mobilization for an economic transformation on the scale of society.

This historical experience does not, any more than the theoretical analysis set out above, encourage us to see the Muslim religion in the present period as a factor likely to mobilize the masses for economic construction, especially when the latter is seen to be necessarily revolutionary, destroying established structures. That Islam is the only factor in the name of which one can mobilize the poor, who are inaccessible to any other ideology, is declared by activists such as the Algerian ex-Minister Amar Ouzegane. He records the attachment to Islam manifested by the poor peasant masses of his own country. This attachment is an established fact, just as in other parts of the

Muslim world, and there is no question of attacking it. To believe, however, that it must inevitably prevent the masses in question from being susceptible to other appeals on other planes is an illusion. It must be seen that this attachment, before being an expression of faith, and although it may indeed lead many souls towards values that are strictly religious in character, is none the less fundamentally a *national*, and a *class*, phenomenon. The poor saw in Islam that which distinguished them from the foreign oppressor and from the Europeanized upper strata, disloyal in deed or in spirit. The Muslim 'clergy', largely poor, and treated without respect by the occupying power, faithful to the values of the traditional society in which they lived, were their own people, providing them with leadership and speaking to them in their own language, a language at their own level. With the coming of independence, however, the 'clergy' gradually rises in the social scale. The (more or less exploiting) upper strata increasingly proclaim their attachment to Islam, in a frenzied search for an ideological guarantee for their social and material advantages. The more successful the 'clergy' become in raising their standard of living, or even merely in becoming integrated in the nation, the less will Islam serve as an exclusive slogan for the disinherited.

The latter may be ready – perhaps for a long time yet, in certain regions and so far as certain strata are concerned – to react violently against those who attack their traditions (whatever these may be) or against those who are denounced to them as intending to do this. They may follow ideologists who sanctify the squalor and poverty in which they live, so long as nobody takes it into his head quite simply to rid them of these conditions. But one must not fall dupe to the usual illusion of travellers and intellectuals; faced with a way of life that seems to them inaccessible to the categories they are familiar with, and populations their dialectic cannot grasp (they are sometimes ignorant of the language altogether, and always of the people's speech), they are quick to suspect the existence of a monolithic block, self-enclosed, which nothing can cause to evolve. This is an illusion shown up by the entire historical experience of the last hundred years. In fact, only a short period is often needed, if a radical change takes place in living conditions, to bring about far-reaching changes in forms of behaviour that have remained fixed for thousands of years.[26] The disinherited (and the rest) will not be mobilized by just any form of Islam; what above all needs to be offered to them, with or without Islam, is a future prospect that means progress in the conditions under which they live. They will mobilize themselves if this prospect is sufficiently close, practicable and attractive. A link with exalting ideas-that-become-forces may, in addition, add zeal to this mobilization, making men ready for a certain period to sacrifice their immediate interests as individuals upon the altar of the collective progress that lies ahead – provided this is not too distant and does not seem too fantastic. It is above all essential that the sacrifices demanded of them should not seem excessively one-sided, that they do not see privileged persons evading or even profiting by the sacrifices they make, even while boasting of their virtue, piety or devotion. At the moment when I am writing these lines we can see the Syrian peasants of the plain of Ḥomṣ and Ḥamāh, disinherited if anyone is, and convinced that they are good Muslims, coming forward to defend by force the government of a party that proclaims its secular character and whose chief ideologist is a Christian Arab, under attack from the traders and craftsmen of the towns who are strongly backed by the *ulemas*. The Friday sermons of the latter have little effect on these disinherited ones, as compared with the concrete benefits that the Baath party promised them and that it has begun to give them.

It is not possible to conceive the role of the Muslim religion as an ideology (whether of the mobilizing variety or not) in the present period otherwise than in a context of class struggle. The Muslim world is specific but it is not exceptional. It will not escape from the general laws that govern human history. Its future is a future of struggles – between classes (or, more broadly, between social groups) and between nations (or, more broadly, between total societies). These struggles may be mitigated or appeased; it may be that they can be made to take the form of peaceful contests. The ideologist will perhaps be able to hover above the battle, turn his attention away from it, pursue his researches or his meditations outside or beyond these struggles, and declare that they are of no importance. Appeals to Allah, to the Muslim soul, to the solidarity of the traditional *umma* or of the nation may disguise these struggles, always to the advantage of certain groups – but they will not succeed in suppressing them.

Struggles between political clans lacking any difference in social basis may, in circumstances such as the first period of Algerian independence (as also, for example, in Russia in the years following Stalin's death) take the place of social struggles for a while. As soon, however, as democratization, even of a very relative kind, takes place, and a political class, even if it be not very large, starts to play a part, the conflicting clans are obliged to equip themselves with programmes, and these usually make play with the advantages that various social groups either do, or do not, enjoy.

A period devoted above all to a form of economic construction that implies a radical overturning of old structures cannot proceed without class struggles, even when the ruling group tries to blur the fact by proclaiming that it is working for the common interest (which may be true). The rulers will strive to lay the foundations of industrialization, the infrastructure of an independent modern country, to create cadres at all levels, and therefore to develop education and to fight against under-employment and poverty, factors of weakness and dependence for any state that wishes to be independent and strong. On the one hand, however, this cannot be done without encroaching on the interests and habits of the beneficiaries of the old structure. Hence a struggle has to be waged against them, which implies the use of ideologies by both sides. On the other, this normally implies, as we learn from the experience of history, that the group in power, and the class made up of those to whom it entrusts the levers of control, benefit from privileges arising from the power they possess, as also from the material advantages they enjoy.

For a certain time, perhaps quite a long one, these privileges may not provoke any very marked challenge. If the ruling group carries out its promises, if the general standard of life of the majority gradually improves, if the essential values to which the nation is attached are not betrayed; if, moreover, a certain social mobility is ensured, enabling the less fortunate to make their way at least into the periphery of the ruling circle, then the advantages held by the latter may for a long time seem to most people to be a deserved reward for the function they perform, which is accessible, moreover, to all capable and ambitious individuals. However, the less favoured classes will, through the activity of the rulers, increasingly rise to a level at which their demands will grow, together with their means of backing these demands. It is difficult, with our experience of history, to suppose that the more favoured strata will yield gracefully to these demands (which may in part be utopian). The advantages enjoyed by these more favoured strata will progressively appear less as a functional reward than as manifestations of a structure of privilege and exploitation. Here, too, there will probably be competition, challenge and struggle. Despite Mao Tse-tung's formula, which is only a pious wish, nothing guarantees that these contradictions, at first non-antagonistic, will not develop to the stage of antagonism, which may be violent. These struggles will doubtless be marked by the usual to-ings and fro-ings. The authorities may succeed in calming them down by means of concessions, or in inflaming them by clumsy actions; external struggles may cause them to become of secondary concern. They will nevertheless continue to be there, latent and subjacent. This seems to be valid regardless of the ideological context, whether in societies adhering to a religious creed or in those professing a humanistic faith. It is improbable, however, that ideologies will fail to play a part in these struggles when they arise.

The 'utilization' of Islam as an ideology is conceivable only in this context. How can it be seen as a factor of struggle against the conservative classes, at one stage or another? In the past it certainly played a role in class struggles, alongside its strictly religious role and its role as a national symbol in the struggles against foreign domination. As a factor of national identity it served as a banner (concurrently with other factors) in the fight against the foreigner. It was then reduced to a simple, stirring slogan, without any recourse being had to dogma or faith: 'We are Muslims, heirs to a glorious and honourable patrimony, members of a community that was founded upon just, good and sound principles. We must not submit to others who are not as good as we are.' It may still on occasion serve the same purpose. For it to be able to serve to mobilize for socialist construction it would have to be translatable into specific, clear, combative, mobilizing slogans. Through these slogans, each individual would have to see himself confronted with an immediate duty to perform, each in his place. The enemy would have to be clearly indicated as 'adversaries of Allah', in accordance with a classical Islamic formula, even if they outwardly professed the Muslim faith. Who cannot see how hard it would be to realize these conditions today? How can one proclaim: 'In the name of Islam, such and such property must be socialized,' when the owners of this property are paragons of devotion, when the majority of the religious are ready to proclaim (and rightly) that Islam sanctifies private property, when Islam is bound up historically in everyone's mind with that traditional society of which the practically untouchable status of private property is, after all, one of the fundamentals? How can one denounce as adversaries of Islam all these personalities whose attachment to Muslim practices and beliefs is obvious, demonstrative, even ostentatious, and when none of these their beliefs or practices is being attacked?

In the past, to be sure, on a number of occasions, ideological movements have been seen which proclaimed themselves the only ones faithful to the true spirit of Islam – to Islam in its pure, original form – and which hurled their supporters, roused to fanaticism, into battle against the majority of the Muslims of their time, whom they denounced as hypocrites, pretendedly devout, inwardly infidels, at bottom adversaries of Allah. But these were themselves religious movements, organized around new religious cadres, new clergy who opposed one religion to another. Even if the new movement were declared to be practically identical with the original movement of Islam, it nevertheless had its own religious practices, its own holy writings, even if these were only commentaries on the Koran (but commentaries with a definite tendency), its own dogmas, even if these were regarded as mere refinements of the Koran's body of dogma. It was then possible, for example, to proclaim as adversaries of Allah those *ulemas* who looked too tolerantly upon the veneration of saints, and to destroy the cupolas raised above the tombs of the latter, including the Prophet's own tomb. All this might well be associated with denunciation of the privileges of wealth and power identified with those who had distorted true Islam. But the revolt against official Islam had to be linked with the proclamation of *a new Islam*, even if the latter were supposed to be a mere return to the primitive form. Where today can new prophets be found? Who will assemble around him in prayer and veneration, with a new theology, adherents who will be ready – while building socialism, of course – to denounce and attack such and such a rite or belief, and those who hold to them? To believe this to be possible one needs to possess that total ignorance of the present climate of the Muslim world which is shown by certain scholars or ideologists, in their naïve conviction that the Muslim masses are still living in the religious atmosphere of the Middle Ages.

An effective ideology of socialist construction, if this requires struggles (and it does), must be an ideology in which the enemy of this construction can be denounced as an adversary of the highest values to which this ideology appeals. Now, the nationalist ideology and the religious ideology alike contain in the present state of things a thousand possibilities for the reactionaries to present themselves as being, on the contrary, the best defenders of faith and fatherland. The ideology of socialist construction must give socialist construction an essential place among its highest values. This can be done by the nationalist ideology, since socialism can easily be presented as the condition for the nation's strength and well-being; but it is hard for religion to do the same thing, since *its* highest values are super-terrestrial.

We are no longer at the stage of national religions. True, the great wave of religious universalism that swept forward from the eighth century BC onward, supplanting national religions, has in many cases undergone a re-nationalizing process of involution, sometimes on the scale of supra-national communities, with a curious arrangement of tiers of national loyalties. Catholicism subtended in practice, as well as a Christian, white, European–American 'nationalism', also French, German, etc., nationalisms – which produced some amazing consequences, as during the war of 1914–18. But we are now in a phase of return to a purer universalism and a greater clarification of strictly religious values. Religion nowadays essentially appears, in everyone's minds, as giving guidance to the individual's attitude to supernatural values. This may not be incompatible with mobilization to secure man's well-being on earth. It may even be possible to base an ethic of struggle upon it, as has been shown by the activity of Left-wing Christians in France in recent years. But the connection maintained with religious cadres whose attitude is quite different in character sets obstacles in the way of consistent revolutionary action. We have seen this in Europe, with the evolution undergone by those movements that called themselves 'Christian-Socialist', and in the Islamic world with those that sheltered beneath the banner of Muslim socialism. In so far as these movements introduced no religious innovation, but regarded as their brethren in God all the members of their church or of their *umma*, they inevitably found themselves in a position of inferiority on the social plane to the secular socialist parties, if the latter enjoyed normal opportunities to compete with them. Their choices were inevitably less radical because their religious and moral principles forbade them to assume an uncompromising and implacable virulence towards their brethren in the faith, even if these were exploiters and oppressors. This 'moderation', even if it was only relative, attracted to them, especially in revolutionary periods, a clientèle of privileged and semi-privileged elements, calm and moderate minded persons, and this clientèle in its turn, following the usual laws governing political groups, diluted the party's radicalism still further.

This process, so obvious in Europe, has already been seen at work in the Muslim world. It is likely to become still more marked as the class struggle intensifies. Already we can see that the ruling strata will make use of Islam to give religious endorsement to their conservative attitudes. They have plenty of facilities for doing that. It is open to them, as it is not to the 'progressives', to appeal to tradition. True, the archaic traditions that prevail in ways of life and social relations have, historically, nothing specifically Muslim about them. But they have been sanctified by Islam, and it is easy to mobilize religious fanaticism, however lacking in justification this may be, against those who would interfere with them. The ruling classes have ways of influencing ministers of religion, to whom independence and economic progress make it possible to give a place among the privileged, rescuing them from the poverty (and closeness to the masses) to which the colonial régimes often confined many of them. The 'clergy' are naturally tempted to play upon the moralistic string that is always ready to vibrate in favour of a resigned attitude. Peace and good understanding within the community means in practice renunciation of demands and acceptance of established situations. Justifications can be found in the sacred writings, and the choices made with religious endorsement can always be camouflaged under modern names, full of attraction for the masses, such as Muslim socialism. One can, of course, fight against this attitude on its own ground of claims to possess the backing of religion But there is no concealing from oneself that it *is* at a certain advantage on that ground. And the imprecision of the sacred writings where economic matters are concerned makes it hard to set up with authority a clearly 'progressive' interpretation in opposition to these 'reactionary' ones.

If this attitude is predominant and the Muslim religion is monopolized by *de facto* reactionary elements, what will happen? This is not hard to foresee, in the light of our historical experience. The certain consequence will be a detachment of the masses from their traditional faith, in proportion as they emerge from their material, cultural and moral wretchedness and break with their age-old resignation, and as the pressure, already very appreciable, of the demands of the modern world, and of the modern ideal of social justice makes itself felt. In this event, Islam will be a barrier against the rise of the forces of change, and this barrier will not hold. It will suffer a crisis like that of Christianity in the nineteenth century, and this despite the extra strength it will draw from its role as a *national* religion.

Islam will not be able to escape, even partially, from this crisis unless it undergoes a profound reconversion, an *aggiornamento*. For this to happen it would be necessary for believing Muslims to appear who would fight against reactionary interpretations of Islam wrapped in the folds of the banner of religion, tradition and traditional morality. They would have to give up all intolerance towards those who do without Allah in deciding what action to take, and who are averse to giving a lip-service to dogmas that is justified only by social necessity. They would have to apply themselves to drawing from the Koran and the Muslim tradition values that are applicable to the modern world, and in the first place to those strata of the modern world that call for the abolition of privilege and exploitation. This they would have to do not by seeking in the scriptures economic precepts and a social system that are not to be found there, and which could in any case only be unsuitable for modern conditions, but by drawing from them valid precepts of social morality, and accomplishing within the religious framework an organic synthesis (and not a juxtaposition) between traditional religious values and the humanist values which exalt (*inter alia*) economic construction, the only way to ensure a worthwhile life for the members of the community. Thus, and only thus, could Islam continue to give reasons for its continued existence to some people in the countries that were Muslim and which are involved in the hard tasks of economic construction, alongside those who believe that they have no need of God in order to regulate their lives and the life of their country.

Whatever happens, with or without Islam, with or without a progressive tendency in Islam, the future of the Muslim world is in the long run a future of struggle. On earth, struggles begin and are fought out for earthly aims, but under the banner of ideas. The idea that has taken possession of Europe, and subsequently of the world, during the last two hundred years, is that happiness on earth is possible, that progress towards this happiness is going on, and that it is worth while to fight for a mankind free from exploitation and oppression. Willy-nilly, nationalist and religious ideologies have had to integrate this idea, the former frequently by restricting and twisting it for the benefit of one single national community. It was developed into a supra-national secular ideology first in the form of the 'liberal-humanitarian' ideology (to use Mannheim's terminology), with mobilizing forms such as French Jacobinism, in a number of countries (including in the East) and in a variety of periods. This may perhaps still occur. But the use made of this ideology to provide cover for domination by the powers of money, and especially by American 'Big Business', and also to disguise domination by Europe, has done it a very great deal of harm. And it is not well adapted to radical transformations of economic structure.

Marxist ideology, despite the deviations it has suffered, has emerged as the most complete type of secular ideology mobilizing men for progress in the modern world. It has succeeded in arousing millions of individuals to readiness for extreme sacrifice. The sociological concepts and scientific discoveries developed by Marx and the Marxists have exposed the principal mystifications behind which lurk exploitation and oppression, even if the ideological mechanism has prevented them from unveiling all manifestations of the mystifying process. No struggle against exploitation and oppression can overlook this contribution; and the values brought to the forefront by the Marxist movement, in a form that has not been surpassed, continue to be the essential values that are capable of mobilizing modern man. Whether or not they are integrated in new syntheses, they are still the lever with which the Prometheus or Archimedes of today can lift up the universe. The peoples and the rulers of what was the Dār al-Islām have every interest in looking this truth in the face. To the innumerable *grandes illusions* that are always being offered afresh by ideologists, rhetoricians and conjurers (behind whom stand the oppressors, and exploiters, either actual or potential); to the great multiform Maya indefatigably creating ever-renewed myths, may they prefer the austere appeal to clear thinking. 'Ye shall know the truth, and the truth shall make you free,' said Jesus, whom the Muslims called 'Isā, son of Maryam'. And the Koran adds: 'Opinion [*zann*] avails nothing against the truth.'

Afterword (1973)

Every writer of a book of this kind must, I suppose, experience a few years after its publication the same ambivalent feelings that affect me now. It is rare for the writer to be completely satisfied or dissatisfied with his work. One would like to recast some formulations. Some arguments would be improved, it seems, if they were to be modified. The writer is inclined to add, or to cut – but he is afraid that in doing so he may destroy the logicality that his exposition had in its original form, and render hardly recognizable, or even cripple, a certain confident vigour that distinguished it. One must either do the whole work afresh, or leave it as it stands.

These considerations – and, to a still greater extent, lack of time – make it impossible for me to undertake even a moderately thorough revision of the text and notes, now that the opportunity to do so has been offered me by the fourth printing of this austere book. On the occasion of previous printings I took care to correct the few small slips that had been pointed out to me or which I had noticed by chance. For this printing I have had the benefit of the comments made by an exceptionally conscientious translator, Mr Brian Pearce. While diligently polishing, in late 1972, his translation of this book, which is to appear in 1974, he drew my attention to a number of misprints, some rather obscure formulations, a questionable translation of a phrase of Marx's (itself not altogether clear), and other such points. I have made the necessary corrections and improvements.

It would undoubtedly be useful to discuss the most intelligent and understanding of the reviews which have been published of my book. That, however, would involve too much work. There have, of course, been some cases where reviewers have mis-understood. The unconditional admirers of Max Weber, for instance, reacted as though I had opposed Weber's theses as a whole, or some major concept of his. I did not intend to do this here, whatever my fundamental views on the matter. I merely criticized certain particular assertions made by Weber, and adduced facts to refute them. Anyone who wants to answer my criticisms should show me either that these facts do not exist, or that they have a significance different from that which I ascribe to them, or else that they are contradicted by other facts – and not just oppose me by acclaiming the value of Weber's concepts. It could also be maintained that, although my criticism is a valid one, Weber did give expression to an under-lying truth, even if in an inadequate or misleading way, as is held to be the case by J. Gabel ('Une lecture marxiste de la sociologie religieuse de Max Weber', in *Cahiers internationaux de sociologie*, 49, 1969, pp. 51–66), who suggests that we ought to read 'reification' wherever Weber writes 'rationality'.

Reviewers have rightly pointed to some gaps in my biblio-graphy, and, in any case, many works that need to be mentioned saw the light after my book had been written. Regarding the role – exaggerated by Louis Massignon – which the Jews played in the economic (and especially financial) life of the Islamic world (p. 264, n. 35), I ought to have referred, as G. Vajda has made me realize, to the contribution by W. J. Fischel, *Jews in the Economic and Political Life of Medieval Islam* (London, 1937). The new writings that deserve to be mentioned and discussed, in relation to a number of points, are legion. I cannot make additions to my book that would amount, in fact, to a partial revision, if, instead of merely listing titles, the value of the contribution made by each one of them were to be assessed.

I might have discussed more extensively the many contem-porary Muslim writers who have taken up, in a spirit of apologia, the theme of the applicability of the 'social' principles of Islam to present-day society and to the ideal community. These writers are numerous, to be sure, but their arguments are always the same as those advanced by the two or three writers whom I did mention and criticize. In view of the influence he had, and the important, even symbolic, role played by his life and his death, I might have analysed the work of the ideologist of the Muslim Brotherhood, Sayyid Quṭb, whom Nasser hanged for conspiracy in 1966 (see, e.g. Hassan Riad, *L'Égypte nassé-rienne*, Paris, Éditions de Minuit, 1964, pp. 218 et seq.)

In connexion with the much wider-ranging discussion of the relations between religious ideology and economic life, some people, who did not think my book worth reading with much care, asked how I could possibly be so lacking in common sense as to deny (as it seemed to them) the influence of a phenomenon of such weight as religion upon the whole of social life, and therefore upon the economy. A review written by a friend of mine, Muḥammad-Ṣāleḥ Ṣfia, offers a very aptly expressed reply to this line of argument. Since this may help – more successfully perhaps, than my own formulations – to make clear what I was trying to demonstrate, I will not resist the temptation to quote here what he writes. M. S. Sfia explains (the italics are his own) that I tend to '*assert the neutrality of ideology in relation to the essential lines of force in social evolution*'. He adds:

> It is not that Rodinson underestimates the part that ideas can play in certain circumstances, or that he is unaware that an idea may some-times, as Marx put it, become in its turn a material force that can prove extremely effective. On the contrary, he appreciates the absurdity of the conception of a world of the mind that reflects the material basis passively and epiphenomenally. . . But from his study of the matter. . . he believes that it is possible to infer that this dialectic of the infrastructure and the superstructure constitutes an element in a trajectory of history which, *in the long run and so far as the general tendency of the curve of development is concerned*, shows a direction and a rhythm that are governed in the last analysis by the concrete being of human communities. The dynamic of social structures, he tells us, with flexibility but not without firmness, conforms to the logic of production-relations: the network con-stituted by the latter defines a 'total man' who is at once the product and the maker of his own history. . . (*Studi storici*, year VII, no. 3, July–September 1966, pp. 585–90).

A number of works and discussions have appeared in recent times dealing with the factors in the origin of modern European capitalism. It is not possible for me to set forth my views about them here: that would require too much space. I will merely mention that I have re-examined the general subject of the 'religious conditions of economic life in Islam' in an article of about twenty pages which is to appear at the beginning of a collective work on the economic history of the Near East in the Muslim period, to be published, in their well-known *Handbuch der Orientalistik* series, by Brill, of Leyden. At the outset of this short article I try to define once more the mechanism of the relations between religious ideas and economic life. I show that religious ideas influence the economy through the mediation of a social morality of which they are not the only source, and I seek to determine the levels of this social morality as well as its sources. For the moment I can only refer the reader to this article, which, I hope, will soon be made available.

On the plane of facts, I noticed while writing the article something that seems to me to be important for elucidating the concept of *ribā* in the Koran, and the origins of the ban imposed upon it. The problem of interest, and especially of compound interest, was a matter of great concern in the Christian Orient at the time when Islam arose. In the actual century that saw the Prophet's birth, for example, a very curious homily in Syriac, written by the Syrian Monophysite Bishop Jacob of Saroug (c. 451–521), shows us Satan lamenting the collapse of his authority as a result of the recent disappearance of paganism. In order to recover this power he is going to make use of lending at interest (*rebithā*, a word related to *ribā*): priests and monks will indulge in this practice, and it will be their undoing. Once they have begun it, their orthodoxy, their cult of the true God, will matter little: 'I do not mind,' exclaims the Devil, 'if the priest uses the interest he draws from his money to buy an axe with which to smash the temples of the gods! The love of gold is a greater idol than any idol of a god. . . It is worth as much to me as all those idols put together!'And the Syrian bishop puts into the mouth of the Evil One this very 'Marxist' formulation: 'They have cast down the idols, but they will never cast down the coins that we shall put in their place . . .' (translated and edited by Abbé Martin, in *Zeitschrift der deutschen morgenländischen Gesellschaft*, 29, 1875, pp. 107–47: other references given in A. Baumstark, *Geschichte der syrischen Literatur*, Bonn, Marcus and Weber, 1922, p. 150, n. 4).

General condemnation of lending at interest was, moreover, a commonplace of the Christian morality expounded by the Fathers of the Church. At least in the Eastern world, it is true that the Councils restricted this prohibition to the clergy. On a more realistic plane, however, Justinian (527–65) had, about a century at least before the Prophet of Islam, reduced interest-rates, forbidden compound interest, and made it illegal to exact any interest from the moment when the sum paid by the debtor came to more than double the amount of the capital advanced. (The reference here is to texts of 529 [*Codex*, 4, 32:10, 27], perfected in 535 [*novellae* 121 and 138]: cf. G. Cassimatis, *Les intérêts dans la législation de Justinien et dans le droit byzantin*, Paris, Recueil Sirey, 1931, pp. 61 et seq., and A. Bernard, in *Dictionnaire de théologie catholique*, Vol. XV, 2, Paris, Letouzey et Ané, 1950, cols. 2322 et seq.)

Compound interest had already been forbidden in the Code of Hammurabi (article 93). Regarding the notion of the doubling of the sum lent, which many commentaries mention in connection with *ribā*, it should perhaps be pointed out that this notion figures prominently in the economic traditions of the Ancient East. At the beginning of the second millennium B C, in Babylonia as also in the Assyrian trading agencies in Cappadocia, despite any prohibitions there might have been, lending at compound interest was in fact practised, in the following manner: interest was capitalized every year, or whenever it had accumulated to an amount equivalent to the capital advanced. Consequently, with an interest-rate of 20 per cent, capitalization of interest took place every five years (cf. R. Bogaert, *Les origines antiques de la banque de dépôt* . . . Leyden, A. W. Sijthoff, 1966, pp. 82–3; for Egypt, cf. p. 43).

In Egypt, according to Diodorus Siculus (I, 79), Pharaoh Bocchoris (720–15 BC) issued a law by which 'whoever lent money along with a written bond was forbidden to do more than double the principal from interest' (trans. Oldfather, Loeb Classical Library: *Diodorus Siculus*, Vol. I, London, Heinemann, 1933, p. 271). It can be noted, moreover, by consulting, e.g., the concise account given by E. Szlechter, 'Le prêt dans l'Ancien Testament et dans les codes mésopotamiens d'avant Hammourabi' (in *La Bible et l'Orient*, *Travaux du*

Premier Congrès d'Archèologie et d'Orientalisme Bibliques, Paris, P.U.F., 1955, pp. 16–25), that the 'tricks' used for getting round the ban on interest are just as old as the ban itself.

Notes and References

FOREWORD

1. This gap was to some degree filled while I was writing this book. The modern period of the economic history of the Muslim world is covered by Z. Y. Hershlag's recent work, *Introduction to the Modern Economic History of the Middle East*, Leiden, Brill, 1964, pp. xiv + 419. This textbook is not altogether satisfactory, but nevertheless it contains many facts, figures and documents. I was able to refer to it only to a limited extent.

CHAPTER I: THE PROBLEM STATED

1. Cf. the opinions of the modernist reformers Muḥammad ʿAbdūh and Rashīd Riḍā, in J. Jomier, *Le Commentaire coranique du Manâr*, Paris, G. P. Maisonneuve, 1954 (Coll. Islam d'hier et d'aujourd'hui, 11), pp. 226 et seq.; for Turkey, cf. Aḥmed Naẓmī, *Naẓer-i Islāmda zenginlighin mewqiʿī*, Istanbul, 1340–42 (1921–3), quotations from which will be found in W. Björkman, 'Kapitalentstehung und -anlage im Islam', in *Mitteilungen des Seminars für orientalische Sprachen*, 32, 1929, 2. Abteilung, pp. 80–98.

2. For example, M. Hamidullah, 'Islam's solution of the basic economic problems: the position of labour', in *Islamic Culture*, 10, 1936, pp. 213–33; 'Le Monde musulman devant l'économie moderne', in *Cahiers de l'Institut de Science Économique Appliquée*, suppl. no. 120 (series V, no. 3), Dec. 1961, pp. 23–41; and the various other writings of this author: all the literature of the Muslim Brotherhood, cf. F. Bertier, 'L'Idéologie politique des Frères musulmans', in *Temps modernes*, No. 83, Sept. 1952, pp. 541–56 (important extracts in *Orient*, No. 8, 4th quarter of 1958, pp. 43–57); and the translation of a pamphlet by their founder, Ḥasan al-Bannā, 'Vers la lumière', trans. by J. Marel

in *Orient*, No. 4, 4th quarter of 1957, pp. 37–62, pp. 52 et seq., 61 et seq.: all modernist-reformist apologetical literature, cf., e.g., J. Jomier, op. cit., pp. 217 et seq.: all the official Pakistani publications (e.g. the report of the commission on the *zakāt*, from which I have given a quotation in my article 'The Life of Muḥammad and the Sociological Problem of the Beginnings of Islam', in *Diogenes*, No. 20, Winter, 1957, pp. 28–51) and the private ones as well. This is repeated *ad nauseam* in thousands of books, articles and pamphlets.

3. Thus, L. Massignon, who has passed from formulations that, though open to criticism, were still cautious ('from the social standpoint, Islam is attractive for its very egalitarian conception of the contribution everyone has to make, through the tithe, to the resources of the community; it is hostile to unrestrained stock-exchange speculation, to bank-capital, state loans, indirect taxes on goods of primary necessity . . . it holds an intermediate position between the doctrines of bourgeois capitalism and the Communism of the Bolshevists' – 1939), to summary statements that go much too far ('Islam does not bow down before any idol, neither the Power of Gold nor the technical cruelty of the police state' – 1953). The references for these passages are as follows: *Situation de l'Islam* (Paris, Geuthner, 1939), *in fine* = *Opera Minora I*, Beirut, Dar al-Maaref, 1963, pp. 11–52, on p. 52; 'Le Mouvement intellectuel contemporain en Proche-Orient', in *Hesperia*, Zurich, Bd. 4, H. 10, 1953, pp. 71–8 = *Opera Minora I*, pp. 224–31, on p. 226 of the latter edition. However, in his article 'Archaïsme et Modernisme en Islam: à propos d'une nouvelle structure du travail humain', in *Cahiers de l'I.S.E.A.*, suppl. no. 120 (series V, no. 3), Dec. 1961, pp. 7–22, taking up again some ideas of his that are to some extent contradictory to those I have just set out, he attributes the economic decadence of the Islamic world to the sin committed in the Middle Ages by the Abbasid Caliphate in organizing a 'modern international economy' (p. 8) of a sort rather similar to capitalism, based on 'colonialist' exploitation, with the help of Jewish bankers who assumed all the responsibility for the sin of usury. These are views that are extremely debatable and weakly supported, despite the erudition of this remarkable Islamic specialist, whose intelligence and learning are unequalled and whose moral sense is admirable, but who has been led astray to an ever greater extent by his mystical conception of the facts of history. It is at any rate possible to deduce from this that Islam in itself has not always been wholly inimical to capitalism. L. Massignon's

usual position is transformed with naïvety (and some distortion) into a Pythagorean table by J.-P. Roux, in *L'Islam en Asie*, Paris, Payot, 1958 (Coll. Bibliothèque historique), p. 262: Islam, like Communism, is anti-capitalist and collectivist (in contrast to capitalism, which is, of course, capitalist and individualist), but respects property (what sort?), just as capitalism does. J. Austruy, *L'Islam face au développement économique*, Paris, Editions Ouvrières, 1961, states that 'the traditional mentality of Islam has not been favourable to the development of capitalism' (p. 60), but considers that 'the profound conception of property' is in Islam especially 'adapted to the new function that modern economic growth assigns to it,' in contrast 'to the role ascribed to it by the working of liberal economics' (pp. 95 et seq.), so that 'the special sense of the collective which is characteristic of Islam may today become a factor in economic progress' (p. 98), in a direction *sui generis*, neither capitalist nor socialist. These views appear again in his other book, *Structure économique et civilisation: l'Égypte et le destin économique de l'Islam*, Paris, S.E.D.E.S., 1960, and, in condensed form, in his article 'Vocation économique de l'Islam', in *Cahiers de l'I.S.E.A.*, No. 106 (Series V, no. 2), Oct. 1960, pp. 151–212. I shall have a number of occasions to return to the ideas of this writer, who represents well enough the standpoint opposite to the views I maintain in this book. It needs to be mentioned at the outset that his ideas are developed on the basis of a very inadequate knowledge of the facts, with a documentation largely consisting of bad books by pseudo-scholars, themselves at second or third hand. Conclusions that are somewhat similar, but with a richer and sounder documentary basis, are put forward by J. Hans, *Homo oeconomicus islamicus*, Klagenfurt and Vienna, J. L. Sen, 1952; *Dynamik und Dogma im Islam*, 2nd edn, Leiden, Brill, 1960, (cf. pp. 71 et seq.).

4. A view upheld by (in succession to many others) the magistrate R. Charles, an amateur and ill-informed student of Islam: 'The fatalist attitude of the Muslims is well known to have had extremely grave consequences; it has checked the spirit of initiative, paralysed material activity, plunged the countries concerned into lethargy' (*L'Âme musulmane*, Paris, Flammarion, 1958, p. 71). More sweepingly, Renan denounced the 'stupefying' consequences of the brutal domination of Muslim dogma (E. Renan, *L'Islamisme et la science*, Paris, Calmann-Levy, 1883). Cf. my critique, *L'Islam, doctrine de progrès ou de réaction*, Paris, Union rationaliste, 1961 (= *Cahiers rationalistes*, no. 199, Dec. 1961).

5. E.g. Hans E. Tütsch, 'Arab Unity and Arab Dissensions', in *The Middle East in Transition*, ed. W. Z. Laqueur, London, Routledge and Kegan Paul, 1958, pp. 12–32; N. A. Faris, 'The Islamic Community and Communism', in the same symposium, pp. 351–9 (reprinted from *The Islamic Review*); R. Charles, *L'Évolution de l'Islam*, Paris, Calmann-Levy, 1960 (Coll. Questions d'Actualité), p. 188. Greater caution is shown by B. Lewis in his contribution to *The Middle East in Transition* (op. cit.), pp. 311–24 (reprinted from *International Affairs*, 30, January 1954, pp. 1–12). On the way in which the question should be presented, cf. my 'Problématique de l'étude des rapports entre Islam et Communisme', in *Colloque sur la sociologie musulmane, Actes, 11–14 Sept. 1961*, Brussels, Centre pour l'étude des problèmes du monde musulman contemporain, 1962, pp. 119–49.

6. Thus, the great Islamic scholar C. H. Becker, in an all-too-brief exposition, 'Islam und Wirtschaft', in *Archiv für Wirtschaftsforschung im Orient*, Weimar, 1, 1916, pp. 66–7, reprinted in his *Islamstudien, Vom Werden und Wesen der islamischen Welt*, I, Leipzig, Quelle u.Meyer, 1924, pp. 54–65; and W. Björkman, op. cit. Both are well informed as regards Islamology, but ill served by the looseness of the economic concepts they employ. The little book by the economist Alfred Rühl, *Vom Wirtschaftsgeist im Orient*, Leipzig, Quelle u.Meyer, 1925, viii + 92 pp., devoted to Algeria, is spoilt by certain scientific assumptions but is at least free of direct political prejudices. To be read is the very honest and intelligent article by G. Destanne de Bernis, 'Islam et développement économique', in *Cahiers de l'I.S.E.A.*, No. 106 (Series V, no. 2), Oct. 1960, pp. 105–50, which draws upon his knowledge of life in the Tunisian countryside and experiments carried out in this setting. However, he has only a second-hand knowledge of both the historical substratum of the area mentioned and also the other parts of the Muslim world.

7. Above all, Claude Cahen, 'Les facteurs économiques et sociaux dans l'ankylose culturelle de l'Islam', in *Classicisme et Déclin culturel dans l'histoire de l'Islam*, Paris, Besson et Chantemerle, 1957, pp. 195–207, with the subsequent discussion at the colloquium held in Bordeaux in 1956, of which this volume constitutes the proceedings, pp. 208–15. The communications and discussions at a colloquium held in Paris in March 1960 were unfortunately published only in roneotyped form and not made available for sale: *L'Évolution économique, sociale et culturelle des pays d'Islam, s'est-elle montrée défavorable à la formation d'un capitalisme de type occidental?*, Paris, Institut d'études islamiques,

Centre d'études de l'Orient contemporain, École Pratique des Hautes Études, 6e section, no date, 24, 22, 17, 33 ff. The communications were read by R. Brunschvig, J. Berque, P. Marthelot and C. Cahen. The present book is a development of the very short contribution I made to the discussion. I shall have occasion to refer to this publication several times, putting the figures I, II, III, IV, respectively, in front of the page-numbers of its four parts.

8. There is a good discussion of some of these definitions by Maurice Dobb, in his *Studies in the Development of Capitalism*, London, Routledge, 1946, pp. 1–10. For discussion of the meaning of various capitalist 'economic institutions' see, e.g., the textbook by R. H. Blodgett, *Comparative Economic Systems*, New York, Macmillan, 1944, pp. 24–42; also, in a more profound way, F. Perroux, *Le Capitalisme*, 5th edn, Paris, P.U.F., 1962 (Coll. Que sais-je?, No. 315), pp. 9–29. Max Weber combines the two kinds of definition: 'While capitalism of various forms is met with in all the periods of history, the provision of the everyday wants by capitalistic methods is characteristic of the Occident alone and even here has been the inevitable method only since the middle of the nineteenth century.' (M. Weber, *Wirtschaftsgeschichte*, Munich and Leipzig, Duncker u. Humblot, 1923, p. 239: Eng. trans., *General Economic History*, 1950 edn, p. 276.)

9. It is the confusion between the different conceptions covered by the term 'capitalism' in Marx's writings that accounts for reactions like those of the great historian Georges Lefebvre, although he had an attitude of goodwill towards Marxism ('Observations', in *La Pensée*, No. 65, Jan.–Feb. 1956, pp. 22–5: cf. *infra*, note 80 to Chapter 3 of this book). Marx speaks quite clearly of merchant capital (*Capital*, Vol. III, chapter 20) and usurer's capital (ibid., chapter 36) as 'antediluvian' forms of capital existing in Antiquity and the Middle Ages. But then he pokes fun at the 'one blunder after another' committed by Mommsen (*Capital*, I, 1938 London edition, p. 146, n. 1) and at the 'error' committed by 'all the philologists' who speak of capital as existing in Antiquity (*Grundrisse der Kritik der politischen Oekonomie. Rohentwurf*, Berlin, Dietz, 1953, p. 412: Eng. trans., *Pre-Capitalist Economic Formations*, ed. Hobsbawm, p. 118).

10. *Studia o marksowskiej teorii społeczeństwa*, Warsaw, Panstwowe Wydawnictwo Naukowe, 1963, pp. 168 et seq. (A French translation of this important work should be published soon, I hope.)

11. This is also Werner Sombart's definition. Furthermore, as we shall see, Marx used the term 'mode of production' not only in this sense but also, and often, in the sense of what will here be called 'socio-economic formation'.

12. The sector is what Lenin calls an 'element' of the economy in his 1918 pamphlet: *The Chief Task of Our Day: 'Left-Wing' Childishness and the Petty-Bourgeois Mentality* (*Works*, 4th edition, Vol. 27, English edition, pp. 335–6). He quotes this passage and expands it in his better-known 1921 pamphlet *On the Food Tax* (ibid., Vol. 32, pp. 330–31, 344), where he writes of 'elements (constituent parts)'. Stalin referred to the passage in his address of 26 January 1934 to the 17th Congress of the Soviet Communist Party (*Works*, Vol. 13, English edition, p. 316).

13. *Capital*, III, Foreign Languages Publishing House edition, p. 320.

14. Ibid., p. 321.

15. Ibid., p. 580.

16. I have borrowed this term from Jean Bénard, *La Conception marxiste du capital*, Paris, S.E.D.E.S., 1952, p. 244.

17. *Capital*, III, p. 321.

18. Ibid., p. 322.

19. *Die protestantische Ethik und der Geist des Kapitalismus*, in *Gesammelte Aufsätze zur Religionssoziologie*, I, Tübingen, J. C. B. Mohr, 1920, p. 4 (Eng. trans. *The Protestant Ethic and the Spirit of Capitalism*, New York, 1958, pp. 17, 18).

20. Weber does indeed speak elsewhere of various 'non-rational forms of capitalism' (*nichtrationalen Kapitalismus*) to be found outside of modern Europe (*Wirtschaftsgeschichte*, op. cit., p. 286: Eng. trans., p. 334).

21. It will be seen that G. H. Bousquet, though he has a high respect for Max Weber, is unfaithful to his spirit when he requires, in order that one may be allowed to speak of Meccan capitalism, the presence there of double-entry book-keeping (*Hespéris*, 41, 1954, p. 239).

22. *Gesammelte Aufsätze*, op. cit., I, pp. 4–6 (Eng. trans., *The Protestant Ethic* . . ., p. 19).

23. Ibid., p. 7 (English translation, p. 21).

24. Melville J. Herskovits, *Economic Anthropology*, New York, A. A. Knopf, 1952, p. 181; cf. pp. 155–79.

25. Ibid., pp. 225 et seq.

26. *Capital*, Vol. III, F.L.P.H. edn, pp. 581, 584.

27. Herskovits, op. cit., pp. 298 et seq. (the passage quoted is on

page 304). It is in this sense that Marx, listing the general determining factors of all production, writes that

capital is, among other things, also an instrument of production, also past, impersonal labour. Hence capital is a universal, eternal, natural phenomenon; which is true if we disregard the specific properties which turn an 'instrument of production' and 'stored-up labour' into capital.

(*Grundrisse*, op. cit., p. 7: Eng. trans., *Marx's Grundrisse*, ed. Maclellan, London, 1971, p. 19.)

28. R. Thurnwald, *Economics in Primitive Communities*, London, Oxford University Press, 1932, pp. 205 et seq.
29. Herskovits, op. cit., p. 304.
30. Perroux, op. cit., p. 35.

CHAPTER 2: WHAT ISLAM PRESCRIBES

1. Social pressure, either diffused or organized, has made it almost impossible to publish in Arabic, Turkish, Persian, etc., any really critical study of Islam, whether scientific or popular in character. Critical studies by Orientalist scholars have been treated with suspicion even by liberal and progressive elements because they seem marked by a racialist, colonialist desire to denigrate the national religion. This, indeed, has often been the case. It is partly for this reason – Islamism being artificially protected from any criticism – that Muslim theologians have failed to work out a doctrine that would enable us to regard these accounts as being, to some extent at least, legendary in character. They would thereby, however, safeguard the essentials of the Muslim dogma in the way that the Catholic theologians have safeguarded theirs, with their theory of different literary genres. I agree on this point with J. Poirier (in *Cahiers de l'I.S.E.A.*, supplement no. 120 (series V, no. 3), Dec. 1961, pp. 218 et seq.) who nevertheless does not seem to perceive at all the social causes of the present Muslim attitude and so minimizes the difficulty of overcoming them.

2. This has been especially well shown by J. Schacht, *The Origins of Muhammadan Jurisprudence*, Oxford, Clarendon Press, 1950. See also his *Introduction to Islamic Law*, Oxford, Clarendon Press, 1964.

3. The traditions regarding pure facts of history, genealogies and so forth, are doubtless more deserving of consideration, at least for the broad outline of the facts they report. Cf. the discussion in my 'Bilan des études mohammadiennes', in *Revue historique*, 229, 1963, pp. 169–220, on pp. 197 et seq.

4. *Koran*, 4:36/32: 'Do not covet what Allah hath bestowed in bounty upon one more than another.' The context shows that differences of wealth are meant here. Cf. also 16:73/71. But the same expressions are used in other places for other kinds of inequality. Cf., e.g., 17:22/21; 4:38/34.

5. 34:33/34. Cf. the list of passages cited by D. Santillana, *Istituzioni di diritto musulmano malichita*, II, Rome, Istituto per l'Oriente, 1938, p. 62, n. 256.

6. 8:28; 13:9, and the index to Blachère's (French) translation under the word '*fortune*'.

7. 28:26 et seq.

8. 18:76/77.

9. 36:20/21; 52:40, and elsewhere.

10. The question is summed up by W. Heffening at the beginning of the article '*tidjāra*' in *Encyclopedia of Islam*, 1st edition, Vol. IV, English version, Leiden, Brill, and London, Luzac, 1934, p. 747.

11. M. Hamidullah, in *Cahiers de l'I.S.E.A.*, supplement no. 120 (Series V, no. 3), Dec. 1961, pp. 26 et seq.

12. Cf. especially the article '*ribā*' by J. Schacht in *Encyclopedia of Islam*, 1st edition (op. cit.), Vol. III (English edition, 1936), pp. 1148–50, and the remarkable theses of F. Arin, *Recherches historiques sur les opérations usuraires et aléatoires en droit musulman*, Paris, A. Pedone, 1909, pp. 13–22, and Benali Fekar, *L'Usure en droit musulman*, Paris, A. Rousseau, 1908. Cf. also M. Gaudefroy-Demombynes, *Mahomet*, Paris, Albin Michel, 1957, pp. 609–11, and W. Montgomery Watt, *Muhammad at Medina*, Oxford, Clarendon Press, 1956, pp. 296–8. However, Watt's view that the polemic in the Koran against the practice called *ribā* is directed solely at the Jews does not stand up even to a mere reading of the relevant passages of the Koran. On the Prophet's fiscal institutions as a whole, see especially the lengthy monograph by L. Caetani, in *Annali dell'Islam*, Vol. V, Milan, Hoepli, 1912, pp. 287–319.

13. In this paragraph I am merely paraphrasing up to this point the chapter on property in the book by the Christian philosopher and Islamic scholar L. Gardet, *La Cité musulmane; vie sociale et politique*, Paris, J. Vrin, 1954 (Coll. Études musulmanes, I), pp. 79–90.

14. According to the Ḥanbalite school, he has only to undertake to pay the price of it as soon as he is able; if he kills the owner who is defending his property by force he is released from any penal responsibility; if he is killed, he is considered as having died a martyr (*shahīd*). (Cf. H. Laoust, *Le Précis de droit d'Ibn Qudāmā*, Beirut, Institut français de Damas, 1950, p. 231). Similarly, according to the Shīʿites, refusal to give food to a starving man amounts in effect to complicity in the killing of a Muslim (Abū l-Qāsim Jaʿfar ibn Muḥammad al-Hillii, *sharāʾiʿ al-Islām* Calcutta, 1839, p. 407: French trans. by A. Querry, *Droit musulman*, Paris, 1871–2, Vol. II, p. 244).

15. As examples available in translation of how hiring, and especially wage-labour, are dealt with in religious law, cf. Khalīl ibn Isḥāq, *Abrégé de la loi musulmane selon le rite de l'imām Mālek*, trans. G.-H. Bousquet, Vol. III, *Le Patrimoine*, Algiers, Maison des Livres, and Paris, A. Maisonneuve, 1961, pp. 128–33; (especially) D. Santillana, op. cit., pp. 254–75; E. Sachau,

Muhammedanisches Recht nach schafiitischer Lehre, Stuttgart and Berlin, W. Spemann, 1897, pp. 539–60; A. Querry, op. cit., Vol. I, pp. 543–56; H. Laoust, op. cit., pp. 117–19, etc.

16. Cf. especially D. Santillana, op. cit., II, pp. 56, 259 et seq., 270 (and in the index, p. 663, under '*alea*'); compare C. Cardahi, *Droit et Morale*, Vol. II, Beirut, Imprimerie Catholique, 1954 (Coll. Université de Lyon, Annales de la Faculté de Droit de Beyrouth), pp. 353 et seq.

17. Dārimī, *Sunan* XVIII, 8, and in other collections, with slight variations (references in Wensinck, *A Handbook of Early Muhammadan Tradition*, Leiden, Brill, 1927, under the word 'barter').

18. Cf. B. Lewis, *The Arabs in History*, 3rd edn, London, Hutchinson, 1964, pp. 91 et seq.; W. Heffening, art. cit., p. 786; there is a good selection of *ḥadīths* of this sort by H. Ritter, in *Der Islam*, 7, 1917, pp. 28–31, based on Suyūṭī.

19. Zaid ibn ʿAlī, *Corpus iuris . . .*, ed. E. Griffini, Milan, Hoepli, 1919, no. 539.

20. Cf. H. Ritter, art. cit., pp. 29, 32.

21. M. Hamidullah, art. cit., p. 27.

22. D. Santillana, op. cit., Vol. I, 1926, pp. 318 et seq.

23. Cf. J. Schacht, art. cit. (see note 12); F. Arin, op. cit., pp. 22 et seq. and passim; B. Fakar, op. cit., pp. 29, 33 et seq., etc.; D. Santillana, op. cit., II, pp. 60 et seq., 177 et seq.; J. Schacht, *The Origins . . .* (op. cit.), pp. 67, 108, 313, and especially p. 251. Exact references to the *ḥadīth* will be found in E. Cohn, *Der Wucher (ribā) in Qorʾān, Chadīth und Fiqh*, Berlin, 1903. A recent account, concise but clear and sound, is given in Y. Linant de Bellefonds, *Traité de droit musulman comparé*, Vol. I, Paris and The Hague, Mouton, 1965 pp. 217–23. Present-day tendencies in interpretation are reflected clearly enough in the brief account by Zaydān Abū l-makārim, *binaʾ al-iqtiṣād fi l-Islām*, Cairo, Dār al-ʿorūba, 1959, pp. 107 et seq. The reference for prohibition of *ribā* has been given as the farewell speech by the Prophet in March 632, three months before his death. Cf. R. Blachère, 'L'Allocution de Mahomet lors du pèlerinage d'adieu', in *Mélanges Louis Massignon*, Damascus, Institut français de Damas, Vol. I, 1956, pp. 223–49, on pp. 242, etc.

24. Cf. e.g., Ghazālī, *iḥyāʾ ʿulūm ad-dīn*, Cairo, 1352/1933, Vol. II, pp. 68 et seq.; abridged analysis by G. H. Bousquet, Paris, Besson, 1955, pp. 125 et seq.

25. There is an abundant literature devoted to developing this theme. I will mention only the most learned of its representa-

tives, who presents the advantage of expounding it in a European language: M. Hamidullah, *Le Prophète de l'Islam*, Paris, Vrin, 1959, Vol. II, pp. 611–25.

26. Naṣīr Ahmed Sheikh, *Some Aspects of the Constitution and Economics of Islam*, Woking, The Woking Muslim Mission and Literary Trust, 1961, pp. 139–229.

27. W. Cantwell Smith, *Islam in Modern History*, Princeton, 1957, p. 234 (Mentor Books edn, New York, 1959, p. 236).

28. There is available in French translation a discussion quoting traditions on this subject in Abū Yūsuf Yaʿqūb, *Le Livre de l'impôt foncier*, trans. E. Fagnan, Paris, Geuthner, 1921, pp. 133–9. Cf. the Mālikite position, in D. Santillana, op. cit., II, pp. 247–54 (rent forbidden only if it takes the form of a share of the crop, but allowed if to be paid in money or movables), the Ḥanabalite position in H. Laoust, op. cit., p. 110 (rent payable in crops allowed), etc. There is a summary in L. Milliot, *Introduction à l'étude du droit musulman*, Paris, Sirey, 1953, pp. 666 et seq.

29. Enumerated by Hamidullah, *Le Prophète* . . . (op. cit.), II, pp. 617 et seq. (to be read critically).

30. Cf. A. Christensen, *L'Iran sous les Sassanides*, 2nd edn, Copenhagen, E. Munsksgaard, and Paris, Geuthner, 1944, pp. 335 et seq., 364 et seq.; O. Klima, *Mazdak, Geschichte einer sozialen Bewegung in sassanidischen Persien*, Prague, Československé Akademie Ved, 1957 (a Marxist study).

31. Cf. e.g., Blachère's (French) translation of the passages listed in the index under the words '*riches*', '*fortune*', '*orgueil*'.

32. H. Grimme, *Mohammed*, Münster in Westfalen, Aschendorff, 1892–5, I, pp. 14 et seq. (but cf. II, pp. 139 et seq.). Criticized pertinently by C. Snouck Hurgronje, 'Une nouvelle biographie de Mohammed', in *Revue de l'Histoire des Religions*, 30, 1894, pp. 48–70, 149–78; reprinted in his *Verspreide Geschriften*, Deel I, Bonn and Leipzig, 1923, pp. 329–62. Cf. L. Caetani, *Annali dell' Islam*, Vol. VIII, Milan, Hoepli, 1918, p. 23, who also speaks of the 'socialist or communist principles' of Mohammed, to which the Prophet remained, he believes, faithful to the end of his days, but which his disciples betrayed; F. Buhl, *Das Leben Muhammads*, 2nd edn, German translation from Danish, Heidelberg, Quelle u. Meyer, 1955, p. 149, n. 58, and M. Rodinson, 'The Life of Muḥammad and the Sociological Problem of the Beginnings of Law', in *Diogenes*, no. 20, Winter, 1957, pp. 28–51.

33. This is what I have tried to show in my *Mahomet*, Paris, Club

français du livre, 1961 (2nd edn, revised, Éditions du Seuil, 1968: Eng. trans., *Mohammed*, Allen Lane The Penguin Press, 1971).

34. There is a good synthesis by J. Leipoldt, *Der soziale Gedanke in der altchristlichen Kirche*, Leipzig, Koehler u. Amelang, 1952, pp. 168 et seq. In French there is P. Bigo, *La Doctrine sociale de l'Église*, Paris, P.U.F., 1965, pp. 27–34, and the collection of passages with a preface by him: *Riches et Pauvres dans l'Église ancienne*, Paris, Grasset, 1962.

35. *Koran*, 9:34 et seq.

36. Ibn Saʿd, *Biographien Muhammeds, seiner Gefährten und der späteren Träger des Islams*, ed. E. Sachau, etc., Bd. IV, Theil 1, Leiden, Brill, 1906, p. 166; cf. I. Goldziher, *Vorlesungen über den Islam*, 2nd edn, Heidelberg, C. Winter, 1925, pp. 137 et seq., French trans. of 1st edn, *Le Dogme et la Loi de l'Islam*, Paris, Geuthner, 1920, pp. 114 et seq.; L. Massignon, *Essai sur les origines du Lexique technique de la mystique musulmane*, 2nd edition, Paris, Vrin, 1954 (Coll. Études musulmanes, II), pp. 145, 158 et seq.; L. Caetani, in *Annali dell' Islam*, Milan, Hoepli, 1905–26, Vol. VII, anno 30 H., paras 154 et seq., Vol. VIII, anno 33 H., para. 23.

37. *Oriente moderno*, 28, 1948, pp. 80 et seq., quoting *al-Ahrām*, 28 March 1948. Along the same line, cf. the somewhat mechanical argument by Mouhssine Barazi, *Islamisme et socialisme*, Paris, Geuthner, 1929 (law thesis).

38. H. A. R. Gibb, 'Government and Islam under the early 'Abbasids', in *L'Élaboration de l'Islam*, Paris, P.U.F., 1961, pp. 115–27, on p. 119.

CHAPTER 3: ECONOMIC PRACTICE IN THE MUSLIM WORLD
OF THE MIDDLE AGES

1. Cf. T. H. Hopkins, 'Sociology and the substantive view of the economy', in *Trade and Market in the Early Empires*, ed. K. Polanyi, C. M. Arensberg and H. W. Pearson, Glencoe, The Free Press, 1957, pp. 297, 299; cf. Polanyi, in the same symposium, pp. 64 et seq.
2. I have here drawn upon an unpublished study by the late Francisco Benet kindly sent me by the author, for which I am very grateful.
3. Cf. H. Lammens, especially in his *La Mecque à la veille de l'hégire*, Beirut, Imprimerie catholique, 1924 (= *Mélanges de l'Université St Joseph*, Vol. IX, part 3), in particular pp. 135 et seq. G. H. Bousquet, 'Une explication marxiste de l'Islam par un ecclésiastique épiscopalien', in *Hespéris*, 41, 1954, pp. 231–47, casts grave doubt on the validity of Lammens' analyses. It is certainly true, and many have commented on this, that Lammens' method is not always above reproach – passages are interpreted somewhat freely, the sources quoted are often far from reliable, the author's partiality is obvious, bold deductions are often made without justification, and his striking formulations about 'Meccan finance' are exaggerated and excessively 'modernizing'. Nevertheless, a kernel of indubitable facts remains, which are confirmed by non-Arabic texts and are, moreover, in accordance with the nature of things. Mecca, a town situated in an arid valley, was unable to sustain its population otherwise than by trade and the exploitation of religious pilgrimages. That this amounted to very little economic activity by the standards of modern Europe is readily admitted. The facts have to be appreciated, however, against the background of a population much less numerous than today. We are well enough informed about caravan cities that led an existence comparable to that of Mecca, such as Palmyra. On the relative trust to be given to our sources, see the discussion in my 'Bilan des études mohammadiennes', in *Revue historique*, Vol. 229, issue 465, January–March 1963, pp. 169–220, especially pp. 196 et seq. Cf., to the same effect, J. Chelhod, *Introduction à la sociologie de l'Islam*, Paris, Besson-Chantemerle, 1958 (Coll. Islam d'hier et d'aujourd'hui, 12), pp. 189–95, in which the treatment is, however, somewhat muddled. Mecca's need to import its food supplies does not come into the question except in so far as the town was unable to get these supplies

in exchange for craft products, or as its inhabitants were not in a position to exact them as landowners possessing estates in the neighbourhood, etc. To this extent they were indeed obliged to pay for their food supplies out of the income they drew from their capitalistic trade or from their control of the sanctuary.

4. *Der Islamische Orient*, Bd. II, *Die Arabische Frage*, Leipzig, R. Haupt, 1909, p. 455: 'The success of the Omayyad clan meant the triumph of capitalism in Arabia.' Cf. p. 449, on Muḥammad's troops, who were 'not an army but groups of capitalist entrepreneurs whom the entrepreneur-in-chief, Mohammed, had persuaded to invest a substantial capital in this business'.

5. A fact well attested not only by the Arabic sources but also by Pliny, *Naturalis Historia*, XII, ch. 32, para. 65. Incense, which was transported from South Arabia to Gaza by camel, in sixty-five stages, was charged with many payments to the leaders of the Beduin clans whose territory had to be traversed. 'All along the route they keep on paying, at one place for water, another for fodder, or the charges for lodging at the halts, and the various *octrois*; so that expenses mount up to 688 denarii per camel before the Mediterranean coast is reached . . .' – which, if I am not mistaken, is equivalent to 2.7 kg of silver. (Pliny, *Natural History*, trans. Rackham, Vol. 4, Harvard, 1945, p. 47.)

6. S. D. Goitein, 'The Rise of the Near-Eastern bourgeoisie in early Islamic times', in *Cahiers d'Histoire Mondiale*, 3, 1956–7, pp. 583–604, on p. 595, where references to sources are given. On a possibly apocryphal story of speculation in Egyptian wheat by Meccan merchants so early as the time of 'Omar, cf. Ibn 'Abd al-Ḥakam, in G. Jacob, 'Die ältesten Spuren des Wechsels', in *Mitteilungen des Seminars für Orientalische Sprachen*, 28, 2 Abt., 1925, pp. 280 et seq.

7. Ibn Khaldūn, *The Muqaddimah*, trans. F. Rosenthal, Vol. II, New York, Pantheon Books, 1958, pp. 336 et seq. The new edition of Ibn Khaldūn by Wāfī (Vol. III, Cairo, 1379/1960, p. 915) gives *daqīq*, 'flour', instead of *raqīq*, 'slaves', which looks like a 'modernizing' apologetical correction. Rosenthal refers the reader, with humour and relevance, to a recently-published book by one Frank V. Fisher, *Buy Low – Sell High: Guidance for the General Reader in Sound Investment Methods and Wise Trading Techniques*, New York, 1952.

8. Ibn Khaldūn, op. cit., trans. Rosenthal, Vol. II, pp. 343 et seq.

The disdainful attitude of the Arab sociologist is similar to that of Plato (*Laws*, IV, 704A; XI, 919C) and Aristotle (*Politics*, VII, 9, 1328B). Cf. M. Rodinson, 'Le Marchand méditerranéen à travers les âges', in *Markets and Marketing as Factors of Development in the Mediterranean Basin*, ed. C. A. O. van Nieuwenhuijze, The Hague, Mouton, 1963, pp. 71–92, on pp. 83 et seq.

9. Ibn Khaldūn, op. cit., trans. Rosenthal, Vol. II, p. 242.

10. Abū l-Faḍl Jaᶜfar ibn ᶜAlī ad-Dimishqī, *Kitāb al-ishāra*, according to H. Ritter, 'Ein arabisches Handbuch der Handelswissenschaft', in *Der Islam*, 7, 1917, pp. 1–91, on pp. 15 et seq., 27, 58, 66 et seq.; see the notes on this work by Cl. Cahen, in *Oriens*, 15, 1962, pp. 160–71.

11. Ibn Khaldūn, op. cit., trans. Rosenthal, Vol. II, p. 313.

12. Abū l-Faḍl Jaᶜfar ibn ᶜAlī ad-Dimishqī, in Ritter, op. cit., p. 5. A similar argument is found in Ibn Abī r-Rabīᶜ (thirteenth century?), cf. Ritter, p. 9, and probably comes originally from a Greek source, the *Economics* (lost in its original form) of the neo-Pythagorean Bryson. (Cf. M. Plessner, *Der Oikonomikos des Neupythagoreers 'Bryson' und sein Einfluss auf die islamische Wissenschaft*, Heidelberg, C. Winter, 1928, passim.) If, however, these Greek theorizings were reproduced (with certain modifications), this means that they must have still seemed valid.

13. Indications will be found here and there in A. Mez, *Die Renaissance des Islams*, Heidelberg, C. Winter, 1922, p. 449 et seq., among others. The facts are assembled by W. Björkman, art. cit., pp. 86 et seq. Cf., e.g., on the wealth of the Abbasid viziers, D. Sourdel, *Le Vizirat ᶜabbāside de 749 à 946*, Damascus, Institut de Damas, 1959–60, Vol. II, pp. 693 et seq.; on the accumulations of wealth in Basra in the eight and ninth centuries, Ch. Pellat, *Le Milieu basrien et la formation de Gāḥiẓ*, Paris, Adrien-Maissonneuve, 1953, pp. 228 et seq.

14. C. Cahen, in *L'Évolution économique, sociale, culturelle*, etc. (see note 7 to Chapter I), IV, pp. 10 et seq. Similarly, the example quoted by Mez (op. cit.), p. 358, from the *Kitāb al-faraj baᶜd ash-shidda*, II, p. 17. A young man who has learned to be prudent invests 50 per cent of his fortune in land, and lives on the income from this; he buries 25 per cent of it, against possible disasters; devotes 20 per cent to restoring and furnishing his house; and entrusts 5 per cent to a merchant, as sleeping partner's capital. But it would be wrong to generalize from this example.

15. Ibn Khaldūn, op. cit., trans. Rosenthal, Vol. II, pp. 283 et seq.
16. Cl. Cahen, in *L'Évolution économique, etc.* (see note 7 to Chapter I), IV, pp. 3, 8.
17. B. Spuler, *Iran in früh-islamischer Zeit*, Wiesbaden, F. Steiner, 1952, pp. 404–8; cf. Mez, op. cit., p. 436.
18. Mez, op. cit., p. 457; M. Rodinson, article '*Ghidhā*'' in *Encyclopedia of Islam*, Vol. II, 2nd edn, Eng. version 1965, pp. 1057–72. On this type of pre-capitalist monoculture, cf. M. Rodinson, 'De l'archéologie à la sociologie historique, notes méthodologiques sur le dernier ouvrage de G. Tchalenko', in *Syria*, 38, 1961, pp. 170–200.
19. W. Hinz, 'Lebensmittelpreise in mittelalterlichen Vorderen Orient', in *Die Welt des Orients*, 2, 1954–9, pp. 52–70.
20. Cf. Ritter, op. cit., pp. 14 et seq., 54 et seq.
21. Cf. the traditions quoted by Ritter, op. cit., pp. 29 et seq. and elsewhere, concerned with the cornering of goods, with fore-stalling (going out to meet the caravans approaching a town in order to do business with them before they reach the market), etc.
22. Abu Dāʾūd, XXII, 49; Tirmidhī, XII, 73; Ibn Māja, XII, 27; Dārimī, XVIII, 13; Aḥmad ibn Ḥanbal, III, 85, 286.
23. This is very clear, for example, from the excellent economic map of Europe and the Near East in the Middle Ages included in the Soviet school atlas *Atlas istorii srednikh vekov*, Moscow, Glavnoye upravlenie geodezii i kartografii pri sovete ministrov S.S.S.R., 1952, map 18, pp. 17–18.
24. S. D. Goitein, 'Artisans en Méditerranée orientale au haut Moyen Age', in *Annales*, 15, 1964, pp. 847–68.
25. What was involved, generally speaking, was something quite different from those consumer loans the prohibition of which in ancient Israelite society and in the Western European society of the Middle Ages has been justified by the fact that they in no way served as a factor in economic activity (cf. A. Dumas, article 'Intérêt et usure', in *Dictionnaire de droit canonique*, Vol. 5, Paris, Letouzey et Ané, 1953, cols 1475–1518, on cols 1475 et seq.; also R. Latouche, *Les Origines de l'économie occidentale (IVe–XIe siècles)*, Paris, Albin Michel, 1956, pp. 63 et seq., 179 et seq. What we have here are indeed credits that develop capitalistic activity by enabling borrowers to engage in profitable enterprises and lenders to accumulate a capital which seems, in many cases at least, to have been re-employed. And this was so no less in Quraysh than in the mediaeval Muslim economy of the classical epoch.

26. Cf. especially, *La Mecque à la veille de l'hégire*, op. cit., pp. 139 (235) et seq.

27. M. Hamidullah, in *Cahiers de l'I.S.E.A.*, suppl. no. 120 (Series V, no. 3), Dec. 1961, p. 35.

28. J. Schacht, *Das Kitāb al-ḥiial wal-mahārig des Abū Bakr Aḥmad . . . al-Hassāf*, dissertation, Hanover, H. Lafaire, 1923 (Coll. Beiträge zur semitischen Philologie und Linguistik, H.4); *Das Kitāb al-ḥijal fil-fiqh (Buch der Rechtskniffe)*, Hanover, H. Lafaire, 1924 (same collection, H.5); *Das Kitāb al-mahārig fil-ḥijal des Muḥammad ibn al-Ḥasan as-Saibānī*, Leipzig, J. C. Hinrichs, 1930 (same collection, H.8).

29. On all this see J. Schacht, art. cit. (note 12 to Chapter II), and D. Santillana, *Istituzioni* (op. cit.), II, pp. 392–7. Cf., earlier, J. Kohler, *Moderne Rechtsfragen bei islamitischen Juristen*, Würzburg, 1885, pp. 5–8.

30. H. Denzinger, *Enchiridion symbolorum*, 26th edn, Freiburg-im-Breisgau, Herder, 1947, para. 1190. This word (from Arabic *bayᶜ mokhāṭara*, literally, 'sale in which risks are incurred') survives in Spanish, in which *mohatra* means 'fraud, deception', as also does the corresponding word in Portuguese, *mofatra*.

31. Whereas there *would* be usury if the objects exchanged, though identical in kind, differed in weight. This is one of the classical definitions of *ribā*. (E.g., if I give two bushels of wheat and receive three bushels of the same.)

32. It would be forbidden, as has just been said, if this operation were regarded as an act of exchange; if, however, it can be presented as two gifts, one following the other, then the position is quite different!

33. Najm ad-dīn Abū l-Qāsim Jaᶜfar ibn Muḥammad al-Hillī (d. 676 or 726), *Kitāb sharā'iᶜ al-Islām*, Calcutta, 1839, p. 170, trans. A. Querry, *Droit musulman* (op. cit.), Vol. I, p. 408, para. 371.

34. Ibid. (Querry), p. 408, n. 3.

35. L. Massignon, 'L'influence de l'Islam au Moyen Age sur la fondation et l'essor des banques juives', in *Bulletin d'études orientales*, I, 1931, pp. 3–12, reprinted in L. Massignon, *Opera Minora*, Vol. I, Beirut, Dar al-Maaref, 1963, pp. 241–9. Massignon has frequently returned to this idea, which he largely derived from reading Werner Sombart's book on the role of the Jews in the development of Western capitalism – a book the ideas in which were later to some extent disavowed by Sombart himself. Cf., earlier, Mez, op. cit., pp. 449 et seq.

36. The bans that applied *within* a given community were usually not applicable as *between* communities.

37. Jāḥiẓ, *Le Livre des avares*, French translation by Ch. Pellat, Paris, G. P. Maisonneuve, 1951, pp. 150, 197–205 (references to the different editions of the Arabic text will be found on pp. 362–3); cf. Ch. Pellat, *Le Milieu basrien et la formation de Gāḥiẓ* (op. cit.), pp. 234 et seq.

38. H. R. Idris, *La Berbérie orientale sous les Zirides, Xe-XIIe siècles*, Paris, Adrien-Maisonneuve, 1962, 2 vols., Vol. II, pp. 653–66.

39. Cf. G. M. Wickens, 'The Saʿādatnāmeh attributed to Nāṣir-i Khusrau', in *The Islamic Quarterly*, 2, 1955, 117–32, 206–21, on pp. 208 et seq. (Chapter xxi).

40. R. Mantran, *Istanbul dans la seconde moitié du XVIIe siècle*, Paris, Adrien-Maisonneuve, 1962 (Coll. Bibliothèque archéologique et historique de l'Institut français d'archéologie d'Istanbul, XII), pp. 112, 173, 175.

41. *Voyages du chevalier Chardin en Perse et autres lieux de l'Orient* . . . , new edition by L. Langlés, Vol. VI, Paris, Le Normant, 1811, pp. 121 et seq.

42. R. Le Tourneau, *Fès avant le protectorat*, Casablanca, Société marocaine de librairie et d'édition, 1949, p. 288.

43. Ibid., p. 450, quoting *Diplomatic and Consular Reports on Trade and Finance, No. 1476* (*Morocco: Report for the Year 1893 on the Trade of Tangier*), Foreign Office Annual Series, London, H.M.S.O., 1894, p. 27.

44. Ibid., pp. 448–50, quoting E. Michaux-Bellaire, 'L'Usure', in *Archives marocaines*, 27, 1927, pp. 313–34, on pp. 319–22.

45. C. Snouck Hurgronje, *Mekka in the Latter Part of the 19th Century*, Eng. trans., Leiden, Brill, and London, Luzac, 1931, pp. 4–5, 30.

46. I quote examples at random. For Syria and the Lebanon, J. Weulersse, *Paysans de Syrie et du Proche-Orient*, Paris, Gallimard, 1946, pp. 125, 196. For Egypt, H. Habib-Ayrout, *Fellahs*, 2nd edn, Cairo, ed. Horus, 1942, pp. 68 et seq. (*Moeurs et coutumes des fellahs*, Paris, Payot, 1938, p. 84); J. Besançon, *L'Homme et le Nil*, Paris, Gallimard, 1957 (Coll. Géographie humaine, 28), pp. 266 et seq.; *L'Égypte indépendante*, Paris, P. Hartmann, 1938, pp. 304 et seq., and, already for the end of the eighteenth century, M. P. S. Girard, *Mémoire sur l'agriculture, l'industrie et le commerce de l'Égypte*, Paris, Imprimerie royale, 1822, pp. 87, 95, 136 (= *Description de l'Égypte*, 1st edn, Vol. VI, *État moderne*, Vol. II, Part 1, Paris,

Imprimerie impériale, 1813, pp. 577, 585, 626; 2nd edn, Vol. XVII, 1824, pp. 173, 190, 270). For Iraq, S. M. Salim, *Marsh Dwellers of the Euphrates Delta*, London, Athlone Press, 1962, pp. 130 et seq.; S. M. Salim, *Al-Chabāyish*, Baghdad, Ar-Rābiṭa Press, 1956–7, Vol. II, pp. 441 et seq.; F. I. Qubain, *The Reconstruction of Iraq, 1950–1957*, London, Atlantic Book Publishing Co., and New York, Praeger, 1958, p. 109. For Morocco, cf. Budgett Meakin, *The Moors*, London, S. Sonnenschein, 1902, pp. 169 et seq.; E. Michaux-Bellaire, 'L'Usure', in *Archives marocaines*, 27, 1927, pp. 313–34; R. Hoffherr and R. Morris, *Revenus et Niveaux de vie indigènes au Maroc*, Paris, Sirey, 1934, pp. 207 et seq. For Algeria, M. Gaffiot, 'L'Usure dans l'Afrique du Nord', in *Outre-Mer*, 7, 1935, pp. 3–26, gives many details and references to earlier publications; cf. also his article 'La répression de l'usure en Algérie' (reference in note 50, *infra*), and the thesis of his pupil E. L. A. Maissiat, *L'Usure en Algérie*, Algiers, Imprimerie Minerva, 1937 (University of Algiers, Faculty of Law). For Kabylia, cf. J-J. Rager, *Les Musulmans algériens en France et dans les pays islamiques*, Paris, Les Belles Lettres, 1950 (Coll. Publications de la Faculté des Lettres d'Alger, 2nd series, Vol. 17), pp. 147 et seq., and the novel by Mouloud Feraoun, *La Terre et le Sang*, Paris, Seuil, 1953 (Coll. Méditerranée), pp. 107 et seq. For Tunisia, cf. René Weill, *Du prêt à intérêt proprement dit et sur gage en Tunisie* (law thesis, Paris, 1902); Ch. Saint-Paul, *La Lutte contre l'usure en Tunisie* (law thesis, Aix, 1914); P. Sebag, *La Tunisie, essai de monographie*, Paris, Éditions Sociales, 1951, p. 106 (according to one official report, Tunisia is 'a country where not a single minute goes by without some transaction being carried out by a usurer'). For Arabia, cf. Ch. M. Doughty, *Arabia Deserta*, London, C.U.P., 1888, II, pp. 355, 388, 412 et seq.; and, *supra*, pp. 58 et seq. For Turkey, cf. A. F. Miller, *Ocherki noveishei istorii Turtsii*, Moscow and Leningrad, Izd. Akademii Nauk, S.S.S.R., 1948, pp. 164 et seq. For Iran, H. Djourabtchi. *Structure économique de l'Iran*, Geneva, Droz, 1955 (Coll. Études d'histoire économique, politique et sociale, XI), pp. 20, 134; A. K. S. Lambton, *Landlord and Peasant in Persia*, London, O.U.P., 1953, pp. 380 et seq.; Nikki R. Keddie, *Historical Obstacles to Agrarian Changes in Iran*, Claremont, California, Society for Oriental Studies, Claremont Graduate School, 1960 (Coll. Claremont Asian Studies No. 8), pp. 5, 15. For Afghanistan, cf. D. N. Wilber, *Afghanistan*, New Haven, H.R.A.F. Press, 1962, pp. 226–62. For Soviet Turkestan, cf.

A. Woeikof, *Le Turkestan russe*, Paris, A. Colin, 1914, pp. 144 et seq., and the *novella* by Sadriddin Aini, *La Mort de L'Usurier*, French translation from a Russian version, Paris, Éditeurs français réunis, 1957 (the *novella*, a portrait of a usurer in pre-1917 Bukhara, which gives the collection its title, is on pp. 50–160). In the former German colony in East Africa, the worst usurers were Arabs and Indian Muslims, according to C. H. Becker (*Islamstudien*, I, p. 63). On the usurers who lend to the peasants at a higher rate the money that they themselves have borrowed from official credit institutions, cf., e.g., the works, quoted above, by J. Weulersse, p. 125, and by A. Woeikof and P. Sebag at the pages mentioned; also, E. Antonini, *Le Crédit et la banque en Égypte* (dissertation), Lausanne, Impr. G. Vaney-Burnier, 1927, pp. 72 et seq. There is a survey of the widespread extent of loans to agriculturalists at usurious rates of interest (generally by the landowner himself) in D. Warriner, *Land and Poverty in the Middle East*, London, Royal Institute of International Affairs, 1948, pp. 135 et seq.

47. Maurice Gaffiot, 'L'Usure dans l'Afrique du Nord' (op. cit.), pp. 9, 18.

48. E. Michaux-Bellaire, op. cit., p. 313.

49. Ibid., p. 327.

50. Report to the President of the French Republic, signed by the Minister of the Interior (R. Salengro) and the Minister of Justice (M. Rucart), setting out the reasons for the decree in question (*Journal officiel*, 18 July 1936, p. 7477). Cf. Maurice Gaffiot, 'La Répression de l'usure en Algérie', in *Troisième Congrès de la Fédération des sociétés savantes de l'Afrique du Nord, Constantine, 30 mars–1er avril, 1937*, Vol. I (= *Revue africaine*, 81, Nos. 372, 373, 3rd and 4th quarters of 1937), pp. 99–125.

51. Benali Fekar, op. cit., pp. 10, 12.

52. The volume of writing on the prohibition of lending at interest in ancient Israel and in Christian society is considerable. I will do no more here than refer the reader to the synthesis provided by the long, three-part article 'Usure' in the *Dictionnaire de théologie catholique*, Vol. XV, 2nd part, Paris, Letouzey et Ané, 1950, cols 2316–90, by A. Bernard (on the formation of the ecclesiastical doctrine on usury, cols 2316–36, with an outline of the facts relating to the Biblical, Greek, Latin, Byzantine and Western early-mediaeval periods), G. Le Bras (excellent synthetic exposition of ecclesiastical doctrine on usury in the classical period, twelfth–fifteenth centuries, cols 2336–72) and

H. du Passage (on Catholic doctrine since the sixteenth century, cols 2372–90).

53. Ibid., col. 2360.

54. Cf. M. Hamidullah, in *Cahiers de l'I.S.E.A.*, suppl. no 120 (series V, no. 3), Dec. 1961, p. 35, following ʿAbd al-Ḥayy al-Kattānī.

55. Leo Africanus, *History and Description of Africa*, Hakluyt Society, 1896, Vol. I, p. 186.

56. Cf. R. Brunschwig, *La Berbérie orientale sous les Hafsides*, Paris, Adrien-Maisonneuve, 1940–7, Vol. II, p. 248. This learned writer seems now to have gone back to the view that the ban on *ribā* 'paralysed the rise of capitalism' (ibid., p. 246); cf. his contribution at the colloquium *L'Évolution économique* ... (note 7 to Chapter I), I, pp. 8–10.

57. Marx, *Capital*, Vol. III, chapter 46 and chapter 47, section 4.

58. Ibid., Vol. III, F.L.P.H. edition, p. 781.

59. Cf., e.g., C. H. Becker, *Islamstudien*, I, Leipzig, Quelle u. Meyer, 1924, pp. 186, 270. The passage in Jāḥiẓ on this question is well-known, cf. the translation by Ch. Pellat (reference in note 37, *supra*), pp. 116 et seq.

60. Cf. J. Hochfeld, *Studia* ... (reference in note 10 to Chapter I), p. 170 et seq.; E. Mandel, *Marxist Economic Theory*, English translation, Vol. I, London, Merlin Press, 1968, pp. 65–8.

61. S. D. Goitein, 'Artisans en Méditerranée orientale au haut Moyen Age', in *Annales*, 15, 1964, pp. 847–68.

62. Gardēzī, *kitāb zayn al-akhbār*, ed. M. Nāẓin, Berlin, 1928, p. 10, quoted in B. Spuler, *Iran in früh-islamischer Zeit*, Wiesbaden, F. Steiner, 1952, pp. 411, 511.

63. Māzarī, quoted in H. R. Idris, op. cit., II, p. 639.

64. Cf. A. Grohmann, art. 'Ṭirāz', in *Encyclopedia of Islam*, 1st edn, English version, Vol. IV, 1934, pp. 785–93.

65. Mez, op. cit., pp. 419 et seq., where his references will be found.

66. Cf. especially, B. Lewis, 'The Islamic Guilds', in *Economic History Review*, 8, 1937, pp. 20–37; H. A. R. Gibb and H. Bowen, *Islamic Society and the West*, Vol. I, Part 1, London, O.U.P., 1950, pp. 281 et seq. A vivid picture is given by R. Mantran, in *La Vie quotidienne à Constantinople au temps de Soliman le Magnifique et de ses successeurs*, Paris, Hachette, 1965, pp. 119–33.

67. R. Mantran, *Istanbul dans la seconde moitié du XVIIe siècle*, Paris, Adrien-Maisonneuve, 1962 (Coll. Bibliothèque archéologique et historique de l'Institut français d'archéologie d'Istanbul, Vol. XII), pp. 355, 412.

68. Chabrol, in *Description de l'Égypte, État moderne*, Vol. II, 2nd part, Paris, 1822, pp. 365 et seq., 516 = 2nd edn, Vol. XVIII, 1st part, Paris, 1826, pp. 10 et seq., 323 et seq.; cf. F. M. Atsamba, in *Ocherki po istorii arabskikh stran*, Moscow, 1959, p. 6.

69. M. P. S. Girard, *Mémoire sur l'agriculture, l'industrie et le commerce de l'Égypte*, Paris, 1822, p. 102 = *Description de l'Égypte, État moderne*, Vol. II, 1st part, Paris, 1813, p. 592; 2nd edn, Vol. XVII, Paris, 1824, p. 203.

70. Girard, ibid., pp. 96, 120 et seq., 220 = *Descr. de l'Égypte*, ibid., pp. 586, 610 et seq., 710; 2nd edn., Vol. XVII, pp. 190 et seq., 238 et seq., 435 et seq.

71. Girard, ibid., pp. 105 et seq. = *Descr. de l'Égypte*, ibid., pp. 595 et seq.; 2nd edn., Vol. XVII, pp. 209 et seq. Cf. Atsamba, op. cit., p. 10.

72. The theoretician of trade Ja'far ibn 'Alī classifies in three categories the ways in which one may acquire goods: by force, like the state and like criminals; by skill, like craftsmen, members of the liberal professions and traders; and by mixed ways. In this last category, characterized by the mixture of force and skill, belong trade as carried on by the state, using measures of authority, and also trade as carried on by big capitalists who dominate the market through selling on a massive scale, thereby forcing down the market price to the detriment of the small-scale trader (quoted in Ritter, art. cit., p. 6). On the state sector, cf. W. Björkman, art. cit., p. 93.

73. S. D. Goitein, art. cit. in note 6, *supra*. In the manual of commerce by Ja'far ibn 'Alī ad-Dimishqī, already referred to several times, and which is supposed to have been written in the eleventh or the twelfth century, it is typical that different advice is given to the bonder depending on whether he has to deal with a weak state or a strong one, a just state or a tyrannical one. In the case of a government that is tyrannical and strong, it is best to carry on one's trading activity in secret; if one lives under a government that is just and weak, dealings should be restricted to lightweight goods, easy to conceal; where the government is tyrannical and weak, it is best to get out as quickly as possible (Ritter, art. cit., pp. 15 et seq.)

74. Cf. Rodinson, art. cit. in note 8, *supra*, pp. 79 et seq.

75. Cf. Rodinson, art. cit. ('De l'archéologie . . .') in note 18, *supra*, pp. 195 et seq.

76. Cf. E. Mandel, *Marxist Economic Theory*, Eng. trans., Vol. I, Chapter 4, 'The development of capital': *The Transition from*

Feudalism to Capitalism, symposium by P. Sweezy, H. K. Takahashi, M. Dobb, R. Hilton, C. Hill, London, Fore Publications, no date (articles published in *Science and Society* between 1950 and 1953).

77. *Political Economy: a textbook issued by the Institute of Economics of the Academy of Sciences of the U.S.S.R.*, 2nd edition, Eng. trans., London, 1957, pp. 42–3.

78. A. Belyaev, in *Cahiers d'histoire mondiale*, 4, 1957–8, p. 233, with S. D. Goitein's reply on the following page.

79. See the history of the idea in R. Boutruche, *Seigneurie et féodalité*, I, *Le Premier Âge des liens d'homme à homme*, Paris, Aubier, 1959 (Coll. Historique), pp. 11 et seq.

80. Cf., e.g. the 'Observations' of that great historian Georges Lefebvre, in *La Pensée*, 65, January–February 1956, pp. 22–5. He does not deserve the reproach in question, but he does fail to grasp the difference that Marx makes (implicitly, at least, though with imprecisions of nomenclature that can mislead the reader) between (1) development of capital, (2) capitalist mode of production, and (3) capitalist socio-economic formation. R. Boutruche sees the problem of distinguishing between the 'feudal' formation and the economic system underlying it, in Marx's thought, but does not explain this very clearly (op. cit., pp. 18 et seq.).

81. K. Marx, *Grundrisse der Kritik der politischen Oekonomie, Rohentwurf*, Berlin, Dietz, 1953, pp. 375–413. (English translation of this section, with an excellent introduction by E. J. Hobsbawm: *Pre-Capitalist Economic Formations*, London, Lawrence and Wishart, 1964).

82. Ibid., p. 409, line 25 (Eng. trans., p. 114); p. 390, line 24 (Eng. trans., p. 88).

83. See the judicious and able pages from the pen of Claude Cahen, 'Réflexions sur l'usage du mot "féodalité"', in *Recherches internationales à la lumière du marxisme*, no. 37, 1963, pp. 203–14.

84. *Grundrisse*, p. 377, line 11 (Eng., trans. p. 70: *durchaus* rendered as 'entirely').

85. M. Godelier, *La Notion de 'mode de production asiatique' et les schémas marxistes d'évolution des sociétés*, Paris, 1964, 43 roneotyped pages (Coll. Les Cahiers du Centre d'Études et de Recherches Marxistes), summarized in his article 'La Notion de "mode de production asiatique"', in *Les Temps Modernes*, Vol. XX, no. 228, May 1965, pp. 2002–27. See the criticism of this by J. Chesneaux, 'Le Mode de production asiatique; quelques perspectives de recherche', in *La Pensée*, no. 114,

April 1964, pp. 33–55, and the implicit criticism in P. Vidal-Naquet's introduction to the French translation of K. A. Wittfogel's *Oriental Despotism* (*Le Despotisme Oriental*, Paris, Éd. de Minuit, 1964, Coll. Arguments, 23); for a slightly different version of this, see P. Vidal-Naquet, 'Histoire et idéologie, Karl Wittfogel et le concept de "mode de production asiatique"', in *Annales*, 1964, pp. 531–49.

86. Marx, unlike many Marxists, distinguished sharply between property, or ownership (*Eigentum*), and possession (*Besitzung*). His conception of property is strongly influenced by the Roman and Western legal concept. On the Oriental type of community he writes: 'the individual member as such is only the *possessor* of a particular part of it, hereditary or not, for any fraction of property belongs (*gehört*) to no member for himself but only as the direct part of the community . . .': 'the individual is therefore only a possessor. What exists is only *communal* property and *private possessions*'. (*Grundrisse*, p. 380, lines 27–33: *Pre-Capitalist Economic Formations*, p. 75). This 'private possession' may, of course, be regarded as property (ownership) if one gives the latter concept a wider meaning than it has in Roman law – which is what the majority of ethnographers have been led to do. It is not a question of 'primitive communism', in the sense of no kind of private appropriation being known, because 'possession' can even be hereditary, and the collective ownership involved here is essentially ownership of the land. Hence phrases like: 'The property [of the individual in the objective conditions of his labour] mediated by its existence in a community, may appear as *communal property*, which gives the individual only possession and no private property in the soil' (*Grundrisse*, p. 385, lines 30–33: *Pre-Capitalist Economic Formations*, p. 82). I dwelt upon these distinctions in my 'Stalinist' article on Engels's *Origin of the Family*, in *La Pensée*, 66, March–April 1956, pp. 13–15. This is the answer to the ethnographers referred to in that article, as also to more recent and ampler attacks upon the ghost of 'primitive communism', e.g., W. Nippold, *Die Anfänge des Eigentums bei den Naturvölkern und die Entstehung des Privateigentums*, The Hague, Mouton, 1954.

87. *Grundrisse*, p. 397, lines 1–3 (*Pre-Capitalist Economic Formations*, p. 97.)

88. Ibid., p. 385, line 43, to 386, line 10 (p. 88).

89. Ibid., p. 390, lines 25 et seq. (pp. 88–9).

90. Ibid., p. 395, lines 1–6 (pp. 94–5).

91. I will here confine myself to taking the example of the Papuans, who are primitive agriculturists, and very warlike, but among whom wars never result in the subjection and exploitation of the conquered entity. It has been possible to say of one group of them (and it seems a proposition valid for all) that 'the mere idea of land without an owner is quite strange to the Kiwais' (G. Landtman, *The Origin of the Inequality of the Social Classes*, London, Kegan Paul, Trench and Trubner, 1938, p. 6); cf., also by G. Landtman, *The Kiwai Papuans of British New Guinea*, London, Macmillan, 1917, chapters X and XII; R. M. Berndt, in *New Guinea, The Central Highlands* (= *American Anthropologist*, Vol. 66, no. 4, part 2, August 1964), pp. 183–203; L. Pospisil, *The Kapauku Papuans of West New Guinea*, New York, Holt, Rinehart and Winston, 1964, pp. 44 et seq., 49, 55 et seq., etc.

92. Cf., especially, Boutruche, op. cit.

93. E.g., the attempts at classification made by R. Thurnwald, *Economics in Primitive Communities*, London, O.U.P., 1932.

94. R. Brunschwig, art. ''Abd' in *Encyclopedia of Islam*, Vol. I, 2nd edn, English version, 1960, pp. 24–40.

95. The best synthesis of this aspect of the matter is that given by Claude Cahen, 'Contribution à l'histoire de l'*iqṭāᶜ*, in *Annales*, 8, 1953, pp. 25–52.

96. E.g., in the discussion among Soviet historians in June 1960 on the origins of capitalism in the East, the position taken up by L. B. Alayev, in *O genezise kapitalizma v stranakh Vostoka* (*XV–XIX vv.*), *materialy obsuzhdeniya*, Moscow, Izd. Vost. Lit., 1962, pp. 396 et seq., and also the position of I. M. Smilyanskaya with regard to the Arab countries, ibid., pp. 409 et seq.

97. Marx, *Grundrisse*, p. 396, lines 32 et seq. (*Pre-Capitalist Economic Formations*, p. 97).

98. Ibid., pp. 396 et seq. (pp. 98–9).

99. Ibid., p. 406 (p. 110).

100. It is doubtless among the naïve that we should place the scholar of al-Azhar University Zaydān Abū l-makārim, whose book *Binā al-iqtiṣād fī l-Islām* (The economic structure in Islam), Cairo, Dār-al-ᶜurūba, 1959, presents (pp. 4 et seq.) Muslim Arab society as well organized in accordance with the *fiqh* before the 'congealing' effect brought about by Turkish domination, and subsequent colonialism. The Turks would not agree!

101. This point has been developed, sometimes with exaggerations,

but nevertheless on a foundation of incontestable facts, by the Marxists Bendelī Jawzī, *min taʾrīkh al-ḥarakāt al-fikriyya fī l-Islam*, I, *min taʾrīkh al-ḥarakāt al-ijtimāʿiyya* (On the history of ideological movements in Islam, I, On the history of social movements), Jerusalem, Bayt al-maqdis, 1928; and E. A. Belyaev, *Musul'manskoye sektantstvo*, Moscow, 1957. On the social tendencies of the Ismāʿīlī sect, cf., e.g., the points briefly made by B. Lewis, *The Arabs in History*, 3rd edn, London, Hutchinson, 1964, pp. 107 et seq.

102. M. Hamidullah (*Cahiers de l'I.S.E.A.*, suppl. no. 120 [series V, no. 3], Dec. 1961, pp. 28 et seq.) adds to this the Koran's laws on inheritance, which, by restricting testamentary freedom and imposing a division of the heritage among specifically indicated relatives, in accordance with fixed shares, are supposed to have hindered the accumulation of wealth in few hands. In reality these arrangements (inspired by a concern for justice, without any clear realization of what the economic consequences would be) were more effective in preventing the *transmission* than the *formation* of great fortunes. Since enterprises were, in the classical period, mainly family affairs, division of the property of the head of a family among members of his family did not prevent the family firm from continuing to accumulate a certain capital. If the worst came to the worst, the harmful consequences of possible division of a heritage could be palliated by the stratagem of gifts *inter vivos*. Classical Islam invented, moreover, the formula of the *waqf* (the pious foundation in mortmain) belonging to a particular family (*ahlī*), which made it possible legally to keep a fortune undivided on the quite fictitious pretext of a pious intention (cf. e.g., G. Baer, *A History of Landownership in Modern Egypt, 1800–1950*, London, O.U.P., 1962, pp. 115, 163 et seq.) Finally, it must not be forgotten that testamentary freedom was in many cases highly restricted also in a number of parts of mediaeval Europe.

CHAPTER 4: THE INFLUENCE OF MUSLIM IDEOLOGY
GENERALLY IN THE ECONOMIC FIELD

1. *Die protestantische Ethik und der Geist des Kapitalismus*, p. 15: Eng. trans., *The Protestant Ethic and the Spirit of Capitalism*, New York, 1958, p. 30.
2. Cf. especially Weber, *Wirtschaftsgeschichte*, pp. 270, 289 et seq., 300 et seq.: Eng. trans., *General Economic History*, Glencoe, 1927, pp. 312–14, 338–9 352.
3. A relatively up-to-date bibliography is given by R. H. Tawney in his introduction to the Eng. trans. of *Die protestantische Ethik*, p. 4, n. 1. Cf., more recently, *The Reformation, Material or Spiritual?*, ed. Lewis W. Spitz, Boston, D. C. Heath, 1962 (Coll. Problems in European Civilization) and all the first part of the collection of articles by Herbert Luthy, *Le Passé présent*, Monaco, Éditions du Rocher, 1965 (Coll. Preuves).
4. Cf., in R. Blachère's (French translation (in its two forms, *Le Coran*, Paris, G. P. Maisonneuve, later Besson et Chantemerle, 1949–50, 3 vols., and *Le Coran* (*al-Qur'ān*), Paris, Besson, 1957, in one volume), the index, under '*Preuves*', especially 6:57; 40:29/28, and Sura 98, which is actually entitled *al-bayyinat*, 'the evidence'. Cf. also the *baṣā'ir*, translated by Blachère as '*appels à la clairvoyance*' (appeals to clearsightedness) and by Kazimirski as '*preuves évidentes*' (obvious evidence). Cf. O. Pautz, *Muhammeds Lehre von der Offenbarung*, Leipzig, W. Drugulin, 1898, pp. 80–81.
5. Cf. H. Grimme, *Mohammed* (op. cit.), Vol. II, pp. 71 et seq.; M. Gaudefroy-Demombynes, *Mahomet*, Paris, Albin Michel, 1957 (Coll. l'Évolution de l'Humanité, 36), pp. 330 et seq.; Pautz, op. cit., pp. 122 et seq.
6. According to the ideology of the Koran, Islam is indeed 'of all time': all the true prophets, from Adam onward, together with those who hearkened unto them, were Muslims, that is, consistent monotheists who had submitted to God.
7. In the same sense, cf. 10:42/41.
8. Cf., e.g., Gaudefroy-Demombynes, *Mahomet*, pp. 322 et seq.
9. On the meaning of the word, cf. Pautz, op. cit., pp. 93 et seq.
10. '*Caractéristique de Mahomet d'après le Qoran*', in *Recherches de science religieuse*, 20, 1930, pp. 416–38, on p. 430. The whole of my argument is a reply to the objection offered by Y. Moubarac (*Abraham dans le Coran*, Paris, Vrin, 1958, p. 111, n. 1) to this formulation. This writer plainly 'Christianizes' Muḥammad in a certain way. The text from St Paul that he

quotes (*Romans*, 1:19–20) is comparable to the conceptions of Muḥammad, but it cannot be detached from a context that is much more fideistic.

11. Grimme, *Mohammed*, II, p. 105.
12. Pautz, op. cit., pp. 80 et seq.
13. Cf. C. C. Torrey, *The Commercial-Theological Terms in the Koran* (Strasbourg thesis), Leiden, Brill, 1892, iv + 51 pp.
14. Ibid., p. 48.
15. Cf. M. Gaudefroy-Demombynes, 'Le Sens du substantif *ghayb* dans le Coran', in *Mélanges Louis Massignon*, II, Beirut, Institut français de Damas, 1957, pp. 245–50.
16. Grimme, *Mohammed*, II, p. 119.
17. Cf. H. Ringgren, 'The Conception of faith in the Koran', in *Oriens*, 4, 1951, pp. 1–20 on pp. 15 et seq.
18. A story that has been told many times: cf. M. Rodinson, *Mohammed*, Eng. trans., p. 73.
19. I permit myself to quote this *ḥadīth*, which, though perhaps somewhat shocking to the official prudery of scholarly circles, is found in the work of the grave and pious Ṭabarī. It is attributed to the Prophet's first wife, Khadīja, who was the first to believe in him:

She said to the Messenger of God, concerning the possibility of a confirmation of the gift of prophecy with which Allah had honoured him: Cousin, can you tell me of (the presence of) your companion who comes to visit you, when he arrives? He answered: Yes. She said: Good, then, if he comes, tell me. Then Gabriel came to visit him, as he had been doing. The Messenger of God said: Khadīja! Gabriel has come to visit me. She said: Good. Get up, then, cousin, and sit on my left thigh. The Messenger of God rose and sat there. She said: Can you see him? He said: Yes. She said: Move over and sit on my right thigh. The Messenger of God moved and sat where she wished. She said: Can you see him? He said: Yes. She said: Now move again, and sit on my lap. He did as she asked. She said: Can you see him? He said: Yes. Then she began to undress, putting off her veils while the Messenger of God was still sitting on her lap. Then she said: Can you see him? He said: No. Then she said: Cousin, persist, and rejoice in the good news! By Allah, it was really an angel, and not the Devil!

(*Annales*, ed. M. J. de Goeje, etc., Leiden, Brill, 1879–1901, Vol. 3 (1881–2), p. 1152: Cairo edn, 1357–8/1939, Vol. II, p. 50.)

20. Cf. Y. Moubarac, op. cit., pp. 108–18. In my 'Bilan des études mohammadiennes' in *Revue historique*, Vol. 229, issue 465, January–March 1963, pp. 169–220, on p. 215, note 1, criticizing the writer's approach to the question of the 'influences', I did not go into the problem thoroughly, and took for granted his thesis of a difference in kind between the conception of Abraham's conversion found in the Jewish writings and that given in the Koran. On looking more closely at the matter, however, it does not seem to me that the difference is so great. It must nevertheless be pointed out that the Jewish writings in question are eminently representative of *Spätjudentum*, being filled with a Hellenistic spirit that is somewhat different from the Biblical mentality. Cf. J. Bonsirven, *Le Judaïsme palestinien au temps de Jésus-Christ*, Paris, Beauchesne, 1935, II, 48–52.

21. G. Von Rad, *Theologie des Alten Testaments*, Bd. I, 2nd edn., Munich, Kaiser, 1958, pp. 61 et seq., 422 et seq.: French trans., *Théologie de L'Ancien Testament*, I, Geneva, Labor et Fides, 1963, pp. 55 et seq., 367 et seq.

22. Ibid., p. 442 (384).

23. The words 'believe' and 'faith' occur especially often in the later writings. Cf. J. Bonsirven, op. cit., Vol. II, p. 48, n. 3.

24. Cf. H. A. Wolfson, *The Philosophy of the Church Fathers*, Vol. I, Cambridge (Mass.), Harvard U.P., 1956, pp. 19 et seq.

25. Ibid., pp. 97 et seq.

26. The references are conveniently assembled in the *Vocabulaire de théologie biblique*, published under the direction of X. Léon-Dufour, etc., Paris, Éditions du Cerf, 1962, p. 1002a (s.v. '*scandale*').

27. Cl. Tresmontant, *Essai sur la pensée hébraïque*, Paris, Ed. du Cerf, 1953 (Coll. Lectio Divina, 12), pp. 118 et seq.

28. *De praescriptione haereticorum*, VII, 6, 9, 11–13. (Eng. trans., *Tertullian*, trans. C. Dodgson, Oxford, 1842, pp. 441–2.)

29. *De carne Christi*, 5 (Eng. trans., *Tertullian's Treatise on the Incarnation*, trans. Evans, London, S.P.C.K., 1956, p. 19): cf. H. A. Wolfson, op. cit., I, pp. 103, 124 et seq.

30. Cf. Wolfson, op. cit., pp. 127 et seq.

31. T. Andrae, *Der Ursprung des Islams und das Christentum*, Uppsala and Stockholm, Almquist and Wiksell, 1926, pp. 123 et seq.: French trans., *Les Origines de l'Islam et le Christianisme*, Paris, Adrien-Maisonneuve, 1955 (Coll. Initiation à l'Islam, 8), pp. 130 et seq.

32. Cf. H. Ringgren, op. cit., pp. 12 et seq. But the root of this

conception is already to be found in Philo, cf. J. Daniélou, *Philon d'Alexandrie*, Paris, A. Fayard, 1958, p. 148.

33. Cf. R. Roques, *Structures théologiques, de la Gnose à Richard de St Victor*, Paris, P.U.F., 1962 (Coll. Bibliothèque de l'École des Hautes Etudes, Sciences religieuses, 72), pp. 144 et seq., 161 et seq. Note, e.g., the passage from *De divinis nominibus*, II, 9 (648 B) where mention is made of 'that one-ness and that faith which are not learned but experienced in a mysterious way' (*Oeuvres complètes* of Pseudo-Dionysius the Areopagite, trans. M. de Gandillac, Paris, Aubier, 1943, p. 86).

34. Wolfson, op. cit., p. 140.

35. A good summary of the present standpoint of Catholic theology can be found in L. Gardet and M.-M. Anawati, *Introduction à la théologie musulmane, essai de théologie comparée*, Paris, Vrin, 1948 (Coll. Études de philosophie médiévale, 37), pp. 330 et seq., 345 et seq.

36. Cf. Roques, op. cit., pp. 246, 288.

37. 'In many respects faith perceives the invisible things of God in a higher way than natural reason does in proceeding to God from his creatures.' (*Summa theologiae*, II, 2, qu. 2, art. 3: Eng. trans., *The Summa Theologica of St Thomas Aquinas . . .*, Vol. 9, London, 1917, p. 35.

38. 'As, for instance, when a man either has not the will, or not a prompt will, to believe, unless he be moved by human reason: and in this way human reason diminishes the merit of faith.' (Ibid., II, 2, qu. 2, art. 10: Eng. trans., ibid., p. 50.)

39. W. Montgomery Watt, *Muhammad at Mecca*, Oxford, Clarendon Press, 1953, pp. 24 et seq.; cf. M. Rodinson in *Histoire universelle*, Vol. II, Paris, Gallimard, 1957 (Encyclopédie de la Pléiade, IV), p. 26.

40. Cf. H. Ringgren, *Studies in Arabian Fatalism*, Uppsala, A. B. Lundequist, and Wiesbaden, O. Harassowitz, 1955 (Coll. Uppsala Universitets Arsskrift, 1955, 2).

41. H. Grimme, *Mohammed*, II, pp. 105–9; Tor Andrae, *Muhammed, hans liv och hans tro*, Stockholm, Natur och Kultur, 1930, pp. 83 et seq. (Eng. trans., *Mohammed, the Man and his Faith*, London, 1936, pp. 84 et seq.); Goldziher, *Vorlesungen über den Islam*, 2nd edn., Heidelberg, Winter, 1925, pp. 12 et seq., French trans., *Le Dogme et la Loi de l'Islam*, Paris, Geuthner, 1920, pp. 11 et seq.; W. Montgomery Watt, *Free Will and Predestination in Islam*, London, Luzac, 1948, pp. 12–17; Pautz, op. cit., pp. 106 et seq.

42. Grimme, *Mohammed*, II, p. 109, n. 1, basing himself essentially on *Koran* 3:159/165 et seq., and 4:80/78 et seq.
43. M. Hamidullah, *Le Prophète de l'Islam*, Paris, Vrin, 1959, II, p. 515.
44. Cf. the index of R. Blachère's French translation, s.v. '*monde*'.
45. L. Massignon, *Essai sur les origines du lexique technique de la mystique musulmane*, 2nd edn., Paris, Vrin, 1954, pp. 140 et seq.
46. This was well appreciated by the great 13th century mystic Jalāl ad-Dīn Rūmī, quoted by F. Meier, in the symposium *Classicisme et Déclin culturel dans l'histoire de l'Islam*, Paris, Besson-Chantemerle, 1957, p. 232.
47. This idea was justifiably developed in a work that played an important role in the awakening of the Moslem world to modern realities – Shakīb Arslān, *li-mā dhā taʾakhkhara l-Muslimūn wa-li-mā dhā taqaddama ghayru-hum* ('why have the Muslims remained behind while others have progressed'), Cairo, Impr. du Manār, 1349 (1930–31), pp. 68 et seq., which quotes numerous verses of the Koran in which there appear the words ʿ*amala*, 'to work, labour, make', and ʿ*amal* 'work, labour'. The author exaggerates the significance of some of these, but fundamentally he is right. He does not fail to mention, as I also do, what might be called the fatalism of the Gospels (p. 72). For a similar, earlier view, see the great modernistic reformer Muḥammad ʿAbdūh, cf. Osman Amin, *Muḥammad ʿAbduh, essai sur ses idées philosophiques et religieuses*, Cairo, Impr. Misr, 1944, pp. 160 et seq., and many others. It is, of course, commonplace in Muslim modernism to emphasize this tendency in Islam. To quote one more out of a hundred possible examples, the poem by the prince of poets Aḥmad Shawqī (1868–1932), reproduced by Mūḥammad Ḥusayn, *al-ittijāhāt al-wataniyya fī l-adab al-muʿaṣir*, Cairo, *maktabat al-ādāb*, no date (about 1954–6), Vol. I, pp. 341 et seq. It will be seen that the sociologist J. Poirier, who doubtless expresses the ideas current among non-specialists in Islamic studies, is wrong to suspect that the Muslim modernists misinterpret Koranic texts in order to provide sacred backing for their anti-fatalistic attitude (in *Cahiers de l'I.S.E.A.*, suppl. no. 120 [series V, no. 3], Dec. 1961, pp. 213 et seq.) The anti-fatalistic verses are no less valid than the deterministic ones. To such an extent has the 'intrinsic fatalism' of Islam become a dogma for the European public!
48. Translator's note: in the original French edition the author used the Jerusalem Bible version. In this edition the more familiar Authorized Version has been used.

49. *Vocabulaire de théologie biblique*, p. 271 b.
50. This question is treated as a whole by D. B. Macdonald, article '*shir*' in *Encyclopedia of Islam*, 1st edn, English version, Vol. 4, 1934, pp. 409–17.
51. Macdonald (art. cit.) is wrong in seeing Jesus as affected by this charge only in 5:110. He is also affected in 61:6. Moreover, verses 26:153, 185, do not concern Muḥammad, as is said several times, but other prophets.
52. Weber, *Wirtschaftsgeschichte*, Munich and Leipzig, Duncker u. Humblot, 1923, p. 308: Eng. trans. (see note 2), p. 361.
53. Ibid., p. 307 (Eng. trans., p. 360).
54. Cf. Johs. Pedersen, *Israel, its Life and Culture*, London, O.U.P., and Copenhagen, P. Branner, 1926–40, Vol. I–II, pp. 199 et seq.
55. Ibid., pp. 164, 430 et seq., 448 et seq.
56. A good example from this economic field is provided by R. Arnaldez, 'Sur une interprétation économique et sociale des théories de la "zakāt" en droit musulman', in *Cahiers de l'I.S.E.A.*, no. 106 (series V, no. 2), Oct., 1960, pp. 65–86.
57. A good popular exposition will be found in A. Guillaume, *The Traditions of Islam, an Introduction to the Study of the Hadith, Literature*, Oxford, Clarendon Press, 1924, pp. 19 et seq.
58. Cf. A. J. Wensinck, art. '*sunna*', in *Encyclopedia of Islam*, 1st edn, Eng. version, Vol. 4, 1934, pp. 555–7.
59. Cf. J. Schacht, *Esquisse d'une histoire du droit musulman*, Paris, Besson, 1953 (Coll. Institut des Hautes Études Marocaines, Notes et Documents, XI), pp. 65–70.
60. Weber, *Wirtschaftsgeschichte*, p. 289 (Eng. trans., p. 339).
61. Weber, *Die protestantische Ethik* . . ., p. 3 (Eng. trans., p. 16).
62. Cf., e.g., Fr. Olivier-Martin, *Précis d'Histoire du droit français*, 3rd edn, Paris, Dalloz, 1938, pp. 220, 239. Cf. J. Huizinga, *The Waning of the Middle Ages*, London, 1924, pp. 47–8.
63. *Wirtschaftsgeschichte*, p. 290 (Eng. trans., pp. 341–2). On the influence that some special points of Muslim law may have had on economic development, cf. C. H. Becker, *Islamstudien*, I, pp. 60 et seq. None of this is of decisive significance.
64. P. Koschaker, *Europa und das römische Recht*, Munich and Berlin, C. H. Beck, 1953, pp. 57 et seq.
65. *Wirtschaftsgeschichte*, p. 292 (Eng. trans., p. 341).
66. Olivier-Martin, op. cit., paras. 246 et seq., 560 et seq., 585, 591; cf. Koschaker, op. cit., pp. 76 et seq., 120 et seq., 142 et seq., etc.
67. I say no more on this point, on which it is very hard to effect a

precise comparison. The best synthesis for the Muslim world
has been given us by Claude Cahen, 'The Body Politic', in
Unity and Variety in Muslim Civilization, ed. G. E. von
Grunebaum, Chicago, University of Chicago Press, 1955, pp.
132–58.
68. Cf. A. Abel, 'La place des sciences occultes dans la décadence',
in *Classicisme et déclin culturel dans l'histoire de l'Islam* (see
note 46), pp. 291–311. An entire school of present-day French
ethnographers lays great stress on the immersion of the economic activity of peoples of non-European civilization in a
symbolic and magico-religious context. Some of these specialists
have chosen as their field of study rural communities of the
Muslim faith, especially in the Berber-speaking zone (cf., e.g.,
J. Servier, 'Essai sur les bases de l'économie traditionnelle chez
les Berbérophones d'Algérie', in *Cahiers de l'I.S.E.A.*, no. 106
(series V, no. 2), Oct. 1960, pp. 87–103, and, more extensively,
in his book, *Les Portes de l'Année*, Paris, R. Laffont, 1962). A
critique of the conceptions held by this school (whose more
scientifically-minded members – the minority among them –
have contributed valuable observations) still remains to be
made, but this is not the place to attempt it (see, however, pp.
203 et seq., *supra*). It will be enough, for our present purpose,
to say that the magical context has in these cases nothing
Muslim about it – as, indeed, the writers concerned themselves
emphasize – and to add this much, at least, that although large-
scale economy and exchange over a wide area may sometimes
be coloured by magical practices, they are none the less resultant, as a whole, from rational motives. Many European and
American industrialists likewise check on 'what the stars say',
according to certain publications, before they undertake a
particular piece of business on a particular day.
69. This has been developed many times, and often very badly,
in works of popularization – especially badly in the writings of
J. C. Risler and A. Mazahéri, which have been widely read in
France, the latter even being translated into foreign languages.
More reliable accounts will be found in *The Legacy of Islam*,
ed. T. Arnold and A. Guillaume, Oxford, Clarendon Press,
1931; M. Meyerhof, *Le Monde islamique*, Paris, Rieder, 1926,
pp. 29–44 (a very thorough summary by a great authority);
A. S. Atiya, *Crusade, Commerce and Culture*, Bloomington,
Indiana University Press, 1962, pp. 205–50, etc. An honest
outline by a non-specialist that deserves to be recommended is
M. Vintéjoux, *Le Miracle arabe*, preface by L. Massignon,

Paris, Charlot, 1950. Cf., especially, G. Jacob, *Der Einfluss des Morgenlands auf das Abendland, vornehmlich während des Mittelalters*, Hanover, Lafaire, 1924; H. A. R. Gibb, 'The influence of Islamic culture in mediaeval Europe', in *Bulletin of the John Rylands Library*, 38, 1955, pp. 82–98, though the substantial information included and the great intelligence with which it is discussed seem to me, nevertheless, to end in conclusions that are to some degree open to question; A. Abel, 'Le problème des relations entre l'Orient musulman et l'Occident chrétien au Moyen Age', in *Annuaire de l'Institut de Philologie et d'Histoire Orientales et Slaves*, 14, 1954–7, pp. 229–61; and the able summing-up by Charles Singer, 'East and West in Retrospect', which concludes a monumental work, *A History of Technology*, ed. Ch. Singer, E. J. Holmyard, etc., Vol. II, *The Mediterranean Civilizations and the Middle Ages*, Oxford, Clarendon Press, 1956, pp. 753–76.

70. L. Gardet, 'Le monde de l'Islam face à la civilisation technique', in *Bulletin du Cercle Saint Jean-Baptiste*, March 1959, pp. 106–11, on p. 108; cf. P. Rondot, in *Cahiers de l'I.S.E.A.*, no. 106 (series V, no. 2), Oct. 1960, pp. 39 et seq.

71. 'External goods come under the head of things useful for an end ... Hence it must needs be that man's good in their respect consists in a certain measure, in other words, that man seek, according to a certain measure, to have external riches, in so far as they are necessary for him to live in keeping with his condition of life. Wherefore it will be a sin for him to exceed this measure, by wishing to acquire or keep them immoderately.'

(*Summa theologiae*, II, 2, question 118, art. 1, Eng. trans., Vol. 12, 1922, p. 145). Cf., already, Paul in *1 Timothy*, 6:6–10 (repeated by Augustine, *De civitate Dei*, I, 10), calling for contentment with 'having food and raiment' and nothing more (cf. R. Latouche, *Les Origines de l'Économie Occidentale (IVe–XIe siècles)*, Paris, A. Michel, 1956, pp. 62 et seq.).

72. E.g., Ghazālī, *iḥyāʾ ʿulūām ad-din*, Book 27, Cairo, 1352/1933, Vol. III, pp. 200 et seq.; in the abridged analysis by G. H. Bousquet, Paris, Besson, 1955, paras. 109 et seq.

73. C. H. Becker, 'Islam und Wirtschaft', in his *Islamstudien*, I, Leipzig, Quelle u. Meyer, 1924, pp. 54–65, on p. 60. Cf. A. Rühl, *Vom Wirtschaftsgeist in Orient*, Leipzig, Quelle u. Meyer, 1925, pp. 71 et seq.

74. Cf., e.g., R. Gendarme, 'La résistance des facteurs socioculturels au développement économique, l'exemple de l'Islam

en Algérie', in *Revue économique*, March 1959, pp. 220–36, reproduced in his book *L'Économie de l'Algérie*, Paris, A. Colin, 1959, pp. 126–41. It was rightly criticized by G. Destanne de Bernis, in *Cahiers de l'I.S.E.A.*, no. 106 (series V, no. 2), Oct. 1960, pp. 110 et seq.

75. C. H. Becker, 'Islam und Wirtschaft', in his *Islamstudien*, p. 56. Cf. Rühl, *Vom Wirtschaftsgeist* . . ., pp. 38 et seq.

76. L. Gardet, *La Mesure de notre liberté*, Tunis, Bascone et Muscat, 1946 (Coll. Publications de l'Institut des Belles Lettres Arabes, 9), p. 100.

77. L. Gardet, *La Cité musulmane*, Paris, Vrin, 1954 (Coll. Études musulmanes, 1), p. 281.

78. Cf. the excellent article '*djihād*', by E. Tyan, in *Encyclopedia of Islam*, 2nd edition, English version, Vol. 2, 1965, pp. 538–40. Cf., e.g., P. Rondot, in *Cahiers de l'I.S.E.A.*, no. 106 (Series V, no. 2), Oct. 1960, p. 42.

79. L. Gardet, *La Cité musulmane*, p. 281.

80. Cf., e.g., the report of the Pakistani official commission which I quote in my article 'The Life of Muḥammad and the Sociological Problem of the Beginnings of Islam', in *Diogenes*, no. 20, Winter 1957, pp. 28–51, on p. 45, n. 14.

81. L. Gardet, *La Mesure de notre Liberté*, p. 99.

82. Ghazālī, op. cit., Book 35, Vol. IV, p. 228: Bousquet's abridgement, p. 386.

83. Murtaḍā, *ithāf as-sāda*, according to H. Ritter, in *Der Islam*, 7, 1917, p. 32.

84. Ghazālī, op. cit., Book 13, Vol. II, p. 56 (Bousquet's abridgement, para. 54).

85. Ibid., Book 35, Vol. IV, p. 238 (Bousquet's abridgement, p. 389).

86. A good example of this kind of attitude is provided by F. J. Bonjean and Ahmed Deif, *Mansour, histoire d'un enfant du pays d'Égypte*, Paris, Rieder, 1924, pp. 169 et seq.

87. Cf., e.g., Henri Sée, *Science et Philosophie de l'Histoire*, Paris, Alcan, 1928, pp. 302 et seq. and Herbert Lüthy, op. cit.

88. *Cahiers de l'I.S.E.A.*, no. 106 (series V, no. 2), Oct. 1960, pp. 114 et seq.

89. Cf. L. Gardet, 'Raison et foi en Islam', in *Revue thomiste*, 43, 1937, pp. 437–78; 44, 1938, pp. 145–67, 342–78; and the passage from Ghazālī translated and annotated by him, ibid., 44, 1938, pp. 569–78.

90. Cf. F. Meier, 'Soufisme et déclin culturel', in *Classicisme et Déclin Culturel dans l'histoire de l'Islam* (see note 68), pp. 217–41,

particularly pp. 230 et seq., and the discussion on pp. 244 et seq. For the opposite point of view see C. H. Becker, *Islamstudien*, pp. 59 et seq.

91. Cf., e.g., L. M. Garnett, *Mysticism and Magic in Turkey*, London, I. Pitman, 1912, pp. 88 et seq.

92. Cf., e.g., O. L. Barkan, giving a summary in French of his own work, in *Revue de la Faculté des Sciences économiques de l'Université d'Istanbul*, 11th year, nos. 1–4 (Oct. 1949–July 1950), p. 77, n. 9.

93. Cf. Garnett, op. cit., pp. 68 et seq.

94. Cf. A. Gouilly, *L'Islam dans l'Afrique occidentale française*, Paris, Larose, 1952, pp. 121 et seq. For more details on these same *murīds*, who seem somewhat heretical from the standpoint of Islam, cf. A. Bourlon, 'Mourides et Mouridisme 1953', in *Notes et Études sur l'Islam en Afrique noire*, Paris, Peyronnet, 1963, pp. 53–74. In the same symposium, however, the article by F. Quesnot, 'Influence du mouridisme sur le tidjanisme', on pp. 117–25, shows the influence of *murīd* practices on the more orthodox confraternities.

95. C. H. Becker, *Islamstudien*, I, pp. 64 et seq. Cf. Rühl, *Vom Wirtschaftsgeist* . . . op. cit., pp. 44 et seq., 81; R. Brunschvig in *L'Évolution économique* . . . op. cit., I, pp. 9 et seq.

96. Cf. R. Brunschvig in *Classicisme et déclin culturel* . . ., op. cit., pp. 35 et seq.

97. Z. Smogorzewski, 'Un poème abāḍite sur certaines divergences entre les Mālikites et les Abāḍites', in *Rocznyk Orientalistyczny*, 2, 1919–24, pp. 260–68.

98. General synthesizing discussion of the Mzabites from the sociological standpoint will be found in Rühl, *Vom Wirtschaftsgeist* . . ., op. cit., pp. 84–92; P. Bourdieu, *Sociologie de l'Algérie* (Coll. Que sais-je? 802), Paris, P.U.F., 1958, pp. 43–58; 2nd edition, pp. 35–50 (though what is said about dogma needs to be taken with reservations). For Ibāḍism see the article 'Ibāḍiyya' by T. Lewicki, in *Encyclopedia of Islam*, 2nd edn, English version, Vol. 3, 1971, pp. 648–60. The necessary bibliographical references will be found in these works.

99. A. J. Meyer, *Middle Eastern Capitalism*, Harvard, 1959, p. 43.

100. See *supra*, p. 77.

CHAPTER 5: ISLAM AND CAPITALISM IN THE MUSLIM
COUNTRIES TODAY

1. On the concept of dominance, cf. F. Perroux, 'Esquisse d'une
   théorie de l'économie dominante', in *Économie appliquée*, 1,
   1948, pp. 243–300, particularly pp. 251 et seq.
2. A. J. Meyer, op. cit., pp. 45 et seq.
3. While I was correcting the proofs of this book I received a
   valuable collection of articles by Soviet economists, *Rabochy
   klass stran Azii i Afriki, spravochnik*, Moscow, Nauka, 1964.
   The statistics given are taken from various sources, not all of
   them very reliable, for the years 1959–63, broadly speaking.
   From these figures I calculate the following percentages:
   Afghanistan 0.21, Iraq 1.85, Lebanon 3.09, Turkey 4.19,
   Egypt 4.51, Israel (total) 7.60, Tunisia 2.87, Algeria 3.60.
4. C. S. Cooper, *The Modernizing of the Orient*, London T. Fisher
   Unwin, 1915, p. 5.
5. Moustafa Fahmy, *La Révolution de l'industrie en Égypte et ses
   conséquences sociales au XIXe siécle (1800–50)*, Leiden, Brill,
   1954, pp. 84 et seq. Cf. F. M. Atsamba, in *Ocherki po istorii
   arabskikh stran*, Moscow, Izd. Mosk. Univ., 1959, pp. 13 et
   seq.: Z. Y. Hershlag, *Introduction to the Modern Economic
   History of the Middle East*, Leiden, Brill, 1964, pp. 86 et seq.,
   subjects Fahmy's figures to justified criticism.
6. L. A. Fridman, *Kapitalisticheskoye razvitie Egipta (1882–
   1939)*, Moscow, 1963, p. 147; cf. Atsamba, op. cit., pp. 27 et
   seq.
7. A. Abdel-Malek, *Égypte, société militaire*, Paris, Seuil, 1962,
   pp. 20 et seq.; L. A. Fridman, op. cit., pp. 5–21, 151.
8. Abdel-Malek, op. cit., p. 22.
9. Hassan Riad, *L'Égypte nassérienne*, Paris, Minuit, 1964, pp. 76–
   84; cf. Hershlag, *Introduction*, pp. 219 et seq.
10. R. Mantran, *Istanbul dans la seconde moitié du XVIIe siècle*,
    Paris, 1962, pp. 419 et seq.; cf., by the same author, *La Vie
    quotidienne à Constantinople au temps de Soliman le Magnifique
    et de ses successeurs*, Paris, Hachette, 1965, pp. 149–52; H. A. R.
    Gibb and H. Bowen, *Islamic Society and the West*, Vol. I,
    Part 1, London, O.U.P., 1950, p. 296; and *supra*, p. 68.
11. *Journal asiatique*, 6th series, Vol. 5 (86), January–June 1865,
    p. 159.
12. Cf. *Novaya istoriya stran zarubezhnogo vostoka*, Moscow,
    Izd. Mosk. Univ., 1952, Vol. I, p. 317.
13. Hershlag, *Introduction*, p. 71.

14. Mehemet Ali Pasha's reply to the address of the British Consul Barnett, published by René Cattaui Bey, *Le Règne de Mohamed Aly d'après les archives russes en Égypte*, Vol. III, Rome, Reale Società di Geografia d'Egitto, 1936, document No. 277 *bis*, p. 587. A. E. Crouchley frequently stresses the internal weaknesses of Mehemet Ali's industrial statism. He sees the experiment as having been premature: 'its failure was perhaps inevitable'. The weaknesses were there, all right, but one cannot pre-judge how the system might have evolved subsequently. Cf. A. E. Crouchley, *The Economic Development of Modern Egypt*, London, Longmans, Green, 1938, pp. 73–5. He is obliged, in any case, to admit that the collapse of the system resulted from the Treaty of London ('A Century of Economic Development, 1837–1937', in *L'Égypte Contemporaine*, 30, 1939, nos. 182–3, pp. 133–55, on p. 145).

15. Defined in these statistics as 'industrial establishments' are those which represent a total value of at least £T.1,000; make in the course of a year at least 750 daily wage-payments; and employ a motive power of at least five horse power. The source is *Statistique industrielle des années 1913 et 1915*, Istanbul, Ministry of Commerce and Agriculture, 1917, analysed by O. Conker and E. Witmeur, *Redressement économique et industrialisation de la nouvelle Turquie*, Paris, Recueil Sirey, 1937 (Coll. Bibliothèque de l'École Supérieure des Sciences Commerciales et Économiques de l'Université de Liège, 18), pp. 55–9, A. F. Miller, *Ocherki noveishei istorii Turtsii*, Moscow and Leningrad, Izd. Akad. Nauk U.S.S.R., 1948, pp. 17 et seq., and Z. Y. Hershlag, *Introduction*, p. 72. Cf. M. Clerget, *La Turquie, passé et présent*, Paris, A. Colin, 1938, pp. 140 et seq. Out of these 269 enterprises, 22 belonged to the state and only 28 to limited companies.

16. G. Ducousso, *L'Industrie de la soie en Syrie*, Paris, A. Challamel, and Beirut, Impr. catholique, 1913, pp. 53–60.

17. Ibid., pp. 123–8.

18. Ibid., pp. 172 et seq.; cf. D. Chevallier, 'Lyon et la Syrie en 1919, bases d'une intervention', in *Revue historique*, Vol. 224, 1960, pp. 275–320.

19. A. Ruppin, *Syrien als Wirtschaftsgebiet*, 2nd edn, Berlin and Vienna, B. Harz, 1920, p. 172.

20. Frédy Bémont, *L'Iran devant le progrès*, Paris, P.U.F., 1964, p. 122; N. Agasi, 'Sakharnaya promyshlennost' Irana', in *Iran, sbornik statei*, Izd. Vost. Lit., Moscow, 1963, pp. 3–18, on p. 3.

21. K. Boldyrev, in *Novaya istoriya stran zarubezhnogo vostoka*, ed. I. M. Reisner and B. K. Rubtsov, Moscow, Izd. Mosk. Univ., Vol. I, 1953, p. 375; cf. Hershlag, *Introduction*, pp. 144 et seq.; with, as an appendix, pp. 340 et seq., the text of the Anglo-Persian trade treaty of 1801, forerunner of many more.
22. J.-B. Feuvrier, *Trois ans à la cour de Perse*, Paris, F. Juven, 1900, p. 211.
23. *L'Homme et la Terre*, Vol. 5, Hachette, 1905, p. 492.
24. On all this cf. the few facts to be found here and there in A. Malekpur, *Die Wirtschaftsverfassung Irans*, thesis, Berlin, 1935; Amin Banani, *The Modernization of Iran, 1921–1941*, Stanford (California), Stanford U.P., 1961, pp. 137 et seq.; *Novaya istoriya . . .*, I, pp. 375 et seq., and II, pp. 322 et seq.; E. G. Browne, *The Persian Revolution of 1905–1909*, Cambridge, C.U.P., 1910, pp. 31 et seq.; F. Bémont, *L'Iran devant le progrès*, pp. 111 et seq.; Z. Y. Hershlag, *Introduction*, pp. 134 et seq.; etc.
25. Muṣṭafā Kāmil al-Falakī, *Ṭalʿat Ḥarb, baṭal al-istiql-āl al-iqtiṣadī*, Cairo, 1940, p. 18, quoted by L. A. Fridman, in *Ocherki po istorii arabskikh stran*, Moscow, 1959, p. 62.
26. Ziya Gökalp, *iktisadî inkilap için nasıl çalishmalıyız* (from *Küçük Mecmua*, Diyarbekir, no. 33, 1923), Eng. trans. in this writer's *Turkish Nationalism and Western Civilization, Selected Essays*, trans. and ed. N. Berkes, New York, Columbia U.P., 1959, p. 310.
27. Ziya Gökalp, '*Medeniyetimiz*' (from *Yeni Mecmua*, Istanbul, no. 68, 1923), and *Garbe dogru*, from his *Türkçülügün Esaslari*, Ankara, 1923, Eng. trans. in *Turkish Nationalism* (op. cit.), p. 279.
28. Sadri Etem, in *Vakït*, 8 August 1929, translated in *The Turkish Press, 1925–1932*, ed. Lutfy Levonian, Athens, School of Religion, 1932, p. 163.
29. Editorial in *Tanin*, February 1926, ibid., p. 48.
30. Speech at Inebolu, August 1925, translated from the school anthology edited by R. Eshref, M. Sadullah and N. Sadïk, *Cümhuriyet Kïraati*, 4th edition, Kïsïm 8, Istanbul, Tefeyyüz, no date, pp. 17 et seq.
31. J. Parker and C. Smith, *Modern Turkey*, London, Routledge, 1940, pp. 101 et seq. More details in O. Conker and E. Witmeur, op. cit., pp. 158 et seq. Cf. Hershlag, *Introduction*, pp. 187 et seq.
32. Muḥammad Rizā Shāh Pahlavī, *Mission for My Country*, London, 1961, p. 48. (In the French version of this book –

Mémoires du chah d'Iran, Paris, Gallimard, 1961, p. 44 – 'modernization' is rendered as *occidentalisation*, i.e., 'Westernization', 'modern' as *en Occident*, i.e., 'in the West', and the last 'abroad' as *en Europe ou aux États-Unis*, i.e., 'in Europe or the United States' – *Translator's note*.)

33. Cf. Amin Banani, op. cit., pp. 137 et seq.; D. N. Wilber, *Iran, Past and Present*, 4th edn, Princeton, Princeton U.P., 1958, pp. 246 et seq.; Hershlag, *Introduction*, pp. 194–207.

34. Ali Fuad Basgïl, 'La Constitution et le régime politique', in *Turquie*, Paris, Delagrave, 1939 (Coll. La Vie juridique des peuples, 7), p. 23.

35. O. Conker and E. Witmeur, op. cit., p. 70; for more details, see pp. 180 et seq.

36. Programme adopted by the 4th General Congress of the People's Republican Party in May 1935, Article 5d, quoted from Parker and Smith, op. cit., p. 238. Cf. also, Hershlag, *Introduction*, pp. 181 et seq.

37. Muḥammad Riza Shah Pahlavi, op. cit., pp. 153, 157.

38. Report on his mission by Baron de Boislecomte to the Duc de Broglie, 1833, Archives of the French Foreign Ministry, quoted by E. Driault in *Précis d'histoire d'Égypte*, Vol. III, *L'Égypte ottomane, l'expédition française en Égypte, et le règne de Mohammed-Aly (1517–1849)*, Cairo, Impr. de l'Institut français d'archéologie orientale, 1933, pp. 311 et seq.

39. F. M. Atsamba, in *Ocherki po istorii arabskikh stran*, Moscow, 1959, p. 14.

40. A. Abdel-Malek, *Égypte, société militaire*, Paris, Seuil, 1962, p. 80. Rich townsmen become the chief landowners: cf. G. Baer, *A History of Landownership in Modern Egypt, 1800–1950*, London, O.U.P., 1962, p. 70.

41. L. A. Fridman, op. cit., p. 38.

42. Hassan Riad, op. cit., pp. 16–19.

43. Ibid., p. 14.

44. Fridman, op. cit., pp. 48–52.

45. Marx, *Capital*, Vol. III, F.L.P.H. edition, pp. 767–8.

46. Cf. *supra*, p. 67.

47. Cf. M. Rodinson, 'De l'archéologie à la sociologie historique, notes méthodologiques sur le dernier ouvrage de G. Tchalenko', in *Syria*, 38, 1968, pp. 170–200, on pp. 189 et seq.

48. Cf. Hershlag, *Introduction*, pp. 94 et seq.; Mohamed Youssef El-Sarki, *La monoculture du coton en Égypte et le développement économique*, Geneva, Droz, 1964 (Coll. Travaux de droit, d'économie, de sociologie et de sciences politiques, 30).

49. In *O genezise kapitalizma v stranakh vostoka* (*XV–XIX vv.*), *materialy obsuzhdeniya*, Moscow, Izd. Vost. Lit., 1962, p. 407.

50. This phenomenon has particularly impressed those who, like the writer of these lines, succumbed to the tendency mentioned, and became aware of the vanity of it only after the Twentieth Congress of the Soviet Communist Party. It is described as 'ideological extremism' or 'tendency to absolute ideology', and analysed rather well by Pierre Hervé in *La Révolution et les Fétiches*, Paris, La Table Ronde, 1956, p. 10. It is an attitude related to that which Jean-François Revel (in *La Cabale des dévots*, Paris, Julliard, 1962) calls 'devotion', and even more closely to what George Orwell called 'nationalism' ('Notes on nationalism', published in *Polemic 1945*, reproduced in his *England Your England*, London, Secker and Warburg, 1953, pp. 41–67). A French translator rendered Orwell's 'nationalism', significantly, as '*chauvinisme*' (in *Echo*, London, No. 1, August, pp. 66–74).

51. In my articles 'Racisme et Civilisation', in *Nouvelle Critique*, No. 66, June 1955, pp. 120–40, with erratum in No. 70, December 1955, p. 191, and 'Ethnographie et relativisme', in ibid., No. 69, November 1955, pp. 46–63, and in an oral disputation with Sheikh Anta Diop, whose book *Nations nègres et culture*, Paris, Éditions Africaines, 1955, is a monument of this tendency carried to absurd lengths. I must mention, however, that my articles in *La Nouvelle Critique*, while combating the anti-colonialist variety of ideological totalitarianism, connived at the Communist variety, and even (unconsciously) at the latent semi-racialist tendencies of the leaders of the French Communist Party. Aimé Césaire was right to point this out, but my argument is not essentially affected by it. The reply made by C. Lévi-Strauss, in his *Structural Anthropology* (1958: English translation, London, 1968, p. 342, n. 31) deserves to be developed further.

52. *Grundrisse . . .*, p. 405 (Eng. trans., *Pre-Capitalist Economic Formations*, p. 109).

53. In *O genezise kapitalizma . . .*, p. 408.

54. John Bowring, *Report on Egypt and Candia*, in *Parliamentary Papers*, 1840, Vol. XXI, p. 30:

> In many conversations which I have had with Mahomet Ali on the subject of his manufactures, in which I have endeavoured to show him that they were, for the most part, useless, absorbing

his capital and misdirecting labour from more profitable agricultural employment, he has answered me that it was rather for the purpose of accustoming the people to manufacture than for any profit which he expected that he continued his manufacturing operations.

55. A concise but sound survey of the question is given in the article *bidᶜa*, by J. Robson, in *Encyclopedia of Islam*, 2nd edn, Vol. I, English version, 1960, p. 1199.

56. A story often repeated, e.g. (in a lively way), by H. C. Armstrong, *Lord of Arabia*, London, 1934, chapter 73.

57. Cf. e.g., F. J. Tomiche, *L'Arabie séoudite*, Paris, P.U.F., 1962 (Coll. Que sais-je?, no. 1025), pp. 85 et seq., a good summary.

58. Lothrop Stoddard, *The New World of Islam*, New York, Scribner, 1921, pp. 229–30.

59. Leonard G. Ting, 'Chinese modern banks and the finance of government and industry', in *Nankai Social and Economic Quarterly* (Tientsin), Vol. 8, no. 3, Oct. 1935, pp. 578–616, on pp. 609–10.

60. D. K. Lieu, *China's Economic Stabilization and Reconstruction*, New Brunswick, Rutgers U.P., 1948, pp. 49, 51. Cf. M. Lachin, *La Chine capitaliste*, Paris, Gallimard, 1938, pp. 47–61.

61. S. R. Wagel, *Chinese Currency and Banking*, Shanghai, North China Daily News and Herald, 1915, pp. 185, 187.

62. G. C. Allen, *A Short Economic History of Modern Japan, 1867–1937*, 3rd edn, London, 1972, pp. 109–10.

63. E. Herbert Norman, *Japan's Emergence as a Modern State: Political and Economic Problems of the Meiji Period*, New York, International Secretariat, Institute of Pacific Relations, 1940, pp. 110–11; and cf. p. 114.

64. William W. Lockwood, *The Economic Development of Japan: Growth and Structural Change, 1868–1938*, Princeton, Princeton U.P., 1954, p. 209, cf. pp. 199 et seq.

65. Cf. among others, J. M. Keynes, *The General Theory of Employment, Interest and Money*, London, Macmillan, 1960, pp. 239 et seq.

66. Lockwood, op. cit., pp. 295–6.

67. Maurice Dobb, *Studies in the Development of Capitalism*, London, Routledge, 1946, p. 185.

68. Ibid., p. 271.

69. I had already written these lines when I read the elaborate parallel ably drawn between these two situations by the economist A. J. Meyer, *Middle Eastern Capitalism*, Cambridge, Mass., Harvard U.P., 1959, pp. 18–31.

70. J. N. D. Anderson, *Islamic Law in the Modern World*, London, Stevens, 1959, pp. 20–21. On recourse to these jurisdictions which do not follow the *sharīᶜa*, cf. N. J. Coulson, 'Doctrine and practice in Islamic law; an aspect of the problem', in *Bulletin of the School of Oriental and African Studies*, 18, 1956, pp. 211–26, on p. 224.
71. Aristarchi Bey, *Législation ottomane . . .*, Vol. I, Constantinople, Impr. Nicolaïdes, 1873, no. 12, p. 45.
72. Ibid., p. 46.
73. G. Young, *Corps de droit ottoman*, Oxford, Clarendon Press, 1905–6, Vol. VII, pp. 132–4.
74. Aristarchi, op. cit., I, pp. 391–406; cf. Young, op. cit., pp. 136 et seq.
75. Cf. the masterly article by C. A. Nallino, 'Delle assicurazioni in diritto musulmano hanafita', in *Oriente Moderno*, 7, 1927, pp. 446–61, reprinted in this writer's *Raccolta di scritti editi e inediti*, Vol. IV, Rome, Istituto per l'Oriente, 1942, pp. 62–84. It is far-fetched to describe as 'insurance' and even 'social insurance', as M. Hamidullah does (in *Cahiers de l'I.S.E.A.*, suppl. no. 120 [series V, no. 3], December 1961, p. 40, and *Le Prophète de l'Islam*, Paris, Vrin, 1959, pp. 126, 623), the solidarity shown by a clan, or even by the clans among themselves, in paying a ransom for a clan member, or the price of blood owed by him. On a more belated move for religious legitimation of insurance, cf. N. Berkes, *The Development of Secularism in Turkey*, Montreal, McGill U.P., 1964, pp. 398 et seq.
76. A document frequently reproduced, e.g., in A. Ubicini and Pavet de Courteille, *État présent de l'Empire ottoman*, Paris, J. Dumaine, 1876, pp. 241 et seq.
77. Ibid., p. 254.
78. G. Young, *Corps de droit ottoman*, V, pp. 342–50.
79. Belin, in *Journal asiatique*, 6th series, Vol. V (1864), pp. 149 et seq.; cf. the article *ḳā'ime*, by J. H. Mordtmann, in the *Encyclopedia of Islam*, 1st edition, Vol. II, English version, 1927, pp. 643–4, where the rate indicated is 12 per cent, and Hershlag, *Introduction*, p. 59, which gives 9 to 12 per cent. The contradictions in the sources are already pointed out by Mordtmann. I have not had time to pursue research any further on this point.
80. E. Engelhardt, *La Turquie et le Tanzimat . . .*, Paris, Cotillon, 1882–4, Vol. II, p. 258, n. 1; cf. pp. 150 et seq.
81. M. B. C. Collas, *La Turquie en 1861*, Paris, A. Franck, 1861,

pp. 84 et seq.; *La Turquie en 1864*, Paris, E. Dentu, 1864, pp. 123 et seq.

82. Cf. J. Schacht, *Esquisse d'une histoire du droit musulman*, Paris, M. Besson, 1953 (Coll. Inst. des Hautes Études Marocaines, Notes et Documents, XI), pp. 79 et seq.

83. French translation of the text in *Annuaire de législation étrangère*, Vol. XIX, Paris, Cotillon, 1890, p. 868.

84. The following fact speaks volumes. In Egypt in 1848 an Armenian named Alexanian had obtained authority to carry out banking operations, with an interest-rate of 10 per cent, using state funds (those of the traditional *Bayt al-māl!*). The authority was withdrawn, and Alexanian thrown into prison, as a result of a protest by the ʿulamāʾ, backed by certain persons who discovered the impropriety of the proceedings at the moment when they were due to make repayment (E. Antonini, *Le Crédit et la Banque en Égypte*, Lausanne, 1927, pp. 29 et seq.).

85. Cf. Ch. A. Julien, *Histoire de l'Afrique du Nord*, Paris, Payot, 1931, pp. 729 et seq., and A. Ayache, *Le Maroc, bilan d'une colonisation*, Paris, Éditions Sociales, 1956, pp. 57 et seq. I might add the testimony of Louis Massignon, who told me (adding: 'this tends to support your ideas') the indications that were given him in 1904, young and naïve as he was then, by the head of the Banque de Paris et des Pays-Bas, about the intentions of the financiers with regard to Morocco. (I notice that there is an allusion to this in *Cahiers de l'I.S.E.A.*, suppl. no. 120 [series V, no. 3], Dec. 1961, p. 11.)

86. Cf. the close analysis given by G. Ayache, 'Aspects de la crise financière au Maroc après l'expédition espagnole de 1860', in *Revue historique*, 220, 1958, pp. 271–310, on p. 295.

87. *Revue du monde musulman*, 5, 1908, p. 428; cf. p. 425. The original Arabic text, with a German translation, was given by G. Kampffmeyer, 'Eine marokkanische Staatsurkunde', in *Der Islam*, 3, 1912, pp. 68–90. ʿAbd al-ʿAzīz's grandfather, Sīdī Muḥammad, being obliged to borrow money from Britain in order to pay the substantial war-indemnity demanded by Spain in 1860, had this loan at interest legitimized by the ʿulamāʾ. Recourse was had to a ḥīla. Cf. J. L. Miège, *Le Maroc et l'Europe (1830–1894)*, II, Paris, P.U.F., 1961, p. 380.

88. It seems pointless to give a lot of references on the development of banking in all the countries of Islam. At random, let us note that even in distant Afghanistan, an economically backward country where the influence of religious personages is

very strong, four credit institutions have been founded since 1948, and these exist 'primarily to make low-interest loans available to small businesses, farmers, animal breeders, cottage and home industries, builders and small factory establishments'. (D. N. Wilber, *Afghanistan*, New Haven, H.R.A.F. Press, 1962, p. 217.) Some subtle observations on the attitude of the different strata of the Muslim population of Syria and the Lebanon towards bank interest, in the first third of this century, will be found in the work by Sa'id B. Himadeh, *Monetary and Banking System of Syria*, Beirut, American University of Beirut, 1935 (Coll. Publications of the Faculty of Arts and Sciences, No. 6), pp. 21 et seq., 189 et seq.

89. Benali Fekar, *L'Usure* . . ., pp. 128 et seq., deploring that he has not found it possible 'to put his hand on the *fetāwi* . . . of the men of learning who gave permission to Muslim governments to contract state loans'. This seems to be the source of I. Goldziher, *Vorlesungen über den Islam*, 2nd edn, 1925, p. 260 (French translation of 1st edition, *Le Dogme et la Loi de l'Islam*, 1920, p. 218).

90. According to B. Fekar, op. cit., p. 127. The lecture appeared in *al-Liwāʾ* (Cairo) 'quite recently', writes Fekar without giving more details. I have not been able to see the journal in question.

91. Mohamed Kamal Amin Malache, *Les Instruments de circulation et les institutions de crédit en Égypte* (law thesis), Paris, P.U.F., 1930, pp. 145 et seq.; E. Antonini, *Le Crédit et la banque en Égypte*, dissertation, Lausanne, Impr. G. Vaney-Burnier, 1927 (University of Lausanne, École des Hautes Études Commerciales), p. 79. According to Antonini, the first bureaux of the Post Office Savings Bank, numbering 28, were inaugurated on 1 March 1901. There was also, forming part of this Savings Bank system, a service of deposits without dividend, for the use of those who were firmly resolved not to play tricks with the ban on *ribā*.

92. J. Jomier, *Le Commentaire coranique du Manār*, Paris, G. P. Maisonneuve, 1954 (Coll. Islam d'hier et d'aujourd'hui, XI), pp. 222 et seq. I am most grateful to Father Jomier for having resumed at my request, in order to find this text, his investigations in Cairo which he had given up. Nevertheless, they remained unsuccessful.

93. Muṣṭafā ash-Shāṭir al-Miṣrī, in the journal *al-Mumtāz*, Cairo, no. 241, 13 *jumādā* I 1323 (16 July 1905), reprinted in Muḥammad Rashīd Riḍā, *taʾrīkh al-ustādh al-imām*, III, Cairo, maṭb. al-Manār, AH 1324. The journal is said to have

echoed these discussions, which had taken place 'during the last two years'.

94. B. Fekar, op. cit., p. 119. The journal *al-Liwā'* for 10 November 1906, reported that deposits in the Egyptian savings banks on 31 October amounted to £300,429 held by 56,408 depositors (*Revue du monde musulman*, 1, 1906–7, p. 422). More complete figures are given in E. Antonini, op. cit., p. 81. Were they founded in 1904 (as Fekar says, pp. 211 et seq.) or in 1901 (cf. *supra*, n. 91)?

95. Fekar, op. cit., pp. 211 et seq.

96. *Revue du Monde musulman*, 4, 1908, pp. 433 et seq.

97. Rashīd Riḍā, in *al-Manār*, 9, 1324/1906, p. 345. I follow fairly closely the translation given by Fekar, p. 120; cf. J. Jomier, op. cit., pp. 226 et seq.

98. Rashīd Riḍā, *tafsīr al-qur'ān*, Vol. IV, Cairo, 1325 (1945–6), p. 131; cf. Jomier, p. 227.

99. Rashīd Riḍā, in *al-Manār*, op. cit., p. 346. I keep fairly close to the translation given by Fekar, p. 120.

100. Sir Malcolm Darling, *The Punjab Peasant in Prosperity and Debt*, 4th edn, London, O.U.P., 1947, p. 198.

101. Review by M. Hamidullah of J. Hans, *Homo OEconomicus Islamicus* (Vienna, 1952), in *Islamic Quarterly*, 2, 1955, p. 143.

102. Ibid., p. 144. Adopting a more aggressive tone, Sheikh Aḥmad Shākir addresses Muslims with an indignation that testifies to the scale of the evil he is denouncing:

> Consider, O Muslims, if you be [truly] Muslims, the lands of Islam in all parts of the world, except for a very few of them. They have been afflicted with laws that are impious and accursed, copied from the pagan and libertine laws of Europe, allowing *ribā* either openly in the letter and spirit (of the legislation), or by means of trickery with words, calling *ribā* by the name of 'interest'. Things have come to such a pass that we see people who claim to be Muslims figuring among the champions of these laws, while others, ignorant of religious law, defend this 'interest' and accuse the Muslim *'ulamā'* of ignorance and dull conservatism if they do not agree to these attempts at legitimizing *ribā*.

> (*'umdat at-tafsīr*, II, 196 et seq., note, as given in Zaydān Abū l-makārim, *Binā al-iqtiṣād fi l-Islām*, Cairo, dār al-'urūba, 1959, p. 177.)

103. M. Hamidullah, in *Islamic Quarterly*, 2, 1955, p. 143.

104. Ibid., p. 143; the same writer, in *Cahiers de l'I.S.E.A.*, suppl. no. 120 (series V, no. 3), Dec. 1961, pp. 35 et seq.
105. M. Hamidullah, in *Islamic Quarterly*, 2, 1955, p. 144.
106. Nāṣir Aḥmed Sheikh, *Some Aspects of the Constitution and the Economics of Islam*, Woking (Surrey), The Woking Muslim Mission and Literary Trust, 1961, pp. 29 et seq.; cf. A. Chapy, 'Islam dans la constitution du Pakistan', in *Orient*, No. 3, July 1957, pp. 120–27.
107. Article 29, para. f of the Constitution (cf., e.g., the translation by V. Vacca, in *Oriente Moderno*, 37, 1957, pp. 493–551, on p. 498).
108. *L'Express* (Paris), No. 692, 21–27 September 1964, p. 37.
109. Nāṣir Aḥmed Sheikh, op. cit., pp. 226 et seq.
110. C. A. Nallino, *Raccolta di scritti editi e inediti*, Vol. I, *L'Arabia Saʿūdiana (1938)*, Rome, 1939, p. 101; A. D'Emilia, 'Intorno al codice di commercio dall' Arabia saudiana', in *Oriente moderno*, 32, 1952, pp. 316–25, especially p. 322, n. 2.
111. Financial agreement of 29 January 1950 (text translated in *Oriente Moderno*, 30, 1950, pp. 19 et seq.). The same applied to the subsequent agreement of 9 November 1955 (ibid., 35, 1955, pp. 591 et seq. and 36, 1956, p. 98) according to J. Hans, *Dynamik und Dogma in Islam*, 2nd edn, Leiden, Brill, 1960, p. 103 (giving the date as 1956). On the other hand, the well-informed economic newspaper *Le Commerce du Levant*, published in Beirut, reported on 31 August 1960, that the Saudi Soama Trading Co., of Jedda, said to be partly owned by King Saʿud, was suggesting to the Tokyo Metropolitan Bank, with a view to investment in Japan, a loan of $100 million for 25 years at 8 per cent annual interest (*Cahiers de l'Orient contemporain*, issue 43, May–August 1960, p. 159). Perhaps it is all right to break the Law when dealing with pagans!
112. M. Hamidullah (in *Cahiers de l'I.S.E.A.*, suppl. no. 120 [series V, no. 3], pp. 37 et seq.) suggests, on the one hand, that the banks pay their depositors (in respect of long-term deposits) a variable 'dividend' only at the end of each financial year, after calculating their profits, instead of promising them, regardless of circumstances, a fixed interest; and, on the other, that they make loans to entrepreneurs and others, in return for the right to participate in any profits that may accrue, and after securing guarantees against ill-success on the part of the debtors. He also proposes that the Muslim governments set up a monetary fund to operate in the same way ('A suggestion for an interest-free Islamic monetary fund', in *Islamic Review*, Vol. 43, no. 6, June

1955, pp. 11 et seq.). These solutions are not contrary to traditional Muslim law, he affirms. No doubt he is quite right there. They are merely contrary to the *purpose* that he himself has assigned to the traditional ban, namely, to stop wealth accumulating in a few men's hands. 'There is not much difference between interest and commercial gain', he adds; 'just as admiration for a statue and adoration of it as an idol differ only in the attitudes of mind of individuals, and one would be licit and the other illicit without there being much outward difference between them' (*Cahiers* . . ., p. 39). Perhaps so; but in the case of interest the attitude of mind (desire for profit) could not be concealed. There would be no great outward difference here, either. In reality, what we see in this case is merely a desperate effort to preserve some formal validity for a precept that is inapplicable in present-day economic circumstances, and in this way to justify *a posteriori* its presence in the sacred *corpus* of Islam.

113. F. Perroux, *Le Capitalisme*, Paris, P.U.F., 1962 (Coll. Que sais-je?, 315), pp. 25 et seq.

114. Marx, *Introduction to the Critique of Political Economy*, London, 1971, pp. 191–2.

115. Marx, *Capital*, Vol. I, London, 1938, p. 521.

116. Cf. M. Rodinson, 'Marxisme et racisme', in *La Nef*, new series, nos. 19–20, Sept.–Dec. 1964, pp. 49–60.

117. Bibliographical and other references regarding attempts at a typology of entrepreneurs will be found in Yusuf A. Sayigh, *Entrepreneurs of Lebanon: The Role of a Business Leader in a Developing Economy*, Cambridge, Mass., Harvard U.P., 1962, pp. 28 et seq., 174.

118. J. Austruy, 'Vocation économique de l'Islam', in *Cahiers de l'I.S.E.A.*, No. 106, Oct. 1960 (Series V, no. 2), pp. 151–212, on p. 167.

119. Ibid., p. 158, n. 24.

120. A. A. I. El-Gritly, *The Structure of Modern Industry in Egypt*, Cairo, Government Press, 1948 (also in *L'Égypte Contemporaine*, 38, 1947, issue nos 241–2), pp. 391 et seq.; cf. Morroe Berger, *The Arab World Today*, London, 1962, p. 243.

121. Berger, op. cit., pp. 243 et seq.

122. See especially Ch. Issawi, 'The Entrepreneur Class', in *Social Forces in the Middle East*, ed. S. N. Fisher, Ithaca, Cornell U.P., 1955, pp. 116–36, on pp. 127 et seq.; A. J. Meyer, *Middle Eastern Capitalism*, pp. 38 et seq.; Y. A. Sayigh, *Entrepreneurs of Lebanon*, pp. 69 et seq.

123. Cf. A. J. Meyer, 'Entrepreneurship, the missing link in the Arab states?', in *Middle East Economic Papers*, Beirut, 1954, pp. 121–32; Y. A. Sayigh, op. cit., pp. 127 et seq.; Ch. Issawi, 'The Entrepreneur Class' (see note 122), pp. 131 et seq.; Ch. Issawi, *Egypt at Mid-Century, an economic survey*, London, O.U.P., 1954, pp. 168 et seq. See also A. P. Alexander, 'Industrial entrepreneurship in Turkey, its origin and growth', in *Economic Development and Cultural Change*, 8, 1960, pp. 349–65; A. J. Meyer, 'Entrepreneurship and economic development in the Middle East', in *The Public Opinion Quarterly*, 22, 1958, pp. 391–6.

124. Cf. A. Ajdari, 'Influence des valeurs traditionnelles sur la mentalité économique dans les pays musulmans du Moyen-Orient', in *Développement et civilisation*, no. 10, April–June 1962, pp. 55–79, and the books and articles by J. Austruy, already quoted.

125. Cf., e.g. A. Bonne, 'Incentive for economic development in Asia', in *Annals for the American Academy of Political and Social Science*, Philadelphia, 276, 1951, pp. 12–19. On the aspiration towards a strong government, cf. D. Lerner, *The Passing of Traditional Society: Modernizing the Middle East*, Glencoe, Ill., The Free Press, 1958, pp. 280 et seq., etc.

126. J. Berque, *Les Arabes d'hier à demain*, Paris, Seuil, 1960, p. 77.

127. Ibid., p. 78. Cf. A. J. Meyer, 'Entrepreneurship, the missing link in the Arab states?' (see note 123), p. 128: El-Gritly, *The Structure* . . ., pp. 455, n. 1 (where the comparison with India is noteworthy), and 465.

128. Berque, p. 76.

129. Ibid., p. 107.

130. Ibid., p. 52.

131. Zaki Badaoui, *La Législation du travail*, 3rd edn, Alexandria, Éd. du Journal du Commerce et de la Marine, 1951, p. 3.

132. H. B. Butler, *Report on Labour Conditions in Egypt, with suggestions for future social legislation*, Cairo, Government Press, 1932, p. 9 of the English part of the text.

133. The text of the law will be found in Z. Badaoui's collection, op. cit., pp. 174–82.

134. El-Gritly, *The Structure* . . ., p. 538; cf. also Issawi, *Egypt at Mid-Century*, pp. 175 et seq.

135. Cf. e.g., D. Lerner, op. cit.; Issawi, 'The Entrepreneur Class' (see note 122); Y. A. Sayigh, op. cit., pp. 129 et seq.

136. This is, for instance, admitted eventually by one of the best authorities on the economic history of modern Egypt, although

some signs of a different view appeared earlier in his work: 'The main obstacle to the development of Egyptian industry in the past has been the competition of foreign products and the lack of government support in the form of protective tariffs.' (A. E. Crouchley, *The Economic Development of Modern Egypt*, London, Longmans, Green, 1938, p. 250.)

137. Y. A. Sayigh, op. cit., pp. 122 et seq., 131 et seq.

138. I use here the translation given by J. Declareuil, *Rome et l'organisation du droit*, Paris, Renaissance du Livre, 1924 (Coll. l'Évolution de l'Humanité, no. 19), p. 177, modifying it as regards the meaning of *abutor* in accordance with the comments of authorities on Roman Law.

139. Ibid., pp. 203 et seq., 380 et seq. I have merely paraphrased the very clear survey given in E. Perrot and L. Levet, *Précis élémentaire de droit romain*, 2nd edn, Paris, Recueil Sirey, 1937, pp. 171 et seq. Cf. also, e.g., R. von Mayr, *Römische Rechtsgeschichte*, 1/2, Leipzig, Göschen, 1912 (Coll. Sammlung Göschen, 578), p. 54; IV, Berlin and Leipzig, Göschen, 1913 (same coll., 697), pp. 108 et seq.

140. Thomas Aquinas, *Summa theologica*, II: 2, qu. 22, art. 5, and qu. 66, art. 2 (English translation in op. cit., Vols. 9 and 10). Cf. the use of the Dominican's own expressions by Leo XIII in his encyclical of 1891, *Rerum Novarum* (see *Les Textes pontificaux sur la démocratie et la société moderne*, ed. G. Michon, Paris, Rieder, 1928, p. 154). A typical example of the conceptions held by Catholics of that time is provided by L. Garriguet, *La Propriété privée*, Paris, Bloud, 1907 (Coll. Science et Religion, 154–5). Cf. P. Bigo, *La Doctrine Sociale de l'Église*, Paris, P.U.F., 1965, which is basically similar (though with more subtlety and learning) to the writings of the Muslim apologists.

141. L. Milliot, *Introduction à l'étude du droit musulman*, Paris, Recueil Sirey, 1953, p. 495. This book, which serves as one of the main sources for those who theorize about the intrinsic characteristics of Islam, is particularly open to criticism from a number of points of view, especially for its legalistic pedantry, its lack of historical sense, and its very scrappy information regarding works that have revolutionized the history of Muslim law, notably those, of major importance, from the pen of J. Schacht. It is a handy book, but not one to be trusted. (One cannot but subscribe to the severe criticism of it made by G. H. Bousquet, in *Revue algérienne, tunisienne et marocaine de législation et de jurisprudence*, 69th year, no. 6, Nov.–Dec. 1953, pp. 223–8). The information given in it needs to be qualified by

the much better informed notes supplied in the invaluable little textbook of P. José López Ortiz, *Derecho Musulmán*, Barcelona, Labor, 1932 (Coll. Coleccion Labor, no. 322), pp. 175–85, and the lengthy treatise by D. Santillana, *Istituzioni di diritto musulmano malichita con reguardo anche al sistema sciafiita*, 2nd edition, I, Rome, no date, pp. 308–26, 352–406, 429–33 (in 1st edition, Rome, 1926, pp. 245–60, 279–318, 340–43). Cf. also, on Muslim law regarding misuse of property rights, M. Morand, *Études de droit musulman algérien*, Algiers, A. Jourdan, 1910, pp. 297–310.

142. F. Olivier-Martin, *Précis d'histoire du droit francais*, 3rd edn, Paris, Dalloz, 1938, p. 243.

143. G. Destanne de Bernis, 'Islam et développement économique', in *Cahiers de l'I.S.E.A.*, No. 106 (series V, no. 2), Oct. 1960, pp. 105–50, on p. 143.

144. J. Austruy, 'Vocation économique de l'Islam', art. cit., p. 190.

145. As is noted even by L. Milliot, *Introduction . . .*, p. 497, despite his propensity to emphasize the divergences between Western and Islamic countries.

146. Austruy, 'Vocation . . .', pp. 188 et seq.

147. Ibid., p. 188. Austruy is merely playing with words when he confronts the conception of ownership found in the works of economists like F. Perroux with the term '*social* ownership of the means of production' (a commonplace, in any case, in Marxist writing) which appears in the textbook *Political Economy* published by the Academy of Sciences of the U.S.S.R. There is more here than merely a different interpretation (p. 189) of one and the same notion. That which is appropriated remains, in the former case – in the last analysis, and despite the restrictions imposed on its use – under the control of the individual who appropriates it. In the U.S.S.R. it is under the exclusive control of the state.

148. Cf. M. Rodinson, 'L'Islam et les nouvelles indépendances', in *Partisans*, No. 10, May–June 1963, pp. 99–117.

149. G. Destanne de Bernis, 'Islam et développement économique . . .', art. cit., p. 144.

150. J. Poirier, 'Droit musulman et développement économique, la tradition et la théorie juridique devant l'innovation', in *Cahiers de l'I.S.E.A.*, suppl. no. 120 (series V, no. 3), Dec. 1961, pp. 191–224, on p. 222.

151. Muṣṭafā as-Sibāʿī, *ishtirākiyyat al-Islām*, 3rd edn, Cairo, ad-dār al-qawmiyya li-ṭ-ṭibāʿa wa-n-nashr, no date (Coll. ikhtarnā laka, 113), pp. 114 et seq.

Notes and References 293

152. Ibid., pp. 114–18.
153. Ibid., p. 118.
154. E. F. Gautier, *Moeurs et coutumes des musulmans*, Paris, Payot, 1931, p. 17.
155. Austruy, 'Vocation . . .', art. cit., p. 158.
156. Berque, op. cit., p. 270.
157. A. J. Meyer, *Middle Eastern Capitalism*, p. 37.
158. Cf. the remarkable analysis of the effect produced on Ottoman opinion of the time by the French Revolution, in B. Lewis, 'The impact of the French Revolution on Turkey, some notes on the transmission of ideas', in *Cahiers d'histoire mondiale*, Vol. I, no. 1, July 1953, pp. 105–25.

CHAPTER 6: CONCLUSIONS AND PROSPECTS

1. M. Rodinson, 'La pensée d'Avicenne', in *La Pensée*, No. 45, Nov.–Dec. 1952, pp. 83–93; no. 46. Jan.–Feb. 1953, pp. 51–7; no. 47, March–April 1953, pp. 85–99. The reader who has the courage to refer to this article is requested, until I can re-publish it in an up-dated form more adequate to my present thinking, to put between parentheses (at the very least) the 'Stalinist' formulations to be found in it.

2. Henry Corbin, *Histoire de la philosophie islamique, I. Des origines jusqu'à la mort d'Averroës (1198)*, in collaboration with Seyyed Hossein Nasr and Osman Yahya, Paris, Gallimard, 1964, 384 pp. (Coll. Idées, 38).

3. Lucien Sebag, *Marxisme et Structuralisme*, Paris, Payot, 1964 (Coll. Bibliothèque scientifique, Collection Science de l'Homme), p. 170.

4. Roland Barthes, 'Éléments de sémiologie', in *Communications*, No. 4, Paris, Éd. du Seuil, 1964, pp. 91–135, on p. 102.

5. Sebag, op. cit., p. 221.

6. Ferdinand de Saussure, *Cours de linguistique générale*, 4th edn, Paris, Payot, 1949 (Coll. Bibliothèque scientifique), pp. 208, 210. (English translation, *Course in General Linguistics*, New York, McGraw Hill, 1966, pp. 151, 153.)

7. I have tried to show the interaction between all these planes in my biography of a great man, *Mahomet*, Paris, Club français du livre, 1961 (Coll. Portraits de l'histoire, 32) (2nd edn, revised, Éd. du Seuil, 1968: Eng. trans., *Mohammed*, Allen Lane The Penguin Press, 1971). If this attempt possesses any value, it does not lie in the discovery of new factors previously unperceived, but in the showing of connections between factors that are already well known.

8. An advantageous technical borrowing, and even a non-technical one, from a civilization regarded as being superior, is inescapably effected once a certain level is reached. In the Muslim world the lateness of such borrowings was not due to the 'hesitations' of intellectuals, as P. Rondot supposes (*Cahiers de l'I.S.E.A.*, No. 106, Oct. 1960 (series V, no. 2), p. 52). The Muslim ideology did no more, at most, than delay their adoption. It was unable to prevent them. And the consequences were immense. Let me make the point in passing that technical aptitudes are apparently distributed more or less equally among all the races of mankind. It is cultural factors that either favour or hinder their development. If held back by cultural circumstances, they always tend

to assert themselves and flourish as soon as these circumstances become more favourable. Hence the (unconsciously racialist) naïvety of J. Austruy's amazement at the existence of Muslim technicians (op. cit., pp. 176, et seq.)

9. Luc de Heusch, 'Pour une dialectique de la sacralité du pouvoir', in *Le Pouvoir et le Sacré*, Brussels, Centre de Sociologie, 1962 (*Annales du Centre d'étude des religions*, I), pp. 15–47, on pp. 15 et seq.

10. L. Dumont, *La Civilisation indienne et nous, esquisse de sociologie comparée*, Paris, A. Colin, 1964 (Coll. Cahiers des Annales, 23), especially pp. 31–54.

11. Particularly in his book *Le Mythe de l'éternel retour, archétypes et répétition*, Paris, Gallimard, 1949 (Coll. Les Essais, 34).

12. *Histoire de la philosophie islamique I* (see note 2). A very idealistic conception of Muslim history is also defended (not without some original and interesting observations) by C. A. O. van Nieuwenhuijze, *Cross-Cultural Studies*, The Hague, Mouton, 1963 (Coll. Publications of the Institute of Social Studies, series major, Vol. V), especially in Chapter ix ('Social Aspects of Economic Development in the Arab States', pp. 222–74).

13. The Arapesh of the mountains of New Guinea have been famous since Margaret Mead wrote about them (*Sex and Temperament in Three Primitive Societies*, Routledge, 1935) for their gentleness, their lack of aggressiveness and ambition, in short their behaviour of the kind traditionally associated with femininity in our societies. They were at peace with their neighbours when they were observed, but 'there are, it is true, traditions of hostile encounters with more warlike beach people [also Arapesh] in former days when the mountain people went down to obtain sea-water for salt' (op. cit., pp. 9–10).

14. Cf. G. Balandier, 'Réflexions sur le fait politique: le cas des sociétés africaines', in *Cahiers internationaux de sociologie*, 37, 1964, pp. 23–50.

15. Cf. e.g., M. Noth, *History of Israel*, London, A. & C. Black, 1958, pp. 104–5.

16. *Le Mythe de l'éternel retour* (see note 11), p. 27; cf. my criticism of this in *La Pensée*, no. 38, Sept.–Oct. 1951, pp. 127–30.

17. John L. La Monte, 'Crusade and Jihad', in *The Arab Heritage*, ed. N. A. Faris, Princeton, 1944, pp. 165–6.

18. Ibid., p. 196.

19. *La Civilisation indienne et nous* (see note 10), p. 53.

20. Ibid., p. 52.

21. Ibid., p. 51.

22. Ibid., p. 19.
23. Van Nieuwenhuijze, *Cross-Cultural Studies* (see note 12), p. 238.
24. J. Berque, *Le Maghreb entre deux guerres*, Paris, Seuil, 1963; cf. my critical comments in *L'Année sociologique*, 3rd series, 1962, pp. 370–2.
25. Cf. F. I. Qubain, *The Reconstruction of Iraq, 1950–1957*, New York, Praeger, 1958; and the excellent critical observations by a member of the Board, M. Ionides, *Divide and Lose: The Arab Revolt of 1955–1958*, London, G. Bles, 1960.
26. Good examples are given by G. Destanne de Bernis, 'Contributions à l'analyse des voies africaines du socialisme: les coopératives rurales', in *Études maghrébines, Mélanges Charles-André Julien*, Paris, P.U.F., 1964, pp. 267–83, and 'Islam et développement économique' (art. cit., note 6).

INDEX

Index

44, 147; state bank, 146; *tartīb* (uniform tax), 146–7
Moses, 14, 78–9, 94, 96; in Koran, 20
Moubarac, Y., 84, 270
Mozabites, 115–16, 277
mubtadi' or *muta°allim* (aprentice), 52
Muḥammad Riẓā Shāh Pahlavī, 127–9, 280–81
Muḥammad, the Prophet, 12, 13, 14, 19, 20, 22, 23, 25, 78, 79, 80, 81, 83, 89, 90–92, 94, 96, 97, 146, 252, 255, 268–69, 273; criteria of *al-bayyināt*, 78; Revelation, 83; monotheism, 91; acceptance of magic, 96
Muḥarram, Decree of (1881), 123
Müller, August, 81
Muslim; religious tradition and modern economics, 2–3; peoples, presuppositions about, 3; state and common lands, 15; community as classless society, 27; empire, economic development, 30; 'common market', 56; ideology transmitted by tradition, 102; rationalism, 103; fatalism, 113; Muslim world, and French and Russian Revolutions, 182

Nakhā°ī, Ibrāhīm an-, 111
Napoleon Bonaparte, 196
Nāṣir Aḥmed Sheikh, 19, 21, 246, 282
Nāṣir-i Khosraw, 40

Oil industry, 138
Orwell, George, on 'nationalism', 282
Ottoman Empire, 36, 109, 114, 119, 122–4, 169, 171; *fermān*

regulating interest rate, 143; Maritime Trade, Code of, 143; *khaṭṭi-i humāyūn* (1856) creating banks, 143–4; *Qā'ime* (floating debt), 144; *evkaf*, 143; and *waqfs* (mortmain foundations), 145; *Mejelle* (Civil Code), 145; legal authorities, 152, 284
Ouzegane, Amar, 225

Pakistan, 153–4, 156; lending by Muslim banks in, 151; *ribā*, aim to eliminate, 154
partnership and wage-labour, 51
Pedersen, Johs., 273
Pellegrin, A., 170
Perroux, François, 158, 246, 248, 278, 289
Philo, 271; on faith and Revelation, 88
Pliny, on tolls, 255
Poirier, J., 177, 181, 249
Polanyi, Karl, 28
political science and history of religions, 203
politicians' decisions and ideologies, 210
post-Koranic ideology; not closed body of doctrine, 99; social consciousness, 100; logic, 104; Bājūrī, 111; no sharp contrast with Christianity, 103; mysticism, 113–14; creative minorities, 116
predestination in Judaism and Christianity, 94–5; *maqdūr*, *maktūb*, 109; *see also* the Koran
price-fixing, 34
production; capitalist, 50–51; Asiatic mode of, 58, 61–2, 66; primitive communal modes of,

About the Author

Maxime Rodinson is Professor of Old Ethiopic and Old South Arabian Languages at the École Pratique des Hautes Études at the Sorbonne. He served in Syria during World War II, and stayed for seven years in Lebanon working as a professor in a Moslem high school and as an official in the French Department of Antiquities for Syria and Lebanon; during this time he traveled frequently in the Middle East. He returned to Paris in 1947 to take charge of Oriental printed books in the National Library, and from 1950 to 1951 he published *Moyen-Orient*, a political monthly on the Middle East. He is the author of *Israel and the Arabs* (1969) and *Mohammed* (1971), published by Pantheon.